American Novel Explication 1991–1995

Compiled by
CATHERINE GLITSCH

With a Foreword by
Donna Gerstenberger and George Hendrick

Archon Books
1998

First published 1998 as an Archon Book,
an imprint of The Shoe String Press, Inc.,
North Haven, Connecticut 06473.

Library of Congress Cataloging-in-Publication Data

Glitsch, Catherine.
American novel explication, 1991–1995 / compiled by Catherine Glitsch;
with a foreword by Donna Gerstenberger and George Hendrick.
p. cm
Includes bibliographical references and index.
ISBN 0-208-02481-6 (lib. bdg.: alk. paper)
1. American fiction—History and criticism—Bibliography. I. Title.
Z1231.F4G58 1998
[PS371]
016.813009—dc21 98-27472
CIP

The paper in this publication meets the minimum
requirements of American National Standard for Information Sciences—
Permanence of Paper for Printed Library Materials, ANSI Z39.48-1984. ♾

Printed in the United States of America

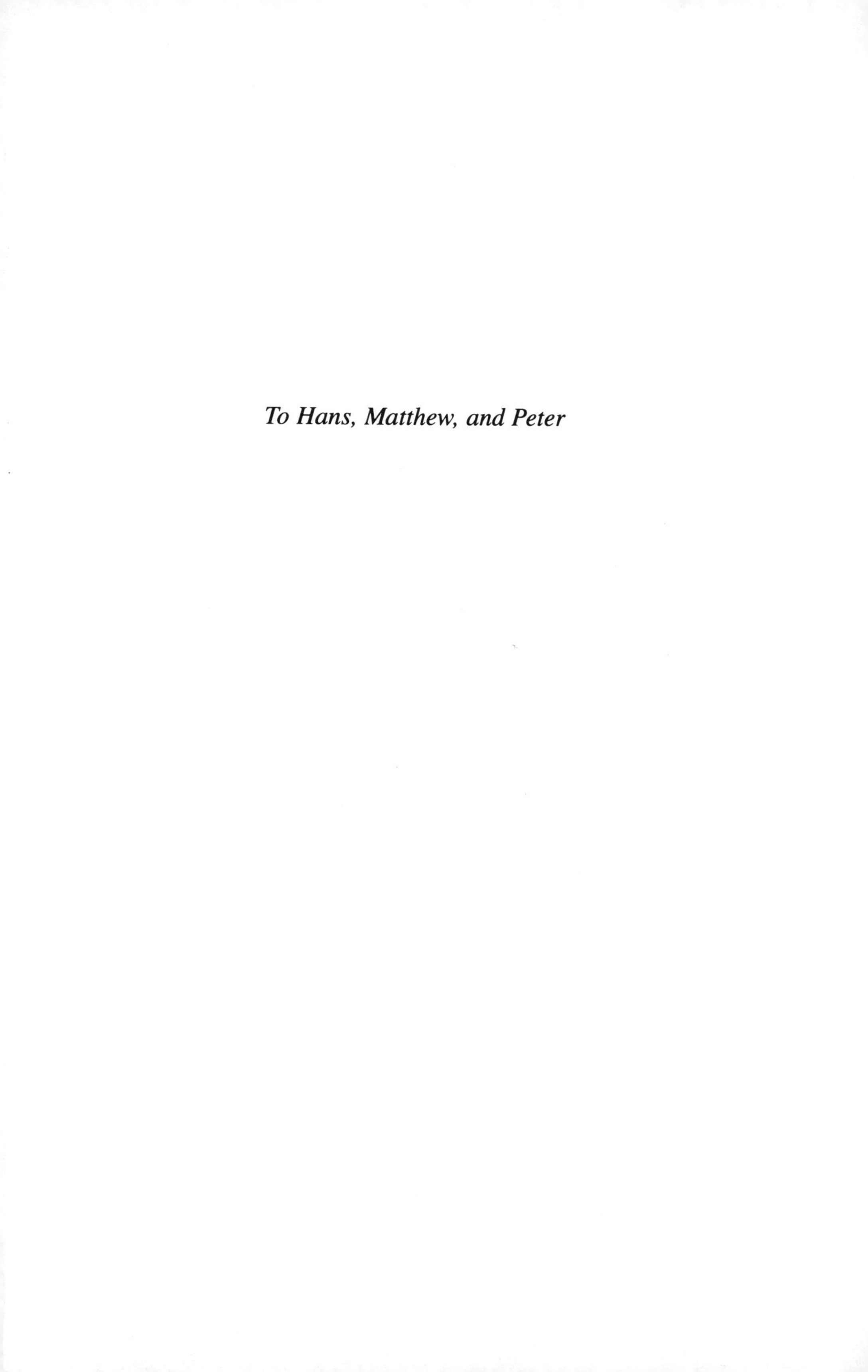

To Hans, Matthew, and Peter

Contents

Foreword

American Novel Explication, 1991–1995, edited by Catherine Glitsch, is part of a new bibliographic series which picks up where the Gerstenberger and Hendrick volumes, *The American Novel 1789–1959: A Checklist of Twentieth Century Criticism* and *The American Novel, Volume II: Criticism Written 1960–1968,* left off. The Shoe String Press, the publisher of this volume, is now planning for future publications of *American Novel Explication* covering the years 1969–1980, 1981–1985, 1986–1990. The series will be kept up to date thereafter in five-year increments.

This volume has several new features, most notably the inclusion of Canadian novelists writing in English and in French. In her preface, Ms. Glitsch concisely and clearly explains how the items of explication are arranged. Her coverage is wide: She has indexed 189 journals and 369 books.

This much-needed series joins *English Novel Explication, Twentieth-Century Short Story Explication: New Series,* and *American Drama Criticism,* all published by Shoe String, as standard bibliographic tools for students and scholars alike.

DONNA GERSTENBERGER
PROFESSOR OF ENGLISH EMERITUS,
UNIVERSITY OF WASHINGTON, SEATTLE

GEORGE HENDRICK
PROFESSOR OF ENGLISH,
UNIVERSITY OF ILLINOIS, URBANA-CHAMPAIGN

Preface

This first volume of *American Novel Explication* covers criticism of American novels found in journals and books published between the years 1991 and 1995. For the purposes of this bibliography, a novel is defined as a fictional prose narrative which is 150 or more pages in length. An "American" novelist is a writer born in the United States or Canada, or who has lived a significant portion of his or her life in the United States or Canada. Some novelists that have become identified as Canadian or U.S. authors are also included even though they do not strictly fit into these categories. For example, Frances Brooke, who was born in Great Britain and lived only a short time in Canada, is included because she is widely considered to be Canada's first novelist.

As in another reference series, *English Novel Explication* by Christian J.W. Kloesel, "explication" is defined as "the interpretation of the *significance* and *meaning* of a novel." This includes examinations of imagery, theme, and symbolism, as well as deconstructionist, linguistic, post-structuralist analyses. It excludes discussions which are solely bibliographical studies, reception studies, publishing histories of a novel, and biographical essays on novelists. Sources consulted in the compilation of *American Novel Explication* include the *MLA International Bibliography*, *Essay and General Literature Index,* and *Uncover.*

The bibliography is alphabetical by novelist with novel titles listed alphabetically within each author's entry. Pen names were chosen as main entries, with "see references" from the authors' given names. Alphabetization is word by word throughout. Authors whose names begin with Mc or Mac are interfiled.

Birth and death dates of novelists, as well as the publication dates of the novels, appear in the main body of the bibliography. A complete index to authors and novel titles appears at the back of the volume. Within each novelist's entry, citations to criticism are alphabetical by the author of the book, journal article, or book article. Novel titles appear in their abbreviated, but recognizable form. For example, Harriet E. Wilson's novel, *Our Nig; or,*

Sketches from the Life of a Free Black, in a Two-Story House, North. Showing that Slavery's Shadow Falls Even There, appears simply as *Our Nig*. Novels written by more than one author, such as Mark Twain's and Charles Dudley Warner's *Gilded Age*, are listed under both authors, as are the citations to criticism on these novels. Main entries for novels originally written in a language other than English appear under the original title with "see references" from the translated title.

In the main body of the volume, as with volumes of the *English Novel Explication* series (cited above), abbreviated titles for books are used in citations. The full citations for books cited can be found at the back of the volume in the "List of Books Indexed" section. When an article from an edited book is cited, the editor and abbreviated title of the book follow the article title and are preceded by the word "in." Books with more than one author or editor have only the first author/editor cited in the main body of the volume. Unedited books about a single novel are cited in their entirety in the main body of the bibliography, as well as appearing in the "List of Books Indexed" section. In most citations, pages cited refer to specific sections in which a novel is discussed, not to the entire article or book. These are not inclusive of footnotes or bibliographies appearing at the end of articles.

For ease of use, all citations to journal articles appear in full, and include the article's author, title, and a complete citation to the journal in which the article appears. Journal abbreviations used are those of the Modern Language Association. A complete list of journal abbreviations appears at the front of the book in the "Journal Abbreviations" section.

Reprints are indicated when possible to further expand the retrieval of information. In the citations to articles which have been reprinted from books, the book in which the article originally appeared is cited in its entirety in the main body of the volume and does not appear in the "List of Books Indexed." Whenever possible, journal abbreviations are not used in citations for journal articles reprinted in a book.

I would like to thank the Humanities and Interlibrary Loan departments of the Houston Public Library, Diantha Thorpe, and my entire family, especially Hans and Matthew Glitsch, and Sheila Curren, for their support and encouragement in completing *American Novel Explication*. I would also like to acknowledge Donna Gerstenberger and George Hendrick, whose bibliography, *American Novel: A Checklist of Twentieth Century Criticism*, inspired me to create *American Novel Explication*. It is my hope that *American Novel Explication* will become a standard bibliography alongside the *English Novel Explication* and *Twentieth-Century Short Story Explication* series published by The Shoe String Press. To that end any comments or suggestions are welcome and can be e-mailed to me at cathy@micronation.com or mailed to The Shoe String Press.

Journal Abbreviations

AAR	*African American Review*
AICRJ	*American Indian Culture and Research Journal*
AIQ	*American Indian Quarterly*
AL	*American Literature: A Journal of Literary History, Criticism, and Bibliography*
ALR	*American Literary Realism*
American Imago	*American Imago*
AmerS	*American Studies*
AmLH	*American Literary History*
AmRev	*Americas Review: A Review of Hispanic Literature and Art of the USA*
ANQ	*ANQ: A Quarterly Journal of Short Articles, Notes, and Reviews*
AQ	*American Quarterly*
ArielE	*ARIEL: A Review of International English Literature*
ArQ	*Arizona Quarterly: A Journal of American Literature, Culture, and Theory*
AS	*American Speech: A Quarterly of Linguistic Usage*
ASch	*American Scholar*
ASInt	*American Studies International*

ATQ	*American Transcendental Quarterly*
BALF	*Black American Literature Forum*
BoundaryII	*Boundary 2: An International Journal of Literature and Culture*
BR/RB	*Bilingual Review/La Revista Bilingue*
BuR	*Bucknell Review: A Scholarly Journal of Letters, Arts and Sciences*
BWVACET	*Bulletin of the West Virginia Association of College English Teachers*
C&L	*Christianity and Literature*
Callaloo	*Callaloo: A Journal of African-American and African Arts and Letters*
CanL	*Canadian Literature*
CathSt	*Cather Studies*
CCrit	*Comparative Criticism: A Yearbook*
CEA	*CEA Critic: An Official Journal of the College English Association*
CEAMag	*CEAMagazine: A Journal of the College English Association, Middle Atlantic Group*
CentR	*Centennial Review*
ChildL	*Children's Literature: Annual of the Modern Language Association Division on Children's Literature and the Children's Literature Association*
ChiR	*Chicago Review*
CI	*Critical Inquiry*
Cithara	*Cithara: Essays in the Judaeo-Christian Tradition*
CLAJ	*College Language Association Journal*
CLAQ	*Children's Literature Association Quarterly*
CLC	*Columbia Library Columns*

CLE	*Children's Literature in Education*
ClioI	*CLIO: A Journal of Literature, History, and the Philosophy of History*
ClQ	*Colby Quarterly*
CLS	*Comparative Literature Studies*
CML	*Classical and Modern Literature*
CollL	*College Literature*
Commentary	*Commentary*
ConL	*Contemporary Literature*
CQ	*Cambridge Quarterly*
CRCL	*Canadian Review of Comparative Literature/Revue Canadienne de Littérature Comparée*
CRevAS	*Canadian Review of American Studies/Revue Canadienne d'Études Américaines*
Crit	*Critique: Studies in Contemporary Fiction*
CritI	*Critical Inquiry*
CritQ	*Critical Quarterly*
DFS	*Dalhousie French Studies*
Diacritics	*Diacritics: A Review of Contemporary Criticism*
Diaspora	*Diaspora: A Journal of Transnational Studies*
DR	*Dalhousie Review*
DUJ	*Durham University Journal*
EAL	*Early American Literature*
EAS	*Essays in Arts and Sciences*
ECCS	*Études Canadiennes/Canadian Studies: Revue interdisciplinaire des Études Canadiennes en France*
ECent	*The Eighteenth Century: Theory and Interpretation*

ECr	*L' Esprit Créateur*
ECW	*Essays on Canadian Writing*
EF	*Études Françaises*
Eire	*Eire-Ireland*
EJ	*English Journal*
ELH	*ELH*
ELit	*Études Littéraires*
ELN	*English Language Notes*
ELWIU	*Essays in Literature*
ES	*English Studies: A Journal of English Language and Literature*
ESC	*English Studies in Canada*
ESQ	*ESQ: A Journal of the American Renaissance*
Expl	*Explicator*
Extrapolation	*Extrapolation: A Journal of Science Fiction and Fantasy*
EWhR	*Edith Wharton Review*
FCB	*Flannery O'Connor Bulletin*
Fiction International	*Fiction International*
FJ	*Faulkner Journal*
FR	*French Review: Journal of the American Association of Teachers of French*
Frontiers	*Frontiers: A Journal of Women Studies*
FSt	*Feminist Studies*
Genders	*Genders*
GPQ	*Great Plains Quarterly*
GrandS	*Grand Street*

HJR	*Henry James Review*
HLB	*Harvard Library Bulletin*
HLQ	*Huntington Library Quarterly: A Journal for the History and Interpretation of English and American Civilization*
HN	*Hemingway Review*
HSL	*University of Hartford Studies in Literature: A Journal of Interdisciplinary Criticism*
IFR	*International Fiction Review*
JAC	*Journal of Advanced Composition*
JACult	*Journal of American Culture*
JAmS	*Journal of American Studies*
JCL	*Journal of Commonwealth Literature*
JCSR	*Journal of Canadian Studies/Revue d'Études Canadiennes*
JELL	*Journal of English Language and Literature*
JML	*Journal of Modern Literature*
JNT	*Journal of Narrative Technique*
JPC	*Journal of Popular Culture*
KR	*Kenyon Review*
L&P	*Literature and Psychology*
Lang&Lit	*Language and Literature: Journal of the Poetics and Linguistics Association*
LCUT	*Library Chronicle of the University of Texas*
Legacy	*Legacy: A Journal of American Women Writers*
LFQ	*Literature/ Film Quarterly*
LJHum	*Lamar Journal of the Humanities*
LnL	*Language and Literature*

MELUS	*MELUS: The Journal of the Society for the Study of the Multi-Ethnic Literature of the United States*
MFS	*MFS: Modern Fiction Studies*
Midamerica	*Midamerica: The Yearbook of the Society for the Study of Midwestern Literature*
MinnR	*Minnesota Review*
MissQ	*Mississippi Quarterly: The Journal of Southern Culture*
MLQ	*Modern Language Quarterly: A Journal of Literary History*
MLS	*Modern Language Studies*
Mosaic	*Mosaic: A Journal for the Interdisciplinary Study of Literature*
MR	*Massachusetts Review: A Quarterly of Literature, the Arts and Public Affairs*
Mythlore	*Mythlore: A Journal of J. R. R. Tolkien, C. S. Lewis, Charles Williams, and the Genres of Myth and Fantasy*
N&Q	*Notes and Queries*
Names	*Names: Journal of the American Name Society*
NCF	*Nineteenth-Century Literature*
NConL	*Notes on Contemporary Literature*
NCS	*Nineteenth-Century Studies*
NDQ	*North Dakota Quarterly*
Neophil	*Neophilologus*
NEQ	*New England Quarterly: A Historical Review of New England Life and Letters*
NewC	*New Criterion*
NLH	*New Literary History: A Journal of Theory and Interpretation*

NMW	*Notes on Mississippi Writers*
Novel	*Novel: A Forum on Fiction*
NWR	*Northwest Review*
ON	*Old Northwest: A Journal of Regional Life and Letters*
PLL	*Papers on Language and Literature: A Journal for Scholars and Critics of Language and Literature*
PMLA	*PMLA: Publications of the Modern Language Association of America*
PQ	*Philological Quarterly*
PR	*Partisan Review*
PVR	*Platte Valley Review*
QS	*Quebec Studies*
RALS	*Resources for American Literary Study*
Raritan	*Raritan: A Quarterly Review*
RCF	*Review of Contemporary Fiction*
Renascence	*Renascence: Essays on Value in Literature*
Representations	*Representations*
RMS	*Renaissance & Modern Studies*
RQ	*Riverside Quarterly*
SAF	*Studies in American Fiction*
SAIL	*Studies in American Indian Literatures: The Journal of the Association for the Study of American Indian Literatures*
SAJL	*Studies in American Jewish Literature*
Salmagundi	*Salmagundi*
SAQ	*South Atlantic Quarterly*
SAR	*Studies in the American Renaissance*

SCL	*Studies in Canadian Literature/Études en Littérature Canadienne*
SCR	*South Carolina Review*
SDR	*South Dakota Review*
SEEJ	*Slavic and East European Journal*
SFolk	*Southern Folklore*
SFS	*Science-Fiction Studies*
Shenandoah	*Shenandoah: The Washington & Lee University Review*
Signs	*Signs: Journal of Women in Culture and Society*
SLitI	*Studies in the Literary Imagination*
SLJ	*Southern Literary Journal*
SNNTS	*Studies in the Novel*
SoAR	*South Atlantic Review*
SoQ	*Southern Quarterly: A Journal of the Arts in the South*
SoR	*Southern Review*
Soundings	*Soundings: An Interdisciplinary Journal*
StQ	*Steinbeck Quarterly*
StTCL	*Studies in Twentieth Century Literature*
Studies	*Studies: An Irish Quarterly Review*
Studies in the Humanities	*Studies in the Humanities*
Style	*Style*
SubStance	*SubStance: A Review of Theory and Literary Criticism*
SWR	*Southwest Review*
Tangence	*Tangence*

TCL	*Twentieth Century Literature: A Scholarly and Critical Journal*
TexasR	*Texas Review*
TSLL	*Texas Studies in Literature and Language*
TSWL	*Tulsa Studies in Women's Literature*
TWN	*Thomas Wolfe Review*
UDR	*University of Dayton Review*
UMSE	*University of Mississippi Studies in English*
UTQ	*University of Toronto Quarterly: A Canadian Journal of the Humanities*
V&I	*Voix et Images: Littérature Québécoise*
Verbatim	*Verbatim: The Language Quarterly*
VN	*Victorian Newsletter*
VQR	*Virginia Quarterly Review: A National Journal of Literature and Discussion*
WAL	*Western American Literature*
WF	*Western Folklore*
WLT	*World Literature Today: A Literary Quarterly of the University of Oklahoma*
WS	*Women's Studies: An Interdisciplinary Journal*
YES	*Yearbook of English Studies*
YJC	*Yale Journal of Criticism: Interpretation in the Humanities*

American Novel Explication

ABBEY, EDWARD (1927–1989)

Brave Cowboy (1956)

Folsom, James K. "Gothicism in the Western Novel," in Mogen, David, ed. *Frontier Gothic*, 38–40.

Good News (1980)

Folsom, James K. "Gothicism in the Western Novel," in Mogen, David, ed. *Frontier Gothic*, 38–40.

Monkey Wrench Gang (1975)

Killingsworth, M. Jimmie. "Realism, Human Action, and Instrumental Discourse." *JAC* 12.1 (1993): 171–200.

Slovic, Scott. "Aestheticism and Awareness: The Psychology of Edward Abbey's *The Monkey Wrench Gang*." *CEA* 55.3 (1993): 54–68.

ABISH, WALTER (1931–)

Alphabetical Africa (1974)

Schirato, Anthony. "Comic Politics and Politics of the Comic: Walter Abish's *Alphabetical Africa*." *Crit* 33.2 (1992): 133–144.

ACKER, KATHY (1948–1997)

Blood and Guts in High School (1978)

Brennan, Karen. "Geography of Enunciation: Hysterical Pastiche in Kathy Acker's Fiction." *BoundaryII* 21.2 (1994): 243–268.

Phillips, Rod. "Purloined Letters: *The Scarlet Letter* in Kathy Acker's *Blood and Guts in High School*." *Crit* 35.3 (1994): 173–180.

Don Quixote (1986)

Walsh, Richard. "Quest for Love and the Writing of Female Desire in Kathy Acker's *Don Quixote*." *Crit* 32.3 (1991): 149–168.

ACOSTA, OSCAR ZETA (1935?–)

Autobiography of a Brown Buffalo (1972)

Thwaites, Jeanne. "Use of Irony in Oscar Zeta Acosta's *Autobiography of a Brown Buffalo*." *AmRev* 20.1 (1992): 73–82.

ADAMS, HENRY (1838–1918)

Democracy (1880)

Ernest, John. "Henry Adams's Double: Recreating the Philosophical Statesman." *JACult* 14.1 (1991): 27–29.

AGEE, JAMES (1909–1955)

Death in the Family (1957)

Carroll, Eugene T. "Mood and Music: Landscape and Artistry in *A Death in the Family*," in Lofaro, Michael A., ed. *James Agee*, 82–102.
Kramer, Victor A. "Urban and Rural Balance in *A Death in the Family*," in Lofaro, Michael A., ed. *James Agee*, 104–117.
Lanier, Lois Elder. "Many Mansions of James Agee," in Lanier, Parks, Jr., ed. *Poetics*, 102–126.
Lowe, James. *Creative Process of James Agee*, 138–140, 141, 145, 146–151, 154.

AIKEN, CONRAD (1899–1973)

Great Circle (1933)

Fleissner, Robert F. "Tsetse Revisited: Prufrock's Michelangelo-Lazarus Nexus Retied in Aiken's *Great Circle*." *NConL* 21.2 (1991): 3–5.

ALBERT, OCTAVIA VICTORIA ROGERS (1853–1889?)

House of Bondage (1890)

Foster, Frances Smith. *Written by Herself*, 160–177.

ALCOTT, LOUISA MAY (1832–1888)

Behind a Mask (1866)

Keyser, Elizabeth Lennox. *Whispers in the Dark*, 46–57.

Jo's Boys (1886)

Brodhead, Richard H. *Cultures of Letters*, 69–70, 71–72.
Keyser, Elizabeth Lennox. *Whispers in the Dark*, 163–180.

Little Men (1871)

Clark, Beverly Lyon. "Domesticating the School Story, Regendering a Genre: Alcott's *Little Men*." *NLH* 26.2 (1995): 323–342.
Keyser, Elizabeth Lennox. *Whispers in the Dark*, 85–99.

Little Women (1868)

Armstrong, Frances. " 'Here Little, and Hereafter Bliss': *Little Women* and the Deferral of Greatness." *AL* 64.3 (1992): 453–474.

Bernstein, Susan Naomi. "Writing and *Little Women:* Alcott's Rhetoric of Subversion." *ATQ* 7.1 (1993): 25–43.

Brodhead, Richard H. *Cultures of Letters*, 89–103.

Crisler, Jesse S. "Alcott's Reading in *Little Women:* Shaping the Autobiographical Self." *RALS* 20.1 (1994): 27–36.

Foster, Shirley. *What Katy Read*, 85–105.

Gaard, Greta. " 'Self-Denial Was All the Fashion': Repressing Anger in *Little Women.*" *PLL* 27.1 (1991): 3–19.

Griswold, Jerry. *Audacious Kids*, 156–166.

Hovet, Grace Ann and Theodore R. Hovet. "TABLEAUX VIVANTS: Masculine Vision and Feminine Reflections in Novels by Warner, Alcott, Stowe, and Wharton." *ATQ* 7.4 (1993): 335–338, 342–344, 352–355.

Keyser, Elizabeth Lennox. *Whispers in the Dark*, 58–82.

Limon, John. *Writing After War*, 183–188.

Showalter, Elaine. *Sister's Choice*, 42–64.

Vrettos, Athena. *Somatic Fictions*, 33–35.

Zwinger, Lynda. *Daughters, Fathers, and the Novel*, 46–75.

Marble Woman (1865)

Keyser, Elizabeth Lennox. *Whispers in the Dark*, 32–45.

Modern Mephistopheles (1877)

Keyser, Elizabeth Lennox. *Whispers in the Dark*, 122–143.

Sanderson, Rena. "*Modern Mephistopheles:* Louisa May Alcott's Exorcism of Patriarchy." *ATQ* 5.1 (1991): 41–55.

Moods (1864)

Keyser, Elizabeth Lennox. *Whispers in the Dark*, 14–31.

Work (1873)

Keyser, Elizabeth Lennox. *Whispers in the Dark*, 100–121.

Lant, Kathleen Margaret and Angela M. Estes. "Feminist Redeemer: Louisa Alcott's Creation of the Female Christ." *C&L* 40.3 (1991): 223–253.

Rigsby, Mary. " 'So Like Women!': Louisa May Alcott's *Work* and the Ideology of Relations," in Harris, Sharon M., ed. *Redefining the Political Novel*, 109–124.

Widdicombe, Toby. " 'Declaration of Independence': Alcott's *Work* as Transcendental Manifesto." *ESQ* 38.3 (1992): 207–229.

ALDRICH, THOMAS BAILEY (1836–1907)

Story of a Bad Boy (1870)

Jacobson, Marcia. *Being a Boy Again*, 27–36.

ALFAU, FELIPE (1902–)

Chromos (1990)

Candau, Antonio. "Literature Is Corny: The Cursi and Felipe Alfau's *Chromos.*" *RCF* 13.1 (1993): 225–228.

Christensen, Peter. "Truth or Temptation? Don Pedro's Refutation of Time in *Chromos.*" *RCF* 13.1 (1993): 229–240.

Rabassa, Gregory. "Power of *Chromos.*" *RCF* 13.1 (1993): 223–224.

Locos (1988)

Shapiro, Anna. "Sixty-One Years of Solitude." *RCF* 13.1 (1993): 203–206.

Sweeney, Susan Elizabeth. "Aliens, Aliases, and Alibis: Alfau's *Locos* as a Metaphysical Detective Story." *RCF* 13.1 (1993): 207–214.

ALGREN, NELSON (1909–1981)

Man with the Golden Arm (1949)

Giles, James R. *Naturalistic Inner-City Novel in America*, 96–117.

ALLEN, PAULA GUNN (1939–)

Woman Who Owned the Shadows (1983)

Bredin, Renae. "'Becoming Minor': Reading *The Woman Who Owned the Shadows.*" *SAIL* 6.4 (1994): 36–50.

Holford, Vanessa. "Re Membering Ephanie: A Women's Re-Creation of Self in Paula Gunn Allen's *The Woman Who Owned the Shadows.*" *SAIL* 6.1 (1994): 99–113.

St. Clair, Janet. "Fighting for Her Life: The Mixed-Blood Woman's Insistence upon Selfhood," in Fleck, Richard F., ed. *Critical Perspectives*, 47–52.

AMYOT, GENEVIÈVE (1945–)

Journal de l'année passée (1978)

Raoul, Valerie. *Distinctly Narcissistic*, 190–194.

ANAYA, RUDOLFO (1937–)

Bless Me, Ultima (1972)

Klein, Dianne. "Coming of Age in Novels by Rudolfo Anaya and Sandra Cisneros." *EJ* 81.5 (1992): 21–26.

Sanders, Scott P. "Southwestern Gothic: On the Frontier between Landscape and Locale," in Mogen, David, ed. *Frontier Gothic*, 60–64.

Taylor, Paul Beekman. "Chicano Translation of Troy: Epic Topoi in the Novels of Rudolfo A. Anaya." *MELUS* 19.3 (1994): 19–32.

Heart of Aztlan (1976)

Taylor, Paul Beekman. "Chicano Translation of Troy: Epic Topoi in the Novels of Rudolfo A. Anaya." *MELUS* 19.3 (1994): 19–32.

Tortuga (1979)

Taylor, Paul Beekman. "Chicano Translation of Troy: Epic Topoi in the Novels of Rudolfo A. Anaya." *MELUS* 19.3 (1994): 19–32.

ANDERSON, SHERWOOD (1876–1941)

Poor White (1920)

Anderson, David D. "Sherwood Anderson and the River." *ON* 15.4 (1991–92): 281–293.

Windy McPherson's Son (1916)

Bidney, Martin. "*Windy McPherson's Son* and Silent McEachern's Son: Sherwood Anderson and *Light in August*." *MissQ* 46.3 (1993): 395–406.

ANTONI, ROBERT (1958–)

Divina Trace (1992)

Hawley, John C. "Robert Antoni's *Divina Trace* and the Womb of Place." *ArielE* 24.1 (1993): 91–104.

AQUIN, HUBERT (1929–1977)

Blackout see *Trou de mémoire*

Hamlet's Twin see *Neige noire*

Neige noire (1974)

Mantovani, Milena. "Réécriture du mythe de l'androgynie dans *Neige noire* d'Hubert Aquin," in Marcato-Falzoni, Franca, ed. *Mythes et mythologies*, 223–238.
Smart, Patricia. *Writing in the Father's House*, 201–202, 211–233.

Prochain épisode (1965)

Green, Mary Jean. "Postmodern Agents: Cultural Representation in Hubert Aquin's *Prochain épisode* and Yolande Villemaire's *Meurtres a blanc*." *UTQ* 63.4 (1994): 584–596.
Shek, Ben-Z. *French-Canadian*, 53–55.
Siemerling, Winfried. *Discoveries of the Other*, 79–94.
Smart, Patricia. *Writing in the Father's House*, 200–201.

Trou de mémoire (1968)

Paterson, Janet M. *Postmodernism*, 43–52.
Raoul, Valerie. *Distinctly Narcissistic*, 233–242.
Shek, Ben-Z. *French-Canadian*, 55–56.
Siemerling, Winfried. *Discoveries of the Other*, 79–82, 95–105.
Smart, Patricia. *Writing in the Father's House*, 200–201.
Söderlind, Sylvia. *MARGIN / ALIAS*, 70–108.

ARNOW, HARRIETTE (1908–1986)

Dollmaker (1954)

Chung, Haeja K. "Harriette Simpson Arnow's Authorial Testimony: Toward a Reading of *The Dollmaker*." *Crit* 36.3 (1995): 211–223.
Cunningham, Rodger. " 'Adjustments an What It Means': The Tragedy of Space in *The Dollmaker*," in Lanier, Parks, Jr., ed. *Poetics*, 127–140.
Devers, James. "Cain and Abel in Harriette Arnow's *The Dollmaker:* A Comment on War." *NConL* 22.3 (1992): 4–5.

Goldsmith, Arnold L. *Modern American Urban Novel*, 84–103.
Harrison, Elizabeth Jane. *Female Pastoral*, 83–99.
Miller, Danny L. " 'For a Living Dog Is Better Than a Dead Lion': Harriette Arnow as Religious Writer." *SoAR* 60.1 (1995): 29–42.

Mountain Path (1936)

Joyner, Nancy Carol. "Poetics of the House in Appalachian Fiction," in Lanier, Parks, Jr., ed. *Poetics*, 20–23.

ASIMOV, ISAAC (1920–1992)

Caves of Steel (1954)

Touponce, William F. *Isaac Asimov*, 47–51.

Currents of Space (1952)

Touponce, William F. *Isaac Asimov*, 64–67.

Foundation (1951)

Touponce, William F. *Isaac Asimov*, 75–78.

Foundation and Earth (1987)

Touponce, William F. *Isaac Asimov*, 89–94.

Foundation and Empire (1952)

Touponce, William F. *Isaac Asimov*, 78–81.

Foundation's Edge (1982)

Touponce, William F. *Isaac Asimov*, 86–89.

God's Themselves (1972)

Touponce, William F. *Isaac Asimov*, 95–97.

Naked Sun (1957)

Touponce, William F. *Isaac Asimov*, 51–54.

Nemesis (1989)

Touponce, William F. *Isaac Asimov*, 98–100.

Pebble in the Sky (1950)

Touponce, William F. *Isaac Asimov*, 67–70.

Prelude to Foundation (1988)

Touponce, William F. *Isaac Asimov*, 71–75.

Robots and Empire (1985)

Touponce, William F. *Isaac Asimov*, 58–61.

Robots of Dawn (1983)

Touponce, William F. *Isaac Asimov*, 54–58.

Second Foundation (1953)

Touponce, William F. *Isaac Asimov*, 81–85.

Stars Like Dust (1951)

Touponce, William F. *Isaac Asimov*, 62–64.

ATTANASIO, A. A. (1951–)

Radix (1990)

Porush, David. "Prigogine, Chaos, and Contemporary Science Fiction." *SFS* 18.3 (1991): 372–373.

ATTAWAY, WILLIAM (1911–1986)

Blood on the Forge (1941)

Barthold, Bonnie J. *Black Time: Fiction of Africa, the Caribbean, and the United States*. New Haven: Yale University Press, 1981. 167–168. Rpt. in Bloom, Harold, ed. *Modern Black American Fiction Writers*, 25–26.

Conder, John. "Selves of the City, Selves of the South: The City in the Fiction of William Attaway and Willard Motley," in Hakutani, Yoshinobu, ed. *City in African-American Literature*, 113–116.

Ellison, Ralph. "Transition." *Negro Quarterly* 1.1 (1942): 89–90. Rpt. in Bloom, Harold, ed. *Modern Black American Fiction Writers*, 18–19.

Garren, Samuel B. "Playing the Wishing Game: Folkloric Elements in William Attaway's *Blood on the Forge*." *College Language Association Journal* 32.1 (1988): 10–11. Rpt. in Bloom, Harold, ed. *Modern Black American Fiction Writers*, 27–28.

Hamilton, Cynthia. "Work and Culture: The Evolution of Consciousness in Urban Industrial Society in the Fiction of William Attaway and Peter Abrahams." *Black American Literature Forum* 21.1–2 (1987): 155–156. Rpt. in Bloom, Harold, ed. *Modern Black American Fiction Writers*, 26–27.

Hughes, Carl Milton. *Negro Novelist: a Discussion of the Writings of American Negro Novelists 1940–1950*. New York: Citadel Press, 1953. 79–81, 83. Rpt. in Bloom, Harold, ed. *Modern Black American Fiction Writers*, 20–22.

Let Me Breathe Thunder (1939)

Lee, Ulysses. "On the Road." *Opportunity* 17.9 (1939): 283–284. Rpt. in Bloom, Harold, ed. *Modern Black American Fiction Writers*, 17.

ATWOOD, MARGARET (1939–)

Bodily Harm (1981)

Bouson, J. Brooks. *Brutal Choreographies*, 111–134.

Epstein, Grace A. "*Bodily Harm:* Female Containment and Abuse in the Romance Narrative." *Genders* 16 (1993): 80–93.

Howells, Coral Ann. *Margaret Atwood*, 105–125.

Irvine, Lorna. *Collecting Clues: Margaret Atwood's Bodily Harm*. Toronto: ECW Press, 1993.

Kuester, Martin. *Framing Truths*, 126–133.

Mycak, Sonia. "Divided and Dismembered: The Decentered Subject in Margaret Atwood's *Bodily Harm*." *CRCL* 20.3–4 (1993): 469–478.

Parker, Emma. "You Are What You Eat: The Politics of Eating in the Novels of Margaret Atwood." *TCL* 41.3 (1995): 353–354, 357, 358, 361, 362–363.

Rao, Eleonora. *Strategies for Identity*, 13–15, 52–55, 103–107, 108–113, 115–122, 123, 125–127, 142–144, 150–151, 156, 158, 161–162.

White, Rebecca. "Margaret Atwood : Reflections in a Convex Mirror," in Pearlman, Mickey, ed. *Canadian Women*, 57–59.

Wilson, Sharon Rose. *Margaret Atwood's Fairy-Tale*, 198–228.

Cat's Eye (1988)

Ahern, Stephen. " 'Meat Like You Like It': The Production of Identity in Atwood's *Cat's Eye*." *CanL* 137 (1993): 8–17.

Bouson, J. Brooks. *Brutal Choreographies*, 159–184.

Cooke, Nathalie. "Reading Reflections: The Autobiographical Illusion in *Cat's Eye*," in Kadar, Marlene, ed. *Essays on Life Writing*, 162–169.

Cowart, David. "Bridge and Mirror: Replicating Selves in *Cat's Eye*," in D'haen, Theo, ed. *Postmodern*, 125–136.

Givner, Jessie. "Names, Faces and Signatures in Margaret Atwood's *Cat's Eye* and *The Handmaid's Tale*." *CanL* 133 (1992): 62–70, 71–74.

Grace, Sherrill. "Gender as Genre: Atwood's Autobiographical 'I'," in Nicholson, Colin, ed. *Margaret Atwood*, 199–202.

Greene, Gayle. *Changing the Story*, 207–214.

Hite, Molly. "Optics and Autobiography in Margaret Atwood's *Cat's Eye*." *TCL* 41.2 (1995): 135–159.

Howells, Coral. "*Cat's Eye:* Elaine Risley's Retrospective Art," in Nicholson, Colin, ed. *Margaret Atwood*, 204–216.

Howells, Coral Ann. *Margaret Atwood*, 148–160.

Ingersoll, Earl G. "Margaret Atwood's *Cat's Eye*: Re-Viewing Women in a Postmodern World." *ArielE* 22.4 (1991): 17–26.

LeBihan, Jill. "*The Handmaid's Tale, Cat's Eye* and *Interlunar*: Margaret Atwood's Feminist (?) Futures (?)," in Howells, Coral Ann, ed. *Narrative Strategies*, 95–96, 98–99, 103, 105–106.

McCombs, Judith. "Contrary Rememberings: The Creating Self and Feminism in *Cat's Eye*." *CanL* 129 (1991): 9–23.

Osborne, Carol. "Constructing the Self through Memory: *Cat's Eye* as a Novel of Female Development." *Frontiers* 14.3 (1994): 95–112.

Parker, Emma. "You Are What You Eat: The Politics of Eating in the Novels of Margaret Atwood." *TCL* 41.3 (1995): 356, 357–358, 358–359, 362, 363, 365.

Rao, Eleonora. *Strategies for Identity*, 107–108, 115, 155–156, 160–161, 169.

Sharpe, Martha. "Margaret Atwood and Julia Kristeva: Space-Time, the Dissident Woman Artist, and the Pursuit of Female Solidarity in *Cat's Eye*." *ECW* 50 (1993): 174–189.

Strehle, Susan. *Fiction in the Quantum Universe*, 159–189.

White, Rebecca. "Margaret Atwood: Reflections in a Convex Mirror," in Pearlman, Mickey, ed. *Canadian Women*, 61–67.

Wilson, Sharon Rose. *Margaret Atwood's Fairy-Tale*, 295–314.

Edible Woman (1969)

Bouson, J. Brooks. *Brutal Choreographies*, 15–37.

Greene, Gayle. *Changing the Story*, 76–78.

Howells, Coral Ann. *Margaret Atwood*, 42–54.

Parker, Emma. "You Are What You Eat: The Politics of Eating in the Novels of Margaret Atwood." *TCL* 41.3 (1995): 350, 357, 360, 364.
Rao, Eleonora. *Strategies for Identity*, 46–52, 134–139, 139–142, 146–147, 157, 159–160, 165.
Wilson, Sharon Rose. *Margaret Atwood's Fairy-Tale*, 82–96.

Handmaid's Tale (1985)

Booker, M. Keith. *Dystopian Impulse*, 162–169.
Bouson, J. Brooks. *Brutal Choreographies*, 135–158.
Caminero-Santangelo, Marta. "Moving Beyond 'The Blank White Spaces': Atwood's Gilead, Postmodernism, and Strategic Resistance." *SCL* 19.1 (1994): 20–42.
Chen, Zhongming. "Theorising about New Modes of Representation and Ideology in the Postmodern Age: The Practice of Margaret Atwood and Li Ang." *CRCL* 21.3 (1994): 341–352.
Deer, Glenn. *Postmodern Canadian Fiction*, 110–129.
Deer, Glenn. "Rhetorical Strategies in *The Handmaid's Tale:* Dystopia and the Paradoxes of Power." *ESC* 18.2 (1992): 215–233.
Dopp, Jamie. "Subject-Position as Victim-Position in *The Handmaid's Tale.*" *SCL* 19.1 (1994): 43–57.
Evans, Mark. "Versions of History: *The Handmaid's Tale* and its Dedicatees," in Nicholson, Colin, ed. *Margaret Atwood*, 177–187.
Gardner, Laurel J. "Pornography as a Matter of Power in *The Handmaid's Tale.*" *NConL* 24.5 (1994): 5–7.
Givner, Jessie. "Names, Faces and Signatures in Margaret Atwood's *Cat's Eye* and *The Handmaid's Tale.*" *CanL* 133 (1992): 58–62, 71–74.
Grace, Sherrill. "Gender as Genre: Atwood's Autobiographical 'I'," in Nicholson, Colin, ed. *Margaret Atwood*, 195–199.
Greene, Gayle. *Changing the Story*, 205–207.
Hansen, Elaine Tuttle. "Mothers Tomorrow and Mothers Yesterday, But Never Mothers Today: *Woman on the Edge of Time* and *The Handmaid's Tale*," in Daly, Brenda O., ed. *Narrating Mothers*, 28–40.
Howells, Coral Ann. *Margaret Atwood*, 126–147.
Klarer, Mario. "Orality and Literacy as Gender-Supporting Structures in Margaret Atwood's *The Handmaid's Tale.*" *Mosaic* 28.4 (1995): 129–142.
Kuester, Martin. *Framing Truths*, 133–147.
LeBihan, Jill. "*The Handmaid's Tale, Cat's Eye* and *Interlunar*: Margaret Atwood's Feminist (?) Futures (?)," in Howells, Coral Ann, ed. *Narrative Strategies*, 96–98, 99–101, 102–104, 105, 106.
Miner, Madonne. " 'Trust Me': Reading the Romance Plot in Margaret Atwood's *The Handmaid's Tale.*" *TCL* 37.2 (1991): 148–168.
Parker, Emma. "You Are What You Eat: The Politics of Eating in the Novels of Margaret Atwood." *TCL* 41.3 (1995): 354–356, 359, 360, 363, 365–366.
Rao, Eleonora. *Strategies for Identity*, 15–20, 77–85, 128–129, 144–145, 154–155, 158–159.
Reesman, Jeanne Campbell. "Dark Knowledge in *The Handmaid's Tale.*" *CEA* 53.3 (1991): 6–22.
Rosenfelt, Deborah Silverton. "Feminism, "Postfeminism," and Contemporary Women's Fiction," in Howe, Florence, ed. *Tradition and the Talents of Women*, 279, 280–281, 282–283, 286.

Staels, Hilde. "Margaret Atwood's *The Handmaid's Tale:* Resistance through Narrating." *ES* 78.5 (1995): 455–467.

Stein, Karen F. "Margaret Atwood's *The Handmaid's Tale:* Scheherazade in Dystopia." *UTQ* 61.2 (1991–92): 269–279.

Templin, Charlotte. "Atwood's *The Handmaid's Tale*." *Expl* 49.4 (1991): 255–256.

Templin, Charlotte. "Names and Naming Tell an Archetypal Story in Margaret Atwood's *The Handmaid's Tale*." *Names* 41.3 (1993): 143–157.

Tomc, Sandra. " 'The Missionary Position': Feminism and Nationalism in Margaret Atwood's *The Handmaid's Tale*." *CanL* 138–139 (1993): 73–87.

Wein, Toni. "Margaret Atwood's Historical Notes (*The Handmaid's Tale*)." *NConL* 25.2 (1995): 2–3.

White, Rebecca. "Margaret Atwood : Reflections in a Convex Mirror," in Pearlman, Mickey, ed. *Canadian Women*, 59–61.

Wilson, Sharon Rose. *Margaret Atwood's Fairy-Tale*, 271–294.

Lady Oracle (1976)

Bok, Christian. "Sibyls: Echoes of French Feminism in *The Diviners* and *Lady Oracle*." *CanL* 135 (1992): 82–92.

Bouson, J. Brooks. *Brutal Choreographies*, 63–85.

Fee, Margery. *Fat Lady Dances: Margaret Atwood's Lady Oracle.* Toronto: ECW Press, 1993.

Grace, Sherrill. "Gender as Genre: Atwood's Autobiographical 'I'," in Nicholson, Colin, ed. *Margaret Atwood*, 192–195.

Greene, Gayle. *Changing the Story*, 166–190.

Howells, Coral Ann. *Margaret Atwood*, 65–76.

Massé, Michelle A. *In the Name of Love*, 250–264.

Parker, Emma. "You Are What You Eat: The Politics of Eating in the Novels of Margaret Atwood." *TCL* 41.3 (1995): 351, 357, 358, 359, 361–362.

Patton, Marilyn. "*Lady Oracle* : The Politics of the Body." *ArielE* 22.4 (1991): 29–47.

Rao, Eleonora. "Margaret Atwood's *Lady Oracle:* Writing Against Notions of Unity," in Nicholson, Colin, ed. *Margaret Atwood*, 133–149.

Rao, Eleonora. *Strategies for Identity*, 28–39, 64–73, 87–89, 91–95, 127–128, 154, 165, 169.

Ross, Catherine. "Calling Back the Ghost of the Old-Time Heroine: Duncan, Montgomery, Atwood, Laurence and Munro." *SCL* 4.1 (1979): 43–58. Rpt. in Reimer, Mavis, ed. *Such a Simple Little Tale*, 44–49.

Tucker, Lindsey. *Textual Excap(e)ades*, 35–53.

White, Rebecca. "Margaret Atwood : Reflections in a Convex Mirror," in Pearlman, Mickey, ed. *Canadian Women*, 55–57.

Wilson, Sharon Rose. *Margaret Atwood's Fairy-Tale*, 120–135.

Life Before Man (1979)

Beran, Carol. *Living Over the Abyss: Margaret Atwood's Life Before Man*. Toronto: ECW Press, 1993.

Bouson, J. Brooks. *Brutal Choreographies*, 87–109.

Howells, Coral Ann. *Margaret Atwood*, 86–104.

Keefer, Janice Kulyk. "Hope Against Hopelessness: Margaret Atwood's *Life Before Man*," in Nicholson, Colin, ed. *Margaret Atwood*, 153–173.

Parker, Emma. "You Are What You Eat: The Politics of Eating in the Novels of Margaret Atwood." *TCL* 41.3 (1995): 351–353, 359–360, 362–363, 364–365.

Rao, Eleonora. *Strategies for Identity*, 73–77, 113–114, 154, 166, 169, 170–171.
Wilson, Sharon Rose. *Margaret Atwood's Fairy-Tale*, 165–197.

Robber Bride (1993)

Howells, Coral Ann. *Margaret Atwood*, 76–85.

Surfacing (1972)

Bouson, J. Brooks. *Brutal Choreographies*, 39–61.
Granofsky, Ronald. *Trauma Novel*, 114–123.
Howells, Coral Ann. *Margaret Atwood*, 23–32.
Parker, Emma. "You Are What You Eat: The Politics of Eating in the Novels of Margaret Atwood." *TCL* 41.3 (1995): 350–351, 357, 359, 361, 362, 366.
Rao, Eleonora. *Strategies for Identity*, 6–11, 11–13, 21–28, 55–64, 87–91, 100–103, 123–125, 126, 147, 165–166.
Tschachler, Heinz. "Janus, Hitler, the Devil, and Co.: On Myth, Ideology, and the Canadian Postmodern," in D'haen, Theo, ed. *Postmodern*, 33–47.
Ward, David. "*Surfacing:* Separation, Transition, Incorporation," in Nicholson, Colin, ed. *Margaret Atwood*, 94–131.
Wilson, Sharon Rose. *Margaret Atwood's Fairy-Tale*, 97–119.

AUBERT DE GASPÉ, PHILLIPE (1786–1871)

Canadians of Old see *Les anciens Canadiens*

Les anciens Canadiens (1863)

Shek, Ben-Z. *French-Canadian*, 7–9.

AUBERT DE GASPÉ, PHILLIPE (1814–1841)

Le chercheur de trésors see *L'Influence d'un livre*

L'Influence d'un livre (1837)

Grutman, Rainier. "Norme, repertoire, systeme: Les Avatars du premier roman quebecois." *EF* 28.2–3 (1992–93): 83–91.

AUCHINCLOSS, LOUIS (1917–)

Portrait in Brownstone (1962)

Castronovo, David. *American Gentleman*, 59–61.

AUSTER, PAUL (1947–)

City of Glass (1985)

Rowen, Norma. "Detective in Search of the Lost Tongue of Adam: Paul Auster's *City of Glass*." *Crit* 32.4 (1991): 224–234.
Tysh, Chris. "From One Mirror to Another: The Rhetoric of Disaffiliation in *City of Glass*." *RCF* 14.1 (1994): 46–52.

In the Country of Last Things (1987)

Birkerts, Sven. "Reality, Fiction, and *In the Country of Last Things*." *RCF* 14.1 (1994): 66–69.

Washburn, Katharine. "Book at the End of the World: Paul Auster's *In the Country of Last Things*." *RCF* 14.1 (1994): 62–65.
Wesseling, Elisabeth. "*In the Country of Last Things:* Paul Auster's Parable of the Apocalypse." *Neophil* 75.4 (1991): 496–504.

Leviathan (1992)

Osteen, Mark. "Phantoms of Liberty: The Secret Lives of *Leviathan*." *RCF* 14.1 (1994): 87–91.

Moon Palace (1989)

Lewis, Barry. "Strange Case of Paul Auster." *RCF* 14.1 (1994): 55–58.
Weisenburger, Steven. "Inside *Moon Palace*." *RCF* 14.1 (1994): 70–79.

Music of Chance (1990)

Bray, Paul. "Currents of Fate and *The Music of Chance*." *RCF* 14.1 (1994): 83–86.
Irwin, Mark. "Inventing the *Music of Chance*." *RCF* 14.1 (1994): 80–82.

BACH MAI

D'ivoire et d'opium (1985)

Yeager, Jack A. "Bach Mai's Francophone Eurasian Voice: Remapping Margin and Center." *QS* 14 (1992): 49–64.

BACHMAN, RICHARD see KING, STEPHEN

BAILLARGEON, PIERRE (1916–1967)

Les médisances de Claude Perrin (1945)

Raoul, Valerie. *Distinctly Narcissistic*, 95–100.

BAKER, NICHOLSON (1957–)

Mezzanine (1988)

Chambers, Ross. "Meditation and the Escalator Principle (on Nicholson Baker's *The Mezzanine*)." *MFS* 40.4 (1994): 765–806.
Simmons, Philip E. "Toward the Postmodern Historical Imagination: Mass Culture in Walker Percy's *The Moviegoer* and Nicholson Baker's *The Mezzanine*." *ConL* 33.4 (1992): 603–623.

BALDWIN, JAMES (1924–1987)

Another Country (1962)

Bawer, Bruce. "Race and Art: The Career of James Baldwin." *NewC* 10.3 (1991): 23–25.
Cohen, William A. "Liberalism, Libido, Liberation: Baldwin's *Another Country*." *Genders* 12 (1991): 1–21.
Hakutani, Yoshinobu. "If the Street Could Talk: James Baldwin's Search for Love and Understanding," in Hakutani, Yoshinobu, ed. *City in African-American Literature*, 153–154.

Rowden, Terry. "Play of Abstractions: Race, Sexuality, and Community in James Baldwin's *Another Country.*" *SoR* 29.1 (1993): 41–50.
Washington, Bryan R. *Politics of Exile*, 127–142.

Giovanni's Room (1956)

Bawer, Bruce. "Race and Art: The Career of James Baldwin." *NewC* 10.3 (1991): 19–21.
DeGout, Yasmin Y. "Dividing the Mind: Contradictory Portraits of Homerotic Love in *Giovanni's Room.*" *AAR* 26.3 (1992): 425–435.
Frontain, Raymond-Jean. "James Baldwin's *Giovanni's Room* and the Biblical Myth of David." *CEA* 57.2 (1995): 41–87.
Koponen, Wilfrid R. *Embracing Gay Identity*, 53–70.
Mengay, Donald H. "Failed Copy: *Giovanni's Room* and the (Re)Contextualization of Difference." *Genders* 17 (1993): 59–70.
Washington, Bryan R. *Politics of Exile*, 70–91.

Go Tell It on the Mountain (1952)

Allen, Shirley S. "Religious Symbolism and Psychic Reality in Baldwin's *Go Tell It on the Mountain.*" *College Language Association Journal* 19.2 (1975): 175, 177–179. Rpt. in Bloom, Harold, ed. *Major Modern Black American Writers*, 26–27
Allen, Shirley S. "Religious Symbolism and Psychic Reality in Baldwin's *Go Tell It on the Mountain.*" *College Language Association Journal* 19.2 (1975): 175, 177–179. Rpt. in Bloom, Harold, ed. *Modern Black American Fiction Writers*, 39–40.
Bawer, Bruce. "Race and Art: The Career of James Baldwin." *NewC* 10.3 (1991): 18–19.
Campbell, Jane. *Mythic Black Fiction: The Transformation of History*. Knoxville: University of Tennessee Press, 1986. 101–102. Rpt. in Bloom, Harold, ed. *Major Modern Black American Writers*, 29–30.
Campbell, Jane. *Mythic Black Fiction: The Transformation of History*. Knoxville: University of Tennessee Press, 1986. 101–102. Rpt. in Bloom, Harold, ed. *Modern Black American Fiction Writers*, 42–43.
Griffin, Farah Jasmine. *"Who Set You Flowin'?"*, 36–40, 87–91.
Scruggs, Charles. *Sweet Home*, 137–166.
Standley, Fred L. " 'But the City Was Real': James Baldwin's Literary Milieu," in Hakutani, Yoshinobu, ed. *City in African-American Literature*, 145–147.

If Beale Street Could Talk (1974)

Hakutani, Yoshinobu. "If the Street Could Talk: James Baldwin's Search for Love and Understanding," in Hakutani, Yoshinobu, ed. *City in African-American Literature*, 151, 152–153, 159–161, 162–165.
Oates, Joyce Carol. [Review of *If Beale Street Could Talk*]. *New York Times Book Review* (19 May 1974): 1–2. Rpt. in Bloom, Harold, ed. *Major Modern Black American Writers*, 25–26.

Just Above My Head (1979)

Bawer, Bruce. "Race and Art: The Career of James Baldwin." *NewC* 10.3 (1991): 25.
Forrest, Leon. *Relocations of the Spirit*, 263–266.
Harris, Trudier. *Black Women in the Fiction of James Baldwin*. Knoxville: Univer-

sity of Tennessee Press, 1985. 210–211. Rpt. in Bloom, Harold, ed. *Major Modern Black American Writers*, 27–29.

Harris, Trudier. *Black Women in the Fiction of James Baldwin*. Knoxville: University of Tennessee Press, 1985. 210–211. Rpt. in Bloom, Harold, ed. *Modern Black American Fiction Writers*, 40–42.

BALLANTYNE, SHEILA (1936–)

Norma Jean the Termite Queen (1975)

Greene, Gayle. *Changing the Story*, 80–84.

BALLARD, J. G. (1930–)

Hello America (1981)

Cooper, Ken. " 'Zero Pays the House': The Las Vegas Novel and Atomic Roulette." *ConL* 33.3 (1992): 538–539.

BAMBARA, TONI CADE (1939–)

Salt Eaters (1980)

De Weever, Jacqueline. *Mythmaking and Metaphor in Black Women's Fiction.* New York: St. Martin's Press, 1992. 62, 82–83. Rpt. in Bloom, Harold, ed. *Black American Women Fiction Writers*, 27–29.

De Weever, Jacqueline. *Mythmaking and Metaphor in Black Women's Fiction.* New York: St. Martin's Press, 1992. 62, 82–83. Rpt. in Bloom, Harold, ed. *Contemporary Black American Fiction Writers*, 12–14.

Hull, Gloria T. " 'What It Is I Think She's Doing Anyhow': A Reading of Toni Cade Bambara's *The Salt Eaters.*" *Conjuring: Black Women, Fiction, and Literary Tradition.* Ed. Marjorie Pryse and Hortense J. Spillers. Bloomington, IN: Indiana University Press, 1985. 220–221. Rpt. in Bloom, Harold, ed. *Black American Women Fiction Writers*, 9–10.

Kelley, Margot Anne. " 'Damballah Is the First Law of Thermodynamics': Modes of Access to Toni Cade Bambara's *The Salt Eaters.*" *AAR* 27.3 (1993): 479–493.

Kolmar, Wendy K. " 'Dialectics of Connectedness': Supernatural Elements in Novels by Bambara, Cisneros, Grahn, and Erdrich," in Carpenter, Lynette, ed. *Haunting the House of Fiction*, 238–240, 243–245, 246.

Porter, Nancy. "Women's Interracial Friendships and Visions of Community in *Meridian*, *The Salt Eaters,* and *Dessa Rose*," in Howe, Florence, ed. *Tradition and the Talents of Women*, 252, 255–257, 265–266.

Stanford, Ann Folwell. "He Speaks for Whom? Inscription and Reinscription of Women in *Invisible Man* and *The Salt Eaters.*" *MELUS* 18.2 (1992): 17–19, 24–30.

Wideman, John. "Healing of Velma Henry." *New York Times Book Review* (June 1, 1980): 28, Rpt. in Bloom, Harold, ed. *Black American Women Fiction Writers*, 18–19.

BARAKA, AMIRI (1934–)

System of Dante's Hell (1965)

Griffin, Farah Jasmine. *"Who Set You Flowin'?"*, 166–171.

BARNES, DJUNA (1892–1982)

Nightwood (1936)

Allen, Carolyn. "Erotics of Nora's Narrative in Djuna Barnes's *Nightwood*." *Signs* 19.1 (1993): 177–200.

Altman, Meryl. "Book of Repulsive Jews?: Rereading *Nightwood*." *RCF* 13.3 (1993): 160–171.

Backus, Margot Gayle. "'Looking for That Dead Girl': Incest, Pornography, and the Capitalist Family Romance in *Nightwood, The Years* and *Tar Baby*." *American Imago* 51.4 (1994): 525–529.

Harper, Phillip Brian. *Framing the Margins*, 73–89.

Herring, Phillip. "Djuna Barnes and Thelma Wood: The Vengeance of *Nightwood*." *JML* 18.1 (1992): 5–18.

Kaivola, Karen. "'Beast Turning Human': Constructions of the 'Primitive' in *Nightwood*." *RCF* 13.3 (1993): 172–185.

Marcus, Jane. "Laughing at Leviticus: *Nightwood* as Woman's Circus Epic," in Howe, Florence, ed. *Tradition and the Talents of Women*, 211–242.

Nimeiri, Ahmed. "Djuna Barnes's *Nightwood* and 'the Experience of America.'" *Crit* 34.2 (1993): 100–112.

Scott, Bonnie Kime. "Barnes Being 'Beast Familiar': Representation on the Margins of Modernism." *RCF* 13.3 (1993): 41–52.

Ryder (1928)

Stevenson, Sheryl. "*Ryder* as Contraception: Barnes vs. the Reproduction of Mothering." *RCF* 13.3 (1993): 97–106.

BARONDESS, SUE K. see KAUFMAN, SUE

BARTH, JOHN (1930–)

Chimera (1972)

Burke, Ruth E. *Games of Poetics*, 83–92.

End of the Road (1958)

Schaub, Thomas Hill. *American Fiction in the Cold War*, 163–184.

Floating Opera (1956)

Couturier, Maurice. "From Displacement to Compactness: John Barth's *The Floating Opera*." *Crit* 33.1 (1991): 3–21.

LETTERS (1979)

Strehle, Susan. *Fiction in the Quantum Universe*, 124–158.

Sabbatical (1982)

Carmichael, Thomas. "Postmodern Genealogy: John Barth's *Sabbatical* and *The Narrative of Arthur Gordon Pym*." *UTQ* 60.3 (1991): 389–401.

BARTHELME, DONALD (1931–1989)

Dead Father (1975)

Burke, Ruth E. *Games of Poetics*, 95–111.

King (1990)

Molesworth, Charles. "Nasciemento Effect and Barthelme's *The King*." *RCF* 11.2 (1991): 102–107.

Paradise (1986)

Strehle, Susan. *Fiction in the Quantum Universe*, 190–217.

Snow White (1967)

McCaffery, Larry. "Towards an Aesthetics of Trash: A Collaborative, Deconstructive Reading of: Barthelme's *Snow White:* The Aesthetics of Trash." *RCF* 11.2 (1991): 36–49.

BAUM, L. FRANK (1856–1919)

Wonderful Wizard of Oz (1900)

Aman, Reinhold. "Verbal Aggression in *The Wizard of Oz*." *Verbatim* 19.3 (1993): 27–28.

Geer, John G. and Thomas R. Rochon. "William Jennings Bryan on the Yellow Brick Road." *JACult* 16.4 (1993): 59–63.

Gilead, Sarah. "Magic Abjured: Closure in Children's Fantasy Fiction." *PMLA* 106.2 (1991): 278–282.

Griswold, Jerry. *Audacious Kids*, 29–41.

Johnson, Michael. "Ozdyssey in Plato." *Mythlore* 19.4 (1993): 22–27.

BEAGLE, PETER S. (1939–)

Innkeeper's Song (1994)

Kondratiev, Alexei. "Tales Newly Told: A Column on Current Modern Fantasy." *Mythlore* 20.1 (1994): 41, 43.

BEAUCHEMIN, YVES (1941–)

Alley Cat see *Le matou*

Juliette Pomerleau (1989)

Piccione, Marie-Lyne. "*Juliette Pomerleau* ou les facéties d'un récit en trompe-l'oeil." *DFS* 23 (1992): 78–85.

Le matou (1981)

Shek, Ben-Z. *French-Canadian*, 129–131.

BEAULIEU, VICTOR-LÉVY (1945–)

Don Quichotte de la démanche (1974)

Lamontagne, Andre. "Entre le récit de fondation et le récit de l'autre: L'Intertextualite dans *Don Quichotte de la démanche*." *Tangence* 41 (1993): 32–42.

Don Quixote in nighttown see *Don Quichotte de la démanche*

L'héritage (1987)

Blais, Marie-Josee and Jean Morency. "*L'héritage* de Victor-Levy Beaulieu: Un 'Testament' littéraire?" *DFS* 23 (1992): 97–104.

Lewis, Manon. "*L'héritage* oecuménique: Lecture d'une mosaïque religieuse." *Tangence* 41 (1993): 95–111.

Grandfathers see *Les grands-pères* (1971)

Les grands-pères

Smart, Patricia. *Writing in the Father's House*, 194–199.

Monsieur Melville (1978)

Morency, Jean. "Américanite et anthropophagie littéraire dans *Monsieur Melville*." *Tangence* 41 (1993): 54–68.

BEECHER, HENRY WARD (1813–1887)

Norwood (1867)

Castronovo, David. *American Gentleman*, 93–94.

BELLAMY, EDWARD (1850–1898)

Looking Backward (1888)

McClay, Wilfred M. "Edward Bellamy and the Politics of Meaning." *AQ* 64.2 (1995): 264–271.

BELLOW, SAUL (1915–)

Adventures of Augie March (1954)

Hollahan, Eugene. *Crisis-Consciousness*, 213–214.

Solomon, Barbara Probst. "Spanish Journey of Saul Bellow's Fiction." *Salmagundi* 106–107 (1995): 94–99.

Dangling Man (1944)

Hollahan, Eugene. *Crisis-Consciousness*, 210–211.

Dean's December (1982)

Hollahan, Eugene. *Crisis-Consciousness*, 228–229.

Henderson the Rain King (1959)

Byatt, A. S. *Passions of the Mind*, 132–139.

Desai, Anita. "Bellow, the Rain King." *Salmagundi* 106–107 (1995): 63–65.

Hollahan, Eugene. *Crisis-Consciousness*, 215–217.
Lawless, Kimberly J. "*Henderson the Rain King:* A Study of the American Hero." *BWVACET* 13.2 (1991): 153–164.
Quayum, M. A. "Bellow's *Henderson the Rain King* as an Allegory for the Fifties." *ASInt* 33.1 (1995): 65–74.
Singh, Sukhbir. "Bellow's *Henderson the Rain King*." *Expl* 50.2 (1992): 118–120.

Herzog (1964)
Hollahan, Eugene. *Crisis-Consciousness*, 217–221.
Rogers, Franklin R. *Occidental Ideographs*, 256–258.
Siegel, Ben. "Simply Not a Mandarin: Saul Bellow as Jew and Jewish Writer," in Friedman, Melvin J., ed. *Traditions, Voices, and Dreams*, 82–85.

Humboldt's Gift (1975)
Hollahan, Eugene. *Crisis-Consciousness*, 223–228.
Krupnick, Mark. " The Gift." *Salmagundi* 106–107 (1995): 85–88.
Quayam, M. A. "Adopting Emerson's Vision of Equilibrium: Citrine and the Two Opposite Poles of Twentieth-Century Consciousness in *Humboldt's Gift*." *SAJL* 10.1 (1991): 8–23.
Quayum, M. A. "Emerson's 'Humboldt': A Probable Source for Bellow's Von Humboldt Fleisher in *Humboldt's Gift*." *NConL* 22.4 (1992): 7–8.

Mr. Sammler's Planet (1970)
Goldsmith, Arnold L. *Modern American Urban Novel*, 133–152.
Hollahan, Eugene. *Crisis-Consciousness*, 221–223.
Langer, Lawrence L. *Admitting the Holocaust*, 84–87.
Parini, Jay. "Mr. Sammler, Hero of Our Time." *Salmagundi* 106–107 (1995): 66–70.

More Die of Heartbreak (1987)
Hollahan, Eugene. *Crisis-Consciousness*, 229–234.
Safer, Elaine B. "From Poem to Cartoon: Comic Irony in Saul Bellow's *More Die of Heartbreak*." *Crit* 34.4 (1993): 203–219.

Victim (1947)
Hollahan, Eugene. *Crisis-Consciousness*, 211–213.

BENFORD, GREGORY (1941–)

Great Sky River (1987)
Curl, Ruth. "Metaphors of Cyberpunk," in Slusser, George, ed. *Fiction 2000*, 237–244.

Timescape (1980)
Benford, Gregory. "Time and *Timescape*." *SFS* 20.2 (1993): 184–190.

BENSON, MILDRED see CLARK, JOAN

BERESFORD-HOWE, CONSTANCE (1922–)

Book of Eve (1973)
Thompson, Elizabeth. *Pioneer Woman*, 116, 121, 124–125, 129, 134, 135, 150.

BERSIANIK, LOUKY (1930–)

Euguelion see *L'Euguélionne*

L'Euguélionne (1976)
Shek, Ben-Z. *French-Canadian*, 89–91.

BÉSSETTE, GERARD (1920–)

Le libraire (1960)
Raoul, Valerie. *Distinctly Narcissistic*, 170–178.
Shek, Ben-Z. *French-Canadian*, 47.

Le semestre (1979)
Paterson, Janet M. *Postmodernism*, 77–84.

L'incubation (1965)
Jacopin, Paul. "Ivresse et stratégie du discours: *L'incubation* de Gerard Béssette." *ECCS* 35 (1993): 205–213.
Robidoux, Rejean. "Gerard Béssette ou l'exaltation de la parole." *UTQ* 63.4 (1994): 542–544.
Shek, Ben-Z. *French-Canadian*, 48–49.

Not for Every Eye see *Le libraire*

BESTER, ALFRED (1913–1987)

Demolished Man (1953)
Kelleghan, Fiona. "Hell's My Destination: Imprisonment in the Works of Alfred Bester." *SFS* 21.3 (1994): 351–364.

Stars My Destination (1956)
Kelleghan, Fiona. "Hell's My Destination: Imprisonment in the Works of Alfred Bester." *SFS* 21.3 (1994): 351–364.

BIRDSELL, SANDRA (1942–)

Chrome Suite (1992)
Harrison, Dallas. "Sandra Birdsell," in Lecker, Robert, ed. *Canadian Writers and Their Works: Fiction Series* (Vol. 12), 33–34, 58–64.

Missing Child (1989)
Harrison, Dallas. "Sandra Birdsell," in Lecker, Robert, ed. *Canadian Writers and Their Works: Fiction Series* (Vol. 12), 28–33, 51–58.

BIRNEY, EARLE (1904–)

Down the Long Table (1955)
Bok, Christian. "Secular Opiate: Marxism as an Ersatz Religion in Three Canadian Texts." *CanL* 147 (1995): 11–22.

BISHOP, JOHN PEALE (1892–1944)

Many Thousands Gone (1931)
Settle, Mary Lee. "On John Peale Bishop's *Many Thousands Gone*," in Madden, David, ed. *Classics of Civil War Fiction*, 110–116.

BISSOONDATH, NEIL (1955–)

Casual Brutality (1989)

Richards, David. "Burning Down the House: Neil Bissoondath's Fiction," in Howells, Coral Ann, ed. *Narrative Strategies*, 50–53, 56.

BLAIS, MARIE-CLAIRE (1939–)

Angel of Solitude see *L'ange de la solitude*

Anna's World see *Visions d'Anna*

Deaf to the City see *Sourd dans la ville*

La belle bête (1959)

Egloff, Karin M. "Entre la mère-miroir et l'amer voir: Le Regard écorche dans *La belle bête* de Marie-Claire Blais." *QS* 17 (1993–94): 125–133.
Green, Mary Jean. *Marie-Claire Blais*, 8–14.

L'ange de la solitude (1989)

Brown, Anne E. "Sappho's Daughters: Lesbian Identities in Novels by Québécois Women (1960–1990)," in Brown, Anne E., ed. *International Women's Writing*, 38–40.
Dufault, Roseanna Lewis. "Decline of the American Empire According to Marie-Claire Blais." *QS* 13 (1991–92): 47–53.
Green, Mary Jean. *Marie-Claire Blais*, 104–108.

Le loup (1972)

Green, Mary Jean. *Marie-Claire Blais*, 48–53.

Les nuits de l'underground (1978)

Green, Mary Jean. *Marie-Claire Blais*, 96–104.
Perron, Dominique. "Les Discours sociaux dans *Les nuits de l'underground* de Marie-Claire Blais." *CanL* 138–139 (1993): 53–70.

Literary Affair see *Une liaison parisienne*

Mad Shadows see *La belle bête*

Manuscripts of Pauline Archange see *Manuscrits de Pauline Archange*

Manuscrits de Pauline Archange (1968)

Brown, Anne E. "Sappho's Daughters: Lesbian Identities in Novels by Québécois Women (1960–1990)," in Brown, Anne E., ed. *International Women's Writing*, 32–34.
Dufault, Roseanna Lewis. *Metaphors of Identity*, 29– 42.
Green, Mary Jean. *Marie-Claire Blais*, 67–82.
Green, Mary Jean. "Structures de la libération: expérience féminine et forme autobiographique au Québec," in Saint-Martin, Lori, ed. *L'autre lecture* (Tome 1), 191–195.

Nights in the Underground see *Les nuits de l'underground*

Pierre (1982)

Green, Mary Jean. *Marie-Claire Blais*, 35–39.

Season in the Life of Emmanuel see *Une saison dans la vie d'Emmanuel*

Sourd dans la ville (1979)

Green, Mary Jean. *Marie-Claire Blais*, 109–123.
Shek, Ben-Z. *French-Canadian*, 68–70.

St. Lawrence Blues see *Un Joualonais sa Joualonie*

Un Joualonais sa Joualonie (1973)

Green, Mary Jean. *Marie-Claire Blais*, 83–91.
Oore, Irene. "La Quete de l'identité et l'inacheve du devenir dans *Un Joualonais sa joualonie* de Marie-Claire Blais." *SCL* 18.2 (1993): 81–93.

Une liaison parisienne (1976)

Green, Mary Jean. *Marie-Claire Blais*, 91–95.

Une saison dans la vie d'Emmanuel (1965)

Green, Mary Jean. *Marie-Claire Blais*, 15–26.
Nardout-Lafarge, Elisabeth. "Dialogue et théâtralisation chez Ducharme, Blais et Godbout." *FR* 67.1 (1993): 86–88.
Shek, Ben-Z. *French-Canadian*, 66–68.

Visions d'Anna (1982)

Couillard, Marie. "*Visions d'Anna* ou l'écriture du vertige de Marie-Claire Blais." *QS* 17 (1993–94): 117–124.
Green, Mary Jean. *Marie-Claire Blais*, 118–123.

Wolf see *Le loup*

BLAISE, CLARK (1940–)

Lunar Attractions (1979)

O'Rourke, William. *Signs of the Literary Times*, 109–111.

BONTEMPS, ARNA (1902–1973)

Black Thunder (1936)

Reagan, Daniel. "Voices of Silence: The Representation of Orality in Arna Bontemps' *Black Thunder*." *SAF* 19.1 (1991): 71–83.
Sundquist, Eric J. *Hammer of Creation*, 92–134.

BOSWORTH, SHEILA

Almost Innocent (1984)

Donaldson, Susan V. "Consumption and Complicity in Sheila Bosworth's *Almost Innocent*." *SoQ* 30.2–3 (1992): 113–122.

BOURJAILY, VANCE (1922–)

Confessions of a Youth Spent (1960)

Shakir, Evelyn. "Arab Mothers, American Sons: Women in Arab-American Autobiograhies." *MELUS* 17.3 (1991–92): 5–8.

BOWER, B. M. (1874–1940)

Chip of the Flying U (1906)

Yates, Norris. *Gender and Genre*, 22–25, 31–34.

Flying U's Last Stand (1915)

Yates, Norris. *Gender and Genre*, 25–29.

Phantom Herd (1916)

Yates, Norris. *Gender and Genre*, 29–30.

BOWERING, GEORGE (1935–)

Burning Water (1980)

Deer, Glenn. *Postmodern Canadian Fiction*, 97–109.
Kuester, Martin. *Framing Truths*, 106–123.

Caprice (1987)

Colvile, Georgiana M. M. "On Coyote or Canadian Otherness in Robert Kroetsch's *Badlands* and George Bowering's *Caprice*." *RMS* 35 (1992): 134–138.

Short Sad Book (1977)

Kuester, Martin. *Framing Truths*, 96–106.

BOWERING, MARILYN R. (1949–)

To All Appearances a Lady (1989)

Huggan, Graham. "Latitudes of Romance: Representations of Chinese Canada in Bowering's *To All Appearances a Lady* and Lee's *Disappearing Moon Café*." *CanL* 140 (1994): 34–44.

BOWLES, JANE (1917–1973)

Two Serious Ladies (1943)

Gentile, Kathy Justice. "'The Dreaded Voyage into the World': Jane Bowles and Her Serious Ladies." *SAF* 22.1 (1994): 47, 52–59.
Roditi, Edouard. "Fiction of Jane Bowles as a Form of Self-Exorcism." *RCF* 12.2 (1992): 188–190.

BOYD, JOHN (1919–)

Andromeda Gun (1974)

Davis, Robert Murray. *Playing Cowboys*, 106–114.

BRACKENRIDGE, HUGH HENRY (1748–1816)

Modern Chivalry (1815)

Chaden, Caryn. "Dress and Undress in Brackenridge's *Modern Chivalry*." *EAL* 26.1 (1991): 55–72.

Rice, Grantland S. "*Modern Chivalry* and the Resistance to Textual Authority." *AL* 67.2 (1995): 257–281.

BRACKETT, LEIGH (1915–1978)

Tiger Among Us (1957)

Haut, Woody. *Pulp Culture*, 114–119.

BRADBURY, RAY (1920–)

Fahrenheit 451 (1953)

Booker, M. Keith. *Dystopian Impulse*, 106–112.

Seed, David. "Flight from the Good Life: *Fahrenheit 451* in the Context of Postwar American Dystopias." *JAmS* 28.2 (1994): 225–240.

Spencer, Susan. "Post-Apocalyptic Library: Oral and Literate Culture in *Fahrenheit 451* and *A Canticle for Leibowitz*." *Extrapolation* 32.4 (1991): 333–335, 341.

BRADLEY, DAVID (1950–)

Chaneysville Incident (1981)

Hogue, W. Lawrence. "Problematizing History: David Bradley's *The Chaneysville Incident*." *CLAJ* 38.4 (1995): 441–460.

Wilson, Matthew. "The African American Historian: David Bradley's *The Chaneysville Incident*." *AAR* 29.1 (1995): 97–106.

BRADLEY, MARION ZIMMER (1930–)

Firebrand (1987)

Fry, Carrol L. "Goddess Ascending: Feminist Neo-Pagan Witchcraft in Marian Zimmer Bradley's Novels." *JPC* 27.1 (1993): 75–76.

Mists of Avalon (1982)

Fry, Carrol L. "Goddess Ascending: Feminist Neo-Pagan Witchcraft in Marian Zimmer Bradley's Novels." *JPC* 27.1 (1993): 72–75, 77.

Hughes, Melinda. "Dark Sisters and Light Sisters: Sister Doubling and the Search for Sisterhood in *The Mists of Avalon* and *The White Raven*." *Mythlore* 19.1 (1993): 24–27.

Tobin, Lee Ann. "Why Change the Arthur Story? Marion Zimmer Bradley's *The Mists of Avalon*." *Extrapolation* 34.2 (1993): 147–157.

BRAUTIGAN, RICHARD (1935–1984)

Hawkline Monster: A Gothic Western (1974)

Davis, Robert Murray. *Playing Cowboys*, 64–71.

Trout Fishing in America (1967)

Legler, Gretchen. "Brautigan's Waters." *CEA* 54.1 (1991): 67–69.

BREWER, GIL (1922–1983)

13 French Street (1951)

Haut, Woody. *Pulp Culture*, 150–156.

BROCHU, ANDRÉ (1942–)

La vie aux trousses (1993)

Riendeau, Pascal. "Le Champ existentiel ou les avatars d'une construction identitaire: Sur *La vie aux trousses* d'André Brochu." *V&I* 20.3 (1995): 571–586.

BRODY, CATHARINE

Nobody Starves (1932)

Hapke, Laura. *Daughters of the Great Depression*, 125–128.

BRONER, E. M. (1930–)

Her Mothers (1972)

Farr, Cecilia Konchar. "Her Mother's Language," in Daly, Brenda O., ed. *Narrating Mothers*, 94–107.

Tucker, Lindsey. *Textual Excap(e)ades*, 55–70.

BROOKE, FRANCES (1724–1789)

History of Emily Montague (1769)

Benedict, Barbara M. "Margins of Sentiment: Nature, Letter, and Law in Frances Brooke's Epistolary Novels." *ArielE* 23.3 (1992): 13–22.

Howells, Robin. "Dialogism in Canada's First Novel: *The History of Emily Montague*." *CRCL* 20.3–4 (1993): 437–450.

McCarthy, Dermot. "Sisters under the Mink: The Correspondent Fear in *The History of Emily Montague*." *ECW* 51–52 (1993–94): 340–357.

Merrett, Robert. "Politics of Romance in *The History of Emily Montague*." *CanL* 133 (1992): 92–108.

Sellwood, Jane. " 'A Little Acid Is Absolutely Necesssary': Narrative as Coquette in Frances Brooke's *The History of Emily Montague*." *CanL* 136 (1993): 60–79.

History of Lady Julia Mandeville (1763)

Benedict, Barbara M. "Margins of Sentiment: Nature, Letter, and Law in Frances Brooke's Epistolary Novels." *ArielE* 23.3 (1992): 10–13.

BROOKNER, ANITA (1928–)

Family and Friends (1985)

MacLaine, Brent. "Photofiction as Family Album: David Galloway, Paul Theroux and Anita Brookner." *Mosaic* 24.2 (1991): 132, 145–147.

BROSSARD, NICOLE (1943–)

Le désert mauve (1987)

Conley, Katharine. "Spiral as Mobius Strip: Inside/Outside *Le désert Mauve.*" *QS* 18 (1994): 149–158.

Gould, Karen. "Féminisme / postmodernité / esthétique de lecture: *Le désert mauve* de Nicole Broussard," in Saint-Martin, Lori, ed. *L'autre lecture*, (Tome 2), 101–114.

McPherson, Karen S. *Incriminations*, 158–178.

Paterson, Janet M. *Postmodernism*, 111–124.

Perry, Catherine. "L'Imagination créatrice dans *Le désert mauve:* Transfiguration de la réalité dans le projet féministe." *V&I* 19.3 (1994): 585–607.

Servin, Henri. "*Le désert mauve* de Nicole Brossard, ou l'indicible référent." *QS* 13 (1991–92): 55–63.

Mauve Desert see *Le désert mauve*

Picture Theory (1982)

Siemerling, Winfried. *Discoveries of the Other*, 181–204.

BROWN, CHARLES BROCKDEN (1771–1810)

Arthur Mervyn (1800)

Christophersen, Bill. *Apparition in the Glass*, 87–125.

Hinds, Elizabeth Jane Wall. "Charles Brockden Brown and the Frontiers of Discourse," in Mogen, David, ed. *Frontier Gothic*, 114–116.

Edgar Huntly (1799)

Anderson, Douglas. "*Edgar Huntly*'s Dark Inheritance." *PQ* 70.4 (1991): 453–473.

Christophersen, Bill. *Apparition in the Glass*, 126–164.

Gardner, Jared. "Alien Nation: *Edgar Huntly*'s Savage Awakening." *AL* 66.3 (1994): 429–461.

Hamelman, Steve. "Rhapsodist in the Wilderness: Brown's Romantic Quest in *Edgar Huntly.*" *SAF* 21.2 (1993): 171–188.

Hinds, Elizabeth Jane Wall. "Charles Brockden Brown and the Frontiers of Discourse," in Mogen, David, ed. *Frontier Gothic*, 110–114.

Hinds, Elizabeth Jane Wall. "Charles Brockden Brown's Revenge Tragedy: *Edgar Huntly* and the Uses of Property." *EAL* 30.1 (1995): 51–70.

Kamrath, Mark L. "Brown and the Enlightenment: A Study of the Influence of Voltaire's *Candide* in *Edgar Huntly.*" *ATQ* 5.1 (1991): 5–14.

Krause, Sydney J. "Penn's Elm and *Edgar Huntly*: Dark 'Instruction to the Heart.' " *AL* 66.3 (1994): 463–484.

Ormond (1799)

Christophersen, Bill. *Apparition in the Glass*, 55–86.

Cowell, Pattie. "Class, Gender, and Genre: Deconstructing Social Formulas on the Gothic Frontier," in Mogen, David, ed. *Frontier Gothic*, 131–133.

Hinds, Elizabeth Jane Wall. "Charles Brockden Brown and the Frontiers of Discourse," in Mogen, David, ed. *Frontier Gothic*, 121–123.

Weiland (1798)

Christophersen, Bill. *Apparition in the Glass*, 26–54.
Hinds, Elizabeth Jane Wall. "Charles Brockden Brown and the Frontiers of Discourse," in Mogen, David, ed. *Frontier Gothic*, 116–121.
Rombes, Nicholas, Jr. " 'All Was Lonely, Darksome, and Waste': *Wieland* and the Construction of the New Republic." *SAF* 22.1 (1994): 37–46.
Scheiber, Andrew J. " 'The Arm Lifted against Me': Love, Terror, and the Construction of Gender in *Wieland*." *EAL* 26.2 (1991): 173–194.

BROWN, LINDA BEATRICE (1939–)

Rainbow Roun Mah Shoulder (1984)

Tate, Linda. *Southern Weave of Women*, 183–194.

BROWN, RITA MAE (1944–)

Bingo (1988)

Ward, Carol M. *Rita Mae Brown*, 96–109.

High Hearts (1986)

Tate, Linda. *Southern Weave of Women*, 79–91.
Ward, Carol M. *Rita Mae Brown*, 134–154.

In Her Day (1976)

Ward, Carol M. *Rita Mae Brown*, 67–75.

Rubyfruit Jungle (1973)

Roof, Judith. " 'This Is Not for You': The Sexuality of Mothering," in Daly, Brenda O., ed. *Narrating Mothers*, 167–172.
Ward, Carol M. *Rita Mae Brown*, 41–67.

Six of One (1978)

Ward, Carol M. *Rita Mae Brown*, 76–96.

Southern Discomfort (1982)

Ward, Carol M. *Rita Mae Brown*, 110–121.

Sudden Death (1983)

Ward, Carol M. *Rita Mae Brown*, 122–133.

Wish You Were Here (1990)

Ward, Carol M. *Rita Mae Brown*, 155–162.

BROWN, ROSELLEN (1939–)

Civil Wars (1984)

Porter, Nancy. "Women's Interracial Friendships and Visions of Community in *Meridian, The Salt Eaters,* and *Dessa Rose*," in Howe, Florence, ed. *Tradition and the Talents of Women*, 252, 257–260, 265–266.

BROWN, WILLIAM WELLS (1816?–1884)

Clotel (1853)

Bentley, Nancy. "White Slaves: The Mulatto Hero in Antebellum Fiction." *AL* 65.3 (1993):, 506–507.

Dorsey, Peter A. "De-Authorizing Slavery: Realism in Stowe's *Uncle Tom's Cabin* and Brown's *Clotel*." *ESQ* 41.4 (1995): 258–263, 274–282.

Mitchell, Angelyn. "Her Side of His Story: A Feminist Analysis of Two Nineteenth-Century Antebellum Novels—William Wells Brown's *Clotel* and Harriet E. Wilson's *Our Nig*." *ALR* 24.3 (1992): 7–12.

Wright, Lee Alfred. *Identity, Family, and Folklore*, 5–8.

BRUCE, CHARLES (1906–1971)

Channel Shore (1954)

Creelman, David. "Charles Bruce: *The Channel Shore* between Realism and Nostalgia." *DR* 70.4 (1991): 460–479.

BRUNET, BERTHELOT (1901–1948)

Les Hypocrites (1945)

Schwartzwald, Robert. "Of Bohemians, Inverts, and Hypocrites: Berthelot Brunet's Montreal." *QS* 15 (1992–93): 87–98.

BUCKLER, ERNEST (1908–1984)

Mountain and the Valley (1952)

Kuester, Martin. *Framing Truths*, 47–55.

Van Rys, John C. "Diminishing Voice in Buckler's *The Mountain and the Valley*." *SCL* 20.1 (1995): 65–79.

Williams, David. *Confessional Fictions*, 147–173.

BUCKLER, FIELDING (1869–1968)

Call Home the Heart (1932)

Hapke, Laura. *Daughters of the Great Depression*, 166–169.

BUCKLEY, WILLIAM F. (1925–)

Mongoose R.I.P. (1987)

Sarchett, Barry W. "Unreading the Spy Thriller: The Example of William F. Buckley, Jr." *JPC* 26.2 (1992): 135–137.

Saving the Queen (1976)

Sarchett, Barry W. "Unreading the Spy Thriller: The Example of William F. Buckley, Jr." *JPC* 26.2 (1992): 133–134, 136.

Stained Glass (1978)

Sarchett, Barry W. "Unreading the Spy Thriller: The Example of William F. Buckley, Jr." *JPC* 26.2 (1992): 127–139.

BURNETT, FRANCES HODGSON (1849–1924)

Little Lord Fauntleroy (1885)

Griswold, Jerry. *Audacious Kids*, 93–103.
MacLeod, Anne Scott. *American Childhood*, 77–83.

Secret Garden (1911)

Evans, Gwyneth. "Girl in the Garden: Variations on a Feminine Pastoral." *CLAQ* 19.1 (1994): 20–21.
Griswold, Jerry. *Audacious Kids*, 200–214.
Plotz, Judith. "*Secret Garden II:* Or, Lady Chatterly's Lover as Palimpest." *CLAQ* 19.1 (1994): 15–19.
Stolzenbach, Mary M. "Braid Yorkshire: The Language of Myth? An Appreciation of *The Secret Garden* by Frances Hodgson Burnett." *Mythlore* 20.4 (1995): 25–29.

BURROUGHS, EDGAR RICE (1875–1950)

Tarzan of the Apes (1914)

Griswold, Jerry. *Audacious Kids*, 104–120.

BURROUGHS, WILLIAM S. (1914–1997)

Naked Lunch (1959)

Ayers, David. "Long Last Goodbye: Control and Resistance in the Work of William Burroughs." *JAmS* 27.2 (1993): 223–224, 230, 232.

Nova Express (1964)

Ayers, David. "Long Last Goodbye: Control and Resistance in the Work of William Burroughs." *JAmS* 27.2 (1993): 225, 228, 230–231, 232, 234–235.

Soft Machine (1961)

Ayers, David. "Long Last Goodbye: Control and Resistance in the Work of William Burroughs." *JAmS* 27.2 (1993): 224–225, 226, 227, 232.

Ticket That Exploded (1962)

Ayers, David. "Long Last Goodbye: Control and Resistance in the Work of William Burroughs." *JAmS* 27.2 (1993): 227–236.

BURT, KATHARINE NEWLIN

Branding Iron (1919)

Yates, Norris. *Gender and Genre*, 105–109.

Hidden Creek (1920)

Yates, Norris. *Gender and Genre*, 110–111.

Tall Ladder (1932)

Yates, Norris. *Gender and Genre*, 111–114.

BUSCH, FREDERICK (1941–)

Sometimes I Live in the Country (1986)

Grenier, Donald J. *Women Enter the Wilderness*, 59–66.

BUTLER, OCTAVIA E. (1947–)

Kindred (1979)

Kubitschek, Missy Dehn. *Claiming the Heritage*, 24–51.

McKible, Adam. " 'These Are the Facts of the Darky's History': Thinking History and Reading Names in Four African American Texts." *AAR* 28.2 (1994): 228, 233.

Xenogenesis (1977)

Peppers, Cathy. "Dialogic Origins and Alien Identities in Butler's *Xenogenesis*." *SFS* 22.1 (1995): 47–62.

White, Eric. "Erotics of Becoming: *Xenogenesis* and *The Thing*." *SFS* 20.3 (1993): 402–406.

CABLE, GEORGE WASHINGTON (1844–1925)

Grandissimes (1880)

Ladd, Barbara. " 'An Atmosphere of Hints and Allusions': Bras-Coupe and the Context of Black Insurrection in *The Grandissimes*." *SoQ* 29.3 (1991): 63–76.

Limon, John. *Writing After War*, 62–63, 66–67.

John March (1894)

Limon, John. *Writing After War*, 63–65.

Madame Delphine (1881)

McLendon, Jacquelyn. *Politics of Color*, 15–17.

CADIGAN, PAT (1953–)

Synners (1991)

Balsamo, Anne. "Feminism for the Incurably Informed." *SAQ* 92.4 (1993): 681–712.

CAHAN, ABRAHAM (1860–1951)

Rise of David Levinsky (1917)

Weber, Donald. "Outsiders and Greenhorns: Christopher Newman in the Old World, David Levinsky in the New." *AL* 67.4 (1995): 732–741.

CAIN, JAMES M. (1892–1977)

Mildred Pierce (1941)

Fine, David. "Running Out of Space: Vanishing Landscapes in California Novels." *WAL* 26.3 (1991): 212–213.

Postman Always Rings Twice (1934)

Fine, David. "Running Out of Space: Vanishing Landscapes in California Novels." *WAL* 26.3 (1991): 213–214.

CALDWELL, ERSKINE (1903–1987)

God's Little Acre (1933)

Hapke, Laura. *Daughters of the Great Depression*, 20–22.

Watson, Jay. "Rhetoric of Exhaustion and the Exhaustion of Rhetoric: Erskine Caldwell in the Thirties." *MissQ* 46.2 (1993): 215–229.

Tobacco Road (1932)

Watson, Jay. "Rhetoric of Exhaustion and the Exhaustion of Rhetoric: Erskine Caldwell in the Thirties." *MissQ* 46.2 (1993): 215–229.

CALISHER, HORTENSE (1911–)

Age (1987)

Snodgras, Kathleen. *Fiction of Hortense Calisher*, 104–106.

Bobby-Soxer (1986)

Snodgras, Kathleen. *Fiction of Hortense Calisher*, 51–53.

Eagle Eye (1973)

Snodgras, Kathleen. *Fiction of Hortense Calisher*, 45–51.

False Entry (1961)

Snodgras, Kathleen. *Fiction of Hortense Calisher*, 54–61.

Journal from Ellipsia (1965)

Snodgras, Kathleen. *Fiction of Hortense Calisher*, 91–94.

Last Trolley Ride (1966)

Snodgras, Kathleen. *Fiction of Hortense Calisher*, 103–104.

Mysteries of Motion (1983)

Snodgras, Kathleen. *Fiction of Hortense Calisher*, 95–101.

New Yorkers (1969)

Snodgras, Kathleen. *Fiction of Hortense Calisher*, 61–67.

Queenie (1973)

Snodgras, Kathleen. *Fiction of Hortense Calisher*, 40–45.

Saratoga, Hot (1984)

Snodgras, Kathleen. *Fiction of Hortense Calisher*, 85–90.

Standard Dreaming (1972)

Snodgras, Kathleen. *Fiction of Hortense Calisher*, 82–85.

Textures of Life (1963)

Snodgras, Kathleen. *Fiction of Hortense Calisher*, 37–40.

CALLAGHAN, MORLEY (1903–1990)

Loved and the Lost (1951)

Orange, John. *Orpheus in Winter: Morley Callaghan's The Loved and the Lost.* Toronto: ECW Press, 1993.

More Joy in Heaven (1937)

Woodcock, George. *Moral Predicament: Morley Callaghan's More Joy in Heaven.* Toronto: ECW Press, 1993.

Such Is My Beloved (1934)

Avison, Margaret. "Reading Morley Callaghan's *Such Is My Beloved.*" *CanL* 133 (1992): 204–208.

Burbidge, John W. "Religion in Morley Callaghan's *Such Is My Beloved.*" *JCSR* 27.3 (1992): 105–114.

James, William Closson. "Ambiguities of Love in Morley Callaghan's *Such Is My Beloved.*" *CanL* 138–139 (1993): 35–51.

CALLAHAN, SOFIA ALICE (1868–1894)

Wynema (1891)

Ruoff, A. LaVonne Brown. "Justice for Indians and Women: The Protest Fiction of Alice Callahan and Pauline Johnson." *WLT* 66.2 (1992): 249–252.

Van Dyke, Annette. "Introduction to *Wynema, a Child of the Forest*, by Sofia Alice Callahan." *SAIL* 4.2–3 (1992): 123–128.

CAMERON, ANNE (1938–)

Journey (1982)

Davidson, Arnold E. *Coyote Country*, 119–135.

CAMPBELL, MARIA (1940–)

Halfbreed (1973)

Lundgren, Jodi. " 'Being a Half-Breed': Discourses of Race and Cultural Syncreticity in the Works of Three Metis Women Writers." *CanL* 144 (1995): 65–67, 71–74.

CAMPBELL, WILLIAM EDWARD MARCH see MARCH, WILLIAM

CANNON, CORNELIA JAMES (1876–1969)

Red Rust (1928)

Robb, Kenneth A. "Cornelia James Cannon and Walter Havighurst: Undermining the Immigrant Stereotype in Midwestern Fiction," in Noe, Marcia, ed. *Exploring the Midwestern*, 192–201.

CANTWELL, ROBERT (1908–1978)

Land of Plenty (1934)

Hapke, Laura. *Daughters of the Great Depression*, 56–58.

CAO YOUFANG

American Moon (1986)

Wong, Sau-ling Cynthia. "Ethnicizing Gender: An Exploration of Sexuality as Sign in Chinese Immigrant Literature," in Lim, Shirley Geok-lin, ed. *Reading the Literatures of Asian America*, 118–120.

CARD, ORSON SCOTT (1951–)

Ender's Game (1985)

Blackmore, Tim. "Ender's Beginning: Battling the Military in Orson Scott Card's *Ender's Game*." *Extrapolation* 32.2 (1991): 124–142.

Red Prophet (1988)

Attebery, Brian. "Godmaking in the Heartland: The Backgrounds of Orson Scott Card's American Fantasy," in Morse, Donald E., ed. *Celebration of the Fantastic*, 64–65.

Seventh Son (1987)

Attebery, Brian. "Godmaking in the Heartland: The Backgrounds of Orson Scott Card's American Fantasy," in Morse, Donald E., ed. *Celebration of the Fantastic*, 62–63.

Wyrms (1987)

Attebery, Brian. "Godmaking in the Heartland: The Backgrounds of Orson Scott Card's American Fantasy," in Morse, Donald E., ed. *Celebration of the Fantastic*, 67–68.

Townsend, Johnny. "Passion vs. Will: Homosexuality in Orson Scott Card's *Wyrms*." *RQ* 9.1 (1992): 48–55.

CARON, LOUIS (1942–)

Le Coup de poing (1990)

Schick, Constance Gosselin. "Écrire le corps québécois: *Le Coup de poing* de Louis Caron." *FR* 67.6 (1994): 1024–1032.

CARR, CALEB (1955–)

Alienist (1994)

Gonshak, Henry. " 'The Child Is Father to the Man': The Psychopathology of Serial Killing in Caleb Carr's *The Alienist*." *NConL* 25.1 (1995): 12–13.

CASTILLO, ANA (1953–)

Mixquiahuala Letters (1986)

Castillo, Debra A. "Borderliners: Federico Campbell and Ana Castillo," in Higonnet, Margaret R., ed. *Reconfigured Spheres*, 148–150, 152–154, 163–170.

Quintana, Alvina E. "Ana Castillo's *The Mixquiahuala Letters:* The Novelist as Ethnographer," in Calderón, Héctor, ed. *Criticism in the Borderlands*, 72–83.
Rebolledo, Tey Diana. *Women Singing in the Snow*, 117–118.
Yarbro-Bejarano, Yvonne. "Multiple Subject in the Writing of Ana Castillo." *AmRev* 20.1 (1992): 66–68.

Sapogonia (1990)

Gomez-Vega, Ibis. "Debunking Myths: The Hero's Role in Ana Castillo's *Sapogonia.*" *AmRev* 22.1–2 (1994): 244–258.
Yarbro-Bejarano, Yvonne. "Multiple Subject in the Writing of Ana Castillo." *AmRev* 20.1 (1992): 68–69.

CATHER, WILLA (1873–1947)

Alexander's Bridge (1912)

Gerber, Philip. *Willa Cather*, 33–34.

Death Comes for the Archbishop (1927)

Byatt, A. S. *Passions of the Mind*, 210–216.
Gerber, Philip. *Willa Cather*, 62–65.
Urgo, Joseph R. *Willa Cather*, 167–190.
Wagenknecht, Edward. *Willa Cather*, 109–112.

Lost Lady (1923)

Dyck, Reginald. "Frontier Violence in the Garden of America," in Heyne, Eric, ed. *Desert, Garden*, 59–61.
Fisher-Wirth, Ann W. "Reading Marian Forrester." *Legacy* 9.1 (1992): 35–48.
Gerber, Philip. *Willa Cather*, 52–56.
Murphy, John J. "Filters, Portraits, and History's Mixed Bag': *A Lost Lady* and *The Age of Innocence.*" *TCL* 38.4 (1992): 477–484.
Urgo, Joseph R. *Willa Cather*, 73–78, 80–82.
Wagenknecht, Edward. *Willa Cather*, 91–95.

Lucy Gayheart (1935)

Albertini, Virgil. "Cather's *Lucy Gayheart:* A Girl in Motion." *PVR* 19.2 (1991): 37–44.
Chown, Linda. " 'It Came Closer Than That': Willa Cather's *Lucy Gayheart.*" *CathSt* 2 (1993): 118–139.
Gerber, Philip. *Willa Cather*, 69–71.
Urgo, Joseph R. *Willa Cather*, 111–129.
Wagenknecht, Edward. *Willa Cather*, 122–126.

My Antonia (1918)

Dyck, Reginald. "Frontier Violence in the Garden of America," in Heyne, Eric, ed. *Desert, Garden*, 58–59.
Fisher-Wirth, Ann. "Out of the Mother: Loss in My Antonia." *CathSt* 2 (1993): 41–71.
Funda, Evelyn I. " 'The Breath Vibrating Behind It': Intimacy the Storytelling of Antonia Shimerda." *WAL* 29.3 (1994): 195–216.
Gerber, Philip. *Willa Cather*, 43–46.

McElhiney, Annette Bennington. "Willa Cather's Use of a Tripartite Narrative Point of View in *My Antonia*." *CEA* 56.1 (1993): 65–76.

Millington, Richard H. "Willa Cather and 'The Storyteller': Hostility to the Novel in *My Antonia*." *AL* 66.4 (1994): 689–717.

Murphy, David. "Jeich Antonie: Czechs, the Land, Cather, and the Pavelka Farmstead." *GPQ* 14.2 (1994): 85–106.

Pickle, Linda S. "Foreign-Born Immigrants on the Great Plains Frontier in Fiction and Nonfiction," in Heyne, Eric, ed. *Desert, Garden*, 82–86.

Romines, Ann. *Home Plot*, 140–143, 147–150.

Urgo, Joseph R. *Willa Cather*, 54–73.

Wagenknecht, Edward. *Willa Cather*, 79–84.

My Mortal Enemy (1926)

Gerber, Philip. *Willa Cather*, 59–62.

Miller, Robert K. "Strains of Blood: Myra Driscoll and the Romance of the Celts." *CathSt* 169–177.

Urgo, Joseph R. *Willa Cather*, 193–195.

Wagenknecht, Edward. *Willa Cather*, 101–106.

O Pioneers! (1913)

Byatt, A. S. *Passions of the Mind*, 198–203.

Gerber, Philip. *Willa Cather*, 35–38.

Gustafson, Neil. "Getting Back to Cather's Text: The Shared Dream in *O Pioneers!*" *WAL* 30.2 (1995): 151–162.

Mayberry, Susan Neal. "Heroine Marriage: Willa Cather's *O Pioneers!*" *ON* 16.1 (1992): 37–59.

Romines, Ann. *Home Plot*, 144–145.

Rosowski, Susan J. "Willa Cather's Ecology of Place." *WAL* 30.1 (1995): 42–47.

Urgo, Joseph R. *Willa Cather*, 40–54.

Wagenknecht, Edward. *Willa Cather*, 71–74.

One of Ours (1922)

Gerber, Philip. *Willa Cather*, 47–52.

Higonnet, Margaret R. "Women in the Forbidden Zone: War, Women, and Death," in Goodwin, Sarah Webster, ed. *Death and Representation*, 200–201.

Limon, John. *Writing After War*, 200–205.

Urgo, Joseph R. *Willa Cather*, 143–167.

Schaefer, Josephine O'Brien. "Great War and 'This Late Age of World's Experience' in Cather and Woolf," in Hussey, Mark, ed. *Virginia Woolf and War*, 135–138, 140–143.

Wagenknecht, Edward. *Willa Cather*, 85–91.

Professor's House (1925)

Bell, Ian F. A. "Re-Writing America: Origin and Gender in Willa Cather's *The Professor's House*." *YES* 24 (1994): 12–43.

Byatt, A. S. *Passions of the Mind*, 203–209.

Chandler, Marilyn R. *Dwelling in the Text*, 181–214.

Gerber, Philip. *Willa Cather*, 56–59.

Leddy, Michael. "*Professor's House* and the Professor's Houses." *MFS* 38.2 (1992): 444–454.

Schaefer, Josephine O'Brien. "Great War and 'This Late Age of World's Experience' in Cather and Woolf," in Hussey, Mark, ed. *Virginia Woolf and War*, 146–150.

Schubnell, Matthias. "Decline of America: Willa Cather's Spenglerian Vision in *The Professor's House*." *CathSt* 2 (1993): 92–117.
Schwind, Jean. "This Is a Frame-Up: Mother Eve in *The Professor's House*." *CathSt* 2 (1993): 72–91.
Sedgwick, Eve Kosofsky. *Tendencies*, 174–176.
Spindler, Michael. "Cather's *The Professor's House*." *Expl* 51.1 (1992): 31–33.
Stout, Janis P. "Autobiography as Journey in *The Professor's House*." *SAF* 19.2 (1991): 203–215.
Urgo, Joseph R. *Willa Cather*, 15–38.
Wagenknecht, Edward. *Willa Cather*, 95–101.

Sapphira and the Slave Girl (1940)

Gerber, Philip. *Willa Cather*, 71–73.
Harrison, Elizabeth Jane. *Female Pastoral*, 65–82.
Romines, Ann. *Home Plot*, 174–189.
Swift, John N. "Narration and the Maternal 'Real' in *Sapphira and the Slave Girl*." *Legacy* 9.1 (1992): 23–34.
Urgo, Joseph R. *Willa Cather*, 83–97.
Wagenknecht, Edward. *Willa Cather*, 126–131.

Shadows on the Rock (1931)

Gerber, Philip. *Willa Cather*, 66–69.
Romines, Ann. *Home Plot*, 152–163.
Skaggs, Merrill Maguire. "Cather's Use of Parkman's Histories in *Shadows on the Rock*." *CathSt* 2 (1993): 140–155.
Urgo, Joseph R. *Willa Cather*, 97–111.
Wagenknecht, Edward. *Willa Cather*, 112–117.

Song of the Lark (1915)

Dubek, Laura. "Rewriting Male Scripts: Willa Cather and *The Song of the Lark*." *WS* 23.4 (1994): 293–306.
Flannigan, John H. "Thea Kronborg's Vocal Transvestism: Willa Cather and the 'Voz Contralto'." *MFS* 40.4 (1994): 737–763.
Gerber, Philip. *Willa Cather*, 38–43.
Romines, Ann. *Home Plot*, 145–147.
Urgo, Joseph R. *Willa Cather*, 130–143.
Wagenknecht, Edward. *Willa Cather*, 75–79.

CHA, THERESA HAK KYUNG

Dictée (1982)

Chung-Hei Yun. "Beyond 'Clay Walls': Korean American Literature," in Lim, Shirley Geok-lin, ed. *Reading the Literatures of Asian America*, 90–94.

CHABON, MICHAEL (1965(?)–)

Mysteries of Pittsburgh (1988)

Young, Elizabeth. *Shopping in Space*, 75–84.

CHANDLER, RAYMOND (1888–1959)

Big Sleep (1939)

Fine, David. "Running Out of Space: Vanishing Landscapes in California Novels." *WAL* 26.3 (1991): 216–218.

Simpson, Hassell A. " 'A Butcher's Thumb': Oral-Digital Consciousness in *The Big Sleep* and Other Novels of Raymond Chandler." *JPC* 25.1 (1991): 83–90.

Farewell, My Lovely (1940)

Simpson, Hassell A. " 'A Butcher's Thumb': Oral-Digital Consciousness in *The Big Sleep* and Other Novels of Raymond Chandler." *JPC* 25.1 (1991): 84–85, 85–86.

Long Goodbye (1954)

Simpson, Hassell A. " 'A Butcher's Thumb': Oral-Digital Consciousness in *The Big Sleep* and Other Novels of Raymond Chandler." *JPC* 25.1 (1991): 86–87, 89.

CHAPPELL, FRED (1936–)

I Am One of You Forever (1985)

Campbell, Hilbert. "Fred Chappell's Urn of Memory: *I Am One of You Forever.*" *SLJ* 25.2 (1993): 103–111.

Gray, Amy Tipton. "Fred Chappell's *I Am One of You Forever:* The Oneiros of Childhood Transformed," in Lanier, Parks, Jr.,ed. *Poetics*, 28–39.

CHARYN, JEROME (1937–)

Blue Eyes (1975)

Madden, David W. "Isaac Quintet: Jerome Charyn's Metaphysics of Law and Disorder." *RCF* 12.2 (1992): 165–172.

Education of Patrick Silver (1976)

Madden, David W. "Isaac Quintet: Jerome Charyn's Metaphysics of Law and Disorder." *RCF* 12.2 (1992): 165–172.

Going to Jerusalem (1967)

Seed, David. "Performance, Play, and Open Form in *Going to Jerusalem* and *The Tar Baby.*" *RCF* 12.2 (1992): 152–155.

Good Policeman (1990)

Madden, David W. "Isaac Quintet: Jerome Charyn's Metaphysics of Law and Disorder." *RCF* 12.2 (1992): 167–172.

Marilyn in the Wild (1976)

Madden, David W. "Isaac Quintet: Jerome Charyn's Metaphysics of Law and Disorder." *RCF* 12.2 (1992): 165–172.

Secret Isaac (1978)

Madden, David W. "Isaac Quintet: Jerome Charyn's Metaphysics of Law and Disorder." *RCF* 12.2 (1992): 166–172.

Tar Baby (1973)

Seed, David. "Performance, Play, and Open Form in *Going to Jerusalem* and *The Tar Baby.*" *RCF* 12.2 (1992): 155–162.

CHASE-RIBOUD, BARBARA (1939–)

Echo of Lions (1989)

Rushdy, Ashraf H. A. "Representing the Constitution: Embodiments of America in Barbara Chase-Riboud's *Echo of Lions*." *Crit* 36.4 (1995): 258–280.

CHAUVEAU, PIERRE J. O.(1820–1890)

Charles Guérin (1853)

Rouleau, Raymond. "Les Médecins de *Charles Guérin* face au choléra." *V&I* 19.3 (1994): 519–531.

CHEEVER, JOHN (1912–1982)

Bullet Park (1969)

Byrne, Michael D. "Split-Level Enigma: John Cheever's *Bullet Park*." *SAF* 20.1 (1992): 85–97.
Meanor, Patrick. *John Cheever Revisited*, 128–146.
Siabey, Robert M. "Postmodern Myth in John Cheever's *Bullet Park*." *NConL* 24.4 (1994): 2–3.
Stoicheff, Peter. "Chaos of Metafiction," in Hayles, N. Katherine, ed. *Chaos and Order*, 87.

Falconer (1977)

Koponen, Wilfrid R. *Embracing Gay Identity*, 30–41.
Meanor, Patrick. *John Cheever Revisited*, 157–173.

Oh What a Paradise It Seems (1982)

Meanor, Patrick. *John Cheever Revisited*, 174–177.

Wapshot Chronicle (1957)

Castronovo, David. *American Gentleman*, 109–111.
Meanor, Patrick. *John Cheever Revisited*, 58–67.

Wapshot Scandal (1964)

Meanor, Patrick. *John Cheever Revisited*, 67–74.

CHÉNÉ, YOLANDE (1926–)

Peur et amour (1965)

Raoul, Valerie. *Distinctly Narcissistic*, 205–208.

CHESNUTT, CHARLES WADDELL (1858–1932)

Colonel's Dream (1905)

Heermance, J. Noel. *Charles W. Chesnutt: America's First Great Black Novelist*. Hamden, CT: Archon/Shoestring Press, 1974. 7–8. Rpt. in Bloom, Harold, ed. *Major Black American Writers Through the Harlem Renaissance*, 185–186.
Pickens, Ernestine Williams. *Charles W. Chesnutt*, 94–120.

House Behind the Cedars (1900)

Hattenhauer, Darryl. "Racial and Textual Miscegenation in Chesnutt's *The House Behind the Cedars*." *MissQ* 47.1 (1993–94): 26–45.
Sundquist, Eric J. *To Wake the Nations*, 394–400.

Marrow of Tradition (1901)

Gates, Henry Louis, Jr. "Introduction." *Three Classic African American Novels*. New York: Vintage Classics, 1990. xv–xvi. Rpt. in Bloom, Harold, ed. *Major Black American Writers Through the Harlem Renaissance*, 13–14.
Gleason, William. "Voices at the Nadir: Charles Chesnutt and David Bryant Fulton." *ALR* 24.3 (1992): 25–30, 32, 37–38.
Pickens, Ernestine Williams. *Charles W. Chesnutt*, 53–75.
Sundquist, Eric J. *To Wake the Nations*, 271–276, 406–454.
Wolkomir, Michelle J. "Moral Elevation and Egalitarianism: Shades of Gray in Chesnutt's *The Marrow of Tradition*." *CLAJ* 36.3 (1993): 245–259.

CHILD, LYDIA MARIA (1802–1880)

Hobomok (1824)

Petitjean, Tom. "Child's *Hobomok*." *Expl* 53.3 (1995): 145–147.

Romance of the Republic (1867)

Samuels, Shirley. "The Identity of Slavery," in Samuels, Shirley, ed. *Culture of Sentiment*, 168–171.

CHILDRESS, ALICE (1916–1994)

Hero Ain't Nothin' but a Sandwich (1973)

Jennings, La Vinia Delois. *Alice Childress*, 85–97.

Rainbow Jordan (1981)

Jennings, La Vinia Delois. *Alice Childress*, 98–105.

Short Walk (1979)

Jennings, La Vinia Delois. *Alice Childress*, 116–133.

Those Other People (1989)

Jennings, La Vinia Delois. *Alice Childress*, 105–115.

CHOPIN, KATE (1851–1904)

Awakening (1899)

Ammons, Elizabeth. *Conflicting Stories*, 71–77.
Anastasopoulou, Maria. "Rites of Passage in Kate Chopin's *The Awakening*." *SLJ* 23.2 (1991): 19–30.
Bender, Bert. "Kate Chopin's Quarrel with Darwin before *The Awakening*." *JAmS* 26.2 (1992): 185–204.
Bender, Bert. "The Teeth of Desire: *The Awakening* and *The Descent of Man*." *AL* 63.3 (1991): 459–473.
Birnbaum, Michele A. " 'Alien Hands': Kate Chopin and the Colonization of Race." *AL* 66.2 (1994): 301–323.

Budick, Emily Miller. *Engendering Romance*, 130–133.
Budkman, Jacqueline. "Dominant Discourse and the Female Imaginary: A Study of the Tensions between Disparate Discursive Registers in Chopin's *The Awakening*." *ESC* 21.1 (1995): 55–76.
Camfield, Gregg. "Kate Chopin-hauer: Or, Can Metaphysics Be Feminized?" *SLJ* 27.2 (1995): 3–22.
Chandler, Marilyn R. *Dwelling in the Text*, 121–139.
Dawson, Hugh J. "Kate Chopin's *The Awakening*: A Dissenting Opinion." *ALR* 26.2 (1994): 1–18.
DeKoven, Marianne. *Rich and Strange*, 140–148.
Dressler, Mylene. "Edna under the Sun: Throwing Light on the Subject of *The Awakening*." *ArQ* 48.3 (1992): 59–75.
Dyer, Joyce. *The Awakening: A Novel of Beginnings.* New York: Twayne Publishers, 1993.
Foata, Anne. "Aphrodite Redux: Edna Pontellier's Dilemma in *The Awakening* by Kate Chopin." *SoQ* 33.1 (1994): 27–31.
Franklin, Rosemary F. "Poe and *The Awakening*." *MissQ* 47.1 (1993–94): 47–57.
Freeman, Barbara Claire. *Feminine Sublime*, 13–39.
Hollister, Michael. "Chopin's *The Awakening*." *Expl* 52.2 (1994): 90–92.
Kearns, Katherine. "Nullification of Edna Pontellier." *AL* 63.1 (1991): 62–88.
Linkin, Harriet Kramer. " 'Call the Roller of Big Cigars': Smoking Out the Patriarchy in *The Awakening*." *Legacy* 11.2 (1994): 130–142.
Malzahn, Manfred. "Strange Demise of Edna Pontellier." *SLJ* 23.2 (1991): 31–39.
Platizky, Roger. "Chopin's *The Awakening*." *Expl* 53.2 (1995): 99–102.
Schulz, Dieter. "Notes Toward a fin-de-siecle Reading of Kate Chopin's *The Awakening*." *ALR* 25.3 (1993): 69–76.
Seidel, Kathryn. "Art Is an Unnatural Act: Mademoiselle Reisz in *The Awakening*." *MissQ* 46.2 (1993): 199–214.
Showalter, Elaine. *Sister's Choice*, 65–84.
Showalter, Elaine. "Tradition and the Female Talent: *The Awakening* as a Solitary Book," in Walker, Nancy A., ed. *Awakening*, 169–188.
Stange, Margit. "Personal Property: Exchange Value and the Female Self in *The Awakening*," in Walker, Nancy A., ed. *Awakening*, 201–217.
Tate, Linda. *Southern Weave of Women*, 12–13.
Thomas, Heather Kirk. "Kate Chopin's Scribbling Women and the American Literary Marketplace." *SAF* 23.1 (1995): 23–25, 27.
Treichler, Paula A. "Construction of Ambiguity in *The Awakening:* A Linguistic Analysis," in Walker, Nancy A., ed. *Awakening*, 308–328.
Vlasopolos, Anca. "Staking Claims for No Territory: The Sea as Woman's Space," in Higonnet, Margaret R., ed. *Reconfigured Spheres*, 84–86.
Wolff, Cynthia Griffin. "Thanatos and Eros: Kate Chopin's *The Awakening*," in Walker, Nancy A., ed. *Awakening*, 233–258.
Yaeger, Patricia S. " 'A Language Which Nobody Understood': Emancipatory Strategies in *The Awakening*," in Walker, Nancy A., ed. *Awakening*, 270–296.

CHU, LOUIS H. (1915–)

Eat a Bowl of Tea (1961)

Hsiao, Ruth Y. "Facing the Incurable: Patriarchy in *Eat a Bowl of Tea*," in Lim, Shirley Geok-lin, ed. *Reading the Literatures of Asian America*, 151–162.

Li, Shu-yan. "Otherness and Transformation in *Eat a Bowl of Tea* and *Crossings*." *MELUS* 18.4 (1993–94): 100, 102–106.

Ling, Jinqi. "Reading for Historical Specificities: Gender Negotiations in Louis Chu's *Eat a Bowl of Tea*." *MELUS* 20.1 (1995): 35–51.

CHUANG HUA

Crossings (1968)

Li, Shu-yan. "Otherness and Transformation in *Eat a Bowl of Tea* and *Crossings*." *MELUS* 18.4 (1993–94): 100–102, 106–109.

Wong, Sau-ling Cynthia. *Reading Asian American Literature*, 62–63, 67.

CICCHETTI, JANET see "LILLIAN JANET"

CLARK, JOAN (1905–)

Victory of Geraldine Gull (1988)

Davidson, Arnold E. *Coyote Country*, 180–185.

CLARK, WALTER VAN TILBURG (1909–1971)

Ox-Bow Incident (1940)

Budd, John M. "Law and Morality in Billy Budd and *The Ox-Bow Incident*." *CLAJ* 35.2 (1991): 188–190, 196–197.

Heilman, Robert Bechtold. *Workings of Fiction*, 349–365.

Walle, A. H. "Walter Van Tilburg Clark's *Ox Bow Incident:* Prototype for the Anti-heroic Western." *PVR* 23.1 (1995): 50–67.

Track of the Cat (1949)

Folsom, James K. "Gothicism in the Western Novel," in Mogen, David, ed. *Frontier Gothic*, 37–38.

CLARKE, ARTHUR C. (1917–)

Childhood's End (1953)

Slusser, George. "Frankenstein Barrier," in Slusser, George, ed. *Fiction 2000*, 55–57

CLAUSEN, JAN

Sinking, Stealing (1985)

Rosenfelt, Deborah Silverton. "Feminism, 'Postfeminism,' and Contemporary Women's Fiction," in Howe, Florence, ed. *Tradition and the Talents of Women*, 279, 286.

CLEMENS, SAMUEL LANGHORNE see TWAIN, MARK

COHEN, LEONARD (1934–)

Beautiful Losers (1966)

Deer, Glenn. *Postmodern Canadian Fiction*, 47–60.
Siemerling, Winfried. *Discoveries of the Other*, 36–61.
Söderlind, Sylvia. "Canadian Cryptic: The Sacred, the Profane, and the Translatable." *ArielE* 22.3 (1991): 95–97.
Söderlind, Sylvia. *MARGIN / ALIAS*, 41–69.

Death of a Lady's Man (1978)

Siemerling, Winfried. *Discoveries of the Other*, 24–26.

Favorite Game (1963)

Siemerling, Winfried. *Discoveries of the Other*, 28–30.

CONAN, LAURE (1845–1924)

Angéline de Montbrun (1881)

Dufault, Roseanna Lewis. *Metaphors of Identity*, 18–27.
Raoul, Valerie. *Distinctly Narcissistic*, 62–77.
Robert, Lucie. "D'*Angéline de Montbrun* à *La Chair décevante:* la naissance d'une parole féminine autonome dans la littérature québécoise," in Saint-Martin, Lori, ed. *L'autre lecture* (Tome 1), 44–46.
Shek, Ben-Z. *French-Canadian*, 9–13.
Smart, Patricia. *Writing in the Father's House*, 20–61.

CONNELL, EVAN S., JR. (1924–)

Alchemist's Journal (1991)

Bawer, Bruce. "Luther of Science?" *NewC* 9.10 (1991): 30–35.

CONNOR, RALPH (1860–1937)

Glengarry School Days (1902)

Thompson, Elizabeth. *Pioneer Woman*, 106–107.

Man from Glengarry (1901)

Thompson, Elizabeth. *Pioneer Woman*, 97–103, 107–108.

CONROY, JACK (1899–1990)

Disinherited (1933)

Hapke, Laura. *Daughters of the Great Depression*, 43–47.
Morgan, Jack. "Jack Conroy's *The Disinherited*, 1933." *Eire* 27.3 (1992): 122–128.

Jews Without Money (1930)

Hapke, Laura. *Daughters of the Great Depression*, 47–50.

COOK, ROBIN (1940–)

Mutation (1989)

Squier, Susan. "Conceiving Difference: Reproductive Technology and the Construction of Identity in Two Contemporary Fictions," in Benjamin, Marina, ed. *Question of Identity*, 98–106.

COOLIDGE, SUSAN (1835–1905)

What Katy Did (1872)

Foster, Shirley. *What Katy Read*, 107–125.

COOPER, DENNIS (1953–)

Closer (1989)

Young, Elizabeth. *Shopping in Space*, 239–253.

Frisk (1991)

Young, Elizabeth. *Shopping in Space*, 254–259.

COOPER, JAMES FENIMORE (1789–1851)

Deerslayer (1841)

Barnett, Louise K. "Speech in the Wilderness: The Ideal Discourse of *The Deerslayer*," in Heyne, Eric, ed. *Desert, Garden*, 19–28.

Engel, Leonard. "Space and Enclosure in Cooper and Peckinpah: Regeneration in the Open Spaces." *JACult* 14.2 (1991): 87–88.

Kowalewski, Michael. *Deadly Musings*, 64–81.

Rogers, Franklin R. *Occidental Ideographs*, 53–75.

Last of the Mohicans (1826)

Baym, Nina. "How Men and Women Wrote Indian Stories," in Peck, Daniel, ed. *New Essays*, 67–86.

Becker-Theye, Betty. "Cooper and Chateaubriand: The American Wilderness as Simpler/More Complex World." *PVR* 19.2 (1991): 45–53.

Byers, Thomas B. "Difference Cooper Makes: The Cultural Text of *Last of the Mochicans*," in Carlisle, Janice,ed. *Narrative and Culture*, 36–44.

Chapman, Mary. "Infanticide and Cultural Reproduction in Cooper's *The Last of the Mohicans*." *CRevAS* 22.3 (1991): 407–417.

Davis, Randall C. "Fire-Water in the Frontier Romance: James Fenimore Cooper and 'Indian Nature'." *SAF* 22.2 (1994): 220–222.

Folsom, James K. "Gothicism in the Western Novel," in Mogen, David, ed. *Frontier Gothic*, 31–33.

Franklin, Wayne. "Wilderness of Words in *The Last of the Mohicans*," in Peck, Daniel, ed. *New Essays*, 25–45.

Lawson-Peebles, Robert. "Lesson of the Massacre at Fort William Henry," in Peck, Daniel, ed. *New Essays*, 115–138.

Martin, Terence. "From Atrocity to Requiem: History in *The Last of the Mohicans*," in Peck, Daniel, ed. *New Essays*, 47–65.

Pitcher, E.W. "Anticipated Torments and Indian Tortures in *The Last of the Mohicans*." *ANQ* 7.4 (1994): 215–219.

Pitcher, E.W. "Beaver and His Cousin in Cooper's *The Last of the Mohicans*." *ANQ* 8.2 (1995): 11–16.

Robinson, Forrest G. "Uncertain Borders: Race, Sex, and Civilization in *The Last of the Mohicans*." *ArQ* 47.1 (1991): 1–28.

Romero, Lora. "Vanishing Americans: Gender, Empire, and New Historicism." *AL* 63.3 (1991): 385–404.

Romero, Lora. "Vanishing Americans: Gender, Empire, and New Historicism," Samuels, Shirley, ed. *Culture of Sentiment*, 115–116, 119–122, 124–125.

Samuels, Shirley. "Generation through Violence: Cooper and the Making of Americans," in Peck, Daniel, ed. *New Essays*, 87–114.

Sommer, Doris. *Foundational Fictions*, 52, 53–55, 56–59.

Zagarell, Sandra A. "Expanding 'America': Lydia Sigourney's *Sketch of Connecticut*, Catherine Sedgwick's *Hope Leslie*," in Harris, Sharon M., ed. *Redefining the Political Novel*, 59–60.

Monikins (1835)

Michaelsen, Scott. "Cooper's *Monikins:* Contracts, Construction, and Chaos." *ArQ* 48.3 (1992): 1–24.

Oak Openings (1848)

Davis, Randall C. "Fire-Water in the Frontier Romance: James Fenimore Cooper and 'Indian Nature'." *SAF* 22.2 (1994): 222–224.

Pathfinder (1840)

Swearingen, James E. and Joanne Cutting-Gray. "Cooper's *Pathfinder:* Revising Historical Understanding." *NLH* 23.2 (1992): 267–280.

Pioneers (1823)

Davis, Randall C. "Fire-Water in the Frontier Romance: James Fenimore Cooper and 'Indian Nature'." *SAF* 22.2 (1994): 218–220.

Goodman, Nan. "Clear Showing: The Problem of Fault in James Fenimore Cooper's *The Pioneers*." *ArQ* 49.2 (1993): 1–22.

Witkowsky, Paul. "If Prairies Had Trees: East, West, Environmentalist Fiction, and the Great Plains." *WAL* 28.3 (1993): 197–200, 204, 205.

Prairie (1827)

Engel, Leonard. "Space and Enclosure in Cooper and Peckinpah: Regeneration in the Open Spaces." *JACult* 14.2 (1991): 88.

Witkowsky, Paul. "If Prairies Had Trees: East, West, Environmentalist Fiction, and the Great Plains." *WAL* 28.3 (1993): 205.

Spy (1821)

Crawford, T. Hugh. "Cooper's *Spy* and the Theater of Honor." *AL* 63.3 (1991): 405–419.

Rosenberg, Bruce A. "Cooper's *The Spy* and the Popular Spy Novel." *ATQ* 7.2 (1993): 115–125.

Rosenberg, Bruce A. "James Fenimore Coopers's *The Spy* and the Neutral Ground." *ATQ* 6.1 (1992): 5–16.

Wyandotté (1843)

Davis, Randall C. "Fire-Water in the Frontier Romance: James Fenimore Cooper and 'Indian Nature'." *SAF* 22.2 (1994): 224–228.

COOVER, ROBERT (1932–)

Public Burning (1977)

Hollahan, Eugene. *Crisis-Consciousness*, 195–206.

Strehle, Susan. *Fiction in the Quantum Universe*, 66–92.

Walsh, Richard. "Narrative Inscription, History and the Reader in Robert Coover's *The Public Burning*." *SNNTS* 25.3 (1993): 332–346.

Universal Baseball Association (1968)

Burke, Ruth E. *Games of Poetics*, 114–121.
Harper, Phillip Brian. *Framing the Margins*, 156–164.

CORMIER, ROBERT (1925–)

After the First Death (1979)

MacLeod, Anne Scott. *American Childhood*, 193–195.

Chocolate War (1974)

MacLeod, Anne Scott. *American Childhood*, 190–192.

I Am the Cheese (1977)

MacLeod, Anne Scott. *American Childhood*, 192–193.

CORPI, LUCHA (1945–)

Delia's Song (1989)

Rebolledo, Tey Diana. *Women Singing in the Snow*, 121–124.

COTA-CÁRDENAS, MARGARITA (1941–)

Puppet (1985)

Rebolledo, Tey Diana. *Women Singing in the Snow*, 119–121, 172, 174, 180–181.

CRANE, STEPHEN (1871–1900)

Maggie (1893)

Ganal, Keith. "Stephen Crane's *Maggie* and the Modern Soul." *ELH* 60.3 (1993): 759–785.
Giles, James R. *Naturalistic Inner-City Novel in America*, 22–26.
Kowalewski, Michael. *Deadly Musings*, 118–122.
Novotny, George T. "Crane's *Maggie, A Girl of the Streets*." *Expl* 50.4 (1992): 225–228.
Pizer, Donald. "*Maggie* and the Naturalistic Aesthetic of Length." *ALR* 28.1 (1995): 58–65.
Pizer, Donald. *Theory and Practice*, 41–44, 124–132.
Sweeney, Gerard M. "Syphilitic World of Stephen Crane's *Maggie*." *ALR* 24.1 (1991): 79–85.

Red Badge of Courage (1895)

Beidler, Philip D. "Stephen Crane's *The Red Badge of Courage:* Henry Fleming's Courage in Its Contexts." *CLioI* 20.3 (1991): 235–251.
Cox, James. "On Stephen Crane's *The Red Badge of Courage*," in Madden, David, ed. *Classics of Civil War Fiction*, 44–62.
Curran, John E., Jr. " 'Nobody Seems to Know Where We Go': Uncertainty, History, and Irony in *The Red Badge of Courage*." *ALR* 26.1 (1993): 1–12.
Esteve, Mary. " 'Gorgeous Neutrality': Stephen Crane's Documentary Anaesthetics." *ELH* 62.3 (1995): 663–689.

Green, Melissa. "Fleming's 'Escape' in *The Red Badge of Courage:* A Jungian Analysis." *ALR* 28.1 (1995): 80–91

Hattenhauer, Darryl. "Crane's *The Red Badge of Courage.*" *Expl* 50.3 (1992): 160–161.

Limon, John. *Writing After War*, 55–58.

Mulcaire, Terry. "Progressive Visions of War in *The Red Badge of Courage* and *The Principles of Scientific Management.*" *AQ* 43.1 (1991): 46–72.

Pizer, Donald. *Theory and Practice*, 95–100.

CREELEY, ROBERT (1926–)

Island (1963)

Taggart, John. "Ending in Ellipsis, the Sea in Our Ears: Robert Creeley's *The Island.*" *RCF* 15.3 (1995): 127–136.

CREWS, HARRY (1935–)

Body (1990)

Shelton, Frank W. "Harry Crews after a Childhood." *SLJ* 24.2 (1992): 3–10.

CULLEN, COUNTEE (1903–1946)

One Way to Heaven (1932)

Early, Gerald. "Introduction." *My Soul's High Song: The Collected Writings of Countee Cullen, Voice of the Harlem Renaissance.* Ed. Gerald Early. New York: Doubleday, 1991. 59. Rpt. in Bloom, Harold, ed. *Major Black American Writers Through the Harlem Renaissance*, 31–32.

CULLETON, BEATRICE (1949–)

In Search of April Raintree (1983)

Davidson, Arnold E. *Coyote Country*, 186–190.

Hoy, Helen. " 'Nothing but the Truth' Discursive Transparency in Beatrice Culleton." *ArielE* 25.1 (1994): 158–172, 176–177.

Lundgren, Jodi. " 'Being a Half-Breed': Discourses of Race and Cultural Syncreticity in the Works of Three Metis Women Writers." *CanL* 144 (1995): 63–65, 74.

Zwicker, Heather. "Canadian Women of Color in the New World Order: Marlene Nourbese Philip, Joy Kogawa, and Beatrice Culleton Fight Their Way Home," in Pearlman, Mickey, ed. *Canadian Women*, 150–152.

CULLINAN, ELIZABETH (1933–)

House of Gold (1969)

Ward, Catherine. "Wake Homes: Four Modern Novels of the Irish-American Family." *Eire* 26.2 (1991): 85–88.

CUMMINS, MARIA (1827–1866)

Lamplighter (1854)

Goshgarian, G. M. *To Kiss the Chastening Rod*, 159–172.
Lang, Amy Schrager. "Class and the Strategies of Sympathy," in Samuels, Shirley, ed. *Culture of Sentiment*, 129–131.

CURRAN, MARY DOYLE (1917–1981)

Parish and the Hill (1948)

Conboy, Sheila C. "Birth and Death: Female Tradition and the Narrative Voice in Mary Doyle Curran's *The Parish and the Hill*." *MELUS* 18.1 (1993): 61–69.
Ward, Catherine. "Wake Homes: Four Modern Novels of the Irish-American Family." *Eire* 26.2 (1991): 79–82.

DAITCH, SUSAN

Colorist (1985)

Katrovas, Richard. "Into the Heart of Things: Passion and Perception in Susan Daitch's *The Colorist*." *RCF* 13.2 (1993): 121–126.

L.C. (1986)

Allen, Esther. "Sentimental Educations." *RCF* 13.2 (1993): 117–120.
Camhi, Leslie. "Uncertain Physiognomies: Susan Daitch's *L.C.*" *RCF* 13.2 (1993): 97–100.

DARGAN, OLIVE see FIELDING, BURKE

DAVIES, ROBERTSON (1913–)

Fifth Business (1970)

Bonnycastle, Stephen. "Robertson Davies and the Ethics of Monologue," in Cameron, Elspeth, ed. *Robertson Davies*, 140–151, 156–166.
Cude, Wilfred. "Miracle and Art in *Fifth Business* or Who the Devil is Liselotte Vitzlipützli?" in Cameron, Elspeth, ed. *Robertson Davies*, 96–118.
Godard, Barbara. "Writing Paradox, the Paradox of Writing: Robertson Davies," in Cameron, Elspeth, ed. *Robertson Davies*, 236–237, 241, 242, 244, 247–248, 252.
Monk, Patricia. *Mud and Magic Shows: Robertson Davies's Fifth Business*. Toronto: ECW Press, 1992.
Neufeld, James. "Structural Unity in the Deptford Trilogy: Robertson Davies as Egoist," in Cameron, Elspeth, ed. *Robertson Davies*, 129–139.
Roper, Gordon. "Robertson Davies' *Fifth Business* and "That Old Fantastical Duke of Dark Corners, C.G. Jung," in Cameron, Elspeth, ed. *Robertson Davies*, 81–95.
Williams, David. *Confessional Fictions*, 55–84.

Leaven of Malice (1954)

Godard, Barbara. "Writing Paradox, the Paradox of Writing: Robertson Davies," in Cameron, Elspeth, ed. *Robertson Davies*, 235–236, 245, 252.

McPherson, Hugo. "Mask of Satire: Character and Symbolic Pattern in Roberston Davies' Fiction," in Cameron, Elspeth, ed. *Robertson Davies*, 75–77.

Lyre of Orpheus (1988)

Lamont-Stewart, Linda. "Robertson Davies and the Doctrine of the Elite: An Ideological Critique of the Cornish Trilogy," in Cameron, Elspeth, ed. *Robertson Davies*, 274–275, 276, 279, 281–282, 283, 284–289.

Munro, Ian. "Liar of Orpheus: Framing Devices and Narrative Structure in Robertson Davies' Cornish Trilogy," in Cameron, Elspeth, ed. *Robertson Davies*, 260–262, 266–269, 271.

Manticore (1972)

Bonnycastle, Stephen. "Robertson Davies and the Ethics of Monologue," in Cameron, Elspeth, ed. *Robertson Davies*, 151–166.

Godard, Barbara. "Writing Paradox, the Paradox of Writing: Robertson Davies," in Cameron, Elspeth, ed. *Robertson Davies*, 237, 252.

Neufeld, James. "Structural Unity in the Deptford Trilogy: Robertson Davies as Egoist," in Cameron, Elspeth, ed. *Robertson Davies*, 129–139.

Mixture of Frailties (1958)

Godard, Barbara. "Writing Paradox, the Paradox of Writing: Robertson Davies," in Cameron, Elspeth, ed. *Robertson Davies*, 235–236, 240, 244, 252.

Keith, W.J. "*A Mixture of Frailties* and 'Romance'," in Cameron, Elspeth, ed. *Robertson Davies*, 199–212.

McPherson, Hugo. "Mask of Satire: Character and Symbolic Pattern in Robertson Davies' Fiction," in Cameron, Elspeth, ed. *Robertson Davies*, 77–80.

Plant, Richard. "Cultural Redemption in the Work of Robertson Davies," in Cameron, Elspeth, ed. *Robertson Davies*, 219–223.

Thomas, Clara. "Two Voices of *A Mixture of Frailties*," in Cameron, Elspeth, ed. *Robertson Davies*, 182–197.

Rebel Angels (1981)

Godard, Barbara. "Writing Paradox, the Paradox of Writing: Robertson Davies," in Cameron, Elspeth, ed. *Robertson Davies*, 235, 237–238, 239–241, 242, 249, 251–252.

Lamont-Stewart, Linda. "Robertson Davies and the Doctrine of the Elite: An Ideological Critique of the Cornish Trilogy," in Cameron, Elspeth, ed. *Robertson Davies*, 273–274, 276, 278–279, 280–281, 282–284, 288–289, 290–291.

Munro, Ian. "Liar of Orpheus: Framing Devices and Narrative Structure in Robertson Davies' Cornish Trilogy," in Cameron, Elspeth, ed. *Robertson Davies*, 262–265, 270.

Tempest-Tost (1951)

Godard, Barbara. "Writing Paradox, the Paradox of Writing: Robertson Davies," in Cameron, Elspeth, ed. *Robertson Davies*, 243–244, 250.

McPherson, Hugo. "Mask of Satire: Character and Symbolic Pattern in Robertson Davies' Fiction," in Cameron, Elspeth, ed. *Robertson Davies*, 70–74.

What's Bred in the Bone (1985)

Dopp, Jamie. "Metanarrative as Inoculation in *What's Bred in the Bone*." *ESC* 21.1 (1995): 77–94.

Lamont-Stewart, Linda. "Robertson Davies and the Doctrine of the Elite: An Ideological Critique of the Cornish Trilogy," in Cameron, Elspeth, ed. *Robertson Davies*, 276, 279, 281–282, 283, 284.

Munro, Ian. "Liar of Orpheus: Framing Devices and Narrative Structure in Robertson Davies' Cornish Trilogy," in Cameron, Elspeth, ed. *Robertson Davies*, 258–259.

World of Wonders (1975)

Bonnycastle, Stephen. "Robertson Davies and the Ethics of Monologue," in Cameron, Elspeth, ed. *Robertson Davies*, 166–168.

Godard, Barbara. "Writing Paradox, the Paradox of Writing: Robertson Davies," in Cameron, Elspeth, ed. *Robertson Davies*, 238–239, 242, 245, 248–251

Monk, Patricia. "Confessions of a Sorcerer's Apprentice: *World of Wonders* and the Deptford Trilogy of Robertson Davies," in Cameron, Elspeth, ed. *Robertson Davies*, 120–128.

Neufeld, James. "Structural Unity in the Deptford Trilogy: Robertson Davies as Egoist," in Cameron, Elspeth, ed. *Robertson Davies*, 129–139.

DAVIS, REBECCA HARDING (1831–1910)

Dallas Galbraith (1868)

Rose, Jane Atteridge. *Rebecca Harding Davis*, 82–86.

Doctor Warrick's Daughters (1895)

Rose, Jane Atteridge. *Rebecca Harding Davis*, 149–155.

Frances Waldeaux (1896)

Rose, Jane Atteridge. *Rebecca Harding Davis*, 155–159.

John Andross (1873)

Rose, Jane Atteridge. *Rebecca Harding Davis*, 76–81.

Kitty's Choice, (1873)

Rose, Jane Atteridge. *Rebecca Harding Davis*, 98–100.

Law Unto Herself (1877)

Rose, Jane Atteridge. *Rebecca Harding Davis*, 107–111.

Life in the Iron Mills (1861)

Bromell, Nicholas K. *By the Sweat of the Brow*, 113–118.

Lang, Amy Schrager. "Class and the Strategies of Sympathy," in Samuels, Shirley, ed. *Culture of Sentiment*, 132–135, 136–137, 139–140, 141–142.

Rose, Jane Atteridge. *Rebecca Harding Davis*, 13–22.

Margret Howth (1861)

Rose, Jane Atteridge. *Rebecca Harding Davis*, 24–33.

Story of To-day see *Margret Howth*

Waiting for the Verdict (1867)

Rose, Jane Atteridge. *Rebecca Harding Davis*, 69–74.

DE FOREST, JOHN WILLIAM (1826–1906)

Miss Ravenel's Conversion from Secession to Loyalty (1867)

Becker, Stephen. "On John William De Forest's *Miss Ravenel's Conversion from Secession to Loyalty*," in Madden, David, ed. *Classics of Civil War Fiction*, 29–36.

Fick, Thomas H. "Genre Wars and the Rhetoric of Manhood in *Miss Ravenel's Conversion from Secession to Loyalty*." *NCF* 46.4 (1992): 473–494.
Limon, John. *Writing After War*, 79–83.

DE MILLE, JAMES (1833–1880)

Helena's Household (1867)

MacDonald, Bruce F. "*Helena's Household*: James De Mille's Heretical Text." *CanL* 128 (1991): 120–140.
Monk, Patricia. *Gilded Beaver*, 191–194.

Lily and the Cross (1874)

Monk, Patricia. *Gilded Beaver*, 185–187.

Strange Manuscript Found in a Copper Cylinder (1888)

Gerson, Carole. "Contrapuntal Reading of *A Strange Manuscript Found in a Copper Cylinder*." *ECW* 56 (1995): 224–235.
Guth, Gwendolyn. "Reading Frames of Reference: The Satire of Exegesis in James De Mille's *A Strange Manuscript Found in a Copper Cylinder*." *CanL* 145 (1995): 35–59.
Lamont-Stewart, Linda. "Rescued by Postmodernism: The Escalating Value of James De Mille's *A Strange Manuscript Found in a Copper Cylinder*." *CanL* 145 (1995): 21–36.
Milnes, Stephen. "Colonialist Discourse, Lord Featherstone's Yawn and the Significance of the Denouement in *A Strange Manuscript Found in a Copper Cylinder*." *CanL* 145 (1995): 86–104.
Monk, Patricia. *Gilded Beaver*, 233–249.
Multineddu, Flavio. "Tendentious Game with an Uncanny Riddle: *A Strange Manuscript Found in a Copper Cylinder*." *CanL* 145 (1995): 62–81.

DELANY, MARTIN R. (1812–1885)

Blake (1859)

Bienvenu, Germain J. "People of Delany's *Blake*." *CLAJ* 36.4 (1993): 406–429.
Marx, Jo Ann. "Myth and Meaning in Martin R. Delany's *Blake; Or the Huts of America*." *CLAJ* 38.2 (1994): 183–192.
Sundquist, Eric J. *To Wake the Nations*, 183–127.

DELANY, SAMUEL R. (1942–)

Babel-17 (1966)

Malmgren, Carl. "Languages of Science Fiction: Samuel Delany's *Babel-17*." *Extrapolation* 34.1 (1993): 5–17.

Dhalgren (1975)

Jonas, Gerald. [Review of *Dhalgren*]. *New York Times Book Review* (February 12, 1975): 27–28. Rpt. in Bloom, Harold, ed. *Contemporary Black American Fiction Writers*, 17–18.
McEvoy, Seth. *Samuel R. Delany*. New York: Frederick Ungar Publishing Co.,

1984. 105–106, 111–112. Rpt. in Bloom, Harold, ed. *Contemporary Black American Fiction Writers*, 21–22.

Nova (1968)

Meisel, Sandra. "Samuel R. Delany's Use of Myth in *Nova*." *Extrapolation* 12.2 (May 1971): 86–87. Rpt. in Bloom, Harold, ed. *Contemporary Black American Fiction Writers*, 16–17.

Triton (1976)

Booker, M. Keith. *Dystopian Impulse*, 142–146.

DELILLO, DON (1936–)

Americana (1971)

Keesey, Douglas. *Don DeLillo*, 13–33.

End Zone (1972)

Keesey, Douglas. *Don DeLillo*, 34–47.
Limon, John. *Writing After War*, 171–173.

Great Jones Street (1973)

DeCurtis, Anthony. "The Product: Bucky Wunderlick, Rock 'n Roll, and Don DeLillo's *Great Jones Street*," in Lentricchia, Frank, ed. *Introducing Don DeLillo*, 131–141.
Keesey, Douglas. *Don DeLillo*, 48–64.
Osteen, Mark. " 'A Moral Form to Master Commerce': The Economies of DeLillo's *Great Jones Street*." *Crit* 35.3 (1994): 157–172.

Libra (1988)

Brent, Jonathan. "Unimaginable Space of Danilo Kis and Don DeLillo." *RCF* 14.1 (1994): 180–188.
Civello, Paul. "Undoing the Naturalistic Novel: Don DeLillo's *Libra*." *ArQ* 48.2 (1992): 33–55.
Johnston, John. "Superlinear Fiction or Historical Diagram?: Don DeLillo's *Libra*." *MFS* 40.2 (1994): 319–342.
Keesey, Douglas. *Don DeLillo*, 151–176.
Kornick, Joseph. "*Libra* and the Assassination of JFK: A Textbook Operation." *ArQ* 50.1 (1994): 109–32.
Lentricchia, Frank. "*Libra* as Postmodern Critique," in Lentricchia, Frank, ed. *Introducing Don DeLillo*, 193–215.
Michael, Magali Cornier. "Political Paradox within Don DeLillo's Libra." *Crit* 35.3 (1994): 146–156.
Mott, Christopher M. "*Libra* and the Subject of History." *Crit* 35.3 (1994): 131–145.

Mao II (1991)

Bizzini, Silvia Caporale. "Can the Intellectual Still Speak? The Example of Don DeLillo's *Mao II*." *CritQ* 37.2 (1995): 104–117.
Keesey, Douglas. *Don DeLillo*, 177–193.
Scanlan, Margaret. "Writers among Terrorists: Don DeLillo's *Mao II* and the Rushdie Affair." *MFS* 40.2 (1994): 229–247.

Names (1982)

Foster, Dennis A. "Alphabetic Pleasures: *The Names*," in Lentricchia, Frank, ed. *Introducing Don DeLillo*, 157–173.

Harris, Paul A. "Epistemocritique: A Synthetic Matrix." *SubStance* 22.2–3 (1993): 185–203.

Keesey, Douglas. *Don DeLillo*, 116–132.

Players (1977)

Goodheart, Eugene. "Don DeLillo and the Cinematic Real," in Lentricchia, Frank, ed. *Introducing Don DeLillo*, 118–120.

Keesey, Douglas. *Don DeLillo*, 86–100.

Ratner's Star (1976)

Keesey, Douglas. *Don DeLillo*, 65–85.

Running Dog (1978)

Keesey, Douglas. *Don DeLillo*, 101–115.

O'Donnell, Patrick. "Engendering Paranoia in Contemporary Narrative." *BoundaryII* 19.1 (1992): 193–195.

White Noise (1985)

Cantor, Paul A. " 'Adolf, We Hardly Knew You'," in Lentricchia, Frank, ed. *New Essays on White Noise*, 39–62.

Conroy, Mark. "From Tombstone to Tabloid: Authority Figured in *White Noise*." *Crit* 35.2 (1994): 97–110.

Duvall, John N. "(Super) Marketplace of Images: Television as Unmediated Mediation in DeLillo's *White Noise*." *ArQ* 50.3 (1994): 127–152.

Ferraro, Thomas J. "Whole Families Shopping at Night!," in Lentricchia, Frank, ed. *New Essays on White Noise*, 15–38.

Frow, John. "The Last Things Before the Last: Notes on *White Noise*," in Lentricchia, Frank, ed. *Introducing Don DeLillo*, 175–191.

Goodheart, Eugene. "Don DeLillo and the Cinematic Real," in Lentricchia, Frank, ed. *Introducing Don DeLillo*, 121–122, 124–125.

Keesey, Douglas. *Don DeLillo*, 133–150.

King, Noel. "Reading *White Noise:* Floating Remarks." *CritQ* 33.3 (1991): 66–83.

Landon, Brooks. "Overloading Memory in Digital Narrative," in Slusser, George, ed. *Fiction 2000*, 157–158.

Lentricchia, Frank. "Tales of the Electronic Tribe," in Lentricchia, Frank, ed. *New Essays on White Noise*, 87–113.

Moses, Michael Valdez. "Lust Removed from Nature," in Lentricchia, Frank, ed. *New Essays on White Noise*, 63–86.

Porush, David. "Fictions as Dissipative Structures: Prigogine's Theory and Postmodernism's Roadshow," in Hayles, N. Katherine, ed. *Chaos and Order*, 55, 56.

Reeve, N. H. and Richard Kerridge. "Toxic Events: Postmodernism and DeLillo's *White Noise*." *CQ* 23.4 (1994): 303–323.

Saltzman, Arthur M. "Figure in the Static: *White Noise*." *MFS* 40.4 (1994): 807–826.

Wilcox, Leonard. "Baudrillard, DeLillo's *White Noise*, and the End of Heroic Narrative." *ConL* 32.3 (1991): 346–365.

DEMBY, WILLIAM (1922–)

Catacombs (1965)

Jaskoski, Helen. "*Catacombs* and the Debate between the Flesh and the Spirit." *Crit* 35.3 (1994): 181–192.

DENNISON, GEORGE (1925–1987)

Luisa Domic (1985)

Brown, Robert McAfee. *Persuade Us To Rejoice*, 135–138.

DEWBERRY, ELIZABETH see VAUGHN, ELIZABETH DEWBERRY

DICK, PHILIP K. (1928–1982)

Clans of the Alphane Moon (1964)

Palmer, Christopher. "Critique and Fantasy in Two Novels by Philip K. Dick." *Extrapolation* 32.3 (1991): 222–228.

Deus Irae (1976)

Moddelmog, Debra A. *Readers and Mythic Signs*, 57, 58.

Divine Invasion (1981)

Stilling, Roger J. "Mystical Healing: Reading Philip K. Dick's *VALIS* and *The Divine Invasion* as Metapsychoanalytic Novels." *SoAR* 56.2 (1991): 91–106.

Man in the High Castle (1962)

Campbell, Laura E. "Dickian Time in *The Man in the High Castle*." *Extrapolation* 33.3 (1992): 190–201.

Carter, Cassie. "Metacolonization of Dick's *The Man in the High Castle:* Mimicry, Parasitism, and Americanism in the PSA." *SFS* 22.3 (1995): 333–342.

Zhu, Jianjiong. "Reality, Fiction, and Wu in *The Man in the High Castle*," in Ruddick, Nicholas, ed. *State of the Fantastic*, 107–112.

Martian Time Slip (1976)

Palmer, Christopher. "Critique and Fantasy in Two Novels by Philip K. Dick." *Extrapolation* 32.3 (1991): 222–224, 228–233.

Simulacra (1964)

Baudrillard, Jean. "*Simulacra* and Science Fiction." Trans. Arthur B. Evans. *SFS* 18.3 (1991): 309–311.

VALIS (1981)

Palmer, Christopher. "Postmodernism and the Birth of the Author in Philip K. Dick's *VALIS*." *SFS* 18.3 (1991): 330–242.

Stilling, Roger J. "Mystical Healing: Reading Philip K. Dick's *VALIS* and *The Divine Invasion* as Metapsychoanalytic Novels." *SoAR* 56.2 (1991): 91–106.

DICKEY, JAMES (1923–1997)

Alnilam (1987)

Baughman, Ronald. "James Dickey's *Alnilam:* Toward a True Center Point." *SCR* 26.2 (1994): 173–179.

Deliverance (1970)

Bidney, Martin. "Spirit-Bird, Bowshot, Water-Snake, Corpses, Cosmic Love: Reshaping the Coleridge Legacy in Dickey's *Deliverance*." *PLL* 31.4 (1995): 389–405.

Ebersole, Peter. "Dickey's *Deliverance*." *Expl* 49.4 (1991): 249–251.

Grenier, Donald J. *Women Enter the Wilderness*, 20–28.

Kuehl, John R. and Linda K. Keuhl. " 'The Principle of Uncertainty' in *Deliverance*." *SCR* 26.2 (1994): 162–172.

Moorhead, Michael. "Dickey's *Deliverance*." *Expl* 51.4 (1993): 247–248.

Spencer, Susan A. "James Dickey's American Cain." *CLAJ* 36.3 (1993): 291–306.

Tschachler, Heinz. "Janus, Hitler, the Devil, and Co.: On Myth, Ideology, and the Canadian Postmodern," in D'haen, Theo, ed. *Postmodern*, 47–56.

DICKSON, GORDON R. (1923–)

Final Encyclopedia (1984)

Butvin, Susan M. "*Final Encyclopedia:* Gordon R. Dickson's Creative Universe." *Extrapolation* 36.4 (1995): 360–368.

DIDION, JOAN (1934–)

Democracy (1984)

Limon, John. *Writing After War*, 219–220.

Nadel, Alan. "Failed Cultural Narratives: America in the Postwar Era and the Story of Democracy." *BoundaryII* 19.1 (1992): 95–120.

Play It as It Lays (1970)

Cooper, Ken. " 'Zero Pays the House': The Las Vegas Novel and Atomic Roulette." *ConL* 33.3 (1992): 535–536.

Fine, David. "Running Out of Space: Vanishing Landscapes in California Novels." *WAL* 26.3 (1991): 211.

Run River (1963)

Castronovo, David. *American Gentleman*, 197–198.

DISCH, THOMAS (1940–)

Businessman (1984)

Andriano, Joseph. *Our Lady of Darkness*, 142–144.

DOCTOROW, E. L. (1931–)

Big as Life (1966)

Brienza, Susan. "Writing as Witnessing: The Many Voices of E. L. Doctorow," in Friedman, Melvin J., ed. *Traditions, Voices, and Dreams*, 173–174.

Parks, John G. *E. L. Doctorow*, 29–33.

Billy Bathgate (1989)

Baba, Minako. "Young Gangster as Mythic American Hero: E. L. Doctorow's *Billy Bathgate*." *MELUS* 18.2 (1992): 33–46.

Clerc, Charles. "Dutch Shultz's Last Words Revisited." *JML* 18.4 (1993): 463–465.
Grenier, Donald J. *Women Enter the Wilderness*, 110–117.
Parks, John G. *E. L. Doctorow*, 106–120.
Rushdie, Salman. *Imaginary Homelands*, 330–332.

Book of Daniel (1971)

Brienza, Susan. "Writing as Witnessing: The Many Voices of E. L. Doctorow," in Friedman, Melvin J., ed. *Traditions, Voices, and Dreams*, 174–179.
Parks, John G. *E. L. Doctorow*, 34–53.
Parks, John G. "Politics of Polyphony: The Fiction of E. L. Doctorow." *TCL* 37.4 (1991): 456–458.

Loon Lake (1980)

Brienza, Susan. "Writing as Witnessing: The Many Voices of E. L. Doctorow," in Friedman, Melvin J., ed. *Traditions, Voices, and Dreams*, 183–186.
Parks, John G. *E. L. Doctorow*, 71–87.
Parks, John G. "Politics of Polyphony: The Fiction of E. L. Doctorow." *TCL* 37.4 (1991): 460–462.

Ragtime (1975)

Brienza, Susan. "Writing as Witnessing: The Many Voices of E. L. Doctorow," in Friedman, Melvin J., ed. *Traditions, Voices, and Dreams*, 179–183.
Ostendorf, Berndt. "Musical World of Doctorow's *Ragtime*." *AQ* 43.4 (1991): 579–601.
Parks, John G. *E. L. Doctorow*, 56–70.
Parks, John G. "Politics of Polyphony: The Fiction of E. L. Doctorow." *TCL* 37.4 (1991): 458–460.
Wright, Derek. "*Ragtime* Revisited: History and Fiction in Doctorow's Novel." *IFR* 20.1 (1993): 14–16.

Welcome to Hard Times (1960)

Brienza, Susan. "Writing as Witnessing: The Many Voices of E. L. Doctorow," in Friedman, Melvin J., ed. *Traditions, Voices, and Dreams*, 170–172.
Davis, Robert Murray. *Playing Cowboys*, 71–79.
Parks, John G. *E. L. Doctorow*, 23–29.

World's Fair (1985)

Brienza, Susan. "Writing as Witnessing: The Many Voices of E. L. Doctorow," in Friedman, Melvin J., ed. *Traditions, Voices, and Dreams*, 189–192.
Parks, John G. *E. L. Doctorow*, 95–105.

DODGE, MARY MAPES (1831(?)–1905)

Hans Brinker (1865)

Griswold, Jerry. *Audacious Kids*, 187–199.

DONALDSON, STEPHEN R. (1947–)

Illearth War (1978)

Slethaug, Gordon E. " 'The Discourse of Arrogance,' Popular Power, and Anarchy: *The (First) Chronicles of Thomas Covenant the Unbeliever*." *Extrapolation* 34.1 (1993): 48–62.

Lord Foul's Bane (1978)

Slethaug, Gordon E. " 'The Discourse of Arrogance,' Popular Power, and Anarchy: *The (First) Chronicles of Thomas Covenant the Unbeliever.*" *Extrapolation* 34.1 (1993): 48–62.

Power That Preserves (1978)

Slethaug, Gordon E. " 'The Discourse of Arrogance,' Popular Power, and Anarchy: *The (First) Chronicles of Thomas Covenant the Unbeliever.*" *Extrapolation* 34.1 (1993): 48–62.

DONLEAVY, J. P. (1926–)

Ginger Man (1955)

Morse, Donald E. "American Readings of J. P. Donleavy's *The Ginger Man.*" *Eire* 26.3 (1991): 128–138.

DOOLITTLE, HILDA see H. D.

DORRIS, MICHAEL (1945–1997)

Crown of Columbus (1991)

Matchie, Thomas. "Exploring the Meaning of Discovery in *The Crown of Columbus.*" *NDQ* 243–250.

Rayson, Ann. "Shifting Identity in the Work of Louise Erdrich and Michael Dorris." *SAIL* 3.4 (1991): 27–36.

St. Clair, Janet. "Fighting for Her Life: The Mixed-Blood Woman's Insistence upon Selfhood," in Fleck, Richard F., ed. *Critical Perspectives*, 48–52.

Yellow Raft in Blue Water (1987)

Forget, Christopher. "Identity and Narration: The Braided History." *BWVACET* 16 (1994):18–25.

Owens, Louis. *Other Destinies*, 218–224.

St. Clair, Janet. "Fighting for Her Life: The Mixed-Blood Woman's Insistence upon Selfhood," in Fleck, Richard F., ed. *Critical Perspectives*, 47–52.

DOS PASSOS, JOHN (1896–1970)

Big Money (1936)

Casey, Janet Galligani. "Historicizing the Female in *U.S.A.*: Re-Visions of Dos Passos Trilogy." *TCL* 41.3 (1995): 249–263.

Heinimann, David. "Dos Passos and the 'Middle-Class Liberal'" *CRevAS* 23.2 (1993): 149–160.

42nd Parallel (1930)

Casey, Janet Galligani. "Historicizing the Female in *U.S.A.*: Re-Visions of Dos Passos Trilogy." *TCL* 41.3 (1995): 249–263.

Manhattan Transfer (1925)

Goldsmith, Arnold L. *Modern American Urban Novel*, 17–38.

1919 (1932)

Casey, Janet Galligani. "Historicizing the Female in *U.S.A.*: Re-Visions of Dos Passos Trilogy." *TCL* 41.3 (1995): 249–263.

One Man's Initiation–1917 (1920)

Graves, Mark A. "World Based on Brotherhood: Male Bonding, Male Representation, and the War Novels of John Dos Passos." *CLAJ* 38.2 (1994): 233–237.

Streets of Night (1923)

Casey, Janet Galligani. "Nancibel Taylor and the Dos Passos Canon: Reconsidering *Streets of Night*." *SNNTS* 24.4 (1992): 410–422.

Three Soldiers (1921)

Graves, Mark A. "World Based on Brotherhood: Male Bonding, Male Representation, and the War Novels of John Dos Passos." *CLAJ* 38.2 (1994): 237–246.

Limon, John. *Writing After War*, 89–90.

U.S.A. (1938)

McHale, Brian. "Child as Ready-Made: Baby-Talk and the Language of Dos Passos's Children in *U.S.A*," in Goodenough, Elizabeth, ed. *Infant Tongues*, 202–222.

DOUGLAS, ELLEN (1921–)

Can't Quit You Baby (1988)

Tate, Linda. *Southern Weave of Women*, 51–60.

DOWELL, COLEMAN (1925–1985)

Island People (1976)

Heise, Ursula K. "Time Frames: Temporality and Narration in Coleman Dowell's *Island People*." *JNT* 21.3 (1991): 277–279, 280–286.

DREISER, THEODORE (1871–1945)

American Tragedy (1925)

Cassuto, Leonard. "Lacanian Equivocation in *Sister Carrie*, *The 'Genius,'* and *An American Tragedy*," in Gogol, Miriam, ed. *Theodore Dreiser*, 112–128.

Eby, Clare Virginia. "Psychology of Desire: Veblen's 'Pecuniary Emulation' and 'Invidious Comparsion' in *Sister Carrie* and *An American Tragedy*." *SAF* 21.2 (1993): 192–193, 199–206.

Foley, Barbara. "Politics of Poetics: Ideology and Narrative Form in *An American Tragedy* and *Native Son*," in Gates, Henry Louis, Jr., ed. *Richard Wright*, 188–199.

Funk, Robert. "Dreiser's *An American Tragedy*." *Expl* 51.4 (1993): 232–234.

Gerber, Philip. " 'A Beautiful Legal Problem': Albert Levitt on *An American Tragedy*." *PLL* 27.2 (1991): 214–242.

Gerber, Philip. *Theodore Dreiser Revisited*, 77–93.

Gogol, Miriam. " 'That oldest boy don't wanta be here': Fathers and Sons and the Dynamics of Shame in Theodore Dreiser's Novels," in Gogol, Miriam, ed. *Theodore Dreiser*, 102–106.

Hapke, Laura. *Tales of the Working Girl*, 122–123.
Pizer, Donald. "American Naturalism in Its 'Perfected' State: *The Age of Innocence* and *An American Tragedy*," in Bendixen, Alfred, ed. *Edith Wharton*, 127–140.
Pizer, Donald. "Dreiser and the Naturalistic Drama of Consciousness." *JNT* 21.2 (1991): 208–210.
Pizer, Donald. *Theory and Practice*, 64–68, 78–81, 157–166.
Plank, Kathryn M. "Dreiser's Real *American Tragedy*." *PLL* 27.2 (1991): 268–287.

Bulwark (1946)

Gerber, Philip. *Theodore Dreiser Revisited*, 95–111.

Financier (1912)

Brennan, Stephen C. "*Financier:* Dreiser's Marriage of Heaven and Hell." *SAF* 19.1 (1991): 55–69.
James, Harold. "Literary Financier." *ASch* 60.2 (1991): 254–255.

"Genius" (1915)

Cassuto, Leonard. "Lacanian Equivocation in *Sister Carrie*, *The 'Genius,'* and *An American Tragedy*," in Gogol, Miriam, ed. *Theodore Dreiser*, 112–128.
Gammel, Irene. "Sexualizing the Female Body: Dreiser, Feminism, and Foucault," in Gogol, Miriam, ed. *Theodore Dreiser*, 47–48.
Gerber, Philip. *Theodore Dreiser Revisited* 65–76.

Jennie Gerhardt (1910)

Barrineau, Nancy Warner. "Recontextualizing Dreiser: Gender, Class, and Sexuality in *Jennie Gerhardt*," in Gogol, Miriam, ed. *Theodore Dreiser*, 55–73.
Gerber, Philip. *Theodore Dreiser Revisited*, 35–45.
Hapke, Laura. *Tales of the Working Girl*, 81–83.
Pizer, Donald. "Dreiser and the Naturalistic Drama of Consciousness." *JNT* 21.2 (1991): 206–208.
Pizer, Donald. *Theory and Practice*, 59–64, 75–78, 115–118..

Sister Carrie (1900)

Cassuto, Leonard. "Lacanian Equivocation in *Sister Carrie*, *The 'Genius,'* and *An American Tragedy*," in Gogol, Miriam, ed. *Theodore Dreiser*, 112–128.
Eby, Clare Virginia. "Psychology of Desire: Veblen's 'Pecuniary Emulation' and 'Invidious Comparsion' in *Sister Carrie* and *An American Tragedy*." *SAF* 21.2 (1993): 192–199.
Gammel, Irene. "Sexualizing the Female Body: Dreiser, Feminism, and Foucault," in Gogol, Miriam, ed. *Theodore Dreiser*, 37–41, 42, 44–46.
Gerber, Philip. *Theodore Dreiser Revisited*, 21–34.
Hapke, Laura. *Tales of the Working Girl*, 77–81.
Hochman, Barbara. "Portrait of the Artist as a Young Actress: The Rewards of Representation in *Sister Carrie*," in Pizer, Donald, ed. *New Essays on Sister Carrie*, 43–64.
Lehan, Richard. "*Sister Carrie:* The City, the Self, and the Modes of Narrative Discourse," in Pizer, Donald, ed. *New Essays on Sister Carrie*, 65–85.
Orlov, Paul A. "Quest for Self-Fulfillment: A Heideggerian Perspective on Dreiser's *Sister Carrie*," 134–169.
Pitoniak, Thomas. "Present Feelings, Distant Reason: Conscience in *Sister Carrie*." *ALR* 26.3 (1994): 65–81.

Pizer, Donald. "Dreiser and the Naturalistic Drama of Consciousness." *JNT* 21.2 (1991): 204–206.
Pizer, Donald. *Theory and Practice*, 72–75, 91–95.
Riggio, Thomas P. "Carrie's Blues," in Pizer, Donald, ed. *New Essays on Sister Carrie*, 23–41.
Trachtenberg, Alan. "Who Narrates? Dreiser's Presence in *Sister Carrie*," in Pizer, Donald, ed. *New Essays on Sister Carrie*, 87–122.
Zaluda, Scott. "Secrets of Fraternity: Men and Friendship in *Sister Carrie*," in Gogol, Miriam, ed. *Theodore Dreiser*, 77–91.

Titan (1914)

Gammel, Irene. "Sexualizing the Female Body: Dreiser, Feminism, and Foucault," in Gogol, Miriam, ed. *Theodore Dreiser*, 46–47.

DREW, WAYLAND (1932–)

Wabeno Feast (1973)

Atwood, Margaret. *Strange Things*, 81–84.

DU BOIS, W.E.B. (1868–1963)

Dark Princess (1928)

Kostelanetz, Richard. *Politics and the African-American Novel*, 31–35.
Sundquist, Eric J. *To Wake the Nations*, 618–624.

Mansart Builds a School (1959)

Kostelanetz, Richard. *Politics and the African-American Novel*, 35–66.

Ordeal of Mansart (1957)

Kostelanetz, Richard. *Politics and the African-American Novel*, 35–66.

Quest of the Silver Fleece (1911)

Byerman, Keith. "Race and Romance: *The Quest of the Silver Fleece* as Utopian Narrative." *ALR* 24.3 (1992): 58–71.
Campbell, Jane. *Mythic Black Fiction: The Transformation of History*. Knoxville, TN: University of Tennessee Press, 1986. 66–68. Rpt. in Bloom, Harold, ed. *Major Black American Writers Through the Harlem Renaissance*, 59–60.
Kostelanetz, Richard. *Politics and the African-American Novel*, 28–31.

Worlds of Color (1961)

Kostelanetz, Richard. *Politics and the African-American Novel*, 35–66.

DUCHARME, RÉJEAN (1941–)

L'Avalée des avalés (1966)

Nardout-Lafarge, Elisabeth. "Dialogue et théâtralisation chez Ducharme, Blais et Godbout." *FR* 67.1 (1993): 84–86.
Nardout-Lafarge, Elisabeth. "Noms et stéréotypes juifs dans *L'Avalée des avalés*." *V&I* 18.52 (1992): 89–104.
Seyfrid, Brigitte. "Rhétorique et argumentation chez Réjean Ducharme: Les Polémiques berenciennes." *V&I* 18.2 (1993): 334–350.

Le nez qui voque (1967)

Raoul, Valerie. *Distinctly Narcissistic*, 226–233.

Valenti, Jean. "L'Épreuve du *nez qui voque:* Des savoirs partages au ludisme verbale." *V&I* 20.2 (1995): 400–423.

Les enfantômes (1976)

Meadwell, Kenneth W. "Subjectivité et métamorphoses des acteurs feminins dans *Les enfantômes* de Réjean Ducharme." *SCL* 16.2 (1991): 162–181.

L'hiver de force (1973)

Gasquy-Resch, Yannick. "Le Brouillage du lisible: Lecture du paratexte de *L'hiver de force.*" *EF* 29.1 (1993): 37–46.

Popovic, Pierre. "Le Festivalesque (La Ville dans le roman de Réjean Ducharme)." *Tangence* 48 (1995): 116–127.

L'Océantume(1968)

Dufault, Roseanna Lewis. *Metaphors of Identity*, 55–65.

Straight Winter see *L'hiver de force*

Wilde to mild see *L'hiver de force*

DUNBAR, PAUL LAURENCE (1872–1906)

Love of Landry (1900)

Williams, Kenny J. "Masking of the Novelist." *Singer in the Dawn: Reinterpretations of Paul Laurence Dunbar*. Ed. Jay Martin. New York: Dodd, Mead and Co., 1975. 168–169. Rpt. in Bloom, Harold, ed. *Major Black American Writers Through the Harlem Renaissance*, 79.

Sport of the Gods (1902)

Baker, Houston A., Jr. *Blues, Ideology, and Afro-American Literature: A Vernacular Theory*. Chicago: University of Chicago Press, 1984. 124–125, 137–138. Rpt. in Bloom, Harold, ed. *Major Black American Writers Through the Harlem Renaissance*, 80–82.

Rodgers, Lawrence R. "Paul Laurence Dunbar's *The Sport of the Gods*: The Doubly Conscious World of Plantation Fiction, Migration, and Ascent." *ALR* 24.3 (1992): 42–57.

Scruggs, Charles. *Sweet Home*, 38–39, 43–50.

Williams, Kenny J. "Masking of the Novelist." *Singer in the Dawn: Reinterpretations of Paul Laurence Dunbar*. Ed. Jay Martin. New York: Dodd, Mead and Co., 1975. 168–169. Rpt. in Bloom, Harold, ed. *Major Black American Writers Through the Harlem Renaissance*, 78.

Uncalled (1898)

Williams, Kenny J. "Masking of the Novelist." *Singer in the Dawn: Reinterpretations of Paul Laurence Dunbar*. Ed. Jay Martin. New York: Dodd, Mead and Co., 1975. 168–169. Rpt. in Bloom, Harold, ed. *Major Black American Writers Through the Harlem Renaissance*, 78, 79.

DUNCAN, SARA JEANETTE (1861–1922)

American Girl in London (1891)

Dean, Misao. *Different Point of View*, 19, 24–26.

Burnt Offering (1910)

Dean, Misao. *Different Point of View*, 90–93, 110–111, 116–117, 141–142, 146–150.

Dean, Misao. "Paintbrush and the Scalpel: Sara Jeanette Duncan Representing India." *CanL* 132 (1992): 89, 91–92.

Consort (1912)

Dean, Misao. *Different Point of View*, 96–100.

Cousin Cinderella (1908)

Dean, Misao. *Different Point of View*, 26–29, 115–116.

Daughter of Today (1895)

Dean, Misao. *Different Point of View*, 49–50, 54–55, 75–76, 77–78.

His Honor, and a Lady (1896)

Dean, Misao. *Different Point of View*, 93–96.

His Royal Happiness (1914)

Dean, Misao. *Different Point of View*, 85–86, 129–132.

Imperialist (1904)

Dean, Misao. *Different Point of View*, 29–33, 47–49, 73–74, 87–89, 110, 112–114.

Heble, Ajay. " 'This Little Outpost of Empire': Sara Jeannette Duncan and the Decolonization of Canada." *JCL* 26.1 (1991): 215–228.

Ross, Catherine. "Calling Back the Ghost of the Old-Time Heroine: Duncan, Montgomery, Atwood, Laurence and Munro." *Studies in Canadian Literature* 4.1 (1979): 43–58. Rpt. in Reimer, Mavis, ed. *Such a Simple Little Tale*, 40–42.

Thompson, Elizabeth. *Pioneer Woman*, 60–87.

Path of a Star (1899)

Dean, Misao. *Different Point of View*,. 55–57, 73–75, 76–77.

Set in Authority (1906)

Dean, Misao. *Different Point of View*, 36–37, 71–73, 116, 117–119, 141, 143–144.

Dean, Misao. "Paintbrush and the Scalpel: Sara Jeanette Duncan Representing India." *CanL* 132 (1992): 88.

Simple Adventures of a Memsahib (1893)

Dean, Misao. *Different Point of View*, 34–36, 70–71.

Dean, Misao. "Paintbrush and the Scalpel: Sara Jeanette Duncan Representing India." *CanL* 132 (1992): 85–86, 88.

Lawn, Jennifer. "*The Simple Adventures of a Memsahib* and the Prisonhouse of Language." *CanL* 132 (1992): 16–30.

Social Departure (1890)

Dean, Misao. *Different Point of View*, 23–24, 66–68.

Dean, Misao. "Paintbrush and the Scalpel: Sara Jeanette Duncan Representing India." *CanL* 132 (1992): 83–85, 86–87, 89.

Vernon's Aunt (1894)

Dean, Misao. *Different Point of View*, 69–70.

DUNN, KATHERINE (1945–)

Geek Love (1989)

Hayles, N. Katherine. "Life Cycle of Cyborgs: Writing the Posthuman," in Benjamin, Marina, ed. *Question of Identity*, 162.

DYKEMAN, WILMA

Tall Woman (1962)

Gage, Jim. "The 'Poetics of Space' in Wilma Dykeman's *The Tall Woman*," in Lanier, Parks, Jr.,ed. *Poetics*, 67–80.

EDWARDS-YEARWOOD, GRACE

In the Shadow of the Peacock (1988)

Prinz, Jessica Kimball. "Marketable Bodies, Possessive Peacocks, and Text as Excess: Edwards-Yearwood's *In Shadow of the Peacock*." *Callaloo* 15.4 (1992): 1066–1084.

EHLE, JOHN (1925–)

Widow's Trial (1989)

Roberts, Terry. "Character before the Bar: John Ehle's *The Widow's Trial*." *SLitI* 27.2 (1994): 55–62.

EHRLICH, GRETEL (1946–)

Heart Mountain (1988)

Morris, Gregory L. "When East Meets West: The Passions of Landscape and Culture in Gretel Ehrlich's *Heart Mountain*." *GPQ* 12.1 (1992): 50–59.

ÉLIE, ROBERT (1915–1973)

Farewell My Dreams see *La fin des songes*

La fin des songes (1950)

Raoul, Valerie. *Distinctly Narcissistic*, 121–127.

ELIZONDO, SERGIO (1930–)

Surama (1990)

Sanchez, Rosaura. "Discourses of Gender, Ethnicity and Class in Chicano Literature." *AmRev* 20.2 (1992): 86.

ELKIN, STANLEY (1930–)

Bad Man (1967)

Dougherty, David. C. *Stanley Elkin*, 44–52.

Boswell: A Modern Comedy (1964)

Dougherty, David. C. *Stanley Elkin*, 17–26.

Dick Gibson Show (1971)

Dougherty, David. C. *Stanley Elkin*, 63–82.

Franchiser (1976)

Dougherty, David. C. *Stanley Elkin*, 52–62.

George Mills (1982)

Dougherty, David. C. *Stanley Elkin*, 26–39.

Magic Kingdom (1985)

Dougherty, David. C. *Stanley Elkin*, 83–99.

Rabbi of Lud (1987)

Dougherty, David. C. *Stanley Elkin*, 100–111.

ELLIS, BRET EASTON (1964–)

American Psycho (1991)

Applegate, Nancy and Joe Applegate. "Prophet or Pornographer: An Evaluation of Black Humor in *American Psycho*." *NConL* 25.1 (1995): 10–12.

Young, Elizabeth. *Shopping in Space*, 93–122.

Less Than Zero (1985)

Sahlin, Nicki. " 'But This Road Doesn't Go Anywhere': The Existential Drama in *Less Than Zero*." *Crit* 33.1 (1991): 23–42.

Young, Elizabeth. *Shopping in Space*, 21–42, 123–129.

ELLIS, TREY (1962–)

Platitudes (1988)

Favor, J. Martin. " 'Ain't Nothin' Like the Real Thing, Baby': Trey Ellis' Search for New Black Voices." *Callaloo* 16.3 (1993): 694–705.

ELLISON, RALPH (1914– 1994)

Invisible Man (1952)

Adell, Sandra. "Big E(llison)'s Texts and Intertexts: Eliot, Burke, and the Underground Man." *CLAJ* 37.4 (1994): 388–401.

Allen, Caffilene. "World as Possibility: The Significance of Freud's Totem and Taboo in Ellison's *Invisible Man*." *L&P* 41.1–2 (1995): 1–18.

Baumbach, Jonathan. *Landscape of Nightmare: Studies in the Contemporary American Novel*. New York: New York University Press, 1965. 68–69. Rpt. in Bloom, Harold, ed. *Major Modern Black American Writers*, 89–90.

Baumbach, Jonathan. *Landscape of Nightmare: Studies in the Contemporary American Novel*. New York: New York University Press, 1965. 68–69. Rpt. in Bloom, Harold, ed. *Modern Black American Fiction Writers*, 51–52.

Budick, Emily Miller. *Engendering Romance*, 190–193.

Busby, Mark. *Ralph Ellison*, 39–92.

Butler, Robert. "City as Psychological Frontier in Ralph Ellison's *Invisible Man* and Charles Johnson's *Faith and the Good Thing*," in Hakutani, Yoshinobu, ed. *City in African-American Literature*, 123–131, 135–136.

Doyle, Laura. *Bordering on the Body*, 174–205.

Finholt, Richard. *American Visionary Fiction: Mad Metaphysics as Salvation Psychology*. Port Washington, NY: Kennikat Press, 1978. 98–100. Rpt. in Bloom, Harold, ed. *Modern Black American Fiction Writers*, 57–58.

Forrest, Leon. *Relocations of the Spirit*, 126–145.
Gould, Philip. "Ralph Ellison's 'Time-Haunted' Novel." *ArQ* 49.1 (1993): 117–138.
Griffin, Farah Jasmine. *"Who Set You Flowin'?"*, 123–124, 130–134.
Harper, Phillip Brian. *Framing the Margins*, 116–144.
Kester, Gunilla Theander. *Writing the Subject*, 21–44, 45–72.
Kostelanetz, Richard. *Politics and the African-American Novel*, 107–137.
Lee, Kun Jong. "Ellison's *Invisible Man:* Emersonianism Revised." *PMLA* 107.2 (1992): 331–344.
Lyne, William. "Signifying Modernist: Ralph Ellison and the Limits of the Double Consciousness." *PMLA* 107.2 (1992): 319–330.
McSweeney, Kerry. *Invisible Man: Race and Identity*. Boston: Twayne Publishers, 1988. 11–13. Rpt. in Bloom, Harold, ed. *Major Modern Black American Writers*, 98–100.
Margolies, Edward. *Native Sons: A Critical Study of Twentieth-Century Negro American Authors*. Philadelphia: J. B. Lippincott Co., 1968. 130, 133. Rpt. in Bloom, Harold, ed. *Major Modern Black American Writers*, 90–91.
Reed, Brian K. "Iron and the Flesh: History as Machine in Ellison's *Invisible Man*." *CLAJ* 37.3 (1994): 261–273.
Reed, T. V. *Fifteen Jugglers, Five Believers*, 58–86.
Rogers, Franklin R. *Occidental Ideographs*, 241–242.
Rovit, Earl H. "Ralph Ellison and the American Comic Tradition." *Wisconsin Studies in Contemporary Literature* 1.3 (1960): 34–35. Rpt. in Bloom, Harold, ed. *Major Modern Black American Writers*, 87–88.
Rovit, Earl H. "Ralph Ellison and the American Comic Tradition." *Wisconsin Studies in Contemporary Literature* 1.3 (1960): 34–35. Rpt. in Bloom, Harold, ed. *Modern Black American Fiction Writers*, 49–50.
Schaub, Thomas Hill. *American Fiction in the Cold War*, 91–115.
Scruggs, Charles. *Sweet Home*, 100–136.
Stanford, Ann Folwell. "He Speaks for Whom? Inscription and Reinscription of Women In *Invisible Man* and *The Salt Eaters*." *MELUS* 18.2 (1992): 17–19, 20–24.

ENGEL, MARIAN (1933–1985)

Bear (1976)

Atwood, Margaret. *Strange Things*, 104–108.
Howells, Coral Ann. "On Gender and Writing: Marian Engel's *Bear* and Tattooed Woman," in Howells, Coral Ann, ed. *Narrative Strategies*, 73–74, 80.
Verduyn, Christl. *Lifelines*, 117–137.

Glassy Sea (1978)

Verduyn, Christl. *Lifelines*, 138–161.

Honeymoon Festival (1970)

Verduyn, Christl. *Lifelines*, 76–92.

Lunatic Villas (1981)

Verduyn, Christl. *Lifelines*, 162–180.

Monodromos (1973)

Verduyn, Christl. *Lifelines*, 93–116.

No Clouds of Glory (1968)
Verduyn, Christl. *Lifelines*, 62–75.

One Way Street see *Monodromos*

Sarah Bastard's Notebook see *No Clouds of Glory*

ERDRICH, LOUISE (1954–)

Beet Queen (1986)
Bataille, Gretchen M. "Louise Erdrich's *Beet Queen:* Images of the Grotesque on the Northern Plains," in Fleck, Richard F., ed. *Critical Perspectives*, 277–284.
Clayton, Jay. "Narrative Turn in Minority Fiction," in Carlisle, Janice,ed. *Narrative and Culture*, 59–60.
Flavin, Louise. "Gender Construction amid Family Dissolution in Louise Erdrich's *The Beet Queen.*" *SAIL* 7.2 (1995): 17–24.
Meisenhelder, Susan. "Race and Gender in Louise Erdrich's *Beet Queen.*" *ArielE* 25.1 (1994): 45–57.
Owens, Louis. *Other Destinies*, 205–212.
Wong, Hertha D. "Adoptive Mothers and Thrown-Away Children in the Novels of Louise Erdrich," in Daly, Brenda O., ed. *Narrating Mothers*, 187–189, 189–191.
Woodward, Pauline G. "Chance in Louise Erdrich's *The Beet Queen*: New Ways to Find a Family." *ArielE* 26.2 (1995): 109–127.

Crown of Columbus (1991)
Matchie, Thomas. "Exploring the Meaning of Discovery in *The Crown of Columbus.*" *NDQ* 243–250.
Rayson, Ann. "Shifting Identity in the Work of Louise Erdrich and Michael Dorris." *SAIL* 3.4 (1991): 27–36.
St. Clair, Janet. "Fighting for Her Life: The Mixed-Blood Woman's Insistence upon Selfhood," in Fleck, Richard F., ed. *Critical Perspectives*, 48–52.

Love Medicine (1984)
Carr, Susan. "Turtle Mountain/Yoknapatawpha Connection." *BWVACET* 16 (1994): 18–25.
Kroeber, Karl, et. al. "Louise Erdrich's *Love Medicine*," in Fleck, Richard F., ed. *Critical Perspectives*, 268–276.
Owens, Louis. *Other Destinies*, 194–205.
Pittman, Barbara L. "Cross-Cultural Reading and Generic Transformations: The Chronotope of the Road in Erdrich's *Love Medicine.*" *AL* 67.4 (1995): 777–792.
Rosenfelt, Deborah Silverton. "Feminism, "Postfeminism," and Contemporary Women's Fiction," in Howe, Florence, ed. *Tradition and the Talents of Women*, 283–284, 285.
Ruppert, James. "Meditation and Multiple Narrative in *Love Medicine.*" *NDQ* 59.4 (1991): 229–241.
Ruppert, James. *Mediation in Contemporary Native American Fiction*, 131–150.
St. Clair, Janet. "Fighting for Her Life: The Mixed-Blood Woman's Insistence upon Selfhood," in Fleck, Richard F., ed. *Critical Perspectives*, 46–52.
Sarve-Gorham, Kristan. "Power Lines: The Motif of Twins and the Medicine Women of *Tracks* and *Love Medicine.*" *BuR* 39.1 (1995): 167–190.
Schneider, Lissa. "Op; *Love Medicine:* A Metaphor for Forgiveness." *SAIL* 4.1 (1992): 1–13.

Smith, Jeanne. "Transpersonal Selfhood: The Boundaries of Identity in Louise Erdrich's *Love Medicine*." *SAIL* 3.4 (1991): 13–26.

Wong, Hertha D. "Adoptive Mothers and Thrown-Away Children in the Novels of Louise Erdrich," in Daly, Brenda O., ed. *Narrating Mothers*, 177–183, 189–191.

Tracks (1988)

Clarke, Joni Adamson. "Why Bears Are Good to Think and Theory Doesn't Have to Be Murder: Transformation and Oral Tradition in Louise Erdrich's *Tracks*." *SAIL* 4.1 (1992): 28–48.

Cornell, Daniel. "Woman Looking: Revis(ion)ing Pauline's Subject Position in Louise Erdrich's *Tracks*." *SAIL* 4.1 (1992): 49–64.

Flavin, James. "Novel as Performance: Communication in Louise Erdrich's *Tracks*." *SAIL* 3.4 (1991): 1–12.

Kolmar, Wendy K. " 'Dialectics of Connectedness': Supernatural Elements in Novels by Bambara, Cisneros, Grahn, and Erdrich," in Carpenter, Lynette, ed. *Haunting the House of Fiction*, 240–241, 242, 243, 245, 246–248.

Owens, Louis. *Other Destinies*, 212–217.

Peterson, Nancy J. "History, Postmodernism, and Louise Erdrich's *Tracks*." *PMLA* 109.5 (1994): 982–994.

St. Clair, Janet. "Fighting for Her Life: The Mixed-Blood Woman's Insistence upon Selfhood," in Fleck, Richard F., ed. *Critical Perspectives*, 46–52.

Sarve-Gorham, Kristan. "Power Lines: The Motif of Twins and the Medicine Women of *Tracks* and *Love Medicine*." *BuR* 39.1 (1995): 167–190.

Sergi, Jennifer. "Storytelling: Tradition and Preservation in Louise Erdrich's *Tracks*." *WLT* 66.2 (1992): 279–282.

Tusmith, Bonnie. *All My Relatives*, 129–132.

Walker, Victoria. "Note on Perspective in *Tracks*." *SAIL* 3.4 (1991): 37–40.

Wong, Hertha D. "Adoptive Mothers and Thrown-Away Children in the Novels of Louise Erdrich," in Daly, Brenda O., ed. *Narrating Mothers*, 183–186, 189–191.

EVANS, AUGUSTA JANE (1835–1909)

Beulah (1859)

Goshgarian, G. M. *To Kiss the Chastening Rod*, 121–155.

FARMER, PHILIP JOSE (1918–)

Night of Light (1966)

Dudley, Joseph M. "Transformational SF Religions: Philip Jose Farmer's *Night of Light* and Robert Silverberg's *Downward to the Earth*." *Extrapolation* 35.4 (1994): 343–349.

FARRELL, JAMES T. (1904–1979)

Gas-House McGinty (1933)

Pizer, Donald. *Theory and Practice*, 45–49.

Judgment Day (1935)

Butler, Robert. "Farrell's Ethnic Neighborhood and Wright's Urban Ghetto: Two Visions of Chicago's South Side." *MELUS* 18.1 (1993): 106–107.

Goldsmith, Arnold L. *Modern American Urban Novel*, 42–45, 51–54, 55–57.
Hapke, Laura. *Daughters of the Great Depression*, 39–42.

Young Lonigan (1932)

Butler, Robert. "Farrell's Ethnic Neighborhood and Wright's Urban Ghetto: Two Visions of Chicago's South Side." *MELUS* 18.1 (1993): 104–106.
Goldsmith, Arnold L. *Modern American Urban Novel*, 41–42, 45–48, 54–55.

Young Manhood of Studs Lonigan (1934)

Butler, Robert. "Farrell's Ethnic Neighborhood and Wright's Urban Ghetto: Two Visions of Chicago's South Side." *MELUS* 18.1 (1993): 106, 110.
Goldsmith, Arnold L. *Modern American Urban Novel*, 40–41, 45, 48–51, 55.

FAULKNER, JOHN (1901–1963)

Cabin Road (1951)

McDonald, Robert L. " 'On the Edge of the Porch': Entering the Hillfolk's Domain in John Faulkner's *Cabin Road*." *NMW* 24.2 (1992): 89–98.

FAULKNER, WILLIAM (1897–1962)

Absalom, Absalom! (1936)

Batty, Nancy E. "Riddle of *Absalom, Absalom!:* Looking at the Wrong Blackbird?" *MissQ* 47.3 (1994): 461–489.
Bauer, Margaret D. "Sterile New South: An Intertextual Reading of *Their Eyes Were Watching God* and *Absalom, Absalom!*" *CLAJ* 36.4 (1993): 384–405.
Castronovo, David. *American Gentleman*, 167–171.
Chandler, Marilyn R. *Dwelling in the Text*, 245–277.
Dale, Corinne. "*Absalom, Absalom!* and the Snopes Trilogy: Southern Patriarchy in Revision." *MissQ* 45.3 (1992): 321–337.
Dalziel, Pamela. "*Absalom, Absalom!:* The Extension of Dialogic Form." *MissQ* 45.3 (1992): 277–294.
Donnelly, Colleen E. "Compelled to Believe: Historiography and Truth in *Absalom, Absalom!*" *Style* 25.1 (1991): 104–122.
Dunne, Robert. "*Absalom, Absalom!* and the Ripple-Effect of the Past." *UMSE* 10 (1992): 56–66.
Geoffroy, Alain. "Through Rosa's Looking-Glass: Narcissism and Identification in Faulkner's *Absalom, Absalom!*" *MissQ* 45.3 (1992): 313–321.
Godden, Richard. "*Absalom, Absalom!* and Faulkner's Erroneous Dating of the Haitian Revolution." *MissQ* 47.3 (1994): 489–495.
Godden, Richard. "*Absalom, Absalom!* and Rosa Coldfield: Or, What Is in the Dark House." *FJ* 8.2 (1993): 31–66.
Godden, Richard. "*Absalom, Absalom!*, Haiti and Labor History: Reading Unreadable Revolutions." *ELH* 61.3 (1994): 685–720.
Hanson, Elizabeth I. *Margaret Mitchell*, 78–82.
Ladd, Barbara. " 'The Direction of the Howling': Nationalism and the Color Line in *Absalom, Absalom!*" *AL* 66.3 (1994): 525–551.
Lee, Kyhan. "Narration as Tragic Experience in Faulkner's *Absalom, Absalom!*" *JELL* 40.4 (1994): 743–754.
Lindsey, William D. "Order as Disorder: *Absalom, Absalom!*'s Inversion of the

Judaeo-Christian Creation Myth," in Fowler, Doreen, ed. *Faulkner and Religion*, 85–100.

Meeter, Glenn. "Quentin as Redactor: Biblical Analogy in Faulkner's *Absalom, Absalom!*," in Fowler, Doreen, ed. *Faulkner and Religion*, 103–123.

Miller, J. Hillis. "Ideology and Topography in Faulkner's *Absalom, Absalom!*," in Kartiganer, Donald M., ed. *Faulkner and Ideology*, 253–276.

Nicolaisen, Peter. " 'The Dark Land Talking the Voiceless Speech': Faulkner and 'Native Soil'." *MissQ* 45.3 (1992): 260, 263.

Poland, Tim. "Faulkner's *Absalom, Absalom!*." *Expl* 50.4 (1992): 239–241.

Porter, Carolyn. "*Absalom, Absalom!:* (Un)Making the Father," in Weinstein, Philip M., ed. *Cambridge Companion*, 168–195.

Railey, Kevin. "Paternalism and Liberalism: Contending Ideologies in *Absalom, Absalom!*." *FJ* 7.1–2 (1991–92): 115–132.

Rogers, Franklin R. *Occidental Ideographs*, 159–187, 217–219.

Ryan, Heberden W. "Behind Closed Doors: The Unknowable and the Unknowing in *Absalom, Absalom!*" *MissQ* 45.3 (1992): 295–312.

Saldívar, Ramón. "Looking for a Master Plan: Faulkner, Paredes, and the Colonial Postcolonial Subject," in Weinstein, Philip M., ed. *Cambridge Companion*, 96–108.

Simpson, Lewis P. "On William Faulkner's *Absalom, Absalom!*," in Madden, David, ed. *Classics of Civil War Fiction*, 151–173.

Slaughter, Carolyn Norman. "*Absalom, Absalom!:* 'Fluid Cradle of Events (Time)'." *FJ* 6.2 (1991): 65–84.

Toker, Leona. *Eloquent Reticence*, 152–184.

Wagner-Martin, Linda. "Rosa Coldfield as Daughter: Another of Faulkner's Lost Children." *SAF* 19.1 (1991): 1–13.

Westling, Louise. "Women, Landscape, and the Legacy of Gilgamesh in *Absalom, Absalom!* and *Go Down, Moses*." *MissQ* 48.3 (1995): 507–511.

Wilson, Deborah. " 'A Shape to Fill a Lack': *Absalom, Absalom!* and the Pattern of History." *FJ* 7.1–2 (1991–92): 61–81.

As I Lay Dying (1930)

Baldwin, Marc D. "Faulkner's Cartographic Method: Producing the Land through Cognitive Mapping." *FJ* 7.1–2 (1991–92): 193–214.

Blaine, Diana York. "Abjection of Addie and Other Myths of the Maternal in *As I Lay Dying*." *MissQ* 47.3 (1994): 419–439.

Budick, Emily Miller. *Engendering Romance*, 89–95.

Chappel, Deborah K. "Pa Says: The Rhetoric of Faulkner's Anse Bundren." *MissQ* 44.3 (1991): 273–285.

Delville, Michel. "Alienating Language and Darl's Narrative Consciousness in Faulkner's *As I Lay Dying*." *SLJ* 27.1 (1994): 61–72.

Hattenhauer, Darryl. "Geometric Design of *As I Lay Dying*." *ClQ* 30.2 (1994): 146–153.

Hayes, Elizabeth. "Tension between Darl and Jewel." *SLJ* 24.2 (1992): 49–61.

Kaufmann, Michael. *Textual Bodies*, 36–51.

Kaufmann, Michael. "Textual Coffin and the Narrative Corpse of *As I Lay Dying*." *ArQ* 49.1 (1993): 99–116.

Kincaid, Nancy. "As Me and Addie Lay Dying." *SoR* 30.3 (1994): 582–595.

Limon, John. *Writing After War*, 84–86, 115–117, 122–127.

McKee, Patricia. "*As I Lay Dying:* Experience in Passing." *SAQ* 90.3 (1991): 579–632

Matthews, John T. "*As I Lay Dying* in the Machine Age." *BoundaryII* 19.1 (1992): 69–94.

Mellard, James M. "Realism, Naturalism, Modernism: Residual, Dominant, and Emergent Ideologies in *As I Lay Dying*," in Kartiganer, Donald M., ed. *Faulkner and Ideology*, 217–237.

Mellard, James M. "Something New and Hard and Bright: Faulkner, Ideology, and the Construction of Modernism." *MissQ* 48.3 (1995): 459–479.

Merrill, Robert. "Faulknerian Tragedy: The Example of *As I Lay Dying*." *MissQ* 47.3 (1994): 403–418.

Nicolaisen, Peter. " 'The Dark Land Talking the Voiceless Speech': Faulkner and 'Native Soil'." *MissQ* 45.3 (1992): 258–259, 264–267, 269–270.

Nielsen, Paul S. "What Does Addie Bundren Mean, and How Does She Mean It?" *SLJ* 25.1 (1992): 33–39.

O'Donnell, Patrick. "Between the Family and the State: Nomadism and Authority in *As I Lay Dying*." *FJ* 7/1–2 (1991–92): 83–94.

Ownby, Ted. "Snopes Trilogy and the Emergence of Consumer Culture," in Kartiganer, Donald M., ed. *Faulkner and Ideology*, 110–112.

Poland, Tim. "Faulkner's *As I Lay Dying*." *Expl* 49.2 (1991): 118–120.

Sass, Karen R. "At a Loss for Words: Addie and Language in *As I Lay Dying*." *FJ* 6.2 (1991): 9–21.

Woodbery, Bonnie. "Abject in Faulkner's *As I Lay Dying*." *L&P* 40.3 (1994): 26–42.

Flags in the Dust (1973)

Andrews, Karen M. "Toward a 'Culturalist' Approach to Faulkner Studies: Making Connections in *Flags in Dust*." *FJ* 7.1–2 (1991): 13–26.

Irwin, John T. "Horace Benbow and the Myth of Narcissa," in Kartinger, Donald M., ed. *Faulkner and Psychology*, 252–257.

Irwin, John T. "Horace Benbow and the Myth of Narcissa." *AL* 64.3 (1992): 552–556, 561–565.

Jones, Anne Goodwyn. "Desire, Dismemberment: Faulkner and the Ideology of Penetration," in Kartiganer, Donald M., ed. *Faulkner and Ideology*, 163–164.

Limon, John. *Writing After War*, 120–121.

Lucas, Teri. "Medicine—Faulkner's Guide to the Future of Humanity." *UMSE* 10 (1992): 177–180.

Nicolaisen, Peter. " 'The Dark Land Talking the Voiceless Speech': Faulkner and 'Native Soil'." *MissQ* 45.3 (1992): 257, 259, 264.

Hamlet (1940)

Kidd, Millie M. "Dialogic Perspective in William Faulkner's *The Hamlet*." *MissQ* 44.3 (1991): 309–320.

Kowalewski, Michael. *Deadly Musings*, 182–184.

Nicolaisen, Peter. " 'The Dark Land Talking the Voiceless Speech': Faulkner and 'Native Soil'." *MissQ* 45.3 (1992): 255–259, 260, 267–269, 270.

Urgo, Joseph. "Faulkner's Real Estate: Land and Literary Speculation in *The Hamlet*." *MissQ* 48.3 (1995): 443–457.

If I Forget Thee, Jerusalem (1939)

Gutting, Gabriele. "Mysteries of the Map-Maker: Faulkner, *If I Forget Thee, Jerusalem*, and the Secret of a Map." *FJ* 8.2 (1993): 85–93.

Hannon, Charles. "Signification, Simulation, and Containment in *If I Forget Thee, Jerusalem.*" *FJ* 7.1–2 (1991–92): 133–150.

Intruder in the Dust (1948)

Castronovo, David. *American Gentleman*, 171–173.

Nicolaisen, Peter. " 'The Dark Land Talking the Voiceless Speech': Faulkner and 'Native Soil'." *MissQ* 45.3 (1992): 257.

Ownby, Ted. "Snopes Trilogy and the Emergence of Consumer Culture," in Kartiganer, Donald M., ed. *Faulkner and Ideology*, 107–109, 121–122.

Light in August (1932)

Bidney, Martin. "*Ring and the Book* and *Light in August:* Faulkner's Response to Browning." *VN* 81 (1992): 51–59.

Bidney, Martin. "*Windy McPherson's Son* and Silent McEachern's Son: Sherwood Anderson and *Light in August.*" *MissQ* 46.3 (1993): 395–406.

Boker, Pamela A. " 'How Can He Be So Nothungry?': Fetishism, Anorexia, and the Disavowal of the Cultural 'I' in *Light in August.*" *FJ* 7.1–2 (1991–92): 175–191.

Burgess, M. J. "Watching (Jefferson) Watching: *Light in August* and the Aestheticization of Gender." *FJ* 7.1–2 (1991–92): 95–114.

Gray, Richard. "On Privacy: William Faulkner and the Human Subject," in Kartiganer, Donald M., ed. *Faulkner and Ideology*, 60–67.

Hays, Peter L. "Racial Predestination: The Elect and the Damned in *Light in August.*" *ELN* 33.2 (1995): 62–69.

Hlavsa, Virginia V. "Crucifixion in *Light in August:* Suspending Rules at the Post," in Fowler, Doreen, ed. *Faulkner and Religion*, 127–138.

Hlavsa, Virginia V. James. *Faulkner*, 61–208.

Jenkins, Lee. "Psychoanalytic Conceptualizations of Characterization, Or Nobody Laughs in *Light in August*," in Kartinger, Donald M., ed. *Faulkner and Psychology*, 189–218.

Jones, Anne Goodwyn. "Desire, Dismemberment: Faulkner and the Ideology of Penetration," in Kartiganer, Donald M., ed. *Faulkner and Ideology*, 164–165.

Kartiganer, Donald M. " 'What I Chose to Be': Freud, Faulkner, Joe Christmas, and the Abandonment of Design," in Kartinger, Donald M., ed. *Faulkner and Psychology*, 288–313.

Kowalewski, Michael. *Deadly Musings*, 187–193.

Newman, David. " 'The Vehicle Itself Is Unaware': New Criticism the Limits of Reading Faulkner." *MissQ* 48.3 (1995): 481–499.

Nicolaisen, Peter. " 'The Dark Land Talking the Voiceless Speech': Faulkner and 'Native Soil'." *MissQ* 45.3 (1992): 267.

Ownby, Ted. "Snopes Trilogy and the Emergence of Consumer Culture," in Kartiganer, Donald M., ed. *Faulkner and Ideology*, 109–110, 204–205.

Toomey, David. "Human Heart in Conflict: *Light in August*'s Schizophrenic Narrator." *SNNTS* 23.4 (1991): 452–469.

Watkins, Ralph. " 'It Was Like I Was the Woman and She Was the Man': Boundaries, Portals, and Pollution in *Light in August.*" *SLJ* 26.2 (1994): 11–24.

Williams, Michael. "Cross-Dressing in Yoknapatawpha County." *MissQ* 47.3 (1994): 382–386.

Wittenberg, Judith Bryant. "Race in *Light in August:* Wordsymbols and Obverse Reflections," in Weinstein, Philip M., ed. *Cambridge Companion*, 146–167.

Mansion (1959)

Kang, Hee. New Configuration of Faulkner's Feminine: Linda Snopes Kohl in *The Mansion.*" *FJ* 8.1 (1992): 31–41.

Ownby, Ted. "Snopes Trilogy and the Emergence of Consumer Culture," in Kartiganer, Donald M., ed. *Faulkner and Ideology*, 123–124.

Williams, Michael. "Cross-Dressing in Yoknapatawpha County." *MissQ* 47.3 (1994): 378–379, 387–390.

Mosquitoes (1927)

Harrington, Evans. " 'A Passion Week of the Heart': Religion and Faulkner's Art," in Fowler, Doreen, ed. *Faulkner and Religion*, 157–161.

Michel, Frann. "William Faulkner as Lesbian Author," in Morgan, Thaïs E., ed. *Men Writing the Feminine*, 143–150.

Pylon (1935)

Folks, Jeffrey J. *Southern Writers*, 25–35.

Wagner, Vivian. "Gender, Technology, and Utopia in Faulkner's Airplane Tales." *ArQ* 49.4 (1993): 81, 83–84, 87–96.

Yerkes, David. "Reporter's Name in *Pylon* and Why That's Important." *FJ* 6.2 (1991): 3–8.

Zeitlin, Michael. "Faulkner's *Pylon:* The City in the Age of Mechanical Reproduction." *CRevAS* 22.2 (1991): 229–240.

Reivers (1962)

Eyster, Kevin I. "Personal Narrative in Fiction: Faulkner's *The Reivers.*" *WF* 51.1 (1992): 11–21.

Requiem for a Nun (1951)

Nicolaisen, Peter. " 'The Dark Land Talking the Voiceless Speech': Faulkner and 'Native Soil'." *MissQ* 45.3 (1992): 262.

Wittenberg, Judith Bryant. "Temple Drake and La Parole pleine." *MissQ* 48.3 (1995): 421–441.

Wondra, Janet. " 'Play' within a Play: Gaming with Language in *Requiem for a Nun.*" *FJ* 8.1 (1992): 43–59.

Sanctuary (1931)

Boon, Kevin A. "Temple Defiled: The Brainwashing of Temple Drake in Faulkner's *Sanctuary.*" *FJ* 6.2 (1991): 33–50.

Folks, Jeffrey J. *Southern Writers*, 37–47.

Irwin, John T. "Horace Benbow and the Myth of Narcissa." *AL* 64.3 (1992): 544–546, 556–561.

Irwin, John T. "Horace Benbow and the Myth of Narcissa," in Kartinger, Donald M., ed. *Faulkner and Psychology*, 244–246, 260–266.

Kirchdorfer, Ulf. "*Sanctuary:* Temple as a Parrot." *FJ* 6.2 (1991): 51–53.

Kowalewski, Michael. *Deadly Musings*, 162–163, 175–177, 180–181.

Schafer, William J. "Faulkner's Sanctuary: The Blackness of Fairytale." *DUJ* 52.2 (1991): 217–222.

Wilson, Andrew J. "Corruption in Looking: William Faulkner's *Sanctuary* as a Detective Novel." *MissQ* 47.3 (1994): 441–460.

Sartoris (1929)

Castronovo, David. *American Gentleman*, 164–167.

Soldiers' Pay (1926)

Limon, John. *Writing After War*, 117–120.

Nicolaisen, Peter. " 'The Dark Land Talking the Voiceless Speech': Faulkner and 'Native Soil'." *MissQ* 45.3 (1992): 263–264.

Scoblionko, Andrew. "Subjectivity and Homelessness in *Soldier's Pay.*" *FJ* 8.1 (1992): 61–71.

Williams, Michael. "Cross-Dressing in Yoknapatawpha County." *MissQ* 47.3 (1994): 387.

Zeitlin, Michael. "Passion of Margaret Powers: A Psychoanalytic Reading of *Soldiers' Pay.*" *MissQ* 46.3 (1993): 351–372.

Sound and the Fury (1929)

Abel, Marco. "One Goal Is Still Lacking: The Influence of Friedrich Nietzsche's Philosophy on William Faulkner's *The Sound and the Fury.*" *SoAR* 60.4 (1995): 35–52.

Barker, Deborah E. and Ivo Kamps. "Much Ado about Nothing: Language and Desire in *The Sound and the Fury.*" *MissQ* 46.3 (1993): 373–393.

Bauer, Margaret D. "Evolution of Caddy: An Intertextual Reading of *The Sound and the Fury* and Ellen Gilchrist's *The Annunciation.*" *SLJ* 25.1 (1992): 40–51.

Bockting, Ineke. "Mind Style as an Interdisciplinary Approach to Characterisation in Faulkner." *Lang&Lit* 3.3 (1994): 157–174.

Brown, Arthur A. "Benjy, the Reader and Death: At the Fence in *The Sound and the Fury.*" *MissQ* 48.3 (1995): 407–420.

Bryant, Cedric Gael. "Mirroring the Racial 'Other': The Deacon and Quentin Compson in William Faulkner's *The Sound and the Fury.*" *SoR* 29.1 (1993): 30–40.

Budick, Emily Miller. *Engendering Romance*, 80–88.

Castille, Philip Dubuisson. "Dilsey's Easter Conversion in Faulkner's *The Sound and the Fury.*" *SNNTS* 24.4 (1992): 423–433.

Clarke, Deborah. "Of Mothers, Robbery, and Language: Faulkner and *The Sound and the Fury,*" in Kartinger, Donald M., ed. *Faulkner and Psychology*, 56–76.

Donaldson, Susan V. "Reading Faulkner Reading Cowley Reading Faulkner: Authority and Gender in the Compson Appendix." *FJ* 7.1–2 (1991–92): 27–41.

Fant, Gene, Jr. "Faulkner's *The Sound and the Fury.*" *Expl* 52.2 (1994): 104–106.

Fleming, Robert E. "James Weldon Johnson's *God's Trombones* as a Source for Faulkner's Rev'un Shegog." *CLAJ* 36.1 (1992): 24–30.

Forrest, Leon. *Relocations of the Spirit*, 182–188.

Fowler, Doreen. " 'Little Sister Death': *The Sound and the Fury* and Denied Unconscious," in Kartinger, Donald M., ed. *Faulkner and Psychology*, 3–19.

Fowler, Doreen. "Ravished Daughter: Eleusinian Mysteries in *The Sound and the Fury,*" in Fowler, Doreen, ed. *Faulkner and Religion*, 140–155.

Gunn, Giles. "Faulkner's Heterodoxy: Faith and Family in *The Sound and the Fury,*" in Fowler, Doreen, ed. *Faulkner and Religion*, 44–64.

Irwin, John T. "Horace Benbow and the Myth of Narcissa." *AL* 64.3 (1992): 547, 548–549.

Jones, Anne Goodwyn. "Desire, Dismemberment: Faulkner and the Ideology of Penetration," in Kartiganer, Donald M., ed. *Faulkner and Ideology*, 164.

Kowalewski, Michael. *Deadly Musings*, 185–187.

Lester, Cheryl. "Racial Awareness and Arrested Development: *The Sound and the Fury* and the Great Migration (1915–1928)," in Weinstein, Philip M., ed. *Cambridge Companion*, 123–143.

O'Neill, Peter. "Work Ethic in *The Sound and the Fury*." *BWVACET* 13.1 (1991): 81–87.

Potts, Donna L. "Faulkner's *The Sound and the Fury*." *Expl* 52.4 (1994): 236–237.

Railey, Kevin. "Cavalier Ideology and History: The Significance of Quentin's Section in *The Sound and the Fury*." *ArQ* 48.3 (1992): 77–93.

Stoicheff, Peter. "Between Originality and Indebtedness: Allegories of Authorship in William Faulkner's *The Sound and Fury*." *MLQ* 53.4 (1992): 449–463.

Toker, Leona. *Eloquent Reticence*, 19–41.

Visser, Irene. "Faulkner's *The Sound and the Fury*." *Expl* 52.3 (1994): 171–172.

Town (1957)

Little, Anne Colclough. "Reconsidering Maggie, Charles, and Gavin in *The Town*." *MissQ* 46.3 (1993): 463–477.

Towner, Theresa M. " 'It Aint Funny A-Tall': The Transfigured Tales of *The Town*." *MissQ* 44.3 (1991): 321–335.

Unvanquished (1938)

Williams, Michael. "Cross-Dressing in Yoknapatawpha County." *MissQ* 47.3 (1994): 372–382.

Wild Palms see *If I Forget Thee, Jerusalem*

FAUSET, JESSIE REDMON (1882–1961)

Chinaberry Tree (1931)

Carby, Hazel V. *Reconstructing Womanhood: The Emergence of the Afro-American Novelist.* New York: Oxford University Press, 1987. 167–168. Rpt. in Bloom, Harold, ed. *Black American Women Fiction Writers*, 39–40.

Lewis, Vashti Crutcher. "Mulatto Hegemony in the Novels of Jessie Redmon Fauset." *CLAJ* 35.4 (1992): 381–384.

Lewis, Vashti Crutcher. "Mulatto Hegemony in the Novels of Jessie Redmon Fauset." *College Language Association Journal* 35.4 (June 1992): 382–383, 385–386. Rpt. in Bloom, Harold, ed. *Black American Women Fiction Writers*, 42.

Comedy: American Style (1933)

Lewis, Vashti Crutcher. "Mulatto Hegemony in the Novels of Jessie Redmon Fauset." *CLAJ* 35.4 (1992): 384–385.

Lupton, Mary Jane. "Clothes and Closure in Three Novels by Black Women." *Black American Literature Forum* 20.4 (Winter 1986): 412–413. Rpt. in Bloom, Harold, ed. *Black American Women Fiction Writers*, 38–39.

McLendon, Jacquelyn. *Politics of Color*, 50–70.

Wall, Cheryl A. *Women of the Harlem Renaissance*, 80–84.

Plum Bun (1929)

Kubitschek, Missy Dehn. *Claiming the Heritage*, 104–111.

Lewis, Vashti Crutcher. "Mulatto Hegemony in the Novels of Jessie Redmon Fauset." *CLAJ* 35.4 (1992): 379–381.

McDowell, Deborah E. *"The Changing Same"*, 61–77.

McLendon, Jacquelyn . *Politics of Color*, 28–49.

Wall, Cheryl A. *Women of the Harlem Renaissance*, 73–78.

There Is Confusion (1924)

Ammons, Elizabeth. *Conflicting Stories*, 147–151.

Ammons, Elizabeth. *Conflicting Stories: American Women Writers at the Turn into the Twentieth Century.* New York: Oxford University Press, 1991. 151, 154. Rpt. in Bloom, Harold, ed. *Black American Women Fiction Writers*, 40–41.

Lewis, Vashti Crutcher. "Mulatto Hegemony in the Novels of Jessie Redmon Fauset." *CLAJ* 35.4 (1992): 378–379.

McCoy, Beth A. " 'Is This Really What You Wanted Me to Be?': The Daughter's Disintegration in Jessie Redmon Fauset's *There Is Confusion*." *MFS* 40.1 (1994): 101–117.

Wall, Cheryl A. *Women of the Harlem Renaissance*, 66–68.

FEARING, KENNETH (1902–1961)

Big Clock (1946)

Evans, T. Jeff. "Narratology in Kenneth Fearing's *Big Clock*." *JNT* 23.3 (1993): 188–200.

FEINBERG, LESLIE (1949–)

Stone Butch Blues (1993)

Prosser, Jay. "No Place Like Home: The Transgendered Narrative of Leslie Feinberg's *Stone Butch Blues*." *MFS* 41.3–4 (1995): 483–514.

FERN, FANNY (1811–1872)

Rose Clark (1856)

Walker, Nancy A. *Fanny Fern*, 63–79.

Ruth Hall (1854)

Brodhead, Richard H. *Cultures of Letters*, 59.

Grasso, Linda. "Anger in the House: Fanny Fern's *Ruth Hall* and the Redrawing of Emotional Boundaries in Mid-19th Century America." *SAR* 19 (1995): 251–261.

Hamilton, Kristie. "Politics of Survival: Sara Parton's *Ruth Hall* and the Literature of Labor," in Harris, Sharon M., ed. *Redefining the Political Novel*, 86–105.

Walker, Nancy A. *Fanny Fern*, 40–62.

FERNÁNDEZ, ROBERTO G. (1951–)

Raining Backwards (1988)

Deaver, William O., Jr. "*Raining Backwards:* Colonization and the Death of a Culture." *AmRev* 21.1 (1993): 112–117.

FERRO, ROBERT (1941–1988)

Family of Max Desir (1983)

Bergman, David. *Gaiety Transfigured*, 196–200.

FERRON, JACQUES (1921–1985)

Juneberry Tree see *L'amélanchier*

L'amélanchier (1970)

Dufault, Roseanna Lewis. *Metaphors of Identity*, 43–50.

Ross, Mary Ellen. "Réalisme merveilleux et autoreprésentation dans *L'amélanchier* de Jacques Ferron." *V&I* 17.49 (1991): 116–129.

Le ciel de Québec (1969)

Cardinal, Jacques. "Fondation Catholique dans '*Le ciel de Québec*' de Jacques Ferron," in Marcato-Falzoni, Franca, ed. *Mythes et mythologies*, 177–198.

Le salut de l'Irlande (1970)

Cote, Jean R. "Les Canadianismes sous l'éclairage bakhtinien: Quatre emplois différents de Pantoute dans *Le salut de l'Irlande* de Jacques Ferron." *SCL* 18.1 (1993): 18–36.

Penniless Redeemer see *Le ciel de Québec*

FILIATRAULT, JEAN (1919–)

Chaînes (1955)

Raoul, Valerie. *Distinctly Narcissistic*, 127–128.

FINDLEY, TIMOTHY (1930–)

Butterfly Plague (1969)

Gabriel, Barbara. "Performing the Bent Text: Fascism and the Regulation of Sexualities in Timothy Findley's *The Butterfly Plague*." *ESC* 21.2 (1995): 227–250.

York, Lorraine M. "Timothy Findley," in Lecker, Robert, ed. *Canadian Writers and Their Works: Fiction Series* (Vol. 12), 92–96.

Famous Last Words (1981)

Dellamora, Richard. "Becoming Homosexual/Becoming Canadian: Ironic Voice and the Politics of Location in Timothy Findley's *Famous Last Words*," in Hutcheon, Linda, ed. *Double Talking*, 172–200.

Dopp, Jamie. "Reading as Collaboration in Timothy Findley's *Famous Last Words*." *SCL* 20.1 (1995): 1–15.

Kuester, Martin. *Framing Truths*, 69–93.

Williams, David. *Confessional Fictions*, 237–260.

York, Lorraine M. "Timothy Findley," in Lecker, Robert, ed. *Canadian Writers and Their Works: Fiction Series* (Vol. 12), 100–103.

Headhunter (1993)

York, Lorraine M. "Timothy Findley," in Lecker, Robert, ed. *Canadian Writers and Their Works: Fiction Series* (Vol. 12), 112–116.

Last of the Crazy People (1967)

York, Lorraine M. "Timothy Findley," in Lecker, Robert, ed. *Canadian Writers and Their Works: Fiction Series* (Vol. 12), 90–92.

Not Wanted on the Voyage (1984)

Delbaere, Jeanne. "Magic Realism: the Energy of the Margins," in D'haen, Theo, ed. *Postmodern*, 96–97.

Nicholson, Mervyn. "God, Noah, Lord Byron—and Timothy Findley." *ArielE* 23.2 (1992): 87–89, 92–105.

Penee, Donna. *Praying for Rain: Timothy Findley's Not Wanted on the Voyage.* Toronto: ECW Press, 1993.

York, Lorraine M. "Timothy Findley," in Lecker, Robert, ed. *Canadian Writers and Their Works: Fiction Series* (Vol. 12), 103–105.

Telling of Lies (1989)

Bailey, Anne Geddes. "Misrepresentations of Vanessa Van Horne: Intertextual Clues in Timothy Findley's *The Telling of Lies.*" *ECW* 55 (1995): 191–212.

York, Lorraine M. "Timothy Findley," in Lecker, Robert, ed. *Canadian Writers and Their Works: Fiction Series* (Vol. 12), 105–109.

Wars (1977)

Cobley, Evelyn. "Postmodernist War Fiction: Findley's The Wars." *CanL* 147 (1995): 98–124.

Granofsky, Ronald. *Trauma Novel,* 84–95.

Kuester, Martin. *Framing Truths,* 56–69.

Tumanov, Vladimir. "De-Automatization in Timothy Findley's *The Wars.*" *CanL* 130 (1991): 107–115.

Weiss, Allan. "Private and Public in Timothy Findley's *The Wars.*" *CanL* 138–139 (1993): 91–102.

York, Lorraine M. "Timothy Findley," in Lecker, Robert, ed. *Canadian Writers and Their Works: Fiction Series* (Vol. 12), 96–100.

FINNEY, CHARLES G. (1905–1984)

Circus of Dr. Lao (1935)

Whyde, Janet M. "Fantastic Disillusionment: Rupturing Narrative and Rewriting Reality in *The Circus of Dr. Lao.*" *Extrapolation* 35.3 (1994): 230–240.

FISHER, DOROTHY CANFIELD (1879–1958)

Deepening Stream (1930)

Schroeter, Joan G. "Crisis, Conflict, and Constituting the Self: A Lacanian Reading of *The Deepening Stream.*" *ClQ* 27.3 (1991): 148–160.

FITZGERALD, F. SCOTT (1896–1940)

Beautiful and the Damned (1922)

Glaser, Madeleine. "Fitzgerald's *The Beautiful and Damned.*" *Expl* 51.4 (1993): 238–239.

Hook, Andrew. *F. Scott Fitzgerald,* 36–43.

Limon, John. *Writing After War,* 108–110.

Roulston, Robert. *Winding Road to West Egg,* 97–105.

Great Gatsby (1925)

Anderson, Hilton. "From the Wasteland to East Egg: Houses in *The Great Gatsby.*" *UMSE* 9 (1991): 114–118.

Bellenir, Karen. "J. P. Morgan and Gatsby's Name." *SAF* 21.1 (1993): 111–115.

Benet, William Rose. "An Admirable Novel." Rev. of *The Great Gatsby* by F. Scott Fitzgerald. *Saturday Review of Literature* (9 May 1925): 740. Rpt. in Bloom, Harold, ed. *Gatsby*, 7.

Berman, Ronald. *Great Gatsby and Modern Times.* Chicago: University of Illinois Press, 1994.

Bizzell, Patricia. "Pecuniary Emulation of the Mediator in *The Great Gatsby*." *Modern Language Notes* 94.4 (May 1979): 774–783. Rpt. in Bloom, Harold, ed. *Gatsby*, 113–120.

Bradbury, Malcolm. *Modern American Novel.* Oxford: Oxford University Press, 1983. 65–67. Rpt. in Bloom, Harold, ed. *Gatsby*, 51–53.

Breitwieser, Mitchell. "*The Great Gatsby:* Grief, Jazz and the Eye-Witness." *ArQ* 47.3 (1991): 17–70.

Budick, Emily Miller. "Gatsby and Emerson." *Fiction and Historical Consciousness: The American Romance Tradition.* New Haven, CT: Yale University Press, 1989. 143–158. Rpt. in Bloom, Harold, ed. *Gatsby*, 161–177.

Callahan, John F. *Illusions of a Nation: Myth and History in the Novels of F. Scott Fitzgerald.* Urbana, IL: University of Illinois Press, 1972. 53–55. Rpt. in Bloom, Harold, ed. *Gatsby*, 37–39.

Castille, Philip. "Jay Gatsby: The Smuggler as Frontier Hero." *UMSE* 10 (1992): 227–237.

Chandler, Marilyn R. *Dwelling in the Text*, 217–243.

Christensen, Bryce J. "Mystery of Ungodliness." *Christianity and Literature* 36.1 (Fall 1986): 15–23. Rpt. in Bloom, Harold, ed. *Gatsby*, 154–160.

Decker, Jeffrey Louis. "Gatsby's Pristine Dream: The Diminishment of the Self-Made Man in the Tribal Twenties." *Novel* 28.1 (1994): 52–71.

Eyson, A.E. "*The Great Gatsby:* Thirty-six Years After." *Modern Fiction Studies* 7.1 (Spring 1961): 42,44. Rpt. in Bloom, Harold, ed. *Gatsby*, 22–23.

E.K. Rev. of *The Great Gatsby* by F. Scott Fitzgerald. *Literary Digest International Book Review.* May 1925: 426–427. Rpt. in Bloom, Harold, ed. *Gatsby*, 7.

Fetterley, Judith. "*The Great Gatsby:* Fitzgerald's *Droit de Seigneur.*" *Resisting Reader: A Feminist Approach to American Literature.* Bloomington, IN: Indiana University Press, 1978. 74–83, 95–100. Rpt. in Bloom, Harold, ed. *Gatsby*, 103–112.

Frohock, W.M. *Strangers to This Ground: Cultural Diversity in Contemporary American Writing.* Dallas: Southern Methodist University Press, 1961. 54–61. Rpt. in Bloom, Harold, ed. *Gatsby*, 18–22.

Fussell, Edwin S. "Fitzgerald's Brave New World." *ELH* 19.4 (December 1952): 295–297. Rpt. in Bloom, Harold, ed. *Gatsby*, 13–15.

Geismar, Maxwell. *Last of the Provincials: The American Novel 1915–1925.* Boston: Houghton Mifflin, 1947. 316–320. Rpt. in Bloom, Harold, ed. *Gatsby*, 11–13.

Godden, Richard. "Glamor on the Turn." *Journal of American Studies* 16.3 (December 1982): 343–359. Rpt. in Bloom, Harold, ed. *Gatsby*, 121–136.

Gross, Barry Edward. "Jay Gatsby and Myrtle Wilson: A Kinship." *Tennessee Studies in Literature* 8 (1963): 57–60. Rpt. in Bloom, Harold, ed. *Gatsby*, 23–25.

Gross, Dalton and Mary-Jean Gross. "F. Scott Fitzgerald's American Swastika: The Prohibition Underworld and *The Great Gatsby*." *N&Q* 41.3 (1994): 377.

Gross, Dalton and Maryjean Gross. "Fitzgerald's *The Great Gatsby*." *Expl* 53.4 (1995): 230–231.

Gross, Theodore L. "F. Scott Fitzgerald: The Hero in Retrospect." *South Atlantic Quarterly* 67.1 (Winter 1968): 65–68. Rpt. in Bloom, Harold, ed. *Gatsby*, 29–31.

Hart, Jeffrey. "Anything Can Happen: Magical Transformation in *The Great Gatsby.*" *SCR* 25.2 (1993): 37–50.

Hochman, Barbara. "Disembodied Voices and Narrating Bodies in *The Great Gatsby.*" *Style* 28.1 (1994): 95–118.

Hook, Andrew. *F. Scott Fitzgerald*, 48–59.

Kazin, Alfred. *On Native Grounds: An Interpretation of Modern American Literature.* New York: Reynal and Hitchcock, 1942. 321–322. Rpt. in Bloom, Harold, ed. *Gatsby*, 9–10.

Kenner, Hugh. "Promised Land." *Homemade World: The American Modernist Writers.* New York: Knopf, 1975. 23–31. Rpt. in Bloom, Harold, ed. *Gatsby*, 74–80.

Klinkowitz, Jerome. *Practice of Fiction in America: Writers From Hawthorne to the Present.* Ames, IA: Iowa State University Press, 1980. 50–54. Rpt. in Bloom, Harold, ed. *Gatsby*, 43–47.

Kuehl, John. "Scott Fitzgerald: Romantic and Realist." *Texas Studies in Language and Literature* 1.3 (Autumn 1959): 413–416. Rpt. in Bloom, Harold, ed. *Gatsby*, 15–18.

Lehan, Richard. "Inventing Gatsby." *The Great Gatsby: The Limits of Wonder.* Boston: Twayne, 1990. 58–66. Rpt. in Bloom, Harold, ed. *Gatsby*, 189–195.

Limon, John. *Writing After War*, 106–108.

Lindberg, Gary. *The Confidence Man in American Literature.* New York: Oxford University Press, 1982. 134–139. Rpt. in Bloom, Harold, ed. *Gatsby*, 47–51.

Lynn, David H. "Within and Without: Nick Carraway." *Hero's Tale: Narrators in the Early Modern Novel.* New York: St. Martin's Press, 1989. 79–91. Rpt. in Bloom, Harold, ed. *Gatsby*, 178–188.

McCormick, John. *Middle Distance: A Comparative History of American Imaginative Literature 1919–1932.* New York: Free Press, 1971. 37–39. Rpt. in Bloom, Harold, ed. *Gatsby*, 31–33.

Moyer, Kermit W. "*The Great Gatsby:* Fitzgerald's Meditation on American History." *Fitzgerald/Hemingway Annual 1972.* 45–49. Rpt. in Bloom, Harold, ed. *Gatsby*, 33–37.

Okeke-Ezigbo, F. E. "Meyer Wolfsheim's Cuff Buttons: Another Conradian Echo in *The Great Gatsby.*" *NConL* 21.2 (1991): 2–3.

O'Meara, Lauraleigh. "Medium of Exchange: The Blue Coupe Dialogue in *The Great Gatsby.*" *PLL* 30.1 (1994): 73–87.

Pauly, Thomas H. "Gatsby as Gangster." *SAF* 21.2 (1993): 225–236.

Pendleton, Thomas A. *I'm Sorry About the Clock: Chronology, Composition and Narrative Technique in The Great Gatsby.* Selinsgrove, PA: Susquehanna University Press, 1993.

Rogers, Franklin R. *Occidental Ideographs*, 252–255.

Roulston, Robert. *Winding Road to West Egg*, 158–168.

Sarracino, Carmine. "Last Transcendental." *CEA* 54.3 (1992): 37–46.

Scott, Robert Ian. "Entropy vs. Ecology in *The Great Gatsby.*" *Queen's* Quarterly 82.4 (Winter 1975): 559–571. Rpt. in Bloom, Harold, ed. *Gatsby*, 81–92.

Searles, Susan. "Fitzgerald's *The Great Gatsby.*" *Expl* 50.1 (1991): 45–47.

Seshachari, Neila. "*The Great Gatsby:* Apogee of Fitzgerald's Mythopoeia." *Fitzgerald/Heminway Annual 1976.* 96–107. Rpt. in Bloom, Harold, ed. *Gatsby*, 93–102.

Stallman, R.W. "Gatsby and the Hole in Time." *Houses That James Built and Other Literary Studies.* East Lansing, MI: 1964. 131–135, 144–148. [First published in

Modern Fiction Studies 1.4 (November 1955): 2–16.] Rpt. in Bloom, Harold, ed. *Gatsby*, 55–63.

Stouck, David. "*The Great Gatsby* as Pastoral." *Genre* 4.4 (December 1971): 335–347. Rpt. in Bloom, Harold, ed. *Gatsby*, 64–73.

Thornton, Patricia Pacey. "Sexual Roles in *The Great Gatsby.*" *English Studies in Canada* 5.4 (Winter 1979): 461–462. Rpt. in Bloom, Harold, ed. *Gatsby*, 42–43.

Troy, William. "Scott Fitzgerald—the Authority of Failure." *Accent* 6.1 (Autumn 1945): 57–58. Rpt. in Bloom, Harold, ed. *Gatsby*, 10–11.

Turner, Gene. "Nick Carraway, Heroic Responsibility." *BWVACET* 13.2 (1991): 144–152.

Tynan, Kenneth. "Gatsby and the American Dream." *Observer* 14 Oct. 1974: 25. Rpt. in Bloom, Harold, ed. *Gatsby*, 41–42.

Washington, Bryan R. *Politics of Exile*, 40–54.

Wasiolek, Edward. "Sexual Drama of Nick and Gatsby." *IFR* 19.1 (1992): 14–22.

Way, Brian. "Scott Fitzgerald." *New Left Review* 21 (October 1963): 43–44. Rpt. in Bloom, Harold, ed. *Gatsby*, 25–26.

Weinstein, Arnold. "Fiction as Greatness: The Case of Gatsby." *Novel* 19.1 (Fall 1985): 22–38. Rpt. in Bloom, Harold, ed. *Gatsby*, 137–153.

Last Tycoon (1941)

Hook, Andrew. *F. Scott Fitzgerald*, 81–84.

Tender Is the Night (1934)

Cummings, Katherine. *Telling Tales*, 231–278.

Haegert, John. "Repression and Counter-Memory in *Tender Is the Night.*" *ELWIU* 21.1 (1994): 97–115.

Hook, Andrew. *F. Scott Fitzgerald*, 66–70, 74–75.

Limon, John. *Writing After War*, 110–115.

Rogers, Franklin R. *Occidental Ideographs*, 255–256.

Silhol, Robert. "*Tender Is the Night* or the Rape of the Child." *L&P* 40.4 (1994): 40–63.

Stern, Milton R. *Tender is the Night: The Broken Universe.* New York: Twayne Publishers, 1994.

Washington, Bryan R. *Politics of Exile*, 55–69.

Weston, Elizabeth A. *International Theme*, 89–116.

This Side of Paradise (1920)

Hook, Andrew. *F. Scott Fitzgerald*, 26–29.

Roulston, Robert. *Winding Road to West Egg*, 33–40.

FITZGERALD, ZELDA (1899–1948)

Save Me the Waltz (1932)

Davis, Simone Weil. " 'The Burden of Reflecting': Effort and Desire in Zelda Fitzgerald's *Save Me the Waltz.*" *MLQ* 56.3 (1995): 327–361.

Wood, Mary E. "Wizard Cultivator: Zelda Fitzgerald's *Save Me the Waltz* as Asylum Autobiography." *TSWL* 11.2 (1992): 247–264.

FLANAGAN, THOMAS (1923–)

Tenants of Time (1988)

O'Connell, Shaun. "Imagining Eire: History as Fiction in the Novels of Tom Flanagan." *MELUS* 18.1 (1993): 25–28.

Year of the French (1979)

O'Connell, Shaun. "Imagining Eire: History as Fiction in the Novels of Tom Flanagan." *MELUS* 18.1 (1993): 24–25.

FLEMING, MAY AGNES (1840–1880)

Baronet's Bride (1869)

MacMillan, Carrie. *Silenced Sextet*, 65–67.

Eulalie (1864)

MacMillan, Carrie. *Silenced Sextet*, 61–63.

Heir of Charlton see *Shaddeck Light!*

Little Queen (1877)

MacMillan, Carrie. *Silenced Sextet*, 73.

Lost for a Woman (1880)

MacMillan, Carrie. *Silenced Sextet*, 74–79.

Shaddeck Light! (1878)

MacMillan, Carrie. *Silenced Sextet*, 73–74.

Sybil Campbell (1861)

MacMillan, Carrie. *Silenced Sextet*, 59–60.

Twin Sisters (1864)

MacMillan, Carrie. *Silenced Sextet*, 60–61.

FOOTE, SHELBY (1916–)

Follow Me Down (1950)

Phillips, Robert L., Jr. *Shelby Foote*, 88–112.

Love in a Dry Season (1951)

Phillips, Robert L., Jr. *Shelby Foote*, 112–134.

Shiloh (1952)

Phillips, Robert L., Jr. *Shelby Foote*, 68–86.

Tournament (1949)

Phillips, Robert L., Jr. *Shelby Foote*, 50–68.

FORREST, LEON (1937–)

Divine Days (1992)

Cawelti, John G. "Earthly Thoughts on *Divine Days*." *Callaloo* 16.2 (1993): 431–447.

There Is a Tree More Ancient Than Eden (1973)

Warren, Kenneth W. "Thinking beyond Catastrophe: Leon Forrest's *There Is a Tree More Ancient Than Eden*." *Callaloo* 16.2 (1993): 409–418.

Two Wings Veil My Face (1983)

Taylor-Guthrie, Danille. "Sermons, Testifying, and Prayers: Looking beneath the Wings in Leon Forrest's *Two Wings to Veil My Face*." *Callaloo* 16.2 (1993): 419–430.

FOSTER, HANNAH WEBSTER (1758–1840)

Boarding School (1798)

Pettengill, Claire C. "Sisterhood in a Separate Sphere: Female Friendship in Hannah Webster Foster's *The Coquette* and *The Boarding School*." *EAL* 27.3 (1992): 187–200.

Coquette (1797)

Hansen, Klaus P. "Sentimental Novel and Its Feminist Critique." *EAL* 26.1 (1991): 43–45

Harris, Sharon M. "Hannah Webster Foster's *The Coquette:* Critiquing Franklin's America," in Harris, Sharon M., ed. *Redefining the Political Novel*, 1–18.

Pettengill, Claire C. "Sisterhood in a Separate Sphere: Female Friendship in Hannah Webster Foster's *The Coquette* and *The Boarding School*." *EAL* 27.3 (1992):185–200.

Waldstreicher, David. " 'Fallen under My Observation': Vision and Virtue in *The Coquette*." *EAL* 27.3 (1992): 204–218.

FRANK, PAT (1907–1964)

Alas, Babylon (1959)

Porter, Jeffrey L. "Narrating the End: Fables of Survival in the Nuclear Age." *JACult* 41–46.

FREDERIC, HAROLD (1856–1898)

Damnation of Theron Ware (1896)

Becknell, Thomas. "Implication through Reading *The Damnation of Theron Ware*." *ALR* 24.1 (1991): 63–71.

MacFarlane, Lisa Watt. "Resurrecting Man: Desire and *The Damnation of Theron Ware*." *SAF* 20.2 (1992): 127–143.

Michelson, Bruce. "Theron Ware in the Wilderness of Ideas." *ALR* 25.1 (1992): 54–73.

Myers, Robert M. "Antimodern Protest in *The Damnation of Theron Ware*." *ALR* 26.3 (1994): 52–64.

FREEMAN, MARY WILKINS (1852–1930)

Jamesons (1899)

Marchalonis, Shirley. "The Sharp-edged Humor of Mary Wilkins Freeman: *The Jamesons*—and Other Stories," in Marchalonis, Shirley, ed. *Critical Essays*, 224–228.

Pembroke (1893)

Lambert, Deborah G. "Rereading Mary Wilkins Freeman: Autonomy and Sexuality in *Pembroke,*" in Marchalonis, Shirley, ed. *Critical Essays*, 197–206.

Pennell, Melissa McFarland. "The Liberating Will: Freedom of Choice in the Fiction of Mary Wilkins Freeman," in Marchalonis, Shirley, ed. *Critical Essays*, 213–216.

Portion of Labor (1901)

Berkson, Dorothy. " 'A Goddess Behind a Sordid Veil': The Domestic Heroine Meets the Labor Novel in Mary E. Wilkins Freeman's *The Portion of Labor*," in Harris, Sharon M., ed. *Redefining the Political Novel*, 149–166.

Hapke, Laura. *Tales of the Working Girl*, 60–62.

Satz, Martha. "Going to an Unknown Home: Redesign in *The Portion of Labor*," in Marchalonis, Shirley, ed. *Critical Essays*, 185–195.

Shoulders of Atlas (1908)

Pennell, Melissa McFarland. "Liberating Will: Freedom of Choice in the Fiction of Mary Wilkins Freeman," in Marchalonis, Shirley, ed. *Critical Essays*, 216–220.

FRENCH, HARRY W.

Our Boys in India (1883)

Singh, Brijraj. "Henry Willard French and India." *NEQ* 64.4 (1991): 582–584, 587, 590–593.

FRIEDMAN, SANFORD (1928–)

Totempole (1984)

Bergman, David. *Gaiety Transfigured*, 204.

FRITZ, JEAN (1915–)

Homesick (1982)

Walter, Virginia A. "Crossing the Pacific to America: The Uses of Narrative." *CLAQ* 16.2 (1991): 65–66.

FULLER, SAMUEL (1911–)

Quint's World (1988)

Williams, Tony. "Satire in *Quint's World* (by Samuel Fuller)." *NConL* 24.5 (1994): 9–11.

FULTON, DAVID BRYANT

Hanover (1900)

Gleason, William. "Voices at the Nadir: Charles Chesnutt and David Bryant Fulton." *ALR* 24.3 (1992): 32–36, 38, 39.

FURMAN, LUCY (1870–1955)

Glass Window (1925)

Joyner, Nancy Carol. "Poetics of the House in Appalachian Fiction," in Lanier, Parks, Jr.,ed. *Poetics*, 14–17.

GADDIS, WILLIAM (1922–)

Frolic of His Own (1994)

Tabbi, Joseph. "Technology of Quotation: William Gaddis's *J R* and Contemporary Media." *Mosaic* 28.4 (1995): 149, 151–152.

J R (1975)

Strehle, Susan. *Fiction in the Quantum Universe*, 93–123.

Tabbi, Joseph. "Technology of Quotation: William Gaddis's *J R* and Contemporary Media." *Mosaic* 28.4 (1995): 144, 146–147, 148–149, 151, 154–155, 156–162.

Recognitions (1955)

Tabbi, Joseph. "Technology of Quotation: William Gaddis's *J R* and Contemporary Media." *Mosaic* 28.4 (1995): 144, 152–153, 155.

GAGNON, MADELEINE (1938–)

Lueur (1979)

Shek, Ben-Z. *French-Canadian*, 91–93.

GAGNON, MAURICE

Les tours de Babylone (1972)

Colas-Charpentier, Helene. "Four Quebecois Dystopias, 1963–1972." Trans. ABE and Carine Deschanel. *SFS* 20.3 (1993): 390–391.

GAINES, ERNEST J. (1933–)

Autobiography of Miss Jane Pittman (1971)

Babb, Valerie Melissa. *Ernest Gaines*, 76–96.

Byerman, Keith E. "A 'Slow-to-Anger' People: *The Autobiography of Miss Jane Pittman* as Historical Fiction," in Estes, David C., ed. *Critical Reflections*, 107–122.

Doyle, Mary Ellen. "*The Autobiography of Miss Jane Pittman* as Fictional Edited Autobiography," in Estes, David C., ed. *Critical Reflections*, 89–105.

Estes, David C. "Gaines's Humor: Race and Laughter," in Estes, David C., ed. *Critical Reflections*, 240–243.

Folks, Jeffrey J. *Southern Writers*, 132–138.

Gaudet, Marcia. "Miss Jane and Personal Experience Narrative: Ernest Gaine's *The Autobiography of Miss Jane Pittman*." *WF* 51.1 (1992): 23–32.

Jackson, Blyden. "Jane Pittman through the Years: A People's Tale." *American Letters and the Historical Consciousness: Essays in Honor of Lewis P. Simpson.* Ed. J. Gerald Kennedy and Daniel Mark Fogel. Baton Rouge: Louisiana State

University Press, 1987. 255–256. Rpt. in Bloom, Harold, ed. *Contemporary Black American Fiction Writers*, 38–39.

Papa, Lee. " 'His Feet on Your Neck': The New Religion in the Works of Ernest J. Gaines." *AAR* 27.2 (1993): 188, 190–192.

Catherine Carmier (1964)

Babb, Valerie Melissa. *Ernest Gaines*, 45–60.

Griffin, Joseph. "Creole and Singaleese: Disruptive Caste in *Catherine Carmier* and *A Gathering of Old Men*," in Estes, David C., ed. *Critical Reflections*, 30–45.

Gathering of Old Men (1983)

Babb, Valerie Melissa. *Ernest Gaines*, 112–131.

Babb, Valerie Melissa. *Ernest Gaines*. Boston: Twayne, 1991. 113–114. Rpt. in Bloom, Harold, ed. *Contemporary Black American Fiction Writers*, 42–43.

Estes, David C. "Gaines's Humor: Race and Laughter," in Estes, David C., ed. *Critical Reflections*, 243–248.

Griffin, Joseph. "Calling, Naming, and Coming of Age in Ernest Gaines's *A Gathering of Old Men*." *Names* 40.2 (1992): 89–97.

Griffin, Joseph. "Creole and Singaleese: Disruptive Caste in *Catherine Carmier* and *A Gathering of Old Men*," in Estes, David C., ed. *Critical Reflections*, 30–45.

Papa, Lee. " 'His Feet on Your Neck': The New Religion in the Works of Ernest J. Gaines." *AAR* 27.2 (1993): 188–190.

Rickels, Milton and Patricia Rickels. " 'Sound of My People Talking': Folk Humor in *A Gathering of Old Men*," in Estes, David C., ed. *Critical Reflections*, 215–226.

Shannon, Sandra G. "Strong Men Getting Stronger: Gaines's Defense of the Elderly Black Male in *A Gathering of Old Men*," in Estes, David C., ed. *Critical Reflections*, 195–214.

Tusmith, Bonnie. *All My Relatives*, 97–98.

White, Daniel. " 'Haunted by the Idea': Fathers and Sons in *In My Father's House* and *A Gathering of Old Men*," in Estes, David C., ed. *Critical Reflections*, 158–179.

In My Father's House (1978)

Babb, Valerie Melissa. *Ernest Gaines*, 97–111.

Holloway, Karla F.C. "Image, Act, and Identity in *In My Father's House*," in Estes, David C., ed. *Critical Reflections*, 180–193.

Shelton, Frank W. "*In My Father's House*: Ernest Gaines After Jane Pittman." *Southern Review* 17.2 (Spring 1981): 342–343. Rpt. in Bloom, Harold, ed. *Contemporary Black American Fiction Writers*, 35–36.

White, Daniel. " 'Haunted by the Idea': Fathers and Sons in *In My Father's House* and *A Gathering of Old Men*," in Estes, David C., ed. *Critical Reflections*, 158–179.

Lesson Before Dying (1993)

Auger, Philip. "Lesson about Manhood: Appropriating 'The Word' in Ernest Gaines's *A Lesson Before Dying*." *SLJ* 27.2 (1995): 74–85.

Babb, Valerie. "Old-Fashioned Modernism: 'The Changing Same' in *A Lesson Before Dying*," in Estes, David C., ed. *Critical Reflections*, 250–264.

Of Love and Dust (1967)

Babb, Valerie Melissa. *Ernest Gaines*, 61–75.

Estes, David C. "Gaines's Humor: Race and Laughter," in Estes, David C., ed. *Critical Reflections*, 231–240.

Smith, David Lionel. "Bloodlines and Patriarchs: *Of Love and Dust* and Its Revisions of Faulkner," in Estes, David C., ed. *Critical Reflections*, 46–61.

GAITSKILL, MARY (1954–)

Two Girls, Fat and Thin (1991)

Young, Elizabeth. *Shopping in Space*, 176–181.

GALLANT, MAVIS (1922–)

Fairly Good Time (1970)

Smythe, Karen E. *Figuring Grief*, 54–60.

Green Water, Green Sky (1959)

Smythe, Karen E. *Figuring Grief*, 50–54.

What Is to Be Done? (1983)

Bok, Christian. "Secular Opiate: Marxism as an Ersatz Religion in Three Canadian Texts." *CanL* 147 (1995): 11–22.

GALLOWAY, DAVID D. (1937–)

Family Album (1978)

MacLaine, Brent. "Photofiction as Family Album: David Galloway, Paul Theroux and Anita Booker." *Mosaic* 24.2 (1991):132, 135–142.

GARCIA, CRISTINA (1958–)

Dreaming in Cuban (1992)

Alvarez-Borland, Isabel. "Displacements and Autobiography in Cuban-American Fiction." *WLT* 68.1 (1994): 46–47.

GARDNER, JOHN (1933–1982)

Grendel (1971)

Payne, Craig. "Cycle of the Zodiac in John Gardner's *Grendel*." *Mythlore* 18.4 (1991): 61–65.

Payne, Craig. "Redemption of Cain in John Gardner's *Grendel*." *Mythlore* 18.2 (1992): 12–16.

GARRETT, GEORGE (1929–)

Succession (1984)

Betts, Richard A. " 'To Dream of Kings': George Garrett's *The Succession*." *MissQ* 45.1 (1991–92): 53–67.

GASS, WILLIAM H. (1924–)

Tunnel (1995)

Unsworth, John M. "William Gass's *The Tunnel:* The Work in Progress as Post-Modern Genre." *ArQ* 48.1 (1992): 63–84.

Wolcott, James. "Gass Attack." *NewC* 13.6 (1995): 63–67.

GÉRIN-LAJOIE, ANTOINE (1824–1882)

Jean Rivard (1862)

Cambron, Micheline. "Les Bibliothèques de papier d'Antoine Gerin-Lajoie." *EF* 29.1 (1993): 135–150.

Shek, Ben-Z. *French-Canadian*, 5–7.

Smart, Patricia. *Writing in the Father's House*, 81–84.

GERNSBACK, HUGO (1884–1967)

Ralph 124C 41+ (1911)

Westfahl, Gary. " 'Gernsback Continuum' and William Gibson," in Slusser, George, ed. *Fiction 2000*, 90–101.

Westfahl, Gary. " 'This Unique Document': Hugo Gernsback's *Ralph 124C 41 +* and the Genres of Science Fiction." *Extrapolation* 35.2 (1994): 95–119.

GERTLER, T.

Elbowing the Seducer (1984)

Miller, Pat. "When Men Are Men and Women Are Men, Too: On Gender, Art, and Reading T. Gertler's *Elbowing the Seducer.*" *CEA* 56.1 (1993): 22–34.

GIBBONS, KAYE (1960–)

Cure for Dreams (1991)

Branan, Tonita. "Women and 'The Gift for Gab': Revisionary Strategies in *A Cure for Dreams.*" *SLJ* 26.2 (1994): 91–101.

Tate, Linda. *Southern Weave of Women*, 195–204.

GIBSON, GRAEME (1934–)

Perpetual Motion (1982)

Atwood, Margaret. *Strange Things*, 84–85.

GIBSON, WILLIAM (1948–)

Burning Chrome (1986)

Booker, M. Keith. *Dystopian Impulse*, 148–151

Schmitt, Ronald. "Mythology and Technology: The Novels of William Gibson." *Extrapolation* 34.1 (1993): 64–78.

Count Zero (1986)

Booker, M. Keith. *Dystopian Impulse*, 150–151.

Christie, John. "Of AIs and Others: William Gibson's Transit," in Slusser, George, ed. *Fiction 2000*, 178–180.

Csicsery-Ronay, Istvan, Jr. "Antimancer: Cybernetics and Art in Gibson's *Count Zero*." *SFS* 22.1 (1995): 63–86.

Mead, David G. "Technological Transfiguration in William Gibson's Sprawl Novels: *Neuromancer, Count Zero*, and *Mona Lisa Overdrive*." *Extrapolation* 32.4 (1991): 350–359.

Olson, Lance. "Shadow of Spirit in William Gibson's Matrix Trilogy." *Extrapolation* 32.3 (1991): 278–287.

Olson, Lance. *William Gibson*, 85–101.

Schmitt, Ronald. "Mythology and Technology: The Novels of William Gibson." *Extrapolation* 34.1 (1993): 64–78.

Schroeder, Randy. "Neu-Criticizing William Gibson." *Extrapolation* 35.4 (1994): 330–341.

Voller, Jack G. "Neuromanticism: Cyberspace and the Sublime." *Extrapolation* 34.1 (1993): 18–27.

Difference Engine (1990)

Booker, M. Keith. *Dystopian Impulse*, 151–152.

Porush, David. "Prigogine, Chaos, and Contemporary Science Fiction." *SFS* 18.3 (1991): 379–384.

Sussman, Herbert. "Cyberpunk Meets Charles Babbage: *The Difference Engine* as Alternative Victorian History." *VS* 38.1 (1994): 1–23.

Mona Lisa Overdrive (1988)

Alkon, Paul. "Deus Ex Machina," in Slusser, George, ed. *Fiction 2000*, 85–86.

Christie, John. "Of AIs and Others: William Gibson's Transit," in Slusser, George, ed. *Fiction 2000*, 179–181.

Mead, David G. "Technological Transfiguration in William Gibson's Sprawl Novels: *Neuromancer, Count Zero*, and *Mona Lisa Overdrive*." *Extrapolation* 32.4 (1991): 350–359.

Olson, Lance. "Shadow of Spirit in William Gibson's Matrix Trilogy." *Extrapolation* 32.3 (1991): 278–287.

Olson, Lance. *William Gibson*, 103–113.

Schmitt, Ronald. "Mythology and Technology: The Novels of William Gibson." *Extrapolation* 34.1 (1993): 64–78.

Schroeder, Randy. "Neu-Criticizing William Gibson." *Extrapolation* 35.4 (1994): 330–341.

Voller, Jack G. "Neuromanticism: Cyberspace and the Sublime." *Extrapolation* 34.1 (1993): 18–27.

Neuromancer (1984)

Alkon, Paul. "Deus Ex Machina," in Slusser, George, ed. *Fiction 2000*, 78–84.

Booker, M. Keith. *Dystopian Impulse*, 147–151.

Bukatman, Scott. "Gibson's Typewriter." *SAQ* 92.4 (1993): 627–645.

Christie, John. "Of AIs and Others: William Gibson's Transit," in Slusser, George, ed. *Fiction 2000*, 173–178.

Csicsery-Ronay, Istvan, Jr. "Sentimental Futurist: Cybernetics and Art in William Gibson's *Neuromancer*." *Crit* 33.3 (1992): 221–240.

Curl, Ruth. "Metaphors of Cyberpunk," in Slusser, George, ed. *Fiction 2000*, 234–237.

Huntington, John. "Newness, *Neuromancer*, and the End of Narrative," in Slusser, George, ed. *Fiction 2000*, 133–141.

Mead, David G. "Technological Transfiguration in William Gibson's Sprawl Novels: *Neuromancer*, *Count Zero*, and *Mona Lisa Overdrive*." *Extrapolation* 32.4 (1991): 350–359.

Olson, Lance. "Shadow of Spirit in William Gibson's Matrix Trilogy." *Extrapolation* 32.3 (1991): 278–287.

Olson, Lance. *William Gibson*, 63–83.

Schmitt, Ronald. "Mythology and Technology: The Novels of William Gibson." *Extrapolation* 34.1 (1993): 64–78.

Schroeder, Randy. "Neu-Criticizing William Gibson." *Extrapolation* 35.4 (1994): 330–341.

Slusser, George. "Frankenstein Barrier," in Slusser, George, ed. *Fiction 2000*, 62–68.

Voller, Jack G. "Neuromanticism: Cyberspace and the Sublime." *Extrapolation* 34.1 (1993): 18–27.

Westfahl, Gary. " 'The Gernsback Continuum': William Gibson and the Context of Science Fiction," in Slusser, George, ed. *Fiction 2000*, 90–105.

GILCHRIST, ELLEN (1935–)

Annunciation (1983)

Bauer, Margaret D. "Evolution of Caddy: An Intertextual Reading of *The Sound and the Fury* and Ellen Gilchrist's *The Annunciation*." *SLJ* 25.1 (1992): 40–51.

GILMAN, CHARLOTTE PERKINS (1860–1935)

Herland (1915)

Gough, Val. "Lesbians and Virgins: The New Motherhood in *Herland*," in Seed, David, ed. *Anticipations*, 195–215.

Keyser, Elizabeth. "Looking Backward: From *Herland* to *Gulliver's Travels*." *Studies in American Fiction* 11.1 (1983): 31–46. Rpt. in Karpinski, Joanne B., ed. *Critical Essays on Charlotte Perkins Gilman*, 159–171.

Unpunished (1997)

Robinson, Lillian S. "Killing Patriarchy: Charlotte Perkins Gilman, the Murder Mystery, and Post-Feminist Propaganda." *TSWL* 10.2 (1991): 273–285.

GIRARD, RODOLPHE (1879–1956)

Marie Calumet (1904)

Shek, Ben-Z. *French-Canadian*, 13–14.

GLASGOW, ELLEN (1873–1945)

Barren Ground (1925)

Ammons, Elizabeth. *Conflicting Stories*, 171–177.

Bauer, Margaret D. " 'Put Your Heart in the Land': An Intertextual Reading of

Barren Ground and *Gone with the Wind*," in Scura, Dorothy M., ed. *Ellen Glasgow*, 162–180.

Levy, Helen Fiddyment. *Fiction of the Home Place*, 106–113.

Rainwater, Catherine. "Consciousness, Gender, and Animal Signs in *Barren Ground* and *Vein of Iron*," in Scura, Dorothy M., ed. *Ellen Glasgow*, 204–218.

Rainwater, Catherine. "Narration as Pragmatism in Ellen Glasgow's *Barren Ground*." *AL* 63.4 (1991): 664–682.

Raper, Rowan. "*Barren Ground* and the Modern Transition to Southern Modernism," in Scura, Dorothy M., ed. *Ellen Glasgow*, 146–160.

Waters, Mary. "Glasgow's *Barren Ground*." *Expl* 51.4 (1993): 234–236.

Winniford, Lee. "Suppressing the Masculine Metanarrative: The Uncaging of Glasgow's *Barren Ground*." *JNT* 24.2 (1994): 141–152.

Battle-Ground (1902)

Dillard, R. H. W. "On Ellen Glasgow's *The Battle-Ground*," Madden, David, ed. *Classics of Civil War Fiction*, 63–81.

MacKethan, Lucinda H. "Restoring Order: Matriarchal Design in *The Battle-Ground* and *Veil of Iron*," in Scura, Dorothy M., ed. *Ellen Glasgow*, 93–100.

Beyond Defeat (1966)

Levy, Helen Fiddyment. "Coming Home: Glasgow's Last Two Novels," in Scura, Dorothy M., ed. *Ellen Glasgow*, 220–232.

Levy, Helen Fiddyment. *Fiction of the Home Place*, 125–130.

Builders (1919)

Carpenter, Lynette. "Visions of Female Community in Ellen Glasgow's Ghost Stories," in Carpenter, Lynette, ed. *Haunting the House of Fiction*, 136–137.

In This Our Life (1941)

Levy, Helen Fiddyment. "Coming Home: Glasgow's Last Two Novels," in Scura, Dorothy M., ed. *Ellen Glasgow*, 220–232.

Romantic Comedians (1926)

Castronovo, David. *American Gentleman*, 161–162.

Hall, Caroline King Barnard. " 'Telling the Truth about Themselves': Women, Form and Idea in *The Romantic Comedians*," in Scura, Dorothy M., ed. *Ellen Glasgow*, 183–194.

Sheltered Life (1932)

Castronovo, David. *American Gentleman*, 162–164.

Levy, Helen Fiddyment. *Fiction of the Home Place*, 117–118.

Wagner-Martin, Linda. "Glasgow's Time in *The Sheltered Life*," in Scura, Dorothy M., ed. *Ellen Glasgow*, 196–203.

They Stooped to Folly (1929)

Levy, Helen Fiddyment. *Fiction of the Home Place*, 114–117.

Vein of Iron (1935)

Levy, Helen Fiddyment. *Fiction of the Home Place*, 118–125.

MacKethan, Lucinda H. "Restoring Order: Matriarchal Design in *The Battle-Ground* and *Veil of Iron*," in Scura, Dorothy M., ed. *Ellen Glasgow*, 101–104.

Rainwater, Catherine. "Consciousness, Gender, and Animal Signs in *Barren Ground* and *Vein of Iron*," in Scura, Dorothy M., ed. *Ellen Glasgow*, 204–218.

Virginia (1913)

Atteberry, Phillip D. "Framing of Glasgow's *Virginia*," in Scura, Dorothy M., ed. *Ellen Glasgow*, 124–130.

Levy, Helen Fiddyment. *Fiction of the Home Place*, 102–106.

Sawaya, Francesca. " 'The Problem of the South': Economic Determination, Gender Discrimination, and Genre in Glasgow's *Virginia*," in Scura, Dorothy M., ed. *Ellen Glasgow*, 132–144.

Wheel of Life (1906)

Matthews, Pamela R. "Between Ellen and Louise: Female Friendship, Glasgow's Letters to Louise Chandler Moulton, and *The Wheel of Life*," in Scura, Dorothy M., ed. *Ellen Glasgow*, 116–119.

GLASPELL, SUSAN (1882–1948)

Fidelity (1915)

Carpentier, Martha C. "Susan Glaspell's Fiction: *Fidelity* as American Romance." *TCL* 40.1 (1994): 92–113.

GLOSS, MOLLY (1944–)

Jump-Off Creek (1989)

Morris, Gregory. "*The Jump-Off Creek:* Molly Gloss' Novel of Frontier Manners." *SDR* 30.2 (1992): 128–142.

GODBOUT, JACQUES (1933–)

An American Story see *Une Histoire américaine*

D'Amour, P.Q. (1972)

Nardout-Lafarge, Elisabeth. "Dialogue et théâtralisation chez Ducharme, Blais et Godbout." *FR* 67.1 (1993): 88–91.

Paterson, Janet M. *Postmodernism*, 97–110.

Hail Galarneau! see *Salut Galarneau!*

Knife on the Kitchen Table see *Le couteau sur la table*

Le couteau sur la table (1965)

Shek, Ben-Z. *French-Canadian*, 50–51.

Les têtes à Papineau (1981)

Shek, Ben-Z. *French-Canadian*, 110–111.

Salut Galarneau! (1967)

Klementowicz, Michael. "Jacques Godbout's *Salut Galarneau!* Identity and Violence Towards Women." *QS* 14 (1992): 83–91.

Raoul, Valerie. *Distinctly Narcissistic*, 178–187.

Shek, Ben-Z. *French-Canadian*, 51–52.

Une histoire américaine (1986)

Cote, Paul Raymond. "Le Récit et ses miroirs: Les Procédes spéculaires dans *Une histoire américaine* de Jacques Godbout." *CanL* 135 (1992): 97–109.

Hebert, Pierre. "Le Professeur fictif dans quelques romans québecois des années quatre-vingt: Pas facile d'être intellectuel postmoderne!" *UTQ* 63.4 (1994): 600–601, 602–604.
Shek, Ben-Z. *French-Canadian*, 128–129.

GODDEN, RUMER (1907–)

Episode of Sparrows (1955)

Evans, Gwyneth. "Girl in the Garden: Variations on a Feminine Pastoral." *CLAQ* 19.1 (1994): 21–22.

GODFREY, DAVE (1938–)

New Ancestors (1970)

Deer, Glenn. *Postmodern Canadian Fiction*, 61–79.
Söderlind, Sylvia. "Canadian Cryptic: The Sacred, the Profane, and the Translatable." *ArielE* 22.3 (1991): 93–95, 99.
Söderlind, Sylvia. *MARGIN / ALIAS*, 109–142.

GODWIN, GAIL (1937–)

Father Melancholy's Daughter (1991)

Westerlund-Shands, Kerstin. "Pas de D(i)eux: Duplicitous Syntheses in Gail Godwin's *Father Melancholy's Daughter*." *SoQ* 31.3 (1993): 79–87.

Finishing School (1984)

Hill, Jane. *Gail Godwin*, 88–101.

Glass People (1972)

Hill, Jane. *Gail Godwin*, 18–19, 29–38.

Mother and Two Daughters (1982)

Hill, Jane. *Gail Godwin*, 64–88.
Pelzer, Linda C. "Visions and Versions of Self: The Other/Women in *A Mother and Two Daughters*." *Crit* 34.3 (1993): 155–163.

Odd Woman (1974)

Greene, Gayle. *Changing the Story*, 91–102.
Hill, Jane. *Gail Godwin*, 39–53.

Perfectionists (1970)

Hill, Jane. *Gail Godwin*, 18–29.

Southern Family (1987)

Hill, Jane. *Gail Godwin*, 102–133.

Violet Clay (1978)

Hill, Jane. *Gail Godwin*, 39–41, 53–63.

GOLD, MICHAEL (1893–1967)

Jews without Money (1930)

Giles, James R. *Naturalistic Inner-City Novel in America*, 47–69.

GONZALES-BERRY, ERLINDA (1942–)

Paletitas de guayaba (1991)

Rebolledo, Tey Diana. *Women Singing in the Snow*, 75–76, 172–174, 176–181.

GOODIS, DAVID (1917–1967)

Burglar (1953)

Haut, Woody. *Pulp Culture*, 29–31.

Cassidy's Girl (1951)

Haut, Woody. *Pulp Culture*, 27–29.

Dark Passage (1946)

Haut, Woody. *Pulp Culture*, 23–25.

Moon in the Gutter (1953)

Haut, Woody. *Pulp Culture*, 31–33.

Nightfall (1947)

Haut, Woody. *Pulp Culture*, 25–27.

Street of No Return (1954)

Haut, Woody. *Pulp Culture*, 33–34.

GOODMAN, PAUL (1911–1972)

Empire City (1959)

Morton, Donald. "Crisis of Narrative in the Postnarratological Era: Paul Goodman's *The Empire City* as (Post)Modern Intervention." *NLH* 24.2 (1993): 407–424.

GORDON, CHARLES see CONNOR, RALPH

GORDON, MARY (1949–)

Company of Women (1981)

O'Rourke, William. *Signs of the Literary Times*, 105–108.

Men and Angels (1985)

Perry, Ruth. "Mary Gordon's Mothers," in Daly, Brenda O., ed. *Narrating Mothers*, 210–221.

Smiley, Pamela. "Unspeakable: Mary Gordon and the Angry Mother's Voice," in Lashgari, Deidre, ed. *Violence, Silence, and Anger*, 124–134.

Other Side (1989)

Ward, Catherine. "Wake Homes: Four Modern Novels of the Irish-American Family." *Eire* 26.2 (1991): 88–91.

GOVIER, KATHERINE (1948–)

Between Men (1987)

Thompson, Elizabeth. *Pioneer Woman*, 132, 134, 135, 150.

GRAHN, JUDY (1940–)

Mundane's World (1988)

Kolmar, Wendy K. " 'Dialectics of Connectedness': Supernatural Elements in Novels by Bambara, Cisneros, Grahn, and Erdrich," in Carpenter, Lynette, ed. *Haunting the House of Fiction*, 241–242, 243, 244, 245–246.

GRAVEL, FRANÇOIS

La note de passage (1985)

Hebert, Pierre. "Le Professeur fictif dans quelques romans québecois des années quatre-vingt: Pas facile d'être intellectuel postmoderne!" *UTQ* 63.4 (1994): 601–602, 602–604.

GREER, BEN (1948–)

Loss of Heaven (1988)

Grenier, Donald J. *Women Enter the Wilderness*, 82–89.

GREVE, FELIX PAUL see GROVE, FREDERICK PHILIP

GRIGNON, CLAUDE-HENRI (1894–1976)

Man and his Sin see *Un homme et son péché*

Un homme et son péché (1933)

Shek, Ben-Z. *French-Canadian*, 25–27.
Smart, Patricia. *Writing in the Father's House*, 75–77, 98–102.

Woman and the Miser see *Un homme et son péché*

GROULX, LIONEL-ADOLPHE see LESTRES, ALONIÉ DE

GROVE, FREDERICK PHILIP (1879–1948)

Consider Her Ways (1947)

Kuester, Martin. *Framing Truths*, 39–42.
Proietti, Salvatore. "Frederick Philip Grove's Version of Pastoral Utopianism." *SFS* 19.3 (1992): 361–377.

In Search of My Self (1946)

Williams, David. *Confessional Fictions*, 51–54.

Master of the Mill (1944)

Ming Chen, John Z. "Re-Reading Grove: The Influence of Socialist Ideology on the Writer and *The Master of the Mill.*" *CanL* 147 (1995): 25–44.
Proietti, Salvatore. "Frederick Philip Grove's Version of Pastoral Utopianism." *SFS* 19.3 (1992): 361–377.

Maurermeister Ihles Haus (1906)

Gammell, Irene. " 'I'll Be My Own Master': Domestic Conflicts and Discursive Resistance in *Maurermeister Ihles Haus* and *Our Daily Bread.*" *CanL* 135 (1992): 15–17, 17–20, 22–28.

Our Daily Bread (1928)

Gammell, Irene. " 'I'll Be My Own Master': Domestic Conflicts and Discursive Resistance in *Maurermeister Ihles Haus* and *Our Daily Bread.*" *CanL* 135 (1992): 15–17, 20–22, 22–28.
Keith, W.J. "Frederick Philip Grove," in Lecker, Robert, ed. *Canadian Writers and Their Works* (Vol. 4), 46–49.

Search for America (1927)

Williams, David. *Confessional Fictions*, 46–48.

Settlers of the Marsh (1925)

Dahlie, Hallvard. *Isolation and Commitment: Frederick Philip Grove's Settlers of the Marsh*. Toronto: ECW Press, 1993.
Keith, W.J. "Frederick Philip Grove," in Lecker, Robert, ed. *Canadian Writers and Their Works* (Vol. 4), 42–44.
Williams, David. *Confessional Fictions*, 48–51.

Yoke of Life (1930)

Keith, W.J. "Frederick Philip Grove," in Lecker, Robert, ed. *Canadian Writers and Their Works* (Vol. 4), 44–46.

GUÉVREMONT, GERMAINE (1893–1968)

Le Survenant (1945)

Shek, Ben-Z. *French-Canadian*, 30–31.
Smart, Patricia. *Writing in the Father's House*, 103–129.

Marie-Didace (1947)

Smart, Patricia. *Writing in the Father's House*, 103–129.

Outlander see *Le Survenant* and *Marie-Didace* (published in single volume as *Outlander*)

GUNN, JAMES E. (1923–)

Dreamers (1980)

McKitterick, Christopher. "James Gunn and *The Dreamers:* Epitomes of an Evolving Science Fiction." *Extrapolation* 36.4 (1995): 316–332.

H. D. (1886–1961)

Bid Me to Live (1960)

Limon, John. *Writing After War*, 210–215.

HERmione (1981)

Morris, Adalaide. "Science and the Mythopoeic Mind: The Case of H. D.," in Hayles, N. Katherine, ed. *Chaos and Order*, 204–210.

HADLEY, LEE see IRWIN, HADLEY

HAGEDORN, JESSICA (1949–)

Dogeaters (1990)

Evangelista, Susan. "Jessica Hagedorn and Manila Magic." *MELUS* 18.4 (1993–94): 41–52.

HALE, JANET CAMPBELL (1947–)

Jailing of Cecelia Capture (1985)

St. Clair, Janet. "Fighting for Her Life: The Mixed-Blood Woman's Insistence upon Selfhood," in Fleck, Richard F., ed. *Critical Perspectives*, 47–52.

HALE, SARAH JOSEPHA (1788–1879)

Lecturess (1839)

Levander, Caroline Field. "Bawdy Talk: The Politics of Women's Public Speech in *The Lecturess* and *The Bostonians*." *AL* 67.3 (1995): 476–483.

Liberia (1853)

Ryan, Susan M. "Errand into Africa: Colonization and Nation Building in Sarah J. Hale's *Liberia*." *NEQ* 68.4 (1995): 558–583.

HALEY, ALEX (1921–1992)

Roots (1976)

Fieldler, Leslie. "Alex Haley's *Roots*: Uncle Tom Rewrites *Uncle Tom's Cabin*." *What Was Literature? Class Culture and Mass Society*. New York: Simon and Schuster, 1982. 222–225. Rpt. in Bloom, Harold, ed. *Contemporary Black American Fiction Writers*, 52–54.

Gerber, David A. "Haley's *Roots* and Our Own: An Inquiry into the Nature of a Popular Phenomenon." *Journal of Ethnic Studies* 5.3 (1977): 92–94. Rpt. in Bloom, Harold, ed. *Contemporary Black American Fiction Writers*, 51–52.

Othow, Helen Chavis. "*Roots* and the Heroic Search for Identity." *CLA Journal* 26.3 (1983): 313–316. Rpt. in Bloom, Harold, ed. *Contemporary Black American Fiction Writers*, 55–56.

Taylor, Helen. " 'The Griot from Tennessee': The Saga of Alex Haley's *Roots*." *CritQ* 37.2 (1995): 46–62.

HALL, OAKLEY (1920–)

Apaches (1986)

Davis, Robert Murray. *Playing Cowboys*, 55–56

Bad Lands (1978)

Davis, Robert Murray. *Playing Cowboys*, 32, 34–35, 37–39, 48–55, 56–57.

Warlock (1958)

Davis, Robert Murray. *Playing Cowboys*, 32–37, 38–48, 54, 56–57.

HAMMETT, DASHIELL (1894–1961)

Maltese Falcon (1930)

Abrahams, Paul P. "On Re-Reading *The Maltese Falcon.*" *JACult* 18.1 (1995): 97–107.

Red Harvest (1929)

Freedman, Carl and Christopher Kendrick. "Forms of Labor in Dashiell Hammett's *Red Harvest.*" *PMLA* 106.2 (1991): 209–221.

HAND, ELIZABETH (1957–)

Aestival Tide (1992)

Harper, Mary Catherine. "Being a Boundary: The Abject Subjects of Elizabeth Hand's HEL Trilogy." *Extrapolation* 36.3 (1995): 222–242.

Kondratiev, Alexei. "Tales Newly Told: A Column on Current Modern Fantasy." *Mythlore* 19.1 (1993): 21.

Icarus Descending (1993)

Harper, Mary Catherine. "Being a Boundary: The Abject Subjects of Elizabeth Hand's HEL Trilogy." *Extrapolation* 36.3 (1995): 222–242.

Winterlong (1990)

Harper, Mary Catherine. "Being a Boundary: The Abject Subjects of Elizabeth Hand's HEL Trilogy." *Extrapolation* 36.3 (1995): 222–242.

Kondratiev, Alexei. "Tales Newly Told: A Column on Current Modern Fantasy." *Mythlore* 19.1 (1993): 15, 21.

HARINGTON, DONALD (1935–)

Architecture of the Arkansas Ozarks (1975)

Lund, Michael. "Donald Harington's House of Fiction." *ChiR* 38.4 (1993): 110–119.

Choiring of the Trees (1991)

Hughes, Linda K. "Knowing Women and the Fiction of Donald Harington." *ChiR* 38.4 (1993): 104–108.

Lightning Bug (1970)

Hughes, Linda K. "Knowing Women and the Fiction of Donald Harington." *ChiR* 38.4 (1993): 100–104, 105.

HARPER, FRANCES (1825–1911)

Iola Leroy (1892)

Ammons, Elizabeth. *Conflicting Stories*, 20–33.

Ernest, John. "From Mysteries to Histories: Cultural Pedagogy in Frances E. Harper's *Iola Leroy*." *AL* 64.3 (1992): 497–518.

McDowell, Deborah E. *"The Changing Same,"* 34–41, 48–57.

Young, Elizabeth. "Warring Fictions: *Iola Leroy* and the Color of Gender." *AL* 64.2 (1992): 273–297.

HARRIS, THOMAS (1940(?)–)

Red Dragon (1982)

Grixti, Joseph. "Consuming Cannibals: Psychopathic Killers as Archetypes and Cultural Icons." *JACult* 18.1 (1995): 91–95.

Williams, Tony. "Through a Dark Mirror: *Red Dragon*'s Gaze." *NConL* 25.1 (1995): 8–10.

Silence of the Lambs (1988)

Fowler, Douglas. "Aesthete as Serial Killer: Dr. Lecter." *NConL* 25.1 (1995): 2–3.

Grixti, Joseph. "Consuming Cannibals: Psychopathic Killers as Archetypes and Cultural Icons." *JACult* 18.1 (1995): 91–95.

McCarron, Bill. "*Silence of the Lambs* as Secular Eucharist." *NConL* 25.1 (1995): 5–6.

Ziegler, Robert. "Incorporation and Rebirth in *The Silence of the Lambs*." *NConL* 23.2 (1993): 7–9.

HARRISON, SUSAN FRANCES (1859–1935)

Forest of Bourg-Marie (1898)

MacMillan, Carrie. *Silenced Sextet*, 122–127.

Ringfield (1914)

MacMillan, Carrie. *Silenced Sextet*, 129–132.

HASSLER, JON (1933–)

Grand Opening (1987)

Narveson, Robert D. "Catholic-Lutheran Interaction in Keillor's *Lake Wobegon Days* and Hassler's *Grand Opening*," in Noe, Marcia, ed. *Exploring the Midwestern*, 180–190.

HAUSER, MARIANNE (1910–)

Talking Room (1976)

Ziarek, Ewa. " 'Taking Chances': The Feminine Genealogy of Style in Marianne Hauser's *The Talking Room*." *ConL* 33.3 (1992): 480–501.

HAVIGHURST, WALTER (1901–1994)

Winds of Spring (1940)

Robb, Kenneth A. "Cornelia James Cannon and Walter Havighurst: Undermining the Immigrant Stereotype in Midwestern Fiction," in Noe, Marcia, ed. *Exploring the Midwestern*, 192–201.

HAWKES, JOHN (1925–)

Beetle Leg (1951)

Davis, Robert Murray. *Playing Cowboys*, 79–86.

Virginie (1982)

Murphy, Peter F. " 'To Write What Cannot Be Written': The Woman Writer and Male Authority in John Hawkes's *Virginie: Her Two Lives*," in Morgan, Thaïs E., ed. *Men Writing the Feminine*, 77–86.

Whistlejacket (1989)

Cowart, David. " 'Significant, Insignificant': Realist and Postmodernist Art in Hawke's *Whistlejacket*." *MFS* 41.1 (1995): 99–115.

HAWTHORNE, NATHANIEL (1804–1864)

Blithedale Romance (1852)

Brodhead, Richard H. *Cultures of Letters*, 48–52, 55–62, 63–67.

Gable, Harvey L., Jr. "Inappeasable Longings: Hawthorne, Romance, and the Disintegration of Coverdale's Self in *The Blithedale Romance*." *NEQ* 67.2 (1994): 257–278.

Hollinger, Douglas L. "Courtship of Miles Coverdale." *ANQ* 8.3(1995): 8–10.

Hull, Richard. "Critique of Characterization: It Was in Not Knowing That He Loved Her." *Style* 26.1 (1992): 33–49.

Jones, E. Michael. *Angel and the Machine*, 175–186.

Jooma, Minaz. "Spectating the Spectator, Re(ad)dressing the (Ad)Dressor." *ATQ* 7.4 (1993): 321–333.

Kronick, Joseph G. "Romance and the Prose of the World: Hegelian Reflections on Hawthorne and America," in Cowan, Bainard, ed. *Theorizing American Literature*, 168–171.

Lewis, Ffrangcon. "Women, Death and Theatricality in *The Blithedale Romance*." *JAmS* 26.1 (1992): 75–94.

Mackenzie, Manfred. "Colonization and Decolonization in *The Blithedale Romance*." *UTQ* 62.4 (1993): 504–521.

Pfister, Joel. *Production of the Personal Life*, 80–103.

Tanner, Laura E. "Speaking with 'Hands at Our Throats': The Struggle for Artistic Voice in *The Blithedale Romance*." *SAF* 21.1 (1993): 1–19.

Weldon, Roberta F. "Tyrant King and Accused Queen: Father and Daughter in Nathaniel Hawthorne's *The Blithedale Romance*." *ATQ* 6.1 (1992): 31–44.

Fanshawe (1828)

Jones, E. Michael. *Angel and the Machine*, 56–61.

House of Seven Gables (1851)

Baym, Nina. "Hawthorne's Holgrave: The Failure of the Artist Hero." *JEGP* 69.4 (1970): 584–598. Rpt. in Rosenthal, Bernard, ed. *Critical Essays on Hawthorne's The House of Seven Gables*, 63–74.

Brown, Gillian. "Hawthorne, Inheritance, and Women's Property." *SNNTS* 23.1 (1991): 107–118.

Buitenhuis, Peter. *House of the Seven Gables: Severing Family and Colonial Ties.* Boston: Twayne Publishers, 1991.

Campbell, Charles. "Representing Representation: Body as Figure, Frame, and Text," in *The House of the Seven Gables.*" *ArQ* 47.4 (1991): 1–24.

Chandler, Marilyn R. *Dwelling in the Text*, 65–89.

Emery, Allan. "Salem History and *The House of Seven Gables*," in Rosenthal, Bernard, ed. *Critical Essays on Hawthorne's The House of Seven Gables*, 129–146.

Engell, John. "Hawthorne and Two Types of Early American Romance." *SoAR* 57.1 (1992): 33–51.

Flibbert, Joseph. " 'That Look Beneath': Hawthorne's Portrait of Benevolence in *The House of Seven Gables*," in Rosenthal, Bernard, ed. *Critical Essays on Hawthorne's The House of Seven Gables*, 114–127.

Gable, H.L., Jr. "Kaleidoscopic Visions: Images of the Self in *The House of Seven Gables*." *ArQ* 48.1 (1992): 109–134.

Goddu, Teresa. "Circulation of Women in *The House of the Seven Gables*." *SNNTS* 23.1 (1991): 119–127.

Johnson, Claudia D. "Unsettling Accounts in *The House of the Seven Gables*." *ATQ* 5.2 (1991): 83–94.

Jones, E. Michael. *Angel and the Machine*, 157–173.

Knadler, Stephen. "Hawthorne's Genealogy of Madness: *The House of the Seven Gables* and Disciplinary Individualism." *AQ* 47.2 (1995): 280–308.

Kronick, Joseph G. "Romance and the Prose of the World: Hegelian Reflections on Hawthorne and America," in Cowan, Bainard, ed. *Theorizing American Literature*, 183–186.

MacDonald, R. D. "Hawthorne's (Devilish?) Humour and the Ending of *The House of the Seven Gables*." *CRevAS* 22.3 (1991): 367–386.

MacLaine, Brent. "Photofiction as Family Album: David Galloway, Paul Theroux and Anita Booker." *Mosaic* 24.2 (1991): 133–135.

Michelson, Bruce. "Hawthorne's House of Three Stories." *New England Quarterly* 57 (1984): 163–183. Rpt. in Rosenthal, Bernard, ed. *Critical Essays on Hawthorne's The House of Seven Gables*, 76–90.

Pfister, Joel. *Production of the Personal Life*, 145–151, 154–161.

Scheick, William J. "Author's Corpse and the Humean Problem of Personal Identity in Hawthorne's *The House of Seven Gables*." *SNNTS* 24.2 (1992): 131–153.

Scheick, William J. "Author's Corpse and the Humean Problem of Personal Identity in Hawthorne's *The House of Seven Gables*." *Studies in the Novel* 24.2 (1992): 131–153. Rpt. in Rosenthal, Bernard, ed. *Critical Essays on Hawthorne's The House of Seven Gables*, 91–109.

Swann, Charles. "*House of the Seven Gables:* Hawthorne's Modern Novel of 1848." *MLQ* 86.1 (1991): 1–18.

Williams, Susan S. " 'The Aspiring Purpose of an Ambitious Demagogue': Portraiture and *The House of the Seven Gables*." *NCF* 49.2 (1994): 221–244.

Woodson, Thomas. "Salem in *The House of Seven Gables*," in Rosenthal, Bernard, ed. *Critical Essays on Hawthorne's The House of Seven Gables*, 150–164.

Marble Faun (1860)

Dolis, John. "Hawthorne's Gentle Reader: (The Hen) House of (Family) Romance." *ArQ* 47.1 (1991): 29–47.

Greenwald, Elissa. "Hawthorne and Judaism: Otherness and Identity in *The Marble Faun*." *SNNTS* 23.1 (1991): 128–138.

Herbert, T. Walter, Jr. "Erotics of Purity: *The Marble Faun* and the Victorian Construction of Sexuality." *Representations* 36 (1991): 114–132.

Idol, John L. " 'A Linked Circle of Three' Plus One: Nonverbal Communication in *The Marble Faun*." *SNNTS* 23.1 (1991): 139–151.

Jones, E. Michael. *Angel and the Machine*, 190–201.

Kronick, Joseph G. "Romance and the Prose of the World: Hegelian Reflections on Hawthorne and America," in Cowan, Bainard, ed. *Theorizing American Literature*, 187–190.

Nattermann, Udo. "Dread and Desire: 'Europe' in Hawthorne's *The Marble Faun*." *ELWIU* 21.1 (1994): 54–67.

Pfister, Joel. *Production of the Personal Life*, 162–180.

Schiller, Emily. "Choice of Innocence: Hilda in *The Marble Faun*." *SNNTS* 26.4 (1994): 372–391.

Scarlet Letter (1850)

Abel, Darrel. "Hawthorne's Hester." *College English* 13 (March 1952): 303–309. Rpt. in Scharnhorst, Gary, ed. *Critical Response*, 167–175.

Anderson, Douglas. "Jefferson, Hawthorne, and 'The Custom-House'." *NCF* 46.3 (1991): 309–326.

Barszcz, James. "Hawthorne, Emerson and the Forms of the Frontier," in Heyne, Eric, ed. *Desert, Garden*, 47–50.

Baym, Nina. "Passion and Authority in *The Scarlet Letter*." *New England Quarterly* 43 (1970): 209–230. Rpt. in Scharnhorst, Gary, ed. *Critical Response*, 176–193.

Bensick, Carol M. "Dimmesdale and His Bachelorhood: 'Priestly Celibacy' in *The Scarlet Letter*." *SAF* 21.1 (1993): 103–110.

Benstock, Shari. "*The Scarlet Letter* (a)dorée, or the Female Body Embroidered," in Murfin, Ross C., ed. *Scarlet Letter*, 288–302.

Bercovitch, Sacvan. "Hawthorne's A-Morality of Compromise," in Murfin, Ross C., ed. *Scarlet Letter*, 344–357.

Bercovitch, Sacvan. *Office of the Scarlet Letter.* Baltimore, MD: Johns Hopkins University Press, 1991.

Bernstein, Cynthia. "Reading *The Scarlet Letter:* Against Hawthorne's Fictional Interpretive Community." *LnL* 18 (1993): 1–20.

Budick, Emily Miller. *Engendering Romance*, 13–39.

Budick, Emily Miller. "Hester's Skepticism, Hawthorne's Faith: Or, What Does a Woman Doubt? Instituting the American Romance Tradition." *NLH* 22.1 (1991): 199–211.

Budick, Emily Miller. "Sacvan Bercovitch, Stanley Cavell, and the Romance Theory of American Fiction." *PMLA* 107.1 (1992): 78–91.

Clasby, Nancy Tenfelde. "Being True: Logos in *The Scarlet Letter*." *Renascence* 45.4 (1993): 247–256.

Cottle, Samuel. "Scarlet Letter as Icon." *ATQ* 6.4 (1992): 251–261.

Daniel, Janice B. " 'Apples of the Thoughts and Fancies': Nature as Narrator in *The Scarlet Letter*." *ATQ* (1993): 307–318.

Derrick, Scott S. " 'A Curious Subject of Observation and Inquiry': Homoeroticism, the Body, and Authorship in Hawthorne's *The Scarlet Letter*." *Novel* 28.3 (1995): 308–326.

Diehl, Joanne Feit. "Re-Reading *The Letter:* Hawthorne, the Fetish, and the (Family) Romance," in Murfin, Ross C., ed. *Scarlet Letter*, 235–251.

Doubleday, Neal Frank. "Hawthorne's Hester and Feminism." *PMLA* 54 (September 1939): 825–828; Rpt. in Scharnhorst, Gary, ed. *Critical Response*, 153–157.

Dreyer, Eileen. " 'Confession' in *The Scarlet Letter*." *JAmS* 25.1 (1991): 78–81.

Eisinger, Chester E. "Pearl and the Puritan Heritage." *CE* 12 (March 1951): 323–329. Rpt. in Scharnhorst, Gary, ed. *Critical Response*, 158–166.

Gappa, Richard. "Penance and Repentance in *The Scarlet Letter*," in Karolides, Nicholas, ed. *Censored Books*, 449–455.

Gilmore, Michael T. "Hawthorne and the Making of the Middle Class," in Lohmann, Christoph K., ed. *Discovering Difference*, 88–103.

Hoffman, Elizabeth Aycock. "Political Power in *The Scarlet Letter*." *ATQ* 4 (March 1990): 13–29. Rpt. in Scharnhorst, Gary, ed. *Critical Response*, 202–219.

Johnson, Claudia Durst. "Impotence and Omnipotence in *The Scarlet Letter*." *NEQ* 66.4 (1993): 594–612.

Johnson, Claudia Durst. *Understanding the Scarlet Letter: A Student Casebook to Issues, Sources, and Historical Documents.* Westport, CT: Greenwood Press, 1995.

Jones, E. Michael. *Angel and the Machine*, 141–155.

Kimball, Samuel. "Countersigning Aristotle: The Amimetic Challenge of *The Scarlet Letter*." *ATQ* 7.2 (1993): 141–158.

Kronick, Joseph G. "Romance and the Prose of the World: Hegelian Reflections on Hawthorne and America," in Cowan, Bainard, ed. *Theorizing American Literature*, 186–187.

Leverenz, David. "Mrs. Hawthorne's Headache: Reading *The Scarlet Letter*," in Murfin, Ross C., ed. *Scarlet Letter*, 263–274.

Lewis, Charles. "Ironic Romance of New Historicism: *The Scarlet Letter* and *Beloved* Standing in Side by Side." *ArQ* 51.1 (1995): 37–48.

Li, Haipeng. "Hester Prynne and the Folk Art of Embroidery." *UMSE* 10 (1992): 80–85.

Maddox, Lucy. *Removals*, 118–126.

Mathe, Sylvie. "Reader May Not Choose: Oxymoron as Central Figure in Hawthorne's Strategy of Immunity from Choice in *The Scarlet Letter*." *Style* 26.4 (1992): 604–633.

Milliman, Craig A. "Hawthorne's *The Scarlet Letter*." *Expl* 53.2 (1995): 83–85.

Person, Leland S., Jr. "Inscribing Paternity: Nathaniel Hawthorne as a Nineteenth-Century Father." *SAR* 15 (1991): 225–244.

Pfister, Joel. *Production of the Personal Life*, 122–143.

Pimple, Kenneth D. " 'Subtle, but Remorseful Hypocrite': Dimmesdale's Moral Character." *SNNTS* 25.3 (1993): 257–271.

Ragusis, Michael. "Silence, Family Discourse, and Fiction in *The Scarlet Letter*," in Murfin, Ross C., ed. *Scarlet Letter*, 316–329.

Railton, Stephen. *Authorship and Audience*, 107–131.

Reiss, John. "Hawthorne's *The Scarlet Letter*." *Expl* 53.4 (1995): 200–201.

Rogers, Franklin R. *Occidental Ideographs*, 76–99.

Shaw, Peter. *Recovering American Literature*, 23–47.
Sorells, David J. "Hawthorne's *The Scarlet Letter*." *Expl* 53.1 (1994): 23–25.
Sterling, Laurie A. "Paternal Gold: Translating Inheritance in *The Scarlet Letter*." *ATQ* 6.1 (1992): 17–29.
Todd, Robert E. "Magna Mater Archetype in *The Scarlet Letter*." *NEQ* 45 (1972): 421–429. Rpt. in Scharnhorst, Gary, ed. *Critical Response*, 194–201.
Wilton, Marilyn Mueller. "Paradigm and Paramour: Role Reversal in *The Scarlet Letter*," in Scharnhorst, Gary, ed. *Critical Response*, 220–231.

HAXTON, JOSEPHINE see DOUGLAS, ELLEN

HÉBERT, ANNE (1916–)

Children of the Black Sabbath see *Les enfants du sabbat*

First Garden see *Le premier jardin*

In the Shadow of the Wind see *Les fous de bassan*

Kamouraska (1970)

Gingrass, Katharine. "Writing the Unconscious: Dreams and Reverie in Anne Hébert's *Kamouraska*." *QS* 12 (1991): 139–145.
Green, Mary Jean. "Dismantling the Colonizing Text: Anne Hébert's *Kamouraska* and Assia Djebar's *L'Amour, la fantasia*." *FR* 66.6 (1993): 959–966.
Shek, Ben-Z. *French-Canadian*, 102–104.

Le premier jardin (1988)

Campagnoli, Ruggero. "Syndrome Québécois dans '*Le premier jardin*' d'Anne Hébert," in Marcato-Falzoni, Franca, ed. *Mythes et mythologies*, 239–247.
Mitchell, Constantina T. and Paul R. Cote. "Ordre et rite: La Fonction du cortège dans *Le premier jardin* d'Anne Hébert." *FR* 64.3 (1991): 451–461.
Saint-Martin, Lori. "Les Premières Mères, *Le premier jardin*." *V&I* 20.3 (1995): 667–681.

Les enfants du sabbat (1975)

Shek, Ben-Z. *French-Canadian*, 104.

Les fous de bassan (1982)

Boyce, Marie-Dominique. "Création de la mère/mer: Symbole du paradis perdu dans *Les fous de bassan*." *FR* 68.2 (1994): 294–302.
Cote, Paul Raymond and Constantina Mitchell. "*Les fous de bassan* and *Le torrent:* At the Crossroads of Desire and Delusion." *MLS* 21.4 (1991): 78–89.
Lee, Scott. "La Rhétorique de la folie: Métaphore et allégorie dans *Les fous de bassan*." *V&I* 19.2 (1994): 374–393.
O'Reilly, Magessa. "Le Jeu des rythmes dans *Les fous de bassan* d'Anne Hébert." *CanL* 133 (1992): 109–126.
Smart, Patricia. *Writing in the Father's House*, 203–211.

HEINEMANN, LARRY (1944–)

Paco's Story (1986)

Morris, Gregory L. "Telling War Stories' Larry Heinemann's *Paco's Story* and the Serio-Comic Tradition." *Crit* 36.1 (1994): 58–68.

Scott, Grant F. "*Paco's Story* and the Ethics of Violence." *Crit* 36.1 (1994): 69–80.
Slabey, Robert M. "Heinemann's *Paco's Story*." *Expl* 52.3 (1994): 187–189.

HEINLEIN, ROBERT (1907–1988)

Moon Is a Hard Mistress (1966)

Williams, Donna Glee. "Moons of Le Guin and Heinlein." *SFS* 21.2 (1994): 164–172.

Stranger in a Strange Land (1961)

Blackmore, Tim. "Talking with Strangers: Interrogating the Many Texts That Became Heinlein's *Stranger in a Strange Land*." *Extrapolation* 36.2 (1995): 136–150.

Reno, Shaun. "Xuni Indian Tribe: A Model for *Stranger in a Strange Land*'s Martian Culture." *Extrapolation* 36.2 (1995): 151–158.

HELLER, JOSEPH (1923–)

Catch-22 (1961)

Green, Daniel. "World Worth Laughing At: *Catch-22* and the Humor of Black Humor." *SNNTS* 27.2 (1995): 186–196.

Limon, John. *Writing After War*, 139–153.

Lupack, Barbara Tepa. *Insanity as Redemption*, 20–61.

Good As Gold (1979)

Toman, Marshall. "*Good as Gold* and Heller's Family Ethic." *SAJL* 10.2 (1991): 211–224.

Something Happened (1974)

Martin, Robert A. "Joseph Heller's *Something Happened*." *NConL* 22.3 (1992): 11–12.

Tyson, Lois. "Joseph Heller's *Something Happened:* The Commodification of Consciousness and the Postmodern Flight from Inwardness." *CEA* 54.2 (1992): 37–51.

HEMINGWAY, ERNEST (1899–1961)

Across the River and into the Trees (1950)

Meredith, James H. "Rapido River and Hurtgen Forest in *Across the River and into the Trees*." *HN* 14.1 (1994): 60–66.

Nuti, Elisabetta Zingoni. " 'Honorable Pacciardi' Remembered." *HN* 11.1 (1991): 56–57

Death in the Afternoon (1932)

Comley, Nancy R.. *Hemingway's Genders*, 107–136.

Messent, Peter. *Ernest Hemingway*, 137–141.

Farewell to Arms (1929)

Barlowe-Keys, Jamie. "Re-Reading Women: The Example of Catherine Barkley." *HN* 12.2 (1993): 24–35.

Finnegan, Robert Emmett. "Adieu Identity: Mirrors and Newspapers in Hemingway's *A Farewell to Arms.*" *DUJ* 86.2 (1994): 259–270.

Hill, William Thomas. "Roads of the Abruzzi and the Roads of Earthly Paradise in Hemingway's *A Farewell to Arms.*" *Studies in the Humanities* 10 (1994): 25–43.

Limon, John. *Writing After War*, 95–98.

Mandel, Miriam. "Ferguson and Lesbian Love: Unspoken Subplots in *A Farewell to Arms.*" *HN* 14.1 (1994): 18–24.

Messent, Peter. *Ernest Hemingway*, 56–63.

Miller, D. Quentin. " 'In the Late Summer of That Year': The Problem of Time in *A Farewell to Arms.*" *HN* 10.2 (1991): 61–64.

Norris, Margot. "Novel as War: Lies and Truth in Hemingway's *A Farewell to Arms.*" *MFS* 40.4 (1994): 689–710.

Phelan, James. "Concepts of Voice, the Voices of Frederic Henry, and the Structure of *A Farewell to Arms,*" in Scafella, Frank, ed. *Hemingway*, 214–231.

Rovit, Earl and Gerry Brenner. *Ernest Hemingway*, 81–89.

Sloan, Gary. "*Farewell to Arms* and the Sunday-School Jesus." *SNNTS* 25.4 (1993): 449–456.

Spilka, Mark. "Repossessing Papa: A Narcissistic Meditation," in Rosen, Kenneth, ed. *Hemingway Repossessed*, 41–47.

Tyler, Lisa. "Passion and Grief in *A Farewell to Arms:* Ernest Hemingway's Retelling of *Wuthering Heights.*" *HN* 14.2 (1995): 79–96.

Underhill, Linda and Jeanne Nakjavani. "Food for Fiction: Lessons from Ernest Hemingway's Writing." *JACult* 15.2 (1992): 88–89.

Fiesta see *Sun Also Rises*

For Whom the Bell Tolls (1940)

Astro, Richard. "Phlebas Sails the Caribbean: Steinbeck, Hemingway, and the American Waste Land," in French, Warren, ed. *Twenties: Fiction, Poetry, Drama.* DeLand, FL: Everett/Edwards, Inc., 1975. 215–233. Rpt. in Hayashi, Tesumaro, ed. *Steinbeck's Literary Dimension*, 43–44.

Boker, Pamela A. "Negotiating the Heroic Paternal Ideal: Historical Fiction as Transference in Hemingway's *For Whom The Bell Tolls.*" *L&P* 41.1–2 (1995): 85–112.

Gajdusek, Robin. "Artists in Their Art: Hemingway and Velásquez—The Shared Worlds of *For Whom the Bell Tolls* and *Las Meninas,*" in Rosen, Kenneth, ed. *Hemingway Repossessed*, 17–27.

Gajdusek, Robert E. " 'Is He Building a Bridge or Blowing One?': The Repossession of Text by the Author in *For Whom the Bell Tolls.*" *HN* 11.2 (1992): 45–51.

Halliburton, Lloyd. "Hemingway's Use of Maquina in *For Whom the Bell Tolls:* A Reconsideration." *NDQ* 62.2 (1994–95): 183–192.

Hodson, Joel. "Robert Jordan Revisited: Hemingway's Debt to T. E. Lawrence." *HN* 10.2 (1991): 2–16.

Josephs, Allen. "Reality and Invention in *For Whom the Bell Tolls*, or Reflections on the Nature of the Historical Novel," in Rosen, Kenneth, ed. *Hemingway Repossessed*, 87–95.

Limon, John. *Writing After War*, 94–95.

Messent, Peter. *Ernest Hemingway*, 68–75.

Nakjavani, Erik. "Nostalgia, Its Stylistics and Politics in Hemingway's *For Whom the Bell Tolls,*" in Rosen, Kenneth, ed. *Hemingway Repossessed*, 97–113.

Rovit, Earl and Gerry Brenner. *Ernest Hemingway*, 117–127.

Rudat, Wolfgang E. H. "Other War in *For Whom the Bells Tolls:* Maria and Miltonic Gender-Role Battles." *HN* 11.1 (1991): 8–24.

Underhill, Linda and Jeanne Nakjavani. "Food for Fiction: Lessons from Ernest Hemingway's Writing." *JACult* 15.2 (1992): 89–90.

Whitmore, Tony. "Gaiety and Psyche: *For Whom the Bell Tolls.*," in Scafella, Frank, ed. *Hemingway*, 234–243.

Wilhelm, Bernard. "Behind *For Whom the Bell Tolls* and L'Espoir." *NDQ* 60.2 (1992): 1–7.

Garden of Eden (1986)

Burwell, Rose Marie. "Hemingway's *Garden of Eden:* Resistance of Things Past and Protecting the Masculine Text." *TSLL* 35.2 (1993): 198–225.

Comley, Nancy R. *Hemingway's Genders*, 52–68, 88–103.

Eby, Carl. " 'Come Back to the Beach Ag'in, David Honey!': Hemingway's Fetishization of Race in *The Garden of Eden* Manuscripts." *HN* 14.2 (1995): 98–117.

Gajdusek, Robert E. "Cost of Sin in the Garden: A Study of an Amended Theme in *The Garden of Eden.*" *RALS* 19.1 (1993): 1–21.

Kennedy, J. Gerald. "Hemingway's Gender Trouble." *AL* 63.2 (1991): 187–207.

Messent, Peter. *Ernest Hemingway*, 110–123.

Peters, K. J. "Thematic Integrity of *The Garden of Eden.*" *HN* 10.2 (1991): 17–29.

Roe, Steven C. "Opening Bluebeard's Closet: Writing and Aggression in Hemingway's *The Garden of Eden* Manuscript." *HN* 12.1 (1992): 52–65.

Spilka, Mark. "Importance of Being Androgynous," in Scafella, Frank, ed. *Hemingway*, 208–211.

Willingham, Kathy. "Hemingway's *The Garden of Eden:* Writing with the Body." *HN* 12.2 (1993): 46–61.

Islands in the Stream (1970)

Messent, Peter. *Ernest Hemingway*, 79–82.

Rovit, Earl and Gerry Brenner. *Ernest Hemingway*, 169–173.

Sun Also Rises (1926)

Achuff, Louise R. " 'Nice' and 'Pleasant' in *The Sun.*" *HN* 10.2 (1991): 42–46.

Atkins, John. *Art of Ernest Hemingway.* London: Spring Books, 1952. 234–241. Rpt. in Bloom, Harold, ed. *Brett Ashley*, 13–17.

Baker, Carlos. *Hemingway the Writer as Artist.* Princeton: Princeton University Press, 1952. 87–93. Rpt. in Bloom, Harold, ed. *Brett Ashley*, 17–22.

Baldwin, Marc D. " 'To Make It into a Novel . . . Don't Talk About It': Hemingway's Political Unconscious." *JNT* 23.3 (1993): 170–187.

Bardacke, Theodore. "Hemingway's Women: 1950." *Ernest Hemingway the Man and His Work.* Ed. John K. M McCaffery. Cleveland: World Publishing Co, 1950. 342–344. Rpt. in Bloom, Harold, ed. *Brett Ashley*, 12–13.

Baskett, Sam S. "Brett and Her Lovers." *Centennial* Review 22.1 (Winter 1978): 45–69. Rpt. in Bloom, Harold, ed. *Brett Ashley*, 105–122.

Benson, Jackson J. "Roles and the Masculine Writer." *Hemingway . . . The Writer's Art of Self-Defense.* Minneapolis: University of Minnesota Press, 1969. 28–42. Rpt. in Bloom, Harold, ed. *Brett Ashley*, 76–85.

Brooks, Cleanth. *Hidden God: Studies in Hemingway, Faulkner, Yeats, Eliot, and Warren.* New Haven, CT: Yale University Press, 1963. Rpt. in Bloom, Harold, ed. *Brett Ashley*, 29–30.

Burnam, Tom. "Primitivism and Masculinity in the Work of Ernest Hemingway."

Modern Fiction Studies 1.3 (August 1955): 21–22. Rpt. in Bloom, Harold, ed. *Brett Ashley*, 22–23.

Cheatham, George. " 'Sign the Wire with Love': The Morality of Surplus in *The Sun Also Rises*." *HN* 11.2 (1992): 25–30.

Cohen, Milton A. "Circe and Her Swine." *Arizona* Quarterly 41.4 (Winter 1985): 293–305. Rpt. in Bloom, Harold, ed. *Brett Ashley*, 157–165.

Cowan, S. A. "Amateur Boxing in Hemingway's *The Sun Also Rises*." *ELN* 33.1 (1995): 58–61.

Cowley, Malcolm. *Second Flowering: Works and Days of the Lost Generation.* London: Andre Deutsch, 1956. 69, 71–73. Rpt. in Bloom, Harold, ed. *Brett Ashley*, 24–26.

Djos, Matts. "Alcoholism in Ernest Hemingway's *The Sun Also Rises:* A Wine and Roses Perspective on the Lost Generation." *HN* 14.2 (1995): 64–78.

Elliot, Ira. "Performance Art: Jake Barnes and 'Masculine' Signification in *The Sun Also Rises*." *AL* 67.1 (1995): 77–94.

Fieldler, Leslie. *Love and Death in the American Novel.* New York: Criterion Books, 1960. Revised Edition. 319–320. Rpt. in Bloom, Harold, ed. *Brett Ashley*, 27–28.

Frohock, W. M. *Novel of Violence in America.* Dallas: Southern Methodist University Press, 1957. 170–172. Rpt. in Bloom, Harold, ed. *Brett Ashley*, 26–27.

Gale, Robert L. "Hemingway's *The Sun Also Rises*." *Expl* 51.3 (1993): 186–187.

Gladstein, Mimi Reisel. *Indestructible Woman in Faulkner, Hemingway, and Steinbeck.* Ann Arbor, MI: UMI Research Press, 1986. 59–62. Rpt. in Bloom, Harold, ed. *Brett Ashley*, 57–60.

Hattenhauer, Darryl. "More Humor in *The Sun Also Rises*." *HN* 10.2 (1991): 56–57.

Hays, Peter L. "Catullus and *The Sun Also Rises*." *HN* 12.2 (1993): 15–23.

Jain, Sunita. "Of Women and Bitches: A Defence of Two Hemingway Heroines." *Journal of the School Languages* 12.2 (Winter 1975–76): 132–135. Rpt. in Bloom, Harold, ed. *Brett Ashley*, 37–40.

Knight, Karl F. "Hemingway's *The Sun Also Rises*." *Expl* 50.2 (1992): 107–109.

Lewis, Robert W. "Tristan or Jacob?" *Hemingway on Love.* Austin: University of Texas Press, 1965. 19–35. Rpt. in Bloom, Harold, ed. *Brett Ashley*, 63–75.

Limon, John. *Writing After War*, 99–102.

Linebarger, J. M. "Symbolic Hats in *The Sun Also Rises*." *Fitzgerald/Heminway Annual 1972*. 323–324. Rpt. in Bloom, Harold, ed. *Brett Ashley*, 34–35.

Meckier, Jerome. "Hemingway Reads Huxley: An Occasion for Some Observations on the Twenties and the Apostolate of the Lost Generation." *Fitzgerald/Hemingway Annual 1976*. 173, 180–184. Rpt. in Bloom, Harold, ed. *Brett Ashley*, 40–43.

Messent, Peter. *Ernest Hemingway*, 52–56.

Miezner, Arthur. "The Two Hemingways." *Great Experiment in American Literature.* Ed. Carl Bode. New York: Praeger, 1961. 139–140. Rpt. in Bloom, Harold, ed. *Brett Ashley*, 28–29.

Morgan, Kathleen. "Between Two Worlds: Hemingway's Brett Ashley and Homer's Helen of Troy." *CML* 11.2 (1991): 169–180.

Morrow, Patrick D. "Bought Generation." *Genre* 13.1 (Spring 1980): 51–69. Rpt. in Bloom, Harold, ed. *Brett Ashley*, 123–138.

Oates, Joyce Carol. *(Woman) Writer: Occasions and Opportunities.* New York: E.P. Dutton, 1988. 304–309. Rpt. in Bloom, Harold, ed. *Brett Ashley*, 48–51.

Pearsall, Robert Brainard. *Life and Writings of Ernest Hemingway.* Amsterdam: Rodopi, 1973. 72–74. Rpt. in Bloom, Harold, ed. *Brett Ashley*, 36–37.

Rogers, Franklin R. *Occidental Ideographs*, 251–252.

Ross, Charles L. " 'The Saddest Story' Part Two: *The Good Soldier* and *The Sun Also Rises*." *HN* 12.1 (1992): 26–33.

Rovit, Earl and Gerry Brenner. *Ernest Hemingway*, 128–142.

Rovit, Earl. "On Psychic Retrenchment in Hemingway," in Scafella, Frank, ed. *Hemingway*, 181–188.

Rudat, Wolfgang E. H. "Anti-Semitism in *The Sun Also Rises:* Traumas, Jealousies, and the Genesis of Cohn." *American Imago* 49.2 (1992): 263–274.

Rudat, Wolfgang E. H. "Brett's Problem." *Style* 19.3 (Fall 1985): 317–325. Rpt. in Bloom, Harold, ed. *Brett Ashley*, 166–174.

Rudat, Wofgang E. H. "Hemingway on Sexual Otherness: What's Really Funny in *The Sun Also Rises*," in Rosen, Kenneth, ed. *Hemingway Repossessed*, 169–179.

Sarason, Bertram D. "Lady Brett Ashley and Lady Duff Twysden." *Connecticut Review* 2.2 (April 1969): 5–13. Rpt. in Bloom, Harold, ed. *Brett Ashley*, 86–95.

Schmidt, Dolores Barracano. "Great American Bitch." *College English* 32.8 (May 1971): 901–903. Rpt. in Bloom, Harold, ed. *Brett Ashley*, 32–34.

Schorer, Mark. "Background of a Style." *Kenyon Review* 3.1 (Winter 1941): 101–103. Rpt. in Bloom, Harold, ed. *Brett Ashley*, 11–12.

Schwartz, Delmore. *Perspectives USA.* New York Intercultural Publications, 1955. 258–259. Rpt. in Bloom, Harold, ed. *Brett Ashley*, 23–24.

Schwartz, Nina. "Lovers' Discourse in *The Sun Also Rises:* A Cock and Bull Story." *Criticism* 26.1 (Winter 1984): 57–60. Rpt. in Bloom, Harold, ed. *Brett Ashley*, 51–54.

Seltzer, Leon F. "Opportunity of Impotence: Count Mippipopolous in *The Sun Also Rises*." *Renascence* 31.1 (Autumn 1978): 7–9. Rpt. in Bloom, Harold, ed. *Brett Ashley*, 43–45.

Smith, Carol H. "Women and the Loss of Eden." *Ernest Hemingway: The Writer in Context.* Ed. James Nagel. Madison, WI: University of Wisconsin Press, 1984. 132–134. Rpt. in Bloom, Harold, ed. *Brett Ashley*, 54–55.

Spilka, Mark. "Jake and Brett: Wounded Warriors." *Hemingway's Quarrel with* Androgyny. Lincoln: University of Nebraska Press, 1990. 200–208. Rpt. in Bloom, Harold, ed. *Brett Ashley*, 175–183.

Stoneback, H.R. " 'You Sure This Thing Has Trout in It?' Fishing and Fabrication, Omission and 'Vermification' in *The Sun Also Rises*," in Rosen, Kenneth, ed. *Hemingway Repossessed*, 115–128.

Tintner, Adeline R. "Ernest and Henry: Heminway's Lover's Quarrel with James." *Ernest Hemingway: The Writer in Context.* Ed. James Nagel. Madison, WI: University of Wisconsin Press, 1984. 171–172. Rpt. in Bloom, Harold, ed. *Brett Ashley*, 55–57.

Underhill, Linda and Jeanne Nakjavani. "Food for Fiction: Lessons from Ernest Hemingway's Writing." *JACult* 15.2 (1992): 88, 90.

Vopat, Carole Gottlieb. "End of *The Sun Also Rises:* A New Beginning." *Fitzgerald Hemingway Annual* 1972, 245–255. Rpt. in Bloom, Harold, ed. *Brett Ashley*, 96–104.

Wagner-Martin, Linda. "Racial and Sexual Coding in Hemingway's *The Sun Also Rises*." *HN* 10.2 (1991): 39–41.

Wagner-Martin, Linda. "Women in Hemingway's Early Fiction." *College Literature* 7.3 (Fall 1980): 239–247. Rpt. in Bloom, Harold, ed. *Brett Ashley*, 139–147.

Whitlow, Roger. "Bitches and Other Simplistic Assumptions." *Cassandra's Daughters: The Women in Hemingway.* Westport, CT: Greenwood Press, 1984. 49–58. Rpt. in Bloom, Harold, ed. *Brett Ashley*, 148–156.

Young, Philip and Charles W. Mann. "Fitzgerald's *Sun Also Rises:* Notes and Comment." *Fitzgerald/Hemingway Annual 1970.* 1–4. Rpt. in Bloom, Harold, ed. *Brett Ashley*, 31–32.

To a God Unknown (1932)

Astro, Richard. "Phlebas Sails the Caribbean: Steinbeck, Hemingway, and the American Waste Land," in French, Warren, ed. *Twenties: Fiction, Poetry, Drama.* DeLand, FL: Everett/Edwards, Inc., 1975. 215–233. Rpt. in Hayashi, Tesumaro, ed. *Steinbeck's Literary Dimension*, 43–44.

To Have and Have Not (1937)

Astro, Richard. "Phlebas Sails the Caribbean: Steinbeck, Hemingway, and the American Waste Land," in French, Warren, ed. *Twenties: Fiction, Poetry, Drama.* DeLand, FL: Everett/Edwards, Inc., 1975. 215–233. Rpt. in Hayashi, Tesumaro, ed. *Steinbeck's Literary Dimension*, 43–44.

Messent, Peter. *Ernest Hemingway*, 64–68.

Pressman, Richard S. "Individualists or Collectivists? Steinbeck's In Dubious Battle and Hemingway's *To Have and Have Not.*" *StQ* 25.3–4 (1992): 122–123, 127.

HÉMON, LOUIS (1880–1913)

Maria Chapdelaine (1916)

Chovrelat, Genevieve. "*Evangeline* et *Maria Chapdelaine*, soeurs mythiques de la survivance nationale ou soeurs de légende?" *ECCS* 37 (1994): 305–322.

Demers, Patricia. *Seasonal Romance: Louis Hémon's Maria Chapdelaine.* Toronto: ECW Press, 1993.

Fortin, Nicole. "Histoire de seconde main ou les auteurs québecois de *Maria Chapdelaine.*" *Tangence* 44 (1994): 32–55.

Shek, Ben-Z. *French-Canadian*, 16–19.

Smart, Patricia. *Writing in the Father's House*, 69–72, 84–88.

HENTZ, CAROLINE LEE (1800–1856)

Ernest Linwood (1856)

Goshgarian, G. M. *To Kiss the Chastening Rod*, 177–211.

Lovell's Folly (1833)

Bakker, Jan. "Twists of Sentiment in Antebellum Southern Romance." *SLJ* 26.1 (1993): 5–8, 12.

HERBERT, FRANK (1920–1986)

Children of Dune (1976)

Zeender, Marie-Noelle. " 'Moi-peau' of Leto II in Herbert's Atreides Saga." *SFS* 22.2 (1995): 226–231.

Dune (1963)

DiTommaso, Lorenzo. "History and Historical Effect in Frank Herbert's *Dune.*" *SFS* 19.3 (1992): 311–325.

Prieto-Pablos, Juan A. "Ambivalent Hero of Contemporary Fantasy and Science Fiction." *Extrapolation* 32.1 (1991): 66–68, 70, 72–73.

Dune Messiah (1972)

Prieto-Pablos, Juan A. "Ambivalent Hero of Contemporary Fantasy and Science Fiction." *Extrapolation* 32.1 (1991): 68–71.

God Emperor of Dune (1981)

Zeender, Marie-Noelle. " 'Moi-peau' of Leto II in Herbert's Atreides Saga." *SFS* 22.2 (1995): 231–232.

White Plague (1982)

Feehan, Ellen. "Frank Herbert and the Making of Myths: Irish History, Celtic Mythology, and IRA Ideology in *The White Plague*." *SFS* 19.3 (1992): 289–310.

HERBST, JOSEPHINE (1897–1969)

Rope of Gold (1939)

Hapke, Laura. *Daughters of the Great Depression*, 200–203.

HERR, MICHAEL (1940(?)–)

Dispatches (1977)

Ringnalda, Don. *Fighting and Writing*, 71–89.

HERSEY, JOHN (1914–)

Bell for Adano (1944)

Sanders, David. *John Hersey Revisited*, 8–12.

Call (1985)

Sanders, David. *John Hersey Revisited*, 92–100.

Child Buyer (1960)

Sanders, David. *John Hersey Revisited*, 54–61.

Conspiracy (1972)

Sanders, David. *John Hersey Revisited*, 84–87.

Marmut Drive (1953)

Sanders, David. *John Hersey Revisited*, 38–42.

My Petition for More Space (1974)

Sanders, David. *John Hersey Revisited*, 87–89.

Single Pebble (1956)

Sanders, David. *John Hersey Revisited*, 43–48.

Too Far to Walk (1966)

Sanders, David. *John Hersey Revisited*, 73–75.

Under the Eye of the Storm (1967)

Sanders, David. *John Hersey Revisited*, 75–78.

Wall (1950)

Sanders, David. *John Hersey Revisited*, 23–32.

Walnut Door (1977)

Sanders, David. *John Hersey Revisited*, 79–81.

White Lotus (1965)

Sanders, David. *John Hersey Revisited*, 62–71.

War Lover (1959)

Sanders, David. *John Hersey Revisited*, 49–54.

HEYWARD, DUBOSE (1885–1940)

Peter Ashley (1932)

Brown, Rosellen. "On DuBose Heyward's *Peter Ashley*," in Madden, David, ed. *Classics of Civil War Fiction*, 117–130.

Porgy (1925)

Rhodes, Chip. "Writing Up the New Negro: The Construction of Consumer Desire in the Twenties." *JACult* 28.2 (1994): 193–199.

HILDRETH, RICHARD (1807–1865)

Slave (1836)

Bentley, Nancy. "White Slaves: The Mulatto Hero in Antebellum Fiction." *AL* 65.3 (1993): 503, 508–514.

HILLERMAN, TONY (1925–)

Blessing Way (1970)

Roush, Jan. "Developing Art of Tony Hillerman." *WAL* 28.2 (1993): 104.

Dance Hall of the Dead (1973)

Engel, Leonard. "Landscape and Place in Tony Hillerman's Mysteries." *WAL* 28.2 (1993): 114–119.

Dark Wind (1982)

Erisman, Fred. "Tony Hillerman's Jim Chee and the Shaman's Dilemma." *LJHum* 17.1 (1991): 5–13.

Ghostway (1984)

Erisman, Fred. "Tony Hillerman's Jim Chee and the Shaman's Dilemma." *LJHum* 17.1 (1991): 5–13.

Roush, Jan. "Developing Art of Tony Hillerman." *WAL* 28.2 (1993): 105–106.

Listening Woman (1978)

Engel, Leonard. "Landscape and Place in Tony Hillerman's Mysteries." *WAL* 28.2 (1993): 119–121.

People of Darkness (1980)

Erisman, Fred. "Tony Hillerman's Jim Chee and the Shaman's Dilemma." *LJHum* 17.1 (1991): 5–13.

Skinwalkers (1986)

Erisman, Fred. "Tony Hillerman's Jim Chee and the Shaman's Dilemma." *LJHum* 17.1 (1991): 5–13.

Roush, Jan. "Developing Art of Tony Hillerman." *WAL* 28.2 (1993): 106–108.

Talking God (1989)

Roush, Jan. "Developing Art of Tony Hillerman." *WAL* 28.2 (1993): 108.

Thief of Time (1988)

Erisman, Fred. "Tony Hillerman's Jim Chee and the Shaman's Dilemma." *LJHum* 17.1 (1991): 5–13.

HIMES, CHESTER (1909–1984)

Big Gold Dream (1960)

Haut, Woody. *Pulp Culture*, 40–42.

Blind Man with a Pistol (1969)

Walters, Wendy W. "Limited Options: Strategic Maneuverings in Himes's Harlem." *AAR* 28.4 (1994): 622–626.

Heat's On (1961)

Haut, Woody. *Pulp Culture*, 42–46.

If He Hollers Let Him Go (1945)

Harris, Trudier. *Exorcising Blackness: Historical and Literary Lynching and Burning Rituals*. Bloomington: Indiana University Press, 1984. 53–55. Rpt. in Bloom, Harold, ed. *Modern Black American Fiction Writers*, 75–76.

Haut, Woody. *Pulp Culture*, 35–37.

Plan B (1994)

Walters, Wendy W. "Limited Options: Strategic Maneuverings in Himes's Harlem." *AAR* 28.4 (1994): 628–629.

Rage in Harlem (1957)

Haut, Woody. *Pulp Culture*, 38–40.

Real Cool Killers (1959)

Walters, Wendy W. "Limited Options: Strategic Maneuverings in Himes's Harlem." *AAR* 28.4 (1994): 615–622.

HINOJOSA, ROLANDO (1929–)

Becky and Her Friends (1990)

Sanchez, Rosaura. "Discourses of Gender, Ethnicity and Class in Chicano Literature." *AmRev* 20.2 (1992): 82–83.

Claros varones de Belken: Fair Gentlemen of Belken County (1986)

Hernández, Guillermo E. *Chicano Satire*, 89–90, 95–96, 98–101, 102–103.

Dear Rafa see *Mi querido Rafa*

Estampas del valle y otras obras (1973)

Hernández, Guillermo E. *Chicano Satire*, 87–89, 92–95, 96, 104.

Fair Gentleman of Belken County see *Claros varones de Belken*

Klail City y sus alrededores (1976)

Hernández, Guillermo E. *Chicano Satire*, 90, 91–94, 97–98, 101–102.

Mi querido Rafa (1981)

Hernández, Guillermo E. *Chicano Satire*, 104–110.

Partners in Crime (1985)

Hernández, Guillermo E. *Chicano Satire*, 97, 103.

Rites and Witnesses (1982)

Hernández, Guillermo E. *Chicano Satire*, 97, 99–100, 105, 107–108.

Sketches of the Valley see *Estampas del valle y otras obras*

HITCHCOCK, ENOS (1745–1803)

Farmer's Friend (1793)

Dunne, Robert. "Cultivating a Cultural Hybrid: A Consideration of *The Farmer's Friend*." *UDR* 21.1 (1991): 169–176.

HITCHENS, DOLORES (1908(?)–1973)

Sleep with Strangers (1956)

Haut, Woody. *Pulp Culture*, 119–124.

HOBAN, RUSSELL (1925–)

Riddley Walker (1980)

Granofsky, Ronald. *Trauma Novel*, 95–105.
Schwenger, Peter. "Circling Ground Zero." *PMLA* 106.2 (1991): 251–261.

HODGINS, JACK (1938–)

Honorary Patron (1987)

McCaig, Jo Ann. "Lines and Circles: Structure in *The Honorary Patron*." *CanL* 128 (1991): 65–75.

HOFFMAN, ALICE (1952–)

At Risk (1988)

Hogan, Katie. "Speculations on Women and AIDS." *MinnR* 40 (1993): 87–90.

HOGAN, LINDA (1947–)

Mean Spirit (1990)

Blair, Elizabeth. "Politics of Place in Linda Hogan's *Mean Spirit*." *SAIL* 6.3 (1994): 15–21.

Carew-Miller, Anna. "Caretaking and the Work of the Text in Linda Hogan's *Mean Spirit.*" *SAIL* 6.3 (1994): 37–48.
Casteel, Alix. "Dark Wealth in Linda Hogan's *Mean Spirit.*" *SAIL* 6.3 (1994): 49–68.
Musher, Andrea. "Showdown at Sorrow Cave: Bat Medicine and the Spirit of Resistance in *Mean Spirit.*" *SAIL* 6.3 (1994): 23–36.
St. Clair, Janet. "Fighting for Her Life: The Mixed-Blood Woman's Insistence upon Selfhood," in Fleck, Richard F., ed. *Critical Perspectives*, 47–52.
Steinberg, Marc H. "Linda Hogan's *Mean Spirit:* The Wealth, Value, and Worth of the Osage Tribe." *NConL* 25.2 (1995): 7–8.

HOLLERAN, ANDREW (1943(?)–)

Dancer from the Dance (1978)

Koponen, Wilfrid R. *Embracing Gay Identity*, 99–117.

Nights in Aruba (1981)

Bergman, David. *Gaiety Transfigured*, 188–192.

HOLMES, MARY JANE (1825–1907)

Lena Rivers (1856)

Goshgarian, G. M. *To Kiss the Chastening Rod*, 172–177.

HOOKER, FORRESTINE COOPER (1867–1932)

Long, Dim Trail (1920)

Yates, Norris. *Gender and Genre*, 121–125.

HOPKINS, PAULINE E. (1859–1930)

Contending Forces (1900)

Ammons, Elizabeth. *Conflicting Stories*, 77–81.
Campbell, Jane. "Female Paradigms in Frances Harper's *Iola Leroy* and Pauline Hopkin's *Contending Forces.*" *Mythic Black Fiction: The Transformation of History.* Knoxville: University of Tennessee Press, 1986. 39–40. Rpt. in Bloom, Harold, ed. *Black American Women Fiction Writers*, 47–48.
Carby, Hazel V. *Reconstructing Womanhood: The Emergence of the Afro-American Woman Novelist.* New York: Oxford University Press, 1987. 143–144. Rpt. in Bloom, Harold, ed. *Black American Women Fiction Writers*, 49–50.
Scruggs, Charles. *Sweet Home*, 34–35.
Tate, Claudia. "Allegories of Black Female Desire; or, Rereading Nineteenth-Century Sentimental Narratives of Black Female Authority." *Changing Our Own Words: Essays on Criticism, Theory, and Writing by Black Women.* Ed. Cheryl A. Wall. New Brunswick, NJ: Rutgers University Press, 1989. 122–123. Rpt. in Bloom, Harold, ed. *Black American Women Fiction Writers*, 51–53.

Hagar's Daughter (1902)

Bruce, Dickson D., Jr. *Black American Writing from the Nadir: The Evolution of Literary Tradition 1977–1915.* Baton Rouge: Louisiana State University Press,

1989. 150–151. Rpt. in Bloom, Harold, ed. *Black American Women Fiction Writers*, 50–51.

Pamplin, Claire. " 'Race' and Identity in Pauline Hopkin's *Hagar's Daughter*," in Harris, Sharon M., ed. *Redefining the Political Novel*, 169–182.

Of One Blood (1903)

Ammons, Elizabeth. *Conflicting Stories*, 81–84.

Ammons, Elizabeth. "Limits of Freedom: The Fiction of Alice Dunbar-Nelson, Kate Chopin, and Pauline Hopkins." *Conflicting Stories: American Women Writers at the Turn into the Twentieth Century.* New York: Oxford University Press, 1991. 83–85. Rpt. in Bloom, Harold, ed. *Black American Women Fiction Writers*, 53–54.

Gillman, Susan. "The Mulatto, Tragic or Triumphant? The Nineteenth-Century American Race Melodrama," in Samuels, Shirley, ed. *Culture of Sentiment*, 231–236

Otten, Thomas J. "Pauline Hopkins and the Hidden Self of Race." *ELH* 59.1 (1992): 227–256.

Winona (1902)

Tate, Claudia. "Pauline Hopkins: Our Literary Foremother." Pryse, Marjorie, ed. *Conjuring: Black Women, Fiction, and Literary Tradition.* Ed. Marjorie Pryse and Hortense J. Spillers. Bloomington, IN: Indiana University Press, 1985. 60–61. Rpt. in Bloom, Harold, ed. *Black American Women Fiction Writers*, 46–47.

HOSPITAL, JANETTE TURNER (1942–)

Borderline (1985)

Schramm, Margaret K. "Identity and the Family in the Novels of Janette Turner Hospital," in Pearlman, Mickey, ed. *Canadian Women*, 89–92.

Charades (1989)

Schramm, Margaret K. "Identity and the Family in the Novels of Janette Turner Hospital," in Pearlman, Mickey, ed. *Canadian Women*, 92–94.

Ivory Swing (1982)

Huggan, Graham. "Orientalism Reconfirmed? Stereotypes of East-West Encounter in Janette Turner Hospital's *The Ivory Swing* and Yvon Rivard's *Les Silences du corbeau.*" *CanL* 132 (1992): 44–55.

Schramm, Margaret K. "Identity and the Family in the Novels of Janette Turner Hospital," in Pearlman, Mickey, ed. *Canadian Women*, 85–87.

Last Magician (1992)

Schramm, Margaret K. "Identity and the Family in the Novels of Janette Turner Hospital," in Pearlman, Mickey, ed. *Canadian Women*, 94–96.

Tiger in the Tiger Pit (1983)

Schramm, Margaret K. "Identity and the Family in the Novels of Janette Turner Hospital," in Pearlman, Mickey, ed. *Canadian Women*, 87–89.

HOUDE, NICOLE (1945–)

La maison du remous (1986)

Saint-Martin, Lori. "*La maison du remous* de Nicole Houde, ou le roman de la terre au féminin." *QS* 17 (1993–94): 187–199.

HOWARD, MAUREEN (1930–)

Bridgeport Bus (1965)

Ward, Catherine. "Wake Homes: Four Modern Novels of the Irish-American Family." *Eire* 26.2 (1991): 83–85.

HOWELLS, WILLIAM DEAN (1837–1920)

Boy's Town (1890)

Jacobson, Marcia. *Being a Boy Again*, 73–86.

Chance Acquaintance (1873)

Daugherty, Sarah B. "The Ideology of Gender in Howells' Early Novels." *ALR* 25.1 (1992): 8.

Fennel and Rue (1908)

Prioleau, Elizabeth S. "William Dean Howells and the Seductress: From Femme Fatale to Femme Vitale." *HLB* 3.1 (1992): 65–67.

Flight of Pony Baker (1902)

Jacobson, Marcia. *Being a Boy Again*, 86–96.

Forgone Conclusion (1875)

Daugherty, Sarah B. "The Ideology of Gender in Howells' Early Novels." *ALR* 25.1 (1992): 8–10.

Hazard of New Fortunes (1890)

McBride, Christopher. "Howells's *A Hazard of New Fortunes*." *Expl* 53.1 (1994): 37–38.

Parrish, Timothy L. "Haymarket and Hazard: The Lonely Politics of William Dean Howells." *JACult* 17.4 (1994): 23–32.

Parrish, Timothy L. "Howells Untethered: The Dean and 'Diversity.' " *SAF* 23.1 (1995): 101–117.

Peyser, Thomas Galt. "Those Other Selves: Consciousness in the 1890 Publications of Howells and the James Brothers." *ALR* 25.1 (1992): 21–26.

Imperative Duty (1891)

McLendon, Jacquelyn. *Politics of Color*, 17–22.

Wonham, Henry B. "Writing Realism, Policing Consciouness: Howells and the Black Body." *AL* 67.4 (1995): 701–724.

Kentons (1902)

Pattison, Eugene H. "Landscape and the Sense of the Past in William Dean Howell's *The Kentons*." *Midamerica* 20 (1993): 48–58.

Lady of Aroostook (1879)

Crowley, John W. "Paradigms of Addiction in Howells' Novels." *ALR* 25.3 (1993): 4–5.

Daugherty, Sarah B. "The Ideology of Gender in Howells' Early Novels." *ALR* 25.1 (1992): 15–16.

Landlord of Lion's Head (1897)

Crowley, John W. "Paradigms of Addiction in Howells' Novels." *ALR* 25.3 (1993): 6–13.

Haralson, Eric. "Romancing the Beast: Howells' *The Landlord at Lion's Head.*" *ALR* 25.3 (1993): 42–59.

Prioleau, Elizabeth S. "William Dean Howells and the Seductress: From Femme Fatale to Femme Vitale." *HLB* 3.1 (1992): 60–62.

Leatherwood God (1916)

Jones, Joel. "Howells's *The Leatherwood God:* The Model in Method for the American Historical Novel." *Expl* 51.2 (1993): 96–103.

Prioleau, Elizabeth S. "William Dean Howells and the Seductress: From Femme Fatale to Femme Vitale." *HLB* 3.1 (1992): 67–70.

Miss Bellard's Inspiration (1905)

Prioleau, Elizabeth S. "William Dean Howells and the Seductress: From Femme Fatale to Femme Vitale." *HLB* 3.1 (1992): 64–65.

Modern Instance (1882)

Crowley, John W. "Paradigms of Addiction in Howells' Novels." *ALR* 25.3 (1993): 5–6.

Private Theatricals (1876)

Daugherty, Sarah B. "The Ideology of Gender in Howells' Early Novels." *ALR* 25.1 (1992): 10–15.

Prioleau, Elizabeth S. "William Dean Howells and the Seductress: From Femme Fatale to Femme Vitale." *HLB* 3.1 (1992): 53–59.

Rise of Silas Lapham (1885)

Bonnell, Marilyn. "Howell's *The Rise of Silas Lapham.*" *Expl* 49.2 (1991): 97–99.

Bové, Paul A. "Helpless Longing, or, the Lesson of Silas Lapham," in Pease, Donald, ed. *New Essays*, 29–45.

Carter, Everett. "Realists and Jews." *SAF* 22.1 (1994): 85–87.

Cox, James M. "*Rise of Silas Lapham:* The Business of Morals and Manners," in Pease, Donald, ed. *New Essays*, 107–128.

Dimock, Wai-Chee. "Economy of Pain: Capitalism, Humanitarianism, and the Realistic Novel," in Pease, Donald, ed. *New Essays*, 67–90.

Eby, Clare Virginia. "Compromise and Complicity in *The Rise of Silas Lapham.*" *ALR* 24.1 (1991): 39–53.

O'hara, Daniel T. "Smiling Through Pain: The Practice of Self in *The Rise of Silas Lapham,*" in Pease, Donald, ed. *New Essays*, 91–105.

Seelye, John. "Hole in Howells / The Lapse in *Silas Lapham,*" in Pease, Donald, ed. *New Essays*, 47–65.

Young, Arlene. "Triumph of Irony in *The Rise Silas Lapham.*" *SAF* 20.1 (1992): 45–55.

Shadow of a Dream (1890)

Prioleau, Elizabeth S. "William Dean Howells and the Seductress: From Femme Fatale to Femme Vitale." *HLB* 3.1 (1992): 59–60.

Son of Royal Langbirth (1904)

Prioleau, Elizabeth S. "William Dean Howells and the Seductress: From Femme Fatale to Femme Vitale." *HLB* 3.1 (1992): 64.

Story of a Play (1891)

Prioleau, Elizabeth S. "William Dean Howells and the Seductress: From Femme Fatale to Femme Vitale." *HLB* 3.1 (1992): 62–63.

Their Wedding Journey (1872)

Carter, Everett. "Realists and Jews." *SAF* 22.1 (1994): 85.

Daugherty, Sarah B. "The Ideology of Gender in Howells' Early Novels." *ALR* 25.1 (1992): 5–7.

World of Chance (1892)

Daugherty, Sarah B. " 'The Dream of Duty Tormenting Us All': *The World of Chance* and the Decline of Realism." *HLB* 5.1 (1994): 45–52.

HUGHES, DOROTHY B. (1904–1993)

In a Lonely Place (1947)

Haut, Woody. *Pulp Culture*, 124–130.

HUMPHREYS, JOSEPHINE (1945–)

Dreams of Sleep (1984)

Griffith, Michael A. " 'A Deal for the Real World': Josephine Humphreys's *Dreams of Sleep* and the New Domestic Novel." *SLJ* 26.1 (1993): 94–108.

Irons, Susan H. "Josephine Humphreys's *Dreams of Sleep:* Revising Walker Percy's Male Gaze." *MissQ* 47.2 (1994): 287–300.

McKee, Kathryn B. "Rewriting Southern Male Introspection in Josephine Humphreys' *Dreams of Sleep*." *MissQ* 46.2 (1993): 241–254.

Walker, Elinor Ann. " 'Go with What Is Most Terrifying': Reinventing Domestic Space in Josephine Humphrey's *Dreams of Sleep*." *SLitI* 27.2 (1994): 87–104.

Rich in Love (1987)

Jackson, Shelley M. "Josephine Humphreys and the Politics of Postmodern Desire." *MissQ* 47.2 (1994): 275–285.

Walker, Elinor Ann. "Josephine Humphreys's *Rich in Love:* Redefining Southern Fiction." *MissQ* 47.2 (1994): 301–315.

HURST, FANNIE (1889–1968)

Back Street (1931)

Hapke, Laura. *Daughters of the Great Depression*, 120–124.

HURSTON, ZORA NEALE (1891–1960)

Jonah's Gourd Vine (1934)

Brown, Alan. " 'De Beast' Within: The Role of Nature in *Jonah's Gourd Vine*," in Glassman, Steve, ed. *Zora in Florida*, 76–85.

Holloway, Karla. "Emergent Voice: The Word Within Its Texts," in Gates, Henry Louis, Jr., ed. *Zora Neale Hurston*, 69–70.

Karanja, Ayana. "Zora Neale Hurston and Alice Walker: A Transcendent Relationship—*Jonah's Gourd Vine* and *The Color Purple*," in Howard, Lillie P., ed. *Alice Walker and Zora Neale Hurston*, 121–128.

Lowe, John. *Jump at the Sun*, 85–148.

Saunders, James Robert. *Wayward Preacher*, 43–69.

Speisman, Barbara. "Voodoo as Symbol in *Jonah's Gourd Vine*," in Glassman, Steve, ed. *Zora in Florida*, 86–92.

Stanford, Ann Folwell. "Dynamics of Change: Men and Co-Feeling in the Fiction of Zora Neale Hurston and Alice Walker," in Howard, Lillie P., ed. *Alice Walker and Zora Neale Hurston*, 111–114.

Sundquist, Eric J. " 'Drum with the Man Skin': *Jonah's Gourd Vine*," in Gates, Henry Louis, Jr., ed. *Zora Neale Hurston*, 39–66.

Sundquist, Eric J. *Hammer of Creation*, 49–91.

Wall, Cheryl A. "Zora Neale Hurston: Changing Her Own Words," in Gates, Henry Louis, Jr., ed. *Zora Neale Hurston*, 84–89.

Washington, Mary Helen. " 'I Love the Way Janie Crawford Left Her Husbands': Emergent Female Hero," in Gates, Henry Louis, Jr., ed. *Zora Neale Hurston*, 98, 103–105, 106–107.

Wilson, Mary Ann. " 'That Which the Soul Lives By': Spirituality in the Works of Zora Neale Hurston and Alice Walker," in Howard, Lillie P., ed. *Alice Walker and Zora Neale Hurston*, 59–60.

Moses, Man of the Mountain (1939)

Holloway, Karla. "Emergent Voice: The Word Within Its Texts," in Gates, Henry Louis, Jr., ed. *Zora Neale Hurston*, 71–72.

Lowe, John. *Jump at the Sun*, 203–250.

McDowell, Deborah E. "Lines of Descent/Dissenting Lines," in Gates, Henry Louis, Jr., ed. *Zora Neale Hurston*, 232–240.

Plant, Deborah G. *Every Tub*, 124–142.

Stanford, Ann Folwell. "Dynamics of Change: Men and Co-Feeling in the Fiction of Zora Neale Hurston and Alice Walker," in Howard, Lillie P., ed. *Alice Walker and Zora Neale Hurston*, 114–115.

Wall, Cheryl A. "Zora Neale Hurston: Changing Her Own Words," in Gates, Henry Louis, Jr., ed. *Zora Neale Hurston*, 93–95.

Seraph on the Suwanee (1948)

Holloway, Karla. "Emergent Voice: The Word Within Its Texts," in Gates, Henry Louis, Jr., ed. *Zora Neale Hurston*, 73–74.

Howard, Lillie. "*Seraph on the Suwanee,*" in Gates, Henry Louis, Jr., ed. *Zora Neale Hurston*, 267–279.

Lowe, John. *Jump at the Sun*, 259–334.

Wall, Cheryl A. "Zora Neale Hurston: Changing Her Own Words," in Gates, Henry Louis, Jr., ed. *Zora Neale Hurston*, 95–96.

Their Eyes Were Watching God (1937)

Ashe, Bertram D. " 'Why Don't He Like My Hair?': Constructing African-American Standards of Beauty in Toni Morrison's *Song of Solomon* and Zora Neale Hurston's *Their Eyes Were Watching God*." *AAR* 29.4 (1995): 581–585.

Babb, Valerie. "Women and Words: Articulating the Self in *Their Eyes Were Watching God* and *The Color Purple*," in Howard, Lillie P., ed. *Alice Walker and Zora Neale Hurston*, 83–89.

Bauer, Margaret D. "Sterile New South: An Intertextual Reading of *Their Eyes Were Watching God* and *Absalom, Absalom!*" *CLAJ* 36.4 (1993): 384–405.

Bond, Cynthia. "Language, Speech, and Difference in *Their Eyes Were Watching God*," in Gates, Henry Louis, Jr., ed. *Zora Neale Hurston*, 204–217.

Brigham, Cathy. "Talking Frame of Zora Neale Hurston's Talking Book: Storytelling as Dialectic in *Their Eyes Were Watching God.*" *CLAJ* 37.4 (1994): 402–419.

Brown, Sterling A. " 'Luck Is a Fortune.' " *Nation* (16 October 1937): 409–410. Rpt. in Bloom, Harold, ed. *Major Black American Writers Through the Harlem Renaissance*, 104–105.

Cassidy, Thomas. "Janie's Rage: The Dog and the Storm in *Their Eyes Were Watching God.*" *CLAJ* 36.3 (1993): 260–269.

Chinn, Nancy. "Like Love, 'A Moving Thing': Janie's Search for Self and God in *Their Eyes Were Watching God.*" *SoAR* 60.1 (1995): 77–95.

Cornwell, JoAnne. "Searching For Zora in Alice's Garden: Rites of Passage in Hurston's *Their Eyes Were Watching God* and Walker's *The Third Life of Grange Copeland*," in Howard, Lillie P., ed. *Alice Walker and Zora Neale Hurston*, 97–103.

Curren, Erik D. "Should Their Eyes Have Been Watching God?: Hurston's Use of Religious Experience and Gothic Horror." *AAR* 29.1 (1995): 17–25

Dalgarno, Emily. " 'Words Walking without Masters': Ethnography and the Creative Process in *Their Eyes Were Watching God.*" *AL* 64.3 (1992): 519–541.

Daniel, Janice. " 'De Understandin' to Go 'Long Wid It': Realism and Romance in *Their Eyes Were Watching God.*" *SLJ* 24.1 (1991): 66–76.

Davie, Sharon. "Free Mules, Talking Buzzards, and Cracked Plates: The Politics of Dislocation in *Their Eyes Were Watching God.*" *PMLA* 108.3 (1993): 446–459.

Davies, Kathleen. "Zora Neale Hurston's Poetics of Embalmment: Articulating the Rage of Black Women and Narrative Self-Defense." *AAR* 26.1 (1992): 147–158.

Dawson, Emma J. Waters. "Redemption Through Redemption of Self in *Their Eyes Were Watching God* and *The Color Purple*," in Howard, Lillie P., ed. *Alice Walker and Zora Neale Hurston*, 69–77.

Fannin, Alice. "Sense of Wonder: The Pattern for Psychic Survival in *Their Eyes Were Watching God* and *The Color Purple.*" *Zora Neale Hurston Forum* 1.1 (1986): 1–11. Rpt. in Howard, Lillie P., ed. *Alice Walker and Zora Neale Hurston*, 45–52.

Gates, Henry Louis, Jr. "*Their Eyes Were Watching God:* Hurston and the Speakerly Text," in Gates, Henry Louis, Jr., ed. *Zora Neale Hurston*, 164–203.

Hapke, Laura. *Daughters of the Great Depression*, 134–141.

Hattenhauer, Darryl. "Hurston's *Their Eyes Were Watching God.*" *Expl* 50.2 (1992): 111–112.

Holloway, Karla F. C. *Character of the Word: The Texts of Zora Neale Hurston.* Wesport, CT: Greenwood Press, 1987. 39–40. Rpt. in Bloom, Harold, ed. *Black American Women Fiction Writers*, 67–69.

Holloway, Karla F. C. *Character of the Word: The Texts of Zora Neale Hurston.* Wesport, CT: Greenwood Press, 1987. 39–40. Rpt. in Bloom, Harold, ed. *Major Black American Writers Through the Harlem Renaissance*, 113–115.

Holloway, Karla. "Emergent Voice: The Word Within Its Texts," in Gates, Henry Louis, Jr., ed. *Zora Neale Hurston*, 70–71.

Hubbard, Dolan. " '. . . Ah Said Ah'd Save de Text for You': Recontextualizing the Sermon to Tell (Her)Story in Zora Neale Hurston's *Their Eyes Were Watching God.*" *AAR* 27.2 (1993): 167–177.

Jordan, Jennifer. "Feminist Fantasies: Zora Neale Hurston's *Their Eyes Were Watching God.*" *Tulsa Studies in Women's Literature* 7.1 (1988): 106–107, 115. Rpt. in Bloom, Harold, ed. *Black American Women Fiction Writers*, 69–70.

Kaplan, Carla. "Erotics of Talk: 'That Oldest Human Longing' in *Their Eyes Were Watching God.*" *AL* 67.1 (1995): 115–142.
Kubitschek, Missy Dehn. *Claiming the Heritage*, 52–68.
Lowe, John. *Jump at the Sun*, 156–198.
McKay, Nellie. " 'Crayon Enlargements of Life': Zora Neale Hurston's *Their Eyes Were Watching God* as Autobiography." *New Essays on Their Eyes Were Watching God.* Ed. Michael Awkward. New York: Cambridge University Press, 1990. 68–69. Rpt. in Bloom, Harold, ed. *Black American Women Fiction Writers*, 70–71.
Morgan, Kathleen. " 'An Ox upon the Tongue': An Allusion to Aeschylus' *Agamemnon* in Zora Neale Hurston's *Their Eyes Were Watching God.*" *CML* 15.1 (1994): 57–65.
Racine, Maria J. "Voice and Interiority in Zora Neale Hurston's *Their Eyes Were Watching God.*" *AAR* 28.2 (1994): 283–292.
Ramsey, William M. "Compelling Ambivalence of Zora Neale Hurston's *Their Eyes Were Watching God.*" *SLJ* 27.1 (1994): 36–50.
Sheppard, David M. "Living by Comparisons: Janie and Her Discontents." *ELN* 30.2 (1992): 63–74.
Spillers, Hortense J. "Hateful Passion, a Lost Love," in Gates, Henry Louis, Jr., ed. *Toni Morrison*, 220–225.
Tate, Linda. *Southern Weave of Women*, 15–18.
Urgo, Joseph R. " 'The Tune Is the Unity of the Thing': Power and Vulnerability in Zora Neale Hurston's *Their Eyes Were Watching God.*" *SLJ* 23.2 (1991): 40–54.
Vickers, Anita M. "Reaffirmation of African-American Dignity through the Oral Tradition in Zora Neale Hurston's *Their Eyes Were Watching God.*" *CLAJ* 37.3 (1994): 303–315.
Walker, S. Jay. "Zora Neale Hurston's *Their Eyes Were Watching God:* Black Novel of Sexism." *Modern Fiction Studies* 20.4 (1974–75): 520–521. Rpt. in Bloom, Harold, ed. *Black American Women Fiction Writers*, 64–65.
Walker, S. Jay. "Zora Neale Hurston's *Their Eyes Were Watching God:* Black Novel of Sexism." *Modern Fiction Studies* 20.4 (1974–75): 520–521. Rpt. in Bloom, Harold, ed. *Major Black American Writers Through the Harlem Renaissance*, 110–111.
Wall, Cheryl A. "Zora Neale Hurston: Changing Her Own Words," in Gates, Henry Louis, Jr., ed. *Zora Neale Hurston*, 89–93.
Wall, Cheryl A. *Women of the Harlem Renaissance*, 179–195.
Washington, Mary Helen. " 'I Love the Way Janie Crawford Left Her Husbands': Emergent Female Hero," in Gates, Henry Louis, Jr., ed. *Zora Neale Hurston*, 98–103, 105–107.
Willis, Susan. "Wandering: Hurston's Search for Self and Method," in Gates, Henry Louis, Jr., ed. *Zora Neale Hurston*, 114–115, 123–127.
Wilson, Mary Ann. " 'That Which the Soul Lives By': Spirituality in the Works of Zora Neale Hurston and Alice Walker," in Howard, Lillie P., ed. *Alice Walker and Zora Neale Hurston*, 58, 61–63.
Wolff, Maria Tai. "Listening and Living: Reading and Experience in *Their Eyes Were Watching God*," in Gates, Henry Louis, Jr., ed. *Zora Neale Hurston*, 218–229.
Wright, Lee Alfred. *Identity, Family, and Folklore*, 51–56.

HUSTON, NANCY (1953–)

La virevolte (1994)

Fortier, Frances. “La Vie chorégraphiee.” *Tangence* 47 (1995): 125–127.

Slow Emergencies see *La virevolte*

INDIANA, GARY

Horse Crazy (1989)

Young, Elizabeth. *Shopping in Space*, 212–216.

INGALLS, RACHEL (1940–)

Binstead's Safari (1983)

Macdonald, Alan. “Re-Writing Hemingway: Rachel Ingalls's *Binstead's Safari*.” *Crit* 34.3 (1993): 165–170.

IRVING, JOHN (1942–)

Hotel New Hampshire (1981)

Shostak, Debra. “Family Romances of John Irving.” *ELWIU* 21.1 (1994): 129–145.

Prayer for Owen Meaney (1989)

Grenier, Donald J. *Women Enter the Wilderness*, 67–75.

Page, Philip. “Hero Worship and Hermeneutic Dialectics: John Irving's *A Prayer for Owen Meany*.” *Mosaic* 28.3 (1995): 137–156.

Shostak, Debra. “Plot as Repetition: John Irving's Narrative Experiments.” *Crit* 37.1 (1995): 54, 61–69.

World according to Garp (1978)

McKay, Kim. “Double Discourse in John Irving's *The World according to Garp*.” *TCL* 38.4 (1992): 457–475.

Shostak, Debra. “Plot as Repetition: John Irving's Narrative Experiments.” *Crit* 37.1 (1995): 54–61, 68–69.

Wilson, Raymond J., III. “Postmodern Novel: The Example of John Irving's *The World according to Garp*.” *Crit* 34.1 (1992): 49–62.

IRWIN, ANN see IRWIN, HADLEY

IRWIN, HADLEY (pseudonym of Lee Hadley and Ann Irwin)

So Long at the Fair (1988)

Apseloff, Marilyn Fain. “Death in Adolescent Literature: Suicide.” *CLAQ* 16.4 (1991–92): 235–236, 237–238.

ISLAS, ARTURO (1938–1991)

Migrant Souls (1990)

Marquez, Antonio C. “Historical Imagination in Arturo Islas's *The Rain God* and *Migrant Souls*.” *MELUS* 19.2 (1994): 3–15.

Sánchez, Rosaura. "Discourses of Gender, Ethnicity and Class in Chicano Literature." *AmRev* 20.2 (1992): 83–84.

Rain God (1984)

Marquez, Antonio C. "Historical Imagination in Arturo Islas's *The Rain God* and *Migrant Souls*." *MELUS* 19.2 (1994): 3–15.

Sánchez, Rosaura. "Ideological Discourses in Arturo Islas's *The Rain God*," in Calderón, Héctor, ed. *Criticism in the Borderlands*, 114–126.

JACKSON, HELEN HUNT (1830–1885)

Hetty's Strange History (1877)

Schmudde, Carol E. "Sincerity, Secrecy, and Lies: Helen Hunt Jackson's No Name Novels." *SAF* 21.1 (1993): 51–63.

Mercy Philbrick's Choice (1876)

Schmudde, Carol E. "Sincerity, Secrecy, and Lies: Helen Hunt Jackson's No Name Novels." *SAF* 21.1 (1993): 51–63.

JACKSON, SHIRLEY (1916–1965)

Haunting of Hill House (1959)

Lootens, Tricia. " 'Whose Hand Was I Holding?': Familial and Sexual Politics In Shirley Jackson's *The Haunting of Hill House*," in Carpenter, Lynette, ed. *Haunting the House of Fiction*, 166–191.

Road through the Wall (1948)

Hall, Joan Wylie. "Fallen Eden in Shirley Jackson's *The Road through the Wall*." *Renascence* 46.4 (1994): 261–270.

JAKES, JOHN (1932–)

Six-Gun Planet (1970)

Davis, Robert Murray. *Playing Cowboys*, 103–106.

JAMES, C. L. R. (1901–1989)

Minty Alley (1936)

Murdoch, H. Adlai. "James's Literary Dialectic: Colonialism and Cultural Space in *Minty Alley*," in Cudjoe, Selwyn R, ed. *C.L.R. James*, 61–71.

Paul-Emile, Barbara. "Gender Dynamics in James's *Minty Alley*," in Cudjoe, Selwyn R, ed. *C.L.R. James*, 72–78.

JAMES, HENRY (1843–1916)

Ambassadors (1903)

Bell, Millicent. *Meaning in Henry James*, 324–353.

Dalton, Elizabeth. "Recognition and Renunciation in *The Ambassadors*." *PR* 59.3 (1992): 457–468.

Garcia, Claire Oberon. " 'Native-Expatriate' Reads Henry James." *HJR* 16.3 (1995): 299–303.

Garcia, Claire Oberon. "Shopper and the Shopper's Friend: Lambert Strether and Maria Gostrey's Consumer Consciousness." *HJR* 16.2 (1995): 153–171.

Hollahan, Eugene. *Crisis-Consciousness*, 118–126.

Levenson, Michael. *Modernism and the Fate of Individuality*, 13–37, 58–63, 67–77.

Lustig, T. J. *Henry James and the Ghostly*, 194–216.

Menton, Allen W. "Typical Tales of Paris: The Function of Reading in *The Ambassadors*." *HJR* 15.3 (1994): 286–300.

Person, Leland S., Jr. "Henry James, George Sand, and the Suspense of Masculinity." *PMLA* 106.3 (1991): 522–526..

Salmon, Richard. "Secret of the Spectacle: Epistemology and Commodity Display in *The Ambassadors*." *HJR* 14.1 (1993): 43–54.

van Rosevelt, Jan. "Dining with *The Ambassadors*." *HJR* 15.3 (1994): 301–308.

Walker, Pierre A. "Reading the Berne Bears in the End of James's *The Ambassadors*." *MLS* 22.2 (1992): 4–14.

Wutz, Michael. "Word and the Self in *The Ambassadors*." *Style* 25.1 (1991): 89–103.

Yeo, Kyung-woo. " 'Virtuous Attachment' as a Basic Structure in *The Ambassadors*." *JELL* 37.4 (1991): 929–938.

American (1877)

Haralson, Eric. "James's *The American:* A (New)man Is Being Beaten." *AL* 64.3 (1992): 475–495.

Hobbs, Michael. "Reading Newman Reading: Textuality and Possession in *The American*." *HJR* 13.2 (1992): 115–125.

Saum, Lewis O. "Henry James's Christopher Newman: *The American* as Westerner." *HJR* 15.1 (1994): 1–9.

Shackelford, Lynne P. "Forsaking the Bridal Veil: Henry James's Allusion to Correggio's *The Marriage of St. Catherine* in *The American*." *HJR* 13.1 (1992): 78–81.

Sherfick, Kathleen A. "Claire de Cintre in Henry James's *The American* and St. Clare of Assisi." *HJR* 12.2 (1991): 117–119.

Steele, Elizabeth. "Chaucer and Henry James: Surprising Bedfellows." *HJR* 13.2 (1992): 126–142.

Torsney, Cheryl B. "Henry James, Charles Sanders Pierce, and the Fat Capon: Homoerotic Desire in *The American*." *HJR* 14.2 (1993): 166–178.

Weber, Donald. "Outsiders and Greenhorns: Christopher Newman in the Old World, David Levinsky in the New." *AL* 67.4 (1995): 727–732.

Aspern Papers (1888)

Richards, Bernard. "How Many Children Had Juliana Bordereau?" *HJR* 12.2 (1991): 120–128.

Awkward Age (1899)

Carter, Everett. "Realists and Jews." *SAF* 22.1 (1994): 87.

Bostonians (1886)

Bell, Ian F. A. *Henry James and the Past*, 61–144.

Bell, Millicent. *Meaning in Henry James*, 123–151.

Boudreau, Kristin. "Narrative Sympathy in *The Bostonians*." *HJR* 14.1 (1993): 17–33.

Bowen, Jane Wolf. "Architectural Envy: 'A Figure Is Nothing without a Setting' in Henry James's *The Bostonians*." *NEQ* 65.1 (1992): 3–23.

Chandler, Katherine R. "Purchase of Power: The Conclusion of *The Bostonians*." *ELN* 32.3 (1995): 46–54.

Dimock, Wai Chee. "Gender, the Market, and the Non-Trivial in James." *HJR* 15.1 (1994): 24–30.

Edwards, J. A. Craig. "James's *The Bostonians*." *Expl* 49.2 (1991): 100–101.

Levander, Caroline Field. "Bawdy Talk: The Politics of Women's Public Speech in *The Lecturess* and *The Bostonians*." *AL* 67.3 (1995): 476–483.

Limon, John. *Writing After War*, 42–49.

Mizruchi, Susan L. "Reproducing Women in *The Awkward Age*." *Representations* 38 (1992): 101–130.

Scheiber, Andrew J. "Eros, Art, and Ideology in *The Bostonians*." *HJR* 13.3 (1992): 235–252.

Scott, Anthony. "Basil, Olive, and Verena: *The Bostonians* and the Problem of Politics." *ArQ* 49.1 (1993): 49–72.

Shaw, Peter. *Recovering American Literature*, 127–150.

Thomas, Brook. "Construction of Privacy in and around *The Bostonians*." *AL* 64.4 (1992): 719–747.

Europeans (1878)

Bell, Ian F. A. *Henry James and the Past*, 145–205.

Petitjean, Tom. "James's *The Europeans*." *Expl* 52.3 (1994): 155–157.

Raguet-Bouvart, Christine. "Representations of Nature in Henry James's *The Europeans*." *IFR* 19.1 (1992): 1–7.

Golden Bowl (1904)

Alberti, John. "Economics of Love: The Production of Value in *The Golden Bowl*." *HJR* 12.1 (1991): 9–19.

Ash, Beth Sharon. "Narcissism and the Gilded Image: A Psychoanalytic Reading of *The Golden Bowl*." *HJR* 15.1 (1994): 55–90.

Carter, Everett. "Realists and Jews." *SAF* 22.1 (1994): 87–90.

Caws, Mary Ann. "What Can a Woman Do for the Late Henry James?" *Raritan* 14.1 (1994): 1–17.

Grossman, Julie. " 'It's the Real Thing': Henry James, Photography, and *The Golden Bowl*." *HJR* 15.3 (1994): 309–328.

Smith, Irena Auerbuch. "Golden Goal: Toward a Dialogic Imagination in Henry James's Last Completed Novel." *HJR* 16.2 (1995): 172–190.

Stevens, Hugh. "Sexuality and the Aesthetic in *The Golden Bowl*." *HJR* 14.1 (1993): 55–71.

Torsney, Cheryl B. "Specula(riza)tion in *The Golden Bowl*." *HJR* 12.2 (1991): 141–146.

van Slyck, Phyllis. " 'An Innate Preference for the Represented Subject': Portraiture and Knowledge in *The Golden Bowl*." *HJR* 15.2 (1994): 179–189.

Walton, Priscilla L. " 'A Mistress of Shades': Maggie as Reviser in *The Golden Bowl*." *HJR* 13.2 (1992): 143–153.

Zwinger, Lynda. *Daughters, Fathers, and the Novel*, 76–95.

In the Cage (1879)

Gabler-Hover, Janet. "Ethics of Determinism in Henry James's *In the Cage*." *HJR* 13.3 (1992): 253–275.

Veeder, William. "Toxic Mothers, Cultural Criticism: *In the Cage* and Elsewhere." *HJR* 14.3 (1994): 264–272.

Portrait of a Lady (1881)

Andres, Sophia. "Narrative Instability in *The Portrait of a Lady:* Isabel on the Edge of the Social." *JNT* 24.1 (1994): 43–54.

Auchincloss, Louis. *Reading Henry James.* Minneapolis: University of Minnesota Press, 1975. 56–70. Rpt. in James, Henry. *Portrait of a Lady*, 720–728.

Baris, Sharon. "Gender, Judgment, and Presumptuous Readers: The Role of Daniel in *The Portrait of a Lady*." *HJR* 12.3 (1991): 212–230.

Baris, Sharon. "James's Pyrotechnic Display: The Book in Isabel's Portrait." *HJR* 12.2 (1991): 146–153.

Bell, Millicent. *Meaning in Henry James*, 80–122.

Bell, Millicent. *Meaning in Henry James.* Cambridge: Harvard University Press, 1991. 80–122. Rpt. in James, Henry. *Portrait of a Lady*, 748–783.

Buchanan, D. " 'The Candlestick and the Snuffers': Some Thoughts on *The Portrait of a Lady*." *HJR* 16.2 (1995): 121–130.

Budick, Emily Miller. *Engendering Romance*, 40–58.

Chandler, Marilyn R. *Dwelling in the Text*, 91–118.

Feidelson, Charles. "Moment of *The Portrait of a Lady*." *Ventures* 8.2 (1968): 47–55. Rpt. in James, Henry. *Portrait of a Lady*, 711–720.

Gass, William H. "High Brutality of Good Intentions." *Accent* 18 (Winter 1958): 62–71. Rpt. in James, Henry. *Portrait of a Lady*, 692–700.

Hollahan, Eugene. *Crisis-Consciousness*, 115–118.

Holland, Laurence B. *Expense of Vision: Essays on the Craft of Henry James.* Princeton, NJ: Princeton University Press, 1964. 28–42. Rpt. in James, Henry. *Portrait of a Lady*, 700–711.

Kyung Woo, Yeo. "Metaphoric Energy of Silences in *The Portrait of a Lady*." *JELL* 41.4 (1995): 1005–1020.

Lustig, T. J. *Henry James and the Ghostly*, 79–84.

Rogers, Franklin R. *Occidental Ideographs*, 130–158.

Sayres, William G. "Proud Penitent: Madame Merle's Quiet Triumph in Henry James's *The Portrait of a Lady*." *ELWIU* 19.2 (1992): 231–245.

Van Ghent, Dorothy. *English Novel: Form and Function.* New York: Harper and Row Publishers, 1953. 211–228. Rpt. in James, Henry. *Portrait of a Lady*, 677–691.

Veeder, William. "Portrait of a Lack." *New Essays on The Portrait of a Lady*. Ed. Joel Porte. Cambridge: Cambridge University Press, 1990. 95–121. Rpt. in James, Henry. *Portrait of a Lady*, 729–747.

Vopat, Carole. "Becoming a Lady: The Origins and Development of Isabel Archer's Ideal Self." *L&P* 38.1–2 (1992): 38–56.

Warren, Jonathan. "Imminence and Immanence: Isabel Archer's Temporal Predicament in *The Portrait of a Lady*." *HJR* 14.1 (1993): 2–16.

White, Craig Howard. "House of Interest: A Keyword in *The Portrait of a Lady*." *MLQ* 52.2 (1991): 191–207.

Princess Casamassima (1886)

Bell, Millicent. *Meaning in Henry James*, 152–184.

Graham, Wendy. "Henry James's Subterranean Blues: A Rereading of *The Princess Casamassima*." *MFS* 40.1 (1994): 51–84.

Lohn, Linda M. "Neurasthenic Dilemma: Mental Dis-ease and Epistemology in James's *The Princess Casamassima.*" *ATQ* 5.2 (1991): 125–134.

Scanlan, Margaret. "Terrorism and the Realistic Novel: Henry James and *The Princess Casamassima.*" *TSLL* 34.3 (1992): 380–402.

Roderick Hudson (1876)

Born, Brad S. "Henry James's *Roderick Hudson:* A Convergence of Family Stories." *HJR* 12.3 (1991): 199–211.

Brown, Chris. "Discourse of the Alps in *Roderick Hudson.*" *ELWIU* 18.2 (1991): 235–242.

Henke, Richard. "Embarrassment of Melodrama: Masculinity in the Early James." *Novel* 28.3 (1995): 272–278.

Lohn, Linda M. " 'An Abyss of Abysses': Will, Morality, and Artistic Imagination in James's *Roderick Hudson.*" *HJR* 12.2 (1991): 93–100.

Milliman, Craig A. "Fiction of Art: *Roderick Hudson*'s Pursuit of the Ideal." *HJR* 15.3 (1994): 231–241.

Sense of the Past (1917)

Williams, Susan S. "Tell-Tale Representation: James and *The Sense of the Past.*" *HJR* 14.1 (1993): 72–86.

Spoils of Poynton (1897)

Bell, Millicent. *Meaning in Henry James*, 204–222.

Bentley, Nancy. "James and the Tribal Discipline of English Kinship." *HJR* 15.2 (1994): 126–140.

Faulkner, Carol. "Reconsidering Poynton's Innocent Patriarch." *HJR* 15.2 (1994): 141–151.

Tragic Muse (1890)

Brown, Chris. "Satire in *The Tragic Muse.*" *SAF* 23.1 (1995): 3–18.

Jobe, Steven H. "Representation and Performance in *The Tragic Muse.*" *ALR* 26.2 (1994): 32–42.

Macnaughton, William R. "Edith Wharton, *The Reef* and Henry James." *ALR* 26.2 (1994): 50–53.

McWhirter, David. "Restaging the Hurt: Henry James and the Artist as Masochist." *TSLL* 33.4 (1991): 464–491.

Peyser, Thomas Galt. "Those Other Selves: Consciousness in the 1890 Publications of Howells and the James Brothers." *ALR* 25.1 (1992): 28–36.

Wilson, Michael. "Lessons of the Master: The Artist and Sexual Identity in Henry James." *HJR* 14.3 (1994): 257–263.

Washington Square (1881)

Bell, Ian F. A. *Henry James and the Past*, 17–60.

Bell, Millicent. *Meaning in Henry James*, 65–79.

Watch and Ward (1878)

Henke, Richard. "Embarrassment of Melodrama: Masculinity in the Early James." *Novel* 28.3 (1995): 265–272.

What Maisie Knew (1897)

Bell, Millicent. *Meaning in Henry James*, 243–261.

Blum, Virginia L. *Hide and Seek*, 171–197.

Havey, Jonathan. "Kleinian Developmental Narrative and James' *What Maisie Knew.*" *HSL* 23.1 (1991): 34–47.

Kaufman, Marjorie. "Beside Maisie on That Bench in Boulogne." *HJR* 15.3 (1994): 257–263.

McCall, Dan. "What Maisie Saw." *HJR* 16.1 (1995): 48–52.

Michaels, Walter Benn. "Jim Crow Henry James?" *HJR* 16.3 (1995): 286–291.

Munich, Adrienne Auslander. "What Lily Knew: Virginity in the 1890's," in Davis, Lloyd, ed. *Virginal Sexuality*, 150–155.

Teahan, Sheila. "*What Maisie Knew* and the Improper Third Person." *SAF* 21.2 (1993): 127–140.

Wings of the Dove (1902)

Bell, Millicent. *Meaning in Henry James*, 289–323.

Brown, Chris. "Milly Theale's London." *HJR* 14.2 (1993): 215–222.

Larson, Doran. "Milly Bargain: The Homosocial Economy in *The Wings of the Dove.*" *ArQ* 51.1 (1995): 81–107.

Oerlemans, Onno. "Literary Value and *The Wings of the Dove.*" *ESC* 17.2 (1991): 177–196.

Olin-Ammentorp, Julie. " 'A Circle of Petticoats': The Feminization of Merton Densher." *HJR* 15.1 (1994): 38–54.

Sangari, Kumkum. "*Wings of the Dove:* 'Not Knowing, but Only Guessing'." *HJR* 13.3 (1992): 292–305.

Sedgwick, Eve Kosofsky. *Tendencies*, 73–103.

Teaham, Sheila. "Abyss of Language in *The Wings of the Dove.*" *HJR* 14.2 (1993): 204–214.

Vrettos, Athena. *Somatic Fictions*, 111–121.

JANES, PERCY (1922–)

House of Hate (1970)

Shorrocks, Graham; Rodgers, Beverly. "Non-Standard Dialect in Percy Janes' *House of Hate.*" *CanL* 133 (1992): 129–141.

JANOWITZ, TAMA (1957–)

American Dad (1981)

Young, Elizabeth. *Shopping in Space*, 151–156.

JENKINS, LYLL BECERRA DE

Honorable Prison (1988)

Morales-Gudmundsson, Lourdes. "Autobiographical Narrator as Structuring Principle in Becerra De Jenkins's *The Honorable Prison.*" *CLAQ* 16.2 (1991): 69–72.

JEWETT, SARAH ORNE (1849–1909)

Country Doctor (1884)

Levy, Helen Fiddyment. *Fiction of the Home Place*, 45–47.

Roman, Margaret. *Sarah Orne Jewett*, 32–34, 75–80.

Country of the Pointed Firs (1896)

Ammons, Elizabeth. *Conflicting Stories*, 44–58.
Blanchard, Paula. *Sarah Orne Jewett*, 278–300.
Brodhead, Richard H. *Cultures of Letters*, 145–149.
Karpinski, Joanne B. "Gothic Underpinnings of Realism in the Local Colorists' No Man's Land," in Mogen, David ed. *Frontier Gothic*, 143–148.
Leder, Patricia. "Living Ghosts and Women's Religion in Sarah Orne Jewett's *The Country of Pointed Firs*," in Carpenter, Lynette, ed. *Haunting the House of Fiction*, 26–39.
Levy, Helen Fiddyment. *Fiction of the Home Place*, 47–58.
Pryse, Marjorie. "Archives of Female Friendship and the 'Way' Jewett Wrote." *NEQ* 66.1 (1993): 63–66.
Roman, Margaret. *Sarah Orne Jewett*, 207–227.
Romines, Ann. *Home Plot*, 48–90.
Zagarell, Sandra A. "Narrative of Community: The Identification of a Genre," in Clark, VéVé A., ed. *Revising the Word*, 265–270, 272–274.

Deephaven (1877)

Blanchard, Paula. *Sarah Orne Jewett*, 89–102.
Church, Joseph. "Transgressive Daughters in Sarah Orne Jewett's *Deephaven*." *ELWIU* 20.2 (1993): 231–250.
Levy, Helen Fiddyment. *Fiction of the Home Place*, 44–45.
Roman, Margaret. *Sarah Orne Jewett*, 40–54.
Romines, Ann. *Home Plot*, 30–47.
Wittenberg, Judith Bryant. "*Deephaven:* Sarah Orne Jewett's Exploratory Metafiction." *SAF* 19.2 (1991): 153–163.

Marsh Island (1885)

Roman, Margaret. *Sarah Orne Jewett*, 75–80, 110–114.

JOHNSON, CHARLES (1948–)

Faith and the Good Thing (1974)

Butler, Robert. "City as Psychological Frontier in Ralph Ellison's *Invisible Man* and Charles Johnson's *Faith and the Good Thing*," in Hakutani, Yoshinobu, ed. *City in African-American Literature*, 131–136.

Middle Passage (1990)

Goudie, S. X. " 'Leavin' a Mark on the Wor(l)d': Marksmen and Marked Men in *Middle Passage*." *AAR* 29.1 (1995): 109–121.
Rushdy, Ashraf H. A. "Properties of Desire: Forms of Slave Identity in Charles Johnson's *Middle Passage*." *ArQ* 50.2 (1994): 73–106.
Scott, Daniel M., III. "Interrogating Identity: Appropriation and Transformation in *Middle Passage*." *AAR* 29.4 (1995): 645–655.
Walby, Celestin. "African Sacrificial Kingship Ritual and Johnson's *Middle Passage*." *AAR* 29.4 (1995): 657–669.

Oxherding Tale (1982)

Coleman, James W. "Charles Johnson's Quest for Black Freedom in *Oxherding Tale*." *AAR* 29.4 (1995): 631–644.

Gleason, William. "Liberation of Perception: Charles Johnson's *Oxherding Tale.*" *BALF* 25.3 (1991): 705–727.

Hayward, Jennifer. "Something to Serve: Constructs of the Feminine in Charles Johnson's *Oxherding Tale.*" *BALF* 25.3 (1991): 689–703.

Kester, Gunilla Theander. *Writing the Subject*, 108–125.

Little, Jonathan. "Charles Johnson's Revolutionary *Oxherding Tale.*" *SAF* 19.2 (1991): 141–151.

Rushdy, Ashraf H. A., "Phenomenology of the Allmuseri: Charles Johnson and the Subject of the Narrative of Slavery." *AAR* 26.3 (1992): 373–394.

JOHNSON, DENIS (1949–)

Stars at Noon (1986)

Reitenbach, Gail. "Foreign Exchange in Denis Johnson's *The Stars at Noon.*" *ArQ* 47.4 (1991): 27–46.

JOHNSON, DIANE (1934–)

Shadow Knows (1975)

O'Donnell, Patrick. "Engendering Paranoia in Contemporary Narrative." *BoundaryII* 19.1 (1992): 199–204.

JOHNSON, JAMES WELDON (1871–1938)

Autobiography of an Ex-Colored Man (1912)

Faulkner, Howard. "James Weldon Johnson's Portrait of the Artist as Invisible Man." *Black American Literature Forum* 19.4 (1985): 148, 151. Rpt. in Bloom, Harold, ed. *Major Black American Writers Through the Harlem Renaissance*, 133–134.

Kostelanetz, Richard. *Politics and the African-American Novel*, 19–24.

Payne, Ladell. *Black Novelists and the Southern Literary Tradition.* Athens, GA: University of Georgia Press, 1981. 28–29. Rpt. in Bloom, Harold, ed. *Major Black American Writers Through the Harlem Renaissance*, 131–132.

Pisiak, Roxanna. "Irony and Subversion in James Weldon Johnson's *The Autobiography of an Ex-Coloured Man.*" *SAF* 21.1 (1993): 83–96.

Scruggs, Charles. *Sweet Home*, 33–34.

Sundquist, Eric J. *Hammer of Creation*, 3–48.

JOHNSTON, MARY (1870–1936)

Long Roll (1911)

Garrett, George. "On Mary Johnston's *The Long Roll*," in Madden, David, ed. *Classics of Civil War Fiction*, 83–95.

JONES, GAYL (1949–)

Corregidora (1975)

Coser, Stellamaris. *Bridging the Americas*, 125–146.

Dubey, Madhu. *Black Women Novelists*, 72–88.

Dubey, Madhu. "Gayl Jones and the Matrilineal Metaphor of Tradition." *SFS* 20.2 (1995): 251–254, 255–260, 262–264.

Gottfried, Amy S. "Angry Arts: Silence, Speech, and Song in Gayl Jones's *Corregidora*." *AAR* 28.4 (1994): 559–570.

Kubitschek, Missy Dehn. *Claiming the Heritage*, 146–155.

Lee, Valerie Gray. "Use of Folktalk in Novels by Black Women Writers." *CLAJ* 23.3 (1980): 270–271. Rpt. in Bloom, Harold ed. *Black American Women Fiction Writers*, 80–81.

Lee, Valerie Gray. "Use of Folktalk in Novels by Black Women Writers." *CLAJ* 23.3 (1980): 270–271. Rpt. in Bloom, Harold, ed. *Contemporary Black American Fiction Writers*, 66–67.

McKible, Adam. " 'These Are the Facts of the Darky's History': Thinking History and Reading Names in Four African American Texts." *AAR* 28.2 (1994): 226–227, 229–230, 232.

Updike, John. "Selda, Lilia, Ursa, Great Gram, and Other Ladies in Distress." *New Yorker* (18 August 1975): 81–82. Rpt. in Bloom, Harold ed. *Black American Women Fiction Writers*, 74.

Updike, John. "Selda, Lilia, Ursa, Great Gram, and Other Ladies in Distress." *New Yorker* (18 August 1975): 81–82. Rpt. in Bloom, Harold, ed. *Contemporary Black American Fiction Writers*, 60.

Wideman, John. "Frame and Dialect: The Evolution of the Black Voice in American Literature." *American Poetry Review* 5.5 (1976): 35–36. Rpt. in Bloom, Harold ed. *Black American Women Fiction Writers*, 76–77.

Wideman, John. "Frame and Dialect: The Evolution of the Black Voice in American Literature." *American Poetry Review* 5.5 (1976): 35–36. Rpt. in Bloom, Harold, ed. *Contemporary Black American Fiction Writers*, 62–63.

Eva's Man (1976)

Dubey, Madhu. *Black Women Novelists*, 89–105.

Dixon, Melvin. *Ride Out the Wilderness: Geography and Identity in Afro-American Literature*. Urbana: University Press of Illinois, 1987. 117, 120. Rpt. in Bloom, Harold ed. *Black American Women Fiction Writers*, 85–86.

Dixon, Melvin. *Ride Out the Wilderness: Geography and Identity in Afro-American Literature*. Urbana: University Press of Illinois, 1987. 117, 120. Rpt. in Bloom, Harold, ed. *Contemporary Black American Fiction Writers*, 71–72.

Kester, Gunilla Theander. *Writing the Subject*, 73–77, 79–90, 92–94, 95–99.

Lionnet, Françoise. "Geographies of Pain: Captive Bodies and Violent Acts in the Fictions of Myriam Warner-Vieyra, Gayl Jones, and Bessie Head." *Callaloo* 16.1 (1993): 144–145. Rpt. in Bloom, Harold ed. *Black American Women Fiction Writers*, 86–87.

Lionnet, Françoise. "Geographies of Pain: Captive Bodies and Violent Acts in the Fictions of Myriam Warner-Vieyra, Gayl Jones, and Bessie Head." *Callaloo* 16.1 (1993): 144–145. Rpt. in Bloom, Harold, ed. *Contemporary Black American Fiction Writers*, 72–73.

Pinckney, Darryl. [Review of *Eva's Man*]. *New Republic* (19 June 1976): 27–28. Rpt. in Bloom, Harold ed. *Black American Women Fiction Writers*, 75–76.

Pinckney, Darryl. [Review of *Eva's Man*]. *New Republic* (19 June 1976): 27–28. Rpt. in Bloom, Harold, ed. *Contemporary Black American Fiction Writers*, 61–62.

JONES, JAMES (1921–1977)

From Here to Eternity (1951)

Limon, John. *Writing After War*, 129–133.

Thin Red Line (1962)

Limon, John. *Writing After War*,136–139.

JONES, LEROI see BARAKA, AMIRI

JONES, NETTIE (1941–)

Mischief Makers (1989)

Holland, Sharon P. " 'If You Know I Have a History, You Will Respect Me': A Perspective on Afro-Native American Literature." *Callaloo* 17.1 (1994): 338–342.

JONG, ERICA (1942–)

Fear of Flying (1973)

Greene, Gayle. *Changing the Story*, 87–91.

How to Save Your Own Life (1977)

Templin, Charlotte. "Sources for the 'Aging Midget-cum-Literary Critic' in Erica Jong's *How to Save Your Own Life*." *NConL* 21.1 (1991): 12.

JUTRAS, JEANNE D'ARC

Georgie (1978)

Brown, Anne E. "Sappho's Daughters: Lesbian Identities in Novels by Québécois Women (1960–1990)," in Brown, Anne E., ed. *International Women's Writing*, 35–37.

KALER, JAMES OTIS (1848–1912)

Toby Tyler (1881)

Griswold, Jerry. *Audacious Kids*, 167–184.

KANG, YOUNGHILL (1903–1972)

East Goes West (1937)

Wong, Sau-ling Cynthia. *Reading Asian American Literature*, 61–62.

KANTOR, MACKINLAY (1904–1977)

Long Remember (1934)

Macauley, Robie. "On MacKinlay Kantor's *Long Remember*," in Madden, David, ed. *Classics of Civil War Fiction*, 131–140.

KAUFMAN, SUE (1926–1977)

Diary of a Mad Housewife (1967)

Greene, Gayle. *Changing the Story*, 69–71.

KEILLOR, GARRISON (1942–)

Lake Wobegon Days (1985)

Narveson, Robert D. "Catholic-Lutheran Interaction in Keillor's *Lake Wobegon Days* and Hassler's *Grand Opening*," in Noe, Marcia, ed. *Exploring the Midwestern*, 180–190.

Scholl, Peter A. *Garrison Keillor*, 112–135.

KELLEY, EDITH SUMMER (1884–1956)

Weeds (1923)

Ammons, Elizabeth. *Conflicting Stories*, 177–180.

KELLEY, EMMA DUNHAM

Four Girls at Cottage City (1898)

McDowell, Deborah E. *"The Changing Same"*, 27–33.

KELLEY, WILLIAM MELVIN (1937–)

Different Drummer (1962)

Faulkner, Howard J. "Vanishing Race." *CLAJ* 37.3 (1994): 274–292.

KENNEDY, WILLIAM (1928–)

Billy Phelan's Greatest Game (1978)

Kennedy, Liam. "Memory and Hearsay: Ethnic History and Identity in *Billy Phelan's Greatest Game* and *Ironweed*." *MELUS* 18.1 (1993): 72–81.

Michener, Christian. "Martin Daugherty's Victories in *Billy Phelan's Greatest Game*." *PLL* 31.4 (1995): 406–429.

Reilly, Edward C. *William Kennedy*, 61–71.

Ink Truck (1969)

Reilly, Edward C. *William Kennedy*, 31–43.

Ironweed (1983)

Kennedy, Liam. "Memory and Hearsay: Ethnic History and Identity in *Billy Phelan's Greatest Game* and *Ironweed*." *MELUS* 18.1 (1993): 76–81.

Pizer, Donald. *Theory and Practice*, 187–194.

Reilly, Edward C. *William Kennedy*, 73–85.

Taylor, Anya. "*Ironweed*, Alcohol, and Celtic Heroism." *Crit* 33.2 (1992): 107–120.

Yetman, Michael G. "*Ironweed:* The Perils and Purgatories of Male Romanticism." *PLL* 27.1 (1991): 84–104.

Legs (1975)

Reilly, Edward C. *William Kennedy*, 45–59.

Quinn's Book (1988)

Reilly, Edward C. *William Kennedy*, 89–103.

Turner, Tramble T. "*Quinn's Book:* Reconstructing Irish-American History." *MELUS* 18.1 (1993): 31–45.

KEROUAC, JACK (1922–1969)

On the Road (1957)

Goldstein, Norma Walrath. "Kerouac's *On the Road.*" *Expl* 50.1 (1991): 60–62.

Holton, Robert. "Kerouac among the Fallahin: On the Road to the Postmodern." *MFS* 41.2 (1995): 265–283.

Huntley, Helen. "*On the Road*—An American Experience." *BWVACET* 13.2 (1991): 165–173.

Subterraneans (1958)

Panish, Jon. "Kerouac's *The Subterraneans:* A Study of 'Romantic Primitivism'." *MELUS* 19.3 (1994): 107–121.

KERSLAKE, SUSAN (1943–)

Middlewatch (1976)

Delbaere, Jeanne. "Magic Realism: The Energy of the Margins," in D'haen, Theo, ed. *Postmodern*, 79–84.

KESEY, KEN (1935–)

One Flew Over the Cuckoo's Nest (1962)

Goluboff, Benjamin. "Carnival Artist in the *Cuckoo's Nest.*" *NWR* 29.3 (1991): 109–123.

Hague, Theodora-Ann. "Gendered Irony in Ken Kesey's *One Flew Over the Cuckoo's Nest.*" *Cithara* 33.1 (1993): 27–34.

Lupack, Barbara Tepa. *Insanity as Redemption*, 64–98.

McCarron, William E. "Pynchon and Kesey." *NConL* 21.5 (1991): 8–9.

Robinson, Daniel. "Awakening of the Natural Man in *One Flew Over the Cuckoo's Nest.*" *NConL* 21.1 (1991): 4–6.

Sometimes a Great Notion (1964)

Drout, Michael D. C. "Hoisting the Arm of Defiance: Beowulfian Elements in Ken Kesey's *Sometimes a Great Notion.*" *WAL* 28.2 (1993): 131–141.

KESSEL, JOHN (1950–)

Good News from Outer Space (1989)

Kelleghan, Fiona. "Ambiguous News from the Heartland: John Kessel's *Good News from Outer Space.*" *Extrapolation* 35.4 (1994): 281–297.

KILLENS, JOHN OLIVER (1916–1987)

And Then We Heard the Thunder (1963)

Ford, Nick Aaron. *Black Insights: Significant Literature by Black Americans, 1760 to the Present.* Waltham, MA: Ginn and Co., 1971. 319. Rpt. in Bloom, Harold, ed. *Modern Black American Fiction Writers*, 85–86.

Cotillion (1971)

Harris, Norman. *Connecting Times: The Sixties in Afro-American Fiction.* Jackson: University of Mississippi Press, 1988. 140–141, 144–145. Rpt. in Bloom, Harold, ed. *Modern Black American Fiction Writers*, 90–91.

'Sippi (1967)

Wiggins, William H., Jr. "Black Folktales in the Novels of John O. Killens." *Black Scholar* 3.3 (1971): 55, 57. Rpt. in Bloom, Harold, ed. *Modern Black American Fiction Writers*, 87–88.

KIM, RONYOUNG

Clay Walls (1986)

Chung-Hei Yun. "Beyond 'Clay Walls': Korean American Literature," in Lim, Shirley Geok-lin, ed. *Reading the Literatures of Asian America*, 86–90.

KINCAID, JAMAICA (1949–)

Annie John (1985)

Nagel, James. "Desperate Hopes, Desperate Lives: Depression and Self-Realization in Jamaica Kincaid's *Annie John* and *Lucy*," in Friedman, Melvin J., ed. *Traditions, Voices, and Dreams*, 237–245.

Niesen de Abruna, Laura. "Family Connections: Mother and Mother Country in the Fiction of Jean Rhys and Jamaica Kincaid," in Nasta, Susheila, ed. *Motherlands*, 260–261, 273–287.

Simmons, Diane. *Jamaica Kincaid*, 1–2, 60–62, 63–66, 70, 101–119.

Lucy (1990)

Ferguson, Moira. "*Lucy* and the Mark of the Colonizer." *MFS* 39.2 (1993): 237–259.

Nagel, James. "Desperate Hopes, Desperate Lives: Depression and Self-Realization in Jamaica Kincaid's *Annie John* and *Lucy*," in Friedman, Melvin J., ed. *Traditions, Voices, and Dreams*, 245–252.

Simmons, Diane. *Jamaica Kincaid*, 3–4, 62–63, 66–71, 120–134.

KING, STEPHEN (1947–)

Carrie (1975)

Pharr, Mary. "Partners in the *Danse:* Women in Stephen King's Fiction," in Magistrale, Tony, ed. *Dark Descent*, 21, 28.

Weller, Greg. "Masks of the Goddess: The Unfolding of the Female Archetype in Stephen King's *Carrie*," in Magistrale, Tony, ed. *Dark Descent*, 5–17.

Dark Half (1989)

Magistrale, Tony. *Stephen King*, 62–66.

Pharr, Mary. "Partners in the *Danse:* Women in Stephen King's Fiction," in Magistrale, Tony, ed. *Dark Descent, 26.*

Dead Zone (1979)

Pharr, Mary. "Partners in the *Danse:* Women in Stephen King's Fiction," in Magistrale, Tony, ed. *Dark Descent*, 28.

Stanton, Michael N. "Some Ways of Reading *The Dead Zone*," in Magistrale, Tony, ed. *Dark Descent*, 61–72.

Drawing of the Three (1987)

Magistrale, Tony. *Stephen King*, 144–148.

Eyes of the Dragon (1987)

Magistrale, Tony. *Stephen King*, 135–141.

Firestarter (1980)

Pharr, Mary. "Partners in the *Danse:* Women in Stephen King's Fiction," in Magistrale, Tony, ed. *Dark Descent*, 26.

Gunslinger (1984)

Magistrale, Tony. *Stephen King*, 141–144.

It (1986)

Bosky, Bernadette Lynn. "Playing the Heavy: Weight, Appetite, and Embodiment in Three Novels by Stephen King," in Magistrale, Tony, ed. *Dark Descent*, 139–147, 148, 149–151.

Dickerson, Mary Jane. "Stephen King Reading William Faulkner: Memory, Desire, and Time in the Making of *It*," in Magistrale, Tony, ed. *Dark Descent*, 171–185.

Keesey, Douglas. " 'Face of Mr. Flip': Homophobia in the Horror of Stephen King," in Magistrale, Tony, ed. *Dark Descent*, 189–194.

Magistrale, Tony. *Stephen King*, 102–124.

Pharr, Mary. "Partners in the *Danse:* Women in Stephen King's Fiction," in Magistrale, Tony, ed. *Dark Descent*, 30–31.

Reesman, Jeanne Campbell. "Riddle Game: Stephen King's Metafictive Dialogue," in Magistrale, Tony, ed. *Dark Descent*, 161–170.

Long Walk (1979)

Magistrale, Tony. *Stephen King*, 53–56.

Smith, James F. " 'Everybody Pays Even for Things They Didn't Do': Stephen King's Pay-out in the Bachman Novels," in Magistrale, Tony, ed. *Dark Descent*, 101–102.

Misery (1987)

Berkenkamp, Lauri. "Reading, Writing and Interpreting: Stephen King's *Misery*," in Magistrale, Tony, ed. *Dark Descent*, 203–211.

Bosky, Bernadette Lynn. "Playing the Heavy: Weight, Appetite, and Embodiment in Three Novels by Stephen King," in Magistrale, Tony, ed. *Dark Descent*, 152–154.

Magistrale, Anthony. "Art Versus Madness in Stephen King's *Misery*," in Morse, Donald, E., ed. *Celebration of the Fantastic*, 271–278.

Magistrale, Tony. *Stephen King*, 124–132.

Pharr, Mary. "Partners in the *Danse:* Women in Stephen King's Fiction," in Magistrale, Tony, ed. *Dark Descent*, 24–25.

Pet Sematary (1983)

Mustazza, Leonard. "Fear and Pity: Tragic Horror in King's *Pet Sematary*," in Magistrale, Tony, ed. *Dark Descent*, 73–81.

Pharr, Mary. "Partners in the *Danse:* Women in Stephen King's Fiction," in Magistrale, Tony, ed. *Dark Descent*, 26–28.

Rage (1977)

Magistrale, Tony. *Stephen King*, 51–53.

Pourteau, Chris. "Individual and Society: Narrative Structure and Thematic Unity in Stephen King's *Rage*." *JPC* 27.1 (1993): 171–178.

Smith, James F. " 'Everybody Pays Even for Things They Didn't Do': Stephen King's Pay-out in the Bachman Novels," in Magistrale, Tony, ed. *Dark Descent*, 100–101.

Roadwork (1981)

Magistrale, Tony. *Stephen King*, 56–58.

Smith, James F. " 'Everybody Pays Even for Things They Didn't Do': Stephen King's Pay-out in the Bachman Novels," in Magistrale, Tony, ed. *Dark Descent*, 102–103.

Running Man (1982)

Magistrale, Tony. *Stephen King*, 58–60.

Smith, James F. " 'Everybody Pays Even for Things They Didn't Do': Stephen King's Pay-out in the Bachman Novels," in Magistrale, Tony, ed. *Dark Descent*, 103–104.

'Salem's Lot (1978)

Keesey, Douglas. " 'Face of Mr. Flip': Homophobia in the Horror of Stephen King," in Magistrale, Tony, ed. *Dark Descent*, 195, 196.

Pharr, Mary. "Partners in the *Danse:* Women in Stephen King's Fiction," in Magistrale, Tony, ed. *Dark Descent*, 23.

Shining (1977)

Curran, Ronald T. "Complex, Archetype, and Primal Fear: King's Use of Fairy Tales in *The Shining*," in Magistrale, Tony, ed. *Dark Descent*, 33–45.

Keesey, Douglas. " 'Face of Mr. Flip': Homophobia in the Horror of Stephen King," in Magistrale, Tony, ed. *Dark Descent*, 197.

Magistrale, Tony. *Stephen King*, 151–153.

Stand (1978)

Bosky, Bernadette Lynn. "Playing the Heavy: Weight, Appetite, and Embodiment in Three Novels by Stephen King," in Magistrale, Tony, ed. *Dark Descent*, 143, 145–146, 149, 151–152.

Casebeer, Edwin F. "Three Genres of *The Stand*," in Magistrale, Tony, ed. *Dark Descent*, 47–58.

Cooper, Ken. " 'Zero Pays the House': The Las Vegas Novel and Atomic Roulette." *ConL* 33.3 (1992): 536–537.

Keesey, Douglas. " 'Face of Mr. Flip': Homophobia in the Horror of Stephen King," in Magistrale, Tony, ed. *Dark Descent*, 197.

Magistrale, Tony. "Free Will and Sexual Choice in *The Stand.*" *Extrapolation* 34.1 (1993): 30–38.

Pharr, Mary. "Partners in the *Danse:* Women in Stephen King's Fiction," in Magistrale, Tony, ed. *Dark Descent*, 23, 28–30.

Talisman (1984)

Magistrale, Tony. "Science, Politics, and the Epic Imagination: *The Talisman*," in Magistrale, Tony, ed. *Dark Descent*, 113–127.

Magistrale, Tony. *Stephen King*, 68–79, 85.

Thinner (1984)

Magistrale, Tony. *Stephen King*, 61–62.

Smith, James F. " 'Everybody Pays Even for Things They Didn't Do': Stephen King's Pay-out in the Bachman Novels," in Magistrale, Tony, ed. *Dark Descent*, 104–111.

Tommyknockers (1987)

Keesey, Douglas. " 'Face of Mr. Flip': Homophobia in the Horror of Stephen King," in Magistrale, Tony, ed. *Dark Descent*, 198.

Magistrale, Tony. *Stephen King*, 79–85.

Pharr, Mary. "Partners in the *Danse:* Women in Stephen King's Fiction," in Magistrale, Tony, ed. *Dark Descent*, 23–24.

KING, THOMAS (1943–)

Green Grass, Running Water (1993)

Donaldson, Laura E. "Noah Meets Old Coyote; Or, Singing in the Rain: Intertextuality in Thomas King's *Green Grass, Running Water.*" *SAIL* 7.2 (1995): 27–43.

Medicine River (1989)

Davidson, Arnold E. *Coyote Country*, 190–196.

KINGSTON, MAXINE HONG (1940–)

Tripmaster Monkey (1989)

Deeney, John J. "Of Monkeys and Butterflies: Transformation in M. H. Kingston's *Tripmaster Monkey* and D. H. Hwang's *M. Butterfly.*" *MELUS* 18.4 (1993–94): 21–25, 30–37.

Furth, Isabella. "Beee-e-een! Nation, Transformation and the Hyphen of Ethnicity in Kingston's *Tripmaster Monkey.*" *MFS* 40.1 (1994): 33–49.

Lin, Patricia. "Clashing Constructions of Reality: Reading Maxine Hong Kingston's *Tripmaster Monkey: His Fake Book* as Indigenous Ethnography," in Lim, Shirley Geok-lin, ed. *Reading the Literatures of Asian America*, 333–346.

Wong, Sau-ling Cynthia. *Reading Asian American Literature*, 113–114, 206–207.

KINSELLA, W. P. (1935–)

Box Socials (1992)

Murray, Don. "W.P. Kinsella," in Lecker, Robert, ed. *Canadian Writers and Their Works: Fiction Series* (Vol. 12), 178–179.

Iowa Baseball Confederacy (1986)

Murray, Don. "W.P. Kinsella," in Lecker, Robert, ed. *Canadian Writers and Their Works: Fiction Series* (Vol. 12), 176–178.

Shoeless Joe (1982)

Garman, Bryan K. "Myth Building and Cultural Politics in W. P. Kinsella's *Shoeless Joe*." *CRevAS* 24.1 (1994): 41–62.
Jenkins, Clarence. "Kinsella's *Shoeless Joe*." *Expl* 53.3 (1995): 179–180.
Murray, Don. "W.P. Kinsella," in Lecker, Robert, ed. *Canadian Writers and Their Works: Fiction Series* (Vol. 12), 171–176.

KLASS, PERRI (1958–)

Other Women's Children (1990)

Hogan, Katie. "Speculations on Women and AIDS." *MinnR* 40 (1993): 90–92.

KLEIN, A. M. (1909–1972)

Second Scroll (1951)

Simon, Sherry. "A. M. Klein: Une Esthétique de l'hybride." *EF* 28.2–3 (1992–93): 93–104.

KNOWLES, ROBERT EDWARD (1868–1946)

Attic Guest (1909)

Knowles, Robert E. "Critic in the Attic: Religious Doubt, Mind, and Heart in the Fiction." *CanL* 138–139 (1993): 25–31.

Undertow (1906)

Knowles, Robert E. "Critic in the Attic: Religious Doubt, Mind, and Heart in the Fiction." *CanL* 138–139 (1993): 24–25.

KOGAWA, JOY (1935–)

Obasan (1981)

Cheng Lok Chua. "Witnessing the Japanese Canadian Experience in World War II: Processual Structure, Symbolism, and Irony in Joy Kogawa's *Obasan*," in Lim, Shirley Geok-lin, ed. *Reading the Literatures of Asian America*, 97–106.
Davidson, Arnold. *Writing Against the Silence: Joy Kogawa's Obasan*. Toronto: ECW Press, 1993.
Ueki, Teruyo. "*Obasan:* Revelations in a Paradoxical Scheme." *MELUS* 18.4 (1993–94): 5–20.
Wong, Sau-ling Cynthia. *Reading Asian American Literature*, 19–24, 49–50, 138–141.
Zwicker, Heather. "Canadian Women of Color in the New World Order: Marlene Nourbese Philip, Joy Kogawa, and Beatrice Culleton Fight Their Way Home," in Pearlman, Mickey, ed. *Canadian Women*, 147–150.

KONIGSBURG, E. L. (1930–)

About the B'nai Bagels (1969)

Hanks, Dorrel Thomas, Jr. *E. L. Konigsburg*, 33–45.

From the Mixed-up Files of Mrs. Basil E. Frankweiler (1967)

Hanks, Dorrel Thomas, Jr. *E. L. Konigsburg*, 17–31.

(George) (1970)

Hanks, Dorrel Thomas, Jr. *E. L. Konigsburg*, 45–59.

Proud Taste for Scarlet and Miniver (1973)

Hanks, Dorrel Thomas, Jr. *E. L. Konigsburg*, 89–100.

Up from Jericho Tel (1986)

Hanks, Dorrel Thomas, Jr. *E. L. Konigsburg*, 149–161.

KOSINSKI, JERZY (1933–1991)

Being There (1971)

Lupack, Barbara Tepa. *Insanity as Redemption*, 136–153.
Meehan, William F. "Towards Understanding Jerzy Kosinski's Being Here." *NConL* 25.5 (1995): 9–11.

Hermit of 69th Street (1988)

Hawthorne, Mark D. "Allusions to Robert Browning in Jerzy Kosinski's *The Hermit of 69th Street.*" *NConL* 23.4 (1993): 3–5.

Painted Bird (1965)

Granofsky, Ronald. "Circle and Line: Modern and Postmodern Constructs of the Self in Jerzy Kosinski's *The Painted Bird.*" *ELWIU* 18.2 (1991): 254–268.
Granofsky, Ronald. *Trauma Novel*, 67–77.
Sokoloff, Naomi B. *Imagining the Child*, 109–128.

KREINER, PHILIP

Contact Prints (1987)

Davidson, Arnold E. *Coyote Country*, 177–184.

KROETSCH, ROBERT (1927–)

Alibi (1983)

Kuester, Martin. "Kroetsch's Fragments: Approaching the Narrative Structure of His Novels," in D'haen, Theo, ed. *Postmodern*, 151–156.
Tiefensee, Dianne. *"The Old Dualities"*, 55–70.

Badlands (1975)

Butterfield, Bruce A. "Mediator Is the Message: Anna Dawe, Cana-Dawe, and Bad Lands as a State of Mind." *GPQ* 14.3 (1994): 195–206.
Colvile, Georgiana M. M. "On Coyote or Canadian Otherness in Robert Kroetsch's *Badlands* and George Bowering's *Caprice.*" *RMS* 35 (1992): 130–134, 137–138.

Davidson, Arnold E. *Coyote Country*, 74–93.
Deer, Glenn. *Postmodern Canadian Fiction*, 80–96.
Kuester, Martin. "Kroetsch's Fragments: Approaching the Narrative Structure of His Novels," in D'haen, Theo, ed. *Postmodern*, 146–148.
Seaton, Dorothy. 'Post-Colonial as Deconstruction: Land and Language in Kroetsch's *Badlands*." *CanL* 128 (1991): 77–89.
Tiefensee, Dianne. *"The Old Dualities"*, 137–151.
Williams, David. *Confessional Fictions*, 219–236.

But We Are Exiles (1965)

Kuester, Martin. "Kroetsch's Fragments: Approaching the Narrative Structure of His Novels," in D'haen, Theo, ed. *Postmodern*, 138–139.
Spinks, Lee. "Kroetsch's Narcissus: Alienation and Identity in *But We Are Exiles*." *JCL* 29.2 (1993): 3–18.

Gone Indian (1973)

Kirtz, Mary K. "Inhabiting the Dangerous Middle of the Space Between: An Intermodernist Reading of Kroetsch's *Gone Indian*." *GPQ* 14.3 (1994):207–217.
Kuester, Martin. "Kroetsch's Fragments: Approaching the Narrative Structure of His Novels," in D'haen, Theo, ed. *Postmodern*, 144–146.
Snyder, J. R. "Map of Misreading: Gender, Identity, and Freedom in Robert Kroetsch's *Gone Indian*." *SCL* 18.1 (1993): 1–17.
Söderlind, Sylvia. "Canadian Cryptic: The Sacred, the Profane, and the Translatable." *ArielE* 22.3 (1991): 93.
Söderlind, Sylvia. *MARGIN / ALIAS*, 170–199.
Tiefensee, Dianne. *"The Old Dualities"*, 111–115.
Turner, Margaret E. *Imagining Culture*, 81–93.

Studhorse Man (1969)

Beran, Carol L. "*Studhorse Man:* Translating the Boundaries of the Text." *GPQ* 14.3 (1994): 185–194.
Kuester, Martin. "Kroetsch's Fragments: Approaching the Narrative Structure of His Novels," in D'haen, Theo, ed. *Postmodern*, 142–144.
Söderlind, Sylvia. "Canadian Cryptic: The Sacred, the Profane, and the Translatable." *ArielE* 22.3 (1991): 91–93, 98.
Tiefensee, Dianne. *"The Old Dualities"*, 109–110.

What the Crow Said (1978)

Jackman, Christine. "*What the Crow Said:* A Topos of Excess." *SCL* 16.2 (1991): 79–92.
Kuester, Martin. "Kroetsch's Fragments: Approaching the Narrative Structure of His Novels," in D'haen, Theo, ed. *Postmodern*, 148–150.
Tiefensee, Dianne. *"The Old Dualities"*, 115–124, 126–136.
Wall, Kathleen. "What Kroetsch Said: The Problem of Meaning and Language in *What the Crow Said*." *CanL* 128 (1991): 90–105.

Words of My Roaring (1966)

Kuester, Martin. "Kroetsch's Fragments: Approaching the Narrative Structure of His Novels," in D'haen, Theo, ed. *Postmodern*, 139–142.

KROMER, TOM

Waiting for Nothing (1935)

Obropta, Mary. "Kromer's *Waiting for Nothing.*" *Expl* 53.2 (1995): 111–114.

LAIDLAW, MARC (1960–)

Dad's Nuke (1985)

Laidlaw, Marc. "Virtual Surreality: Our New Romance with Plot Devices." *SAQ* 92.4 (1993): 648–651.

Kalifornia (1993)

Laidlaw, Marc. "Virtual Surreality: Our New Romance with Plot Devices." *SAQ* 92.4 (1993): 651–662.

LALONDE, ROBERT (1947–)

Le dernier été des Indiens (1982)

Frédéric, Madeleine. "Quête de l'origine et retour au temps mythique: deux lignes de fuite dans l'oeuvre de Robert Lalonde," in Marcato-Falzoni, Franca, ed. *Mythes et mythologies*, 251, 252.

Le Diable en personne (1989)

Frédéric, Madeleine. "Quête de l'origine et retour au temps mythique: deux lignes de fuite dans l'oeuvre de Robert Lalonde," in Marcato-Falzoni, Franca, ed. *Mythes et mythologies*, 251–252.

L'Ogre de Grand Remous (1992)

Frédéric, Madeleine. "Quête de l'origine et retour au temps mythique: deux lignes de fuite dans l'oeuvre de Robert Lalonde," in Marcato-Falzoni, Franca, ed. *Mythes et mythologies*, 250, 253, 255, 255–256, 257–259.

Une belle journée d'avance (1986)

Frédéric, Madeleine. "Quête de l'origine et retour au temps mythique: deux lignes de fuite dans l'oeuvre de Robert Lalonde," in Marcato-Falzoni, Franca, ed. *Mythes et mythologies*, 249–250, 251, 253, 254, 259–260.

L'AMOUR, LOUIS (1910–1988)

Last of the Breed (1986)

Terrie, Philip G. "*Last of the Breed:* Louis L'Amour's Survivalist Fantasy." *JPC* 25.4 (1992): 23–33.

LANE, MARY E. BRADLEY

Mizora (1881)

Suksang, Duangrudi. "World of Their Own: The Separatist Utopian Vision of Mary E. Bradley Lane's *Mizora*," in Harris, Sharon M., ed. *Redefining the Political Novel*, 128–148.

LANE, ROSE WILDER (1887–1968)

Free Land (1938)

Holtz, William. "Rose Wilder Lane's *Free Land:* The Political Background." *SDR* 30.1 (1992): 46–60.

LANGEVIN, ANDRÉ (1927–)

Dust Over the City see *Poussière sur la ville*

L'Élan d'Amérique (1972)

Söderlind, Sylvia. *MARGIN / ALIAS*, 143–169.

Orphan Street see *Une chaîne dans le parc*

Poussière sur la ville (1953)

Roy, Fernand. "Figures de l'écrit dans le roman," in Duchet, Claude, ed. *Recherche littéraire*, 223–224, 225–226.
Shek, Ben-Z. *French-Canadian*, 40–42.

Une chaîne dans le parc (1974)

Oore, Irene. "L'Experience des limites dans *Une chaîne dans le parc* d'Andre Langevin." *SCL* 17.1 (1992): 78–92.

LAPIERRE, RENÉ

L'Été Rébecca (1985)

Hebert, Pierre. "Le Professeur fictif dans quelques romans québecois des années quatre-vingt: Pas facile d'être intellectuel postmoderne!" *UTQ* 63.4 (1994): 600, 602–604.

LARSEN, NELLA (1891–1964)

Passing (1929)

Ammons, Elizabeth. *Conflicting Stories*, 190–191.
Blackmore, David L. " 'That Unreasonable Restless Feeling': The Homosexual Subtexts of Nella Larsen's *Passing*." *AAR* 26.3 (1992): 475–484.
Blackmore, David L. " 'That Unreasonable Restless Feeling': The Homosexual Subtexts of Nella Larsen's *Passing*." *African Amerian Review* 26.3 (1992): 478–479, 481. Rpt. in Bloom, Harold, ed. *Black American Women Fiction Writers*, 115–116.
Brody, Jennifer DeVere. "Clare Kennedy's 'True' Colors: Race and Class Conflict in Nella Larsen's *Passing*." *Callaloo* 15.4 (1992): 1053–1065.
Grayson, Deborah R. "Fooling White Folks: Or, How I Stole the Show: The Body Politics of Nella Larsen's *Passing*." *BuR* 39.1 (1995): 27–37.
Horton, Merrill. "Blackness, Betrayal, and Childhood: Race and Identity in Nella Larsen's *Passing*." *CLAJ* 38.1 (1994): 31–45.
McDowell, Deborah E. *"The Changing Same"*, 79–97.
McLendon, Jacquelyn. *Politics of Color in the Fiction*, 94–111.
Tate, Claudia. "Nella Larsen's *Passing*: A Problem of Interpretation." *Black Ameri-*

can Literature Forum 14.4 (1980): 143–144. Rpt. in Bloom, Harold, ed. *Black American Women Fiction Writers*, 107–108.

Wall, Cheryl A. *Women of the Harlem Renaissance*, 120–132.

Washington, Mary Helen. "Nella Larsen: Mystery Woman of the Harlem Renaissance." *Ms.* 9.6 (December 1980): 50. Rpt. in Bloom, Harold, ed. *Black American Women Fiction Writers*, 108–109.

Williams, Bettye J. "Nella Larsen: Early Twentieth-Century Novelist of Afrocentric Feminist Thought." *CLAJ* 39.2 (1995): 165–178.

Quicksand (1933)

Barnett, Pamela E. " 'My Picture of You Is, after All, the True Helga Crane': Portraiture and Identity in Nella Larsen's *Quicksand*." *Signs* 20.3 (1995): 575–600.

Bone, Robert. *Negro Novel in America.* New Haven: Yale University Press, 1958. 103–106. Rpt. in Bloom, Harold, ed. *Black American Women Fiction Writers*, 105–107.

Carby, Hazel V. *Reconstructing Womanhood: The Emergence of the Afro-American Woman Novelist.* New York: Oxford University Press, 1987. 173–174. Rpt. in Bloom, Harold, ed. *Black American Women Fiction Writers*, 112–113.

Elkins, Marilyn. "Expatriate Afro-American Women as Exotics," Brown, Anne E., ed. *International Women's Writing*, 264–271.

Griffin, Farah Jasmine. *"Who Set You Flowin'?"*, 154–160.

Kubitschek, Missy Dehn. *Claiming the Heritage*, 93–104.

McDowell, Deborah E. *"The Changing Same"*, 79–97.

McLendon, Jacquelyn. *Politics of Color*, 71–93.

Rhodes, Chip. "Writing Up the New Negro: The Construction of Consumer Desire in the Twenties." *JACult* 28.2 (1994): 199–207.

Saunders, James Robert. *Wayward Preacher*, 9–42.

Silverman, Debra B. "Nella Larsen's *Quicksand:* Untangling the Webs of Exoticism." *AAR* 27.4 (1993): 606–609, 610–614.

Wall, Cheryl A. *Women of the Harlem Renaissance*, 96–114.

Williams, Bettye J. "Nella Larsen: Early Twentieth-Century Novelist of Afrocentric Feminist Thought." *CLAJ* 39.2 (1995): 165–178.

LARUE, MONIQUE (1948–)

Copies conformes (1988)

Ireland, Susan. "Monique Larue's *Copies conformes:* An Original Copy.' *QS* 15 (1992–93): 21–30.

True Copies see *Copies conformes*

LATIF-GHATTAS, MONA (1946–)

Le double conte de l'exil (1990)

Verthuy, Maïr and Lucie Lequin. "L'écriture des femmes migrantes au Québec," in Duchet, Claude, ed. *Recherche littéraire*, 348–350.

LAURENCE, MARGARET (1926–1987)

Diviners (1974)

Bok, Christian. "Sibyls: Echoes of French Feminism in *The Diviners* and *Lady Oracle*." *CanL* 135 (1992): 82–92.

Greene, Gayle. *Changing the Story*, 148–165.
Morley, Patricia. *Margaret Laurence*, 120–139.
Potvin, Elisabeth. " 'A Mystery at the Core of Life': Margaret Laurence and Women's Spirituality." *CanL* 128 (1991): 34–35.
Thompson, Elizabeth. *Pioneer Woman*, 135–157.
Verduyn, Christl. "Contra/diction/s: Language in Laurence's *The Diviners*." *JCSR* 26.3 (1991): 52–67.
Warwick, Susan J. *River of Now and Then: Margaret Laurence's The Diviners*. Toronto: ECW Press, 1993.

Fire-Dwellers (1969)

Greene, Gayle. *Changing the Story*, 73–75.
Morley, Patricia. *Margaret Laurence*, 99–109.
Potvin, Elisabeth. " 'A Mystery at the Core of Life': Margaret Laurence and Women's Spirituality." *CanL* 128 (1991): 32–34.
Stovcl, Nora. *Stacey's Choice: Margaret Laurence's The Fire-Dwellers*. Toronto: ECW Press, 1993.

Jest of God (1966)

Morley, Patricia. *Margaret Laurence*, 88–99.
Potvin, Elisabeth. " 'A Mystery at the Core of Life': Margaret Laurence and Women's Spirituality." *CanL* 128 (1991): 31–32.
Powell, Barbara. "Conflicting Inner Voices of Rachel Cameron." *SCL* 16.1 (1991): 22–35.
Söderlind, Sylvia. "Canadian Cryptic: The Sacred, the Profane, and the Translatable." *ArielE* 22.3 (1991): 90–91, 98–99.
Stovel, Nora. *Rachel's Children: Margaret Laurence's A Jest of God*. Toronto: ECW Press, 1992.
Thompson, Elizabeth. *Pioneer Woman*, 125–132, 134, 135.

Rachel, Rachel see *Jest of God*

Stone Angel (1964)

Comeau, Paul. "Hagar in Hell: Margaret Laurence's Fallen Angel." *CanL* 128 (1991): 11–22.
Davidson, Arnold E. *Coyote Country*, 100.
Potvin, Elisabeth. " 'A Mystery at the Core of Life': Margaret Laurence and Women's Spirituality." *CanL* 128 (1991): 27–30.
Thompson, Elizabeth. *Pioneer Woman*, 115–124, 134.
Williams, David. *Confessional Fictions*, 85–101.

This Side Jordan (1960)

Morley, Patricia. *Margaret Laurence*, 60–67.

LAWTON, VIRGINIA see ROE, VINGIE E.

LAZARRE, JANE (1943–)

Mother Knot (1976)

Reddy, Maureen T. "Maternal Reading: Lazarre and Walker," in Daly, Brenda O., ed. *Narrating Mothers*, 225, 227–228, 234–235.

Powers of Charlotte (1987)

Reddy, Maureen T. "Maternal Reading: Lazarre and Walker," in Daly, Brenda O., ed. *Narrating Mothers*, 226–227, 235–236.

LE GUIN, URSULA K. (1929–)

Always Coming Home (1985)

Brown, Robert McAfee. *Persuade Us To Rejoice*, 139–148.

Dispossessed (1974)

Williams, Donna Glee. "Moons of Le Guin and Heinlein." *SFS* 21.2 (1994): 164–172.

Farthest Shore (1972)

Barrow, Craig and Diana Barrow. "Le Guin's Earthsea: Voyages in Consciousness." *Extrapolation* 32.1 (1991): 36–40.

Left Hand of Darkness (1969)

Barry, Nora and Mary Prescott. "Beyond Words: The Impact of Rhythm as Narrative Technique in *The Left Hand of Darkness*." *Extrapolation* 33.2 (1992): 154–165.

Téhanu (1990)

Littlefield, Holly. "Unlearning Patriarchy: Ursula Le Guin's Feminist Consciousness in *The Tombs of Atuan* and *Téhanu*." *Extrapolation* 36.3 (1995): 251–256.

Tombs of Atuan (1971)

Barrow, Craig and Diana Barrow. "Le Guin's Earthsea: Voyages in Consciousness." *Extrapolation* 32.1 (1991): 32–36

Littlefield, Holly. "Unlearning Patriarchy: Ursula Le Guin's Feminist Consciousness in *The Tombs of Atuan* and *Téhanu*." *Extrapolation* 36.3 (1995): 245–250.

Wizard of Earthsea (1968)

Barrow, Craig and Diana Barrow. "Le Guin's Earthsea: Voyages in Consciousness." *Extrapolation* 32.1 (1991): 21–32.

LEBLANC, LOUISE (1942–)

37 1/2 AA (1983)

Joubert, Lucie. "Le Pastiche pastiche: Une Lecture de *37 1/2 AA* de Louise Leblanc." *SCL* 18.1 (1993): 85–98.

LEE, ANDREA (1953–)

Sarah Phillips (1984)

Elkins, Marilyn. "Expatriate Afro-American Women as Exotics," in Brown, Anne E., ed. *International Women's Writing*, 264–271.

LEE, HARPER (1926–)

To Kill a Mockingbird (1960)

Johnson, Claudia D. "Secret Courts of Men's Hearts: Code and Law in Harper Lee's *To Kill a Mockingbird*." *SAF* 19.2 (1991): 129–139.

Johnson, Claudia Durst. *To Kill a Mockingbird: Threatening Boundaries.* New York: Twayne Publishers, 1994.

Johnson, Claudia Durst. *Understanding To Kill a Mockingbird: A Student Casebook to Issues, Sources, and Historic Documents.* Westport, CT: Greenwood Press, 1994.

LEE, SKY

Disappearing Moon Café (1990)

Huggan, Graham. "Latitudes of Romance: Representations of Chinese Canada in Bowering's *To All Appearances a Lady* and Lee's *Disappearing Moon Café.*" *CanL* 140 (1994): 34–44.

LEIBER, FRITZ (1910–1992)

Conjure Wife (1953)

Byfield, Bruce. " 'Sister Picture of Dorian Grey': The Image of the Female in Fritz Leiber's *Conjure Wife.*" *Mythlore* 17.4 (1991): 24–28.

Our Lady of Darkness (1977)

Andriano, Joseph. *Our Lady of Darkness*, 136.

LEMAY, ALAN (1899–1964)

Searchers (1954)

Folsom, James K. "Gothicism in the Western Novel," in Mogen, David, ed. *Frontier Gothic*, 33–36.

LEMELIN, ROGER (1919–1992)

Au pied de la Pente douce (1944)

Tremblay, Victor-Laurent. " 'Le Mythe des jambes' chez Roger Lemelin." *V&I* 18.2 (1993): 351–370.

Tremblay, Victor-Laurent. "Réévaluer *Au pied de la Pente douce.*" *QS* 17 (1993–94): 151–167.

Town Below see *Au pied de la Pente douce*

L'ENGLE, MADELEINE (1918–)

Many Waters (1986)

Hammond, Wayne G. "Seraphim, Cherubim, and Virtual Unicorns: Order and Being in Madeleine L'Engle's Time Quartet." *Mythlore* 20.4 (1995): 41–45.

Swiftly Tilting Planet (1978)

Hammond, Wayne G. "Seraphim, Cherubim, and Virtual Unicorns: Order and Being in Madeleine L'Engle's Time Quartet." *Mythlore* 20.4 (1995): 41–45.

Wind in the Door (1973)

Hammond, Wayne G. "Seraphim, Cherubim, and Virtual Unicorns: Order and Being in Madeleine L'Engle's Time Quartet." *Mythlore* 20.4 (1995): 41–45.

Wrinkle in Time (1962)

Hammond, Wayne G. “Seraphim, Cherubim, and Virtual Unicorns: Order and Being in Madeleine L’Engle’s Time Quartet.” *Mythlore* 20.4 (1995): 41–45.

LEPROHON, ROSANNA (1829–1879)

Ada Dunmore (1870)

MacMillan, Carrie. *Silenced Sextet*, 43–46.

Antoinette de Mirecourt (1864)

MacMillan, Carrie. *Silenced Sextet*, 36–38.

Armand Durand (1868)

MacMillan, Carrie. *Silenced Sextet*, 40–43.

Clarence Fitz-Clarence (1851)

MacMillan, Carrie. *Silenced Sextet*, 24–26.

Eveleen O’Donnell (1859)

MacMillan, Carrie. *Silenced Sextet*, 28–31.

Florence Fitz-Hardinge (1849)

MacMillan, Carrie. *Silenced Sextet*, 22–23.

Ida Beresford (1848)

MacMillan, Carrie. *Silenced Sextet*, 18–21.

Le Manoir de Villerai (1860)

MacMillan, Carrie. *Silenced Sextet*, 31–35.

Manor House of de Villerai see *Le Manoir de Villerai*

Stepmother (1847)

MacMillan, Carrie. *Silenced Sextet*, 16–18.

LESLEY, CRAIG

River Song (1989)

Davies, J. C. “Euro-American Realism versus Native Authenticity: Two Novels by Craig Lesley.” *SAF* 22.2 (1994): 233–245.

Winterkill (1984)

Davies, J. C. “Euro-American Realism versus Native Authenticity: Two Novels by Craig Lesley.” *SAF* 22.2 (1994): 233–245.

LESTRES, ALONIÉ DE (1878–1967)

Au Cap Blomidon (1932)

Stapinsky, Stephane. “L’Intégration d’un document historique a un récit de fiction: L’Exemple d’*Au Cap Blomidon* de Lionel Groulx.” *V&I* 19.1 (1993): 54–77.

Iron Wedge see *L’Appel de la race*

L'Appel de la race (1923)

Garand, Dominique. "Appeal of the Race: Quand l'antagonisme se fait vérité de l'être." *V&I* 19.1 (1993): 11–38.

LESUEUR, MERIDEL (1900–)

Girl (1978)

Gelfant, Blanche H. " 'Everybody Steals': Language as Theft in Meridel LeSueur's *The Girl*," in Howe, Florence, ed. *Tradition and the Talents of Women*, 183–210.

LEWIS, ALFRED

Home Is an Island (1951)

Suarez, Jose I. "Four Luso-American Autobiographies: A Comparative View." *MELUS* 17.3 (1991–92): 17–18.

LEWIS, SINCLAIR (1885–1951)

Ann Vickers (1933)

Hapke, Laura. *Daughters of the Great Depression*, 209–213.

Arrowsmith (1925)

Hutchisson, James M. "Sinclair Lewis, Paul De Kruif, and the Composition of *Arrowsmith*." *SNNTS* 24.1 (1992): 48–66.

Babbitt (1922)

Reitinger, D. W. "Source for Tanis Judique in Sinclair Lewis's *Babbitt*." *NConL* 23.5 (1993): 3–4.

It Can Happen Here (1935)

Booker, M. Keith. *Dystopian Impulse*, 98–99.

Main Street (1920)

MacDonald, R. D. "Measuring Leacock's Mariposa against Lewis's Gopher Prairie: A Question of Monuments." *DR* 71.1 (1991): 90–94.

Sunshine Sketches of a Little Town (1912)

MacDonald, R. D. "Measuring Leacock's Mariposa against Lewis's Gopher Prairie: A Question of Monuments." *DR* 71.1 (1991): 94–102.

LEWISOHN, LUDWIG (1883–1955)

Case of Mr. Crump (1926)

Greenfield, Robert. " 'Significant Ugliness': *The Case of Mr. Crump* in Perspective." *LCUT* 20.4 (1991): 98–135.

"LILLIAN JANET" (pseudonym of Janet Cicchetti and Lillian Ressler)

Touchstone (1947)

Yates, Norris. *Gender and Genre*, 129–131.

LIPPARD, GEORGE (1822–1854)

New York (1853)

Ashwill, Gary. "Mysteries of Capitalism in George Lippard's City Novels." *ESQ* 40.4 (1994): 293–314.

Quaker City (1845)

Ashwill, Gary. "Mysteries of Capitalism in George Lippard's City Novels." *ESQ* 40.4 (1994): 293–314.

LOCKHART, CAROLINE (1870–1962)

Fighting Shepherdess (1919)

Yates, Norris. *Gender and Genre*, 49–52.

Lady Doc (1912)

Yates, Norris. *Gender and Genre*, 43–49, 53.

"Me—Smith" (1911)

Yates, Norris. *Gender and Genre*, 39–43, 53.

LOCKRIDGE, ROSS, JR. (1914–1948)

Raintree County (1948)

Aaron, Daniel. "On Ross Lockridge, Jr.'s *Raintree County*," in Madden, David, ed. *Classics of Civil War Fiction*, 204–213.

LONDON, JACK (1876–1916)

Burning Daylight (1910)

Furer, Andrew J. "Jack London's New Woman: A Little Lady with a Big Stick." *SAF* 22.2 (1994): 196–200.

Call of the Wild (1903)

Auerbach, Jonathan. " 'Congested Mails': Buck and Jack's 'Call.' " *AL* 67.1 (1995): 51–76.

Daughter of the Snows (1902)

Furer, Andrew J. "Jack London's New Woman: A Little Lady with a Big Stick." *SAF* 22.2 (1994): 188–196.

Iron Heel (1908)

Barley, Tony. "Prediction, Programme and Fantasy in Jack London's *Iron Heel*," in Seed, David, ed. *Anticipations*, 153–170.

Shor, Francis. "*Iron Heel*'s Marginal(ized) Utopia." *Extrapolation* 35.3 (1994): 211–229.

Little Lady of the Big House (1916)

Furer, Andrew J. "Jack London's New Woman: A Little Lady with a Big Stick." *SAF* 22.2 (1994): 200–206.

People of the Abyss (1903)

Giles, James R. *Naturalistic Inner-City Novel in America*, 34–44.

Sea Wolf (1904)

Baskett, Sam S. "Sea Change in *The Sea Wolf*." *ALR* 24.2 (1992): 5–22.

Gair, Christopher. "Gender and Genre: Nature, Naturalism, and Authority in *The Sea-Wolf*," *SAF* 22.2 (1994): 131–147.

Valley of the Moon (1913)

Gair, Christopher. " 'The Way Our People Came': Citzenship, Capitalism and Racial Difference in *The Valley of the Moon*." *SNNTS* 25.4 (1993): 418–435.

Reesman, Jeanne Campbell. "Jack London's New Woman in a New World: Saxon Brown Roberts' Journey into the *Valley of the Moon*." *ALR* 24.2 (1992): 40–54.

LÓPEZ-MEDINA, SYLVIA (1942–)

Cantora (1992)

Rebolledo, Tey Diana. *Women Singing in the Snow*, 129–130.

LORANGER, FRANÇOISE (1913–1995)

Mathieu (1949)

Raoul, Valerie. *Distinctly Narcissistic*, 112–121.

LORD, BETTE BAO (1938–)

In the Year of the Boar and Jackie Robinson (1984)

Walter, Virginia A. "Crossing the Pacific to America: The Uses of Narrative." *CLAQ* 16.2 (1991): 66–67.

LUMPKIN, GRACE (1892(?)–1980)

To Make My Bread (1932)

Hapke, Laura. *Daughters of the Great Depression*, 161–163.

LURIE, ALISON (1926–)

Foreign Affairs (1984)

Costa, Richard Hauer. *Alison Lurie*, 55–60.

Imaginary Friends (1967)

Costa, Richard Hauer. *Alison Lurie*, 69–73.

Love and Friendship (1962)

Costa, Richard Hauer. *Alison Lurie*, 17–21.

Nowhere City (1965)

Costa, Richard Hauer. *Alison Lurie*, 22–25.

Only Children (1979)

Costa, Richard Hauer. *Alison Lurie*, 43–49.

Real People (1969)

Costa, Richard Hauer. *Alison Lurie*, 25–29.

Truth about Lorin Jones (1988)

Costa, Richard Hauer. *Alison Lurie*, 85–91.

War Between the Tates (1974)

Costa, Richard Hauer. *Alison Lurie*, 31–42.

LYTLE, ANDREW (1902–)

Long Night (1936)

Warren, Robert Penn. "On Andrew Lytle's *Long Night*," in Madden, David, ed. *Classics of Civil War Fiction*, 141–150.

Velvet Horn (1957)

Bonds, Ellen. "Storytelling Characters and the Mythmaking Process in Andrew Lytle's *The Velvet Horn*." *SLJ* 25.2 (1993): 69–78.

MCCARTHY, CORMAC (1933–)

All the Pretty Horses (1992)

Bell, Vereen. " 'Between the Wish and the Thing the World Lies Waiting'." *SoR* 28.4 (1992): 920–927.

Cheuse, Alan. "A Note on Landscape in *All The Pretty Horses*." *SoQ* 30.4 (1992): 140–142.

Pilkington, Tom. "Fate and Free Will on the American Frontier: Cormac McCarthy's Western Fiction." *WAL* 27.4 (1993): 318–322.

Witek, Terri. "Reeds and Hides: Cormac McCarthy's Domestic Spaces." *SoR* 30.1 (1994): 136–142.

Blood Meridian (1985)

Daugherty, Leo. "Gravers False and True: *Blood Meridian* as Gnostic Tragedy." *SoQ* 30.4 (1992): 122–133.

Pilkington, Tom. "Fate and Free Will on the American Frontier: Cormac McCarthy's Western Fiction." *WAL* 27.4 (1993): 314–318.

Schopen, Bernard. " 'They Rode Up': *Blood Meridian* and the Art of Narrative." *WAL* 30.2 (1995): 179–194.

Sepich, John Emil. " 'Bloody Dark Pastryman': Cormac McCarthy's Recipe for Gunpowder and Historical Fiction in *Blood Meridian*." *MissQ* 46.4 (1993): 547–563.

Sepich, John Emil. "Dance of History in Cormac McCarthy's *Blood Meridian*." *SLJ* 24.1 (1991): 16–31.

Sepich, John Emil. " 'What Kind of Indians Was Them?': Some Historical Sources in Cormac McCarthy's *Blood Meridian*." *SoQ* 30.4 (1992): 93–110.

Shaviro, Steven. " 'The Very Life of Darkness': A Reading of *Blood Meridian.*" *SoQ* 30.4 (1992): 111–121.
Witek, Terri. "Reeds and Hides: Cormac McCarthy's Domestic Spaces." *SoR* 30.1 (1994): 136–142.

Child of God (1974)

Bartlett, Andrew. "From Voyeurism to Archaeology: Cormac McCarthy's *Child of God.*" *SLJ* 24.1 (1991): 3–15.
Witek, Terri. "Reeds and Hides: Cormac McCarthy's Domestic Spaces." *SoR* 30.1 (1994): 136–142.

Orchard Keeper (1965)

Ragan, David Paul. "Values and Structure in *The Orchard Keeper.*" *SoQ* 30.4 (1992): 10–18.
Witek, Terri. "Reeds and Hides: Cormac McCarthy's Domestic Spaces." *SoR* 30.1 (1994): 136–142.

Outer Dark (1968)

Witek, Terri. "Reeds and Hides: Cormac McCarthy's Domestic Spaces." *SoR* 30.1 (1994): 136–142.

Suttree (1979)

Young, Thomas D., Jr. "Imprisonment of Sensibility: *Suttree.*" *SoQ* 30.4 (1992): 72–92.
Witek, Terri. "Reeds and Hides: Cormac McCarthy's Domestic Spaces." *SoR* 30.1 (1994): 136–142.

MCCARTHY, MARY (1912–1989)

Cannibals and Missionaries (1979)

Gordon, Mary. *Good Boys and Dead Girls*, 61–66.

Company She Keeps (1942)

Crowley, John W. "Mary McCarthy's *The Company She Keeps.*" *Expl* 51.2 (1993): 111–115.

Group (1963)

Castronovo, David. *American Gentleman*, 76–79.

MCCORKLE, JILL (1958–)

Tending to Virginia (1987)

Tate, Linda. *Southern Weave of Women*, 22–33.

MCCOY, HORACE (1897–1955)

They Shoot Horses, Don't They (1970)

Fine, David. "Running Out of Space: Vanishing Landscapes in California Novels." *WAL* 26.3 (1991): 214–215.

MCCUAIG, SANDRA

Blindfold (1990)

Apseloff, Marilyn Fain. "Death in Adolescent Literature: Suicide." *CLAQ* 16.4 (1991–92): 235, 236, 237–238.

MCCULLERS, CARSON (1917–1967)

Heart Is a Lonely Hunter (1940)

Budick, Emily Miller. *Engendering Romance*, 144–161.
Champion, Laurie. "Black and White Christs in Carson McCuller's *The Heart Is a Lonely Hunter*." *SLJ* 24.1 (1991): 47–52.
Rogers, Franklin R. *Occidental Ideographs*, 188–211, 219–221.
Whitt, Jan. "Loneliest Hunter." *SLJ* 24.2 (1992): 26–35.

MCCUNN, RUTHANNE LUM (1946–)

Thousand Pieces of Gold (1981)

Wong, Sau-ling Cynthia. *Reading Asian American Literature*, 123–124.

MCELROY, JOSEPH (1930–)

Lookout Cartridge (1974)

O'Donnell, Patrick. "Engendering Paranoia in Contemporary Narrative." *BoundaryII* 19.1 (1992): 195–198.

MCGIVERN, WILLIAM P. (1922–1982)

But Death Run's Faster (1948)

Haut, Woody. *Pulp Culture*, 144–149.

Odds Against Tomorrow (1957)

Haut, Woody. *Pulp Culture*, 141–144.

MCGUANE, THOMAS (1939–)

Bushwacked Piano (1971)

Westrum, Dexter. *Thomas McGuane*, 31–32, 33–40.

Keep the Change (1990)

Westrum, Dexter. *Thomas McGuane*, 118, 119–130.

Ninety-two in the Shade (1973)

Westrum, Dexter. *Thomas McGuane*, 41–43, 45–52.

Nobody's Angel (1982)

Westrum, Dexter. *Thomas McGuane*, 78–79, 81–88.

Panama (1978)

Westrum, Dexter. *Thomas McGuane*, 68–69, 71–77.

Something to Be Desired (1985)

Westrum, Dexter. *Thomas McGuane*, 89, 90–99.

Sporting Club (1969)

Westrum, Dexter. *Thomas McGuane*, 19–20, 21–29.

MCINERNEY, JAY (1955–)

Bright Lights, Big City (1984)

Young, Elizabeth. *Shopping in Space*, 47–55.

Brightness Falls (1992)

Young, Elizabeth. *Shopping in Space*, 69–74.

Ransom (1985)

Young, Elizabeth. *Shopping in Space*, 55–63

Story of My Life (1988)

De Caro, Frank. "Three Great Lies: Riddles of Love and Death in a Postmodern Novel." *SFolk* 48.3 (1991): 235–254.

Young, Elizabeth. *Shopping in Space*, 63–69.

MCINTOSH, MARIA (1803–1878)

Two Lives (1846)

Levy, Helen Fiddyment. *Fiction of the Home Place*, 37–41.

MCKAY, CLAUDE (1890–1948)

Banana Bottom (1933)

Dixon, Melvin. *Ride Out the Wilderness: Geography and Identity in Afro-American Literature*. Urbana, IL: University of Illinois Press, 1987. 52–53. Rpt. in Bloom, Harold, ed. *Major Black American Writers Through the Harlem Renaissance*, 149–150.

Home to Harlem (1928)

Hapke, Laura. *Daughters of the Great Depression*, 59–61.

Hielgar, Charles J. "Claude McKay's 'If We Must Die,' *Home to Harlem*, and the Hog Trope." *ANQ* 8.3 (1995): 22–25.

Kent, George E. *Blackness and the Adventure of Western Culture*. Chicago: Third World Press, 1972. 46–48. Rpt. in Bloom, Harold, ed. *Major Black American Writers Through the Harlem Renaissance*, 146–148.

MCKINLEY, ROBIN (1952–)

Beauty (1978)

Cadden, Michael. "Illusion of Control: Narrative Authority in Robin McKinley's *Beauty* and *The Blue Sword*." *Mythlore* 76 (1994): 16–19.

Blue Sword (1982)

Cadden, Michael. "Illusion of Control: Narrative Authority in Robin McKinley's *Beauty* and *The Blue Sword.*" *Mythlore* 76 (1994): 16–19.

MACLENNAN, HUGH (1907–1990)

Barometer Rising (1941)

Lacombe, Michèle. "Gender in the Fiction of Thomas H. Raddall," in Young, Alan R., ed. *Time and Place*, 92.

Watch That Ends the Night (1959)

Keith, W. J. *Life Struggle: Hugh Maclennan's The Watch That Ends the Night.* Toronto: ECW Press, 1993.

Pell, Barbara. "Faith and Fiction: Hugh MacLennan's *The Watch That Ends the Night.*" *CanL* 128 (1991): 39–50.

MCMILLAN, TERRY (1951–)

Mama (1987)

Saunders, James Robert. *Wayward Preacher*, 125–144.

See, Carolyn. "Down-and-Out Family, Out of the Mainstream, Wants In." *Los Angeles Times* (23 Feb. 1987): V4. Rpt. in Bloom, Harold, ed. *Contemporary Black American Fiction Writers,* 75–76.

Disappearing Acts (1989)

Davis, Thulani. "Don't Worry, Be Buppie: Black Novelists Head for the Mainstream." *Voice Literary Supplement* 85 (May 1990): 26, 29. Rpt. in Bloom, Harold, ed. *Contemporary Black American Fiction Writers*, 78–80.

Nicholson, David. "Love's Old Sweet Song." *Washington Post Book World* (27 Aug. 1989): 6. Rpt. in Bloom, Harold, ed. *Contemporary Black American Fiction Writers*, 77–78.

MCMURTRY, LARRY (1936–)

Anything for Billy (1988)

Cox, Diana H. "*Anything for Billy:* A Fiction Stranger Than Truth." *JACult* 14.2 (1991): 75–81.

Horseman, Pass By (1958)

Sarll, Pauline. "Boundaries, Borders and Frontiers: A Revisionary Reading of Larry McMurtry's *Horseman, Pass By.*" *JPC* 28.1 (1994): 97–110.

Hud see *Horseman, Pass By*

Last Picture Show (1966)

Crawford, Iain. "Intertextuality in Larry McMurtry's *The Last Picture Show.*" *JPC* 27.1 (1993): 43–54.

Lonesome Dove (1985)

Birchfield, D. L. "Lonesome Duck: The Blueing of a Texas-American Myth." *SAIL* 7.2 (1995): 45–64.

Texasville (1987)

Woodward, Daniel. "Larry McMurtry's *Texasville:* A Comic Pastoral of the Oil-patch." *HLQ* 56.2 (1993): 167–180.

MCNICKLE, D'ARCY (1904–1977)

Surrounded (1936)

Brown, Bill. "Trusting Story and Reading *The Surrounded.*" *SAIL* 3.2 (1991): 22–27.

Larson, Charles R. "*Surrounded,*" in Fleck, Richard F., ed. *Critical Perspectives,* 87–94.

Oaks, Priscilla. "First Generation of Native American Novels," in Fleck, Richard F., ed. *Critical Perspectives,* 82–84

Owens, Louis. *Other Destinies,* 61–78.

Ruppert, James. "Textual Perspectives and the Reader in *The Surrounded,*" in Fleck, Richard F., ed. *Critical Perspectives,* 71–78.

Wind from an Enemy Sky (1979)

Owens, Louis. *Other Destinies,* 80–89.

Ruppert, James. *Mediation in Contemporary Native American Fiction,* 109–130.

MAHEUX-FORCIER, LOUISE (1929–)

Amadou (1963)

Brown, Anne E. "Sappho's Daughters: Lesbian Identities in Novels by Québécois Women (1960–1990)," in Brown, Anne E., ed. *International Women's Writing,* 31–32.

Dufault, Roseanna Lewis, "*Amadou* de Louise Maheux-Forcier: un roman qui défie l'ordre établi," in Saint-Martin, Lori, ed. *L'autre lecture* (Tome 1), 167–175.

Forest for Zoe see *Une Forêt pour Zoé*

L'Ile joyeuse (1964)

Dufault, Roseanna Lewis. *Metaphors of Identity,* 50–54.

Tinder see *Amadou*

Une Forêt pour Zoé (1969)

Brown, Anne E. "Sappho's Daughters: Lesbian Identities in Novels by Québécois Women (1960–1990)," in Brown, Anne E., ed. *International Women's Writing,* 30–31, 32–34.

MAILER, NORMAN (1923–)

American Dream (1965)

Cafagna, Dianne. "Mailer's Moon over *An American Dream.*" *NConL* 22.5 (1992): 3–4.

Cooper, Ken. " 'Zero Pays the House': The Las Vegas Novel and Atomic Roulette." *ConL* 33.3 (1992): 537.

Glenday, Michael K. *Norman Mailer,* 84–100.

Ancient Evenings (1983)

Glenday, Michael K. *Norman Mailer*, 117–126.

Mellard, James M. "Origins, Language, and the Constitution of Reality: Norman Mailer's *Ancient Evenings*," in Friedman, Melvin J., ed. *Traditions, Voices, and Dreams*, 131–149.

Armies of the Night (1968)

Byatt, A. S. *Passions of the Mind*, 139–140.

Reed, T. V. *Fifteen Jugglers, Five Believers*, 87–119.

Stull, James N. *Literary Selves*, 101–117.

Barbary Shore (1963)

Glenday, Michael K. *Norman Mailer*, 62–71.

Deer Park (1955)

Glenday, Michael K. *Norman Mailer*, 72–83.

Executioner's Song (1979)

Merrill, Robert. "Mailer's Sad Comedy: *The Executioner's Song*." *TSLL* 34.1 (1992): 129–148.

O'Donnell, Patrick. "Engendering Paranoia in Contemporary Narrative." *BoundaryII* 19.1 (1992): 184–190.

Pizer, Donald. *Theory and Practice*, 175–181.

Harlot's Ghost (1991)

Glenday, Michael K. *Norman Mailer*, 130–143.

Miami and the Siege of Chicago (1968)

Naked and the Dead (1948)

Glenday, Michael K. *Norman Mailer*, 46–61.

Limon, John. *Writing After War*, 133–136.

Pizer, Donald. *Theory and Practice*, 49–52.

Of a Fire on the Moon (1970)

Tabbi, Joseph. "Mailer's Psychology of Machines." *PMLA* 106.2 (1991): 238–250.

Tough Guys Don't Dance (1984)

Glenday, Michael K. *Norman Mailer*, 126–129.

Merrill, Robert. "Mailer's *Tough Guys Don't Dance* and the Detective Traditions." *Crit* 34.4 (1993): 232–246.

Why Are We in Vietnam? (1967)

Glenday, Michael K. *Norman Mailer*, 100–114.

Limon, John. *Writing After War*, 173–176.

MAILHOT, MICHÈLE

Dis-moi que je vis (1964)

Anderson, M. Jean. "Fuir pour survivre: aliénation et identité chez Michèle Mailhot," in Saint-Martin, Lori, ed. *L'autre lecture* (Tome 1), 159–161, 164.

Le passé composé (1990)

Raoul, Valerie. *Distinctly Narcissistic*, 211–214.

Le portique (1967)

Anderson, M. Jean. "Fuir pour survivre: aliénation et identité chez Michèle Mailhot," in Saint-Martin, Lori, ed. *L'autre lecture* (Tome 1), 158–159, 164.

MAILLET, ANTONINE (1929–)

Les cordes-de-bois (1977)

Maindron, Andre. "Le Petit Prêtre d'Antonine Maillet." *ECCS* 30 (1991): 79–87.

Pélagie-la-Charrette (1979)

O'Reilly, Magessa. "Une Écriture qui célèbre la tradition orale: *Pélagie-la-charrette* d'Antonine Maillet." *SCL* 18.1 (1993): 118–127.
Shek, Ben-Z. *French-Canadian*, 112–114.

Pélagie: The Return to a Homeland see *Pélagie-la-Charrette*

MAJOR, CLARENCE (1936–)

All-Night Visitors (1969)

Coleman, James W. "Clarence Major's *All-Night Visitors*: Calabanic Discourse and Black Male Expression." *AAR* 28.1 (1994): 95–107.
Welburn, Ron. [Review of *All-Night Visitors*]. *Negro Digest* 19.2 (1969): 85, 87. Rpt. in Bloom, Harold, ed. *Contemporary Black American Fiction Writers*, 89–90.

Emergency Exit (1979)

Quartermain, Peter. "Trusting the Reader." *Chicago Review* 32.2 (1980): 66–69. Rpt. in Bloom, Harold, ed. *Contemporary Black American Fiction Writers*, 93–94.

My Amputations (1986)

Klawans, Stuart. " 'I Was a Weird Example of Art': *My Amputations* as Cubist Confession." *AAR* 28.1 (1994): 77–86.
Tate, Greg. [Review of *My Amputations*]. *Voice Literary Supplement* 52 (February 1987): 3. Rpt. in Bloom, Harold, ed. *Contemporary Black American Fiction Writers*, 98.

NO (1973)

Klinkowitz, Jerome. "Clarence Major." *The Life of Fiction*. Urbana, IL: University of Illinois Press, 1977. 97. Rpt. in Bloom, Harold, ed. *Contemporary Black American Fiction Writers*, 91–92.

Reflex and Bone Structure (1975)

Bradfield, Larry D. "Beyond Mimetic Exhaustion: The *Reflex and Bone Structure* Experiement." *Black American Literature Forum* 17.3 (Fall 1983): 120–122. Rpt. in Bloom, Harold, ed. *Contemporary Black American Fiction Writers*, 94–96.

Such Was the Season (1987)

Bell, Bernard W. "Clarence Major's Homecoming Voice in *Such Was the Season*." *AAR* 28.1 (1994): 89–94.

MALAMUD, BERNARD (1914–1986)

Assistant (1957)

Abramson, Edward A. *Bernard Malamud Revisited*, 25–42.

Goldsmith, Arnold L. *Modern American Urban Novel*, 104–118.

Langer, Lawrence L. *Admitting the Holocaust*, 145–146, 150–152.

Purcell, William F. "Demands of Love: The Ending of Bernard Malamud's *The Assistant*." *NConL* 23.5 (1993): 4–5.

Dubin's Lives (1979)

Abramson, Edward A. *Bernard Malamud Revisited*, 101–113.

Magaw, Malcolm O. "Malamud's Dubious Dubin: The Biographer and His Square Walk in Circle." *ClioI* 23.3 (1994): 219–233.

Fixer (1966)

Abramson, Edward A. *Bernard Malamud Revisited*, 58–75.

Langer, Lawrence L. *Admitting the Holocaust*, 145–148.

God's Grace (1982)

Abramson, Edward A. *Bernard Malamud Revisited*, 114–127.

Buchen, Irving H. "Malamud's *God's Grace:* Divine Genesis, Mortal Terminus." *SAJL* 10.1 (1991): 24–34.

Freese, Peter. "Surviving the End: Apocalypse, Evolution, and Entropy in Bernard Malamud, Kurt Vonnegut, and Thomas Pynchon." *Crit* 36.3 (1995): 163–167.

Natural (1952)

Abramson, Edward A. *Bernard Malamud Revisited*, 9–24.

Limon, John. *Writing After War*, 157–160.

New Life (1961)

Abramson, Edward A. *Bernard Malamud Revisited*, 43–57.

MANFRED, FREDERICK (1912–1994)

Golden Bowl (1944)

Quantic, Diane Dufva. "Frederick Manfred's *The Golden Bowl:* Myth and Reality in the Dust Bowl." *WAL* 25.4 (1991): 297–309.

MANGIONE, GERALDO see MANGIONE, JERRE

MANGIONE, JERRE (1909–)

Mount Allegro (1942)

Vitiello, Justin. "Sicilian Folk Narrative versus Sicilian-American Literature: Mangione's *Mount Allegro*." *MELUS* 18.2 (1992): 61–75.

MARCH, WILLIAM (1893–1954)

Bad Seed (1954)

Simmonds, Roy S. "Cathy Ames and Rhoda Penmark: Two Child Monsters." *Mississippi Quarterly* 39 (Spring 1986): 91–101. Rpt. in Hayashi, Tesumaro, ed. *Steinbeck's Literary Dimension*, 103–112.

MARCHESSAULT, JOVETTE (1938–)

Des Cailloux blancs pour les forêts obscures (1987)

Poirier, Martin. "L'Épopée d'une famille hors-la-loi." *Tangence* 47 (1995): 98–111.

La Mère des herbes (1980)

Shek, Ben-Z. *French-Canadian*, 96–97.
Theberge, Ghislaine. "Lecture et imaginaire: Pour une figure de l'Indien dans *La mère des herbes* de Jovette Marchessault." *Tangence* 36 (1992): 85–95.

Mother of the Grass see *La Mère des herbes*

White Pebbles in the Dark Forest see *Des Cailloux blancs pour les forêts obscures*

MARQUAND, J. P. (1893–1960)

H.M. Pulham, Esquire (1941)

Castronovo, David. *American Gentleman*, 105–107.

Wickford Point (1939)

Castronovo, David. *American Gentleman*, 107–109.

MARSHALL, PAULE (1929–)

Brown Girl, Brownstones (1959)

Coser, Stellamaris. *Bridging the Americas*, 60.
Denniston, Dorothy Hamer. *Fiction of Paule Marshall*, 7–32.
Kubitschek, Missy Dehn. *Claiming the Heritage*, 71–77.
LeSeur, Geta. "Monster-Machine and the White Mausoleum: Paule Marshall's Metaphors for Western Materialism." *CLAJ* 39.1 (1995): 49–51, 55–56.
Niesen de Abruña, Laura. "Ambivalence of Mirroring and Female Bonding in Paule Marshall's *Brown Girl, Brownstones*," in Brown, Anne E., ed. *International Women's Writing*, 245–251.
Pettis, Joyce. *Toward Wholeness*, 42–46, 87–90.
Saunders, James Robert. *Wayward Preacher*, 71–104.
Willis, Susan. *Specifying: Black Women Writing the American Experience*. Madison, WI: University of Wisconsin Press, 1987. 74–75. Rpt. in Bloom, Harold, ed. *Black American Women Fiction Writers*, 140–141.
Willis, Susan. *Specifying: Black Women Writing the American Experience*. Madison, WI: University of Wisconsin Press, 1987. 74–75. Rpt. in Bloom, Harold, ed. *Modern Black American Fiction Writers*, 102–103.

Chosen Place, the Timeless People (1969)

Coser, Stellamaris. *Bridging the Americas*, 34–59.
DeLamotte, Eugenia. "Women, Silence, and History in *The Chosen Place, the Timeless People*." *Callaloo* 16.1 (1993): 227–242.
Denniston, Dorothy Hamer. *Fiction of Paule Marshall*, 97–125.
Kapai, Leela. "Dominant Themes and Technique in Paule Marshall's Fiction." *CLA Journal* 16.1 (September 1972): 54–55. Rpt. in Bloom, Harold, ed. *Black American Women Fiction Writers*, 136–137.

Kapai, Leela. "Dominant Themes and Technique in Paule Marshall's Fiction." *CLA Journal* 16.1 (September 1972): 54–55. Rpt. in Bloom, Harold, ed. *Modern Black American Fiction Writers*, 98–99.

Kubitschek, Missy Dehn. *Claiming the Heritage*, 77–85.

LeSeur, Geta. "Monster-Machine and the White Mausoleum: Paule Marshall's Metaphors for Western Materialism." *CLAJ* 39.1 (1995): 51–53, 56–57.

Ogunyemi, Chikwenye Okonjo. "Womanism: The Dynamics of the Contemporary Black Female Novel in English," in Clark, VéVé A., ed. *Revising the Word*, 239.

Pettis, Joyce. *Toward Wholeness*, 47–60, 86–87, 90–93.

Rahming, Melvin. "Towards a Caribbean Mythology: The Function of Africa in Paule Marshall's *The Chosen Place, The Timeless People*." *SLitI* 26.2 (1993): 77–87.

Daughters (1991)

Coser, Stellamaris. *Bridging the Americas*, 66–79.

Denniston, Dorothy Hamer. *Fiction of Paule Marshall*, 146–165.

Pettis, Joyce. "Legacies of Community and History in Paule Marshall's *Daughters*." *SLitI* 26.2 (1993): 89–99.

Pettis, Joyce. *Toward Wholeness*, 60–71, 136–147.

Schaeffer, Susan Fromberg. "Cutting Herself Free." *New York Times Book Review* (27 October 1991): 3, 29. Rpt. in Bloom, Harold, ed. *Modern Black American Fiction Writers*, 105–106.

Praisesong for the Widow (1984)

Cooper, Carolyn. " 'Something Ancestral Recaptured': Spirit Possession as Trope in Selected Feminist Fictions of the African Diaspora," in Nasta, Susheila, ed. *Motherlands*, 81–84.

Coser, Stellamaris. *Bridging the Americas*, 60–65.

Denniston, Dorothy Hamer. *Fiction of Paule Marshall*, 126–145.

Kubitschek, Missy Dehn. *Claiming the Heritage*, 85–88.

LeSeur, Geta. "Monster-Machine and the White Mausoleum: Paule Marshall's Metaphors for Western Materialism." *CLAJ* 39.1 (1995): 53–54, 57–58.

Pettis, Joyce. *Toward Wholeness*, 106–135.

Smith-Wright, Geraldine. "In Spite of the Klan: Ghosts in the Fiction of Black Women Writers," in Carpenter, Lynette, ed. *Haunting the House of Fiction*, 159–164.

Wilentz, Gay Alden. *Binding Cultures*, 99–115.

MARSHALL, WILLIAM (1944–)

Roadshow (1985)

Porush, David. "Fictions as Dissipative Structures: Prigogine's Theory and Postmodernism's Roadshow," in Hayles, N. Katherine, ed. *Chaos and Order*, 61–76.

MARTEL, SUZANNE (1924–)

City Underground see *Quatre Montréalais en l'an 3000*

Quatre Montréalais en l'an 3000 (1963)

Colas-Charpentier, Helene. "Four Quebecois Dystopias, 1963–1972." Trans. ABE and Carine Deschanel. *SFS* 20.3 (1993): 385–387.

MARTIN, VALERIE (1948–)

Mary Reilly (1990)

Cowart, David. *Literary Symbiosis*, 85–104.
Roberts, Bette B. "Strange Case of *Mary Reilly*." *Extrapolation* 34.1 (1993): 39–47.

MASON, BOBBIE ANN (1940–)

In Country (1985)

Blais, Ellen A. "Gender Issues in Bobbie Ann Mason's *In Country*." *SoAR* 56.2 (1991): 107–118.
Booth, David. "Sam's Quest, Emmett's Wound: Grail Motifs in Bobbie Ann Mason's Portrait of America after Vietnam." *SLJ* 23.2 (1991): 98–109.
Dwyer, June. "New Roles, New History and New Patriotism: Bobbie Ann Mason's *In Country*." *MLS* 22.2 (1992): 72–78.
Krasteva, Yonka. "South and The West in Bobbie Ann Mason's *In Country*." *SLJ* 26.2 (1994): 77–90.
Limon, John. *Writing After War*, 216–219.
Morrissey, Thomas J. "Mason's *In Country*." *Expl* 50.1 (1991): 62–64.
Price, Joanna. "Remembering Vietnam: Subjectivity and Mourning in American New Realist Writing." *JAmS* 27.2 (1993): 175–178, 180, 182–186.
Tate, Linda. *Southern Weave of Women*, 132–148.

MATHEWS, JOHN JOSEPH (1894–1979)

Sundown (1934)

Owens, Louis. *Other Destinies*, 48–60.

MATTHIESSEN, PETER (1927–)

At Play in the Fields of the Lord (1965)

Dowie, William. *Peter Matthiessen*, 51–56.

Far Tortuga (1975)

Dowie, William. *Peter Matthiessen*, 91–103.
Raglon, Rebecca. "Fact and Fiction: The Development of Ecological Form in Peter Matthiessen's *Far Tortuga*." *Crit* 35.4 (1994): 245–259.

Killing Mr. Watson (1990)

Dowie, William. *Peter Matthiessen*, 122–129.

Partisans (1955)

Dowie, William. *Peter Matthiessen*, 23–28.

Race Rock (1954)

Dowie, William. *Peter Matthiessen*, 19–23.

Raditzer (1961)

Dowie, William. *Peter Matthiessen*, 26–28.

Snow Leopard (1978)

Dowie, William. *Peter Matthiessen*, 107–113.

MAYNARD, FREDELLE BRUSER (1922–)

Raisins and Almonds (1972)

Dufault, Roseanna Lewis. *Metaphors of Identity*, 66–71.

MEDINA, PABLO (1948–)

Exiled Memories (1990)

Alvarez-Borland, Isabel. "Displacements and Autobiography in Cuban-American Fiction." *WLT* 68.1 (1994): 44–45.

MELVILLE, HERMAN (1819–1891)

Confidence-Man (1857)

Atherton, Eric N. "Blurred Distinctions: The Parable of the Sower and Melville's One-Legged Man." *ANQ* 7.3 (1994): 149–153.

Dolan, Marc. "Four Faces of *The Confidence-Man:* An Academic Blind Man's Zoo." *ESQ* 39.2–3 (1993): 133–160.

Maddox, Lucy. *Removals*, 81–87.

Pimple, Kenneth D. "Personal Narrative, Melville's *The Confidence-Man*, and the Problem of Deception." *WF* 51.1 (1992): 33–50.

Van Cromphout, Gustaaf. "*The Confidence-Man:* Melville and the Problem of Others." *SAF* 21.1 (1993): 37–50.

Israel Potter (1855)

Christophersen, Bill. "*Israel Potter:* Melville's 'Citizen of the Universe.'" *SAF* 21.1 (1993): 21–35.

Davis, Clark. "Body Deferred: *Israel Potter* and the Search for the Hearth." *SAF* 19.2 (1991): 175–187.

Reagan, Daniel. "Charles Knight's London in Melville's *Israel Potter.*" *ESQ* 38.3 (1992): 189–205.

Mardi (1849)

Berthold, Michael C. " 'Born-Free-and-Equal': Benign Cliche and Narrative Imperialism in Melville's *Mardi.*" *SNNTS* 25.1 (1993): 16–27.

Newman, Lea Bertani Vozar. "Melville's Copy of Dante: Evidence of New Connections between the *Commedia* and *Mardi.*" *SAR* 17 (1993): 305–338.

Pottle, Russ. "Monkey before the Whale: 'Signifyin(g)' and Melville's *Mardi.*" *JNT* 23.3 (1993): 136–153.

Thorne, Beverly Hume. "Taji's Yillah: Transcending the Fates in Melville's *Mardi.*" *ELWIU* 19.1 (1992): 61–72.

Weinstein, Cindy. "Calm before the Storm: Laboring through *Mardi.*" *AL* 65.2 (1993): 239–253.

Moby-Dick (1851)

Berthold, Michael C. "*Moby-Dick* and American Slave Narrative." *MR* 36.1 (1994): 135–148.

Birk, John F. "Unsealing the Sphinx: The Pequod's Egyptian Pantheon." *ATQ* 5.4 (1991): 283–299.

Budick, Emily Miller. *Engendering Romance*, 63–69.

Chang, Young-hee. " 'One Seamless Whole': Ishmael's Dual Vision in *Moby-Dick*." *JELL* 37.4 (1991): 939–953.

Crain, Caleb. "Lovers of Human Flesh: Homosexuality and Cannibalism in Melville's Novels." *AL* 66.1 (1994): 40, 42–43, 45–46.

Dameron, J. Lasley. "Melville and Scoresby on Whiteness." *ES* 74.1 (1993): 96–104.

Davis, Clark. "Divided Body: Topographical Dualism in *Moby-Dick*." *ATQ* 5.1 (1991): 31–40.

Forrest, Leon. *Relocations of the Spirit*, 238–239.

Hamilton, Christopher T. "Melville's *Moby Dick*." *Expl* 49.3 (1991): 152–153.

Herreshoff, David Sprague. *Labor Into Art*, 28–68.

Keating, AnnLouise. "Implications of Edwards' Theory of the Will on Ahab's Pursuit of Moby Dick." *ELN* 28.3 (1991): 28–36.

Kowalewski, Michael. *Deadly Musings*, 10–13.

Lakacs, Paul. "Abandonment of Time and Place: History and Narrative, Metaphysics and Exposition in Melville's *Moby-Dick*." *ClioI* 20.2 (1991): 139–155.

Maddox, Lucy. *Removals*, 60–67.

Martin, Robert. "Sleeping with a Savage: Deculturation in *Moby-Dick*." *ATQ* 5.3 (1991): 195–202.

Mulvihill, Alice S. A. "Significance of the 'Old Thunder' Epithet in *Moby Dick*." *ANQ* 7.1 (1994): 22–25.

Onishi, Naoki. "Melville's *Moby-Dick*." *Expl* 50.3 (1992): 148–150.

Person, Leland S., Jr. "Melville's Cassock: Putting on Masculinity in *Moby-Dick*." *ESQ* 40.1 (1994): 1–26.

Phillips, Rod. "Melville's *Moby Dick*." *Expl* 53.2 (1995): 92–95.

Railton, Stephen. *Authorship and Audience*, 152–189.

Rathbun, John W. "*Moby-Dick:* Ishmael's Fictions of Ahab's Romantic Insurgency." *MLS* 21.3 (1991): 3–9.

Roberts, Terry. "Ishmael as Phallic Narrator." *SAF* 20.1 (1992): 99–109.

Sanborn, Geoffrey. "Name of the Devil: Melville's Other 'Extracts' for *Moby-Dick*." *NCF* 47.2 (1992): 212–235.

Shaw, Peter. "Cutting a Classic Down to Size." *VQR* 69.1 (1993): 60–84.

Shaw, Peter. *Recovering American Literature*, 48–74.

Staud, John. " 'What's in a Name?' The Pequod and Melville's Heretical Politics." *ESQ* 38.4 (1992): 338–359.

Straud, John J. "*Moby-Dick* and Melville's Vexed Romanticism." *ATQ* 6.4 (1992): 279–292.

Taketani, Etsuko. "*Moby-Dick*: Gnostic Re-Writing of History." *ATQ* 8.2 (1994): 119–134.

Vick, Marsha C. " 'Defamiliarization' and the Ideology of Race in *Moby-Dick*." *CLAJ* 35.3 (1992): 325–338.

Pierre (1852)

Cervo, Nathan. "Melville's *Pierre*." *Expl* 51.4 (1993): 223–224.

Davis, Clark. "Asceticism and the Fictive in *Pierre*." *ESQ* 38.2 (1992): 143–159.

Hall, Jonathan. "Non-Correspondent Breeze: Melville's Rewriting of Wordsworth in *Pierre*." *ESQ* 39.1 (1993): 1–19.

Hume, Beverly A. "Of Krakens and Other Monsters: Melville's *Pierre.*" *ATQ* 6.2 (1992): 95–107.

Mishra, Vijay. *Gothic Sublime*, 250–254.

Otter, Samuel. "Eden of Saddle Meadows: Landscape and Ideology in *Pierre.*" *AL* 66.1 (1994): 55–81.

Post-Lauria, Sheila. "Genre and Ideology: The French Sensational Romance and Melville's *Pierre.*" *JACult* 15.3 (1992): 1–8.

Rowe, John Carlos. "Romancing the Stone: Melville's Critique of Ideology in *Pierre,*" in Cowan, Bainard, ed. *Theorizing American Literature*, 195–232.

Redburn (1849)

Bernard, Ernest S. "Spontaneous Combustion in *Redburn: Redburn*'s Ultimate Guidebook?" *SNNTS* 23.3 (1991): 348–356.

Bromell, Nicholas K. *By the Sweat of the Brow*, 61–79.

Crain, Caleb. "Lovers of Human Flesh: Homosexuality and Cannibalism in Melville's Novels." *AL* 66.1 (1994): 32–33, 43–44.

Hall, Jonathan L. " 'Every Man of Them Almost Was a Volume of Voyages': Writing the Self in Melville's *Redburn.*" *ATQ* 5.4 (1991): 259–270.

Tassoni, John Paul. "*Redburn*'s Kunstlerroman: Nineteenth-Century Linguistics and Melville's Signification of Delusion." *NCS* 6 (1992): 51–60.

Thomas, Heather Kirk. "Melville's *Redburn.*" *Expl* 50.1 (1991): 16–18.

Typee (1846)

Bergman, David. *Gaiety Transfigured*, 143–149.

Crain, Caleb. "Lovers of Human Flesh: Homosexuality and Cannibalism in Melville's Novels." *AL* 66.1 (1994): 29–32, 33,3 34, 38, 41.

Evelev, John. " 'Made in the Marquesas': *Typee*, Tatooing and Melville's Critique of the Literary Marketplace." *ArQ* 48.4 (1992): 19–28, 37–41.

Harvey, Bruce A. " 'Precepts Graven on Every Breast': Melville's *Typee* and the Forms of the Law." *AQ* 45.3 (1993): 394–424.

Lyons, Paul. "From Man-Eaters to Spam-Eaters: Literary Tourism and the Discourse of Cannibalism from Herman Melville to Paul Theroux." *ArQ* 51.2 (1995): 34–35, 40–42.

Maddox, Lucy. *Removals*, 57–59.

Renker, Elizabeth. "Melville's Spell in *Typee.*" *ArQ* 51.2 (1995): 1–31.

Schueller, Malini Johar. "Colonialism and Melville's South Seas Journeys." *SAF* 22.1 (1994): 3–18.

Shaw, Peter. *Recovering American Literature*, 151–171.

White-Jacket (1850)

Casarino, Cesare. "Gomorrahs of the Deep: Or, Melville, Foucault, and the Question of Heterotopia." *ArQ* 51.4 (1995): 4–12.

Crain, Caleb. "Lovers of Human Flesh: Homosexuality and Cannibalism in Melville's Novels." *AL* 66.1 (1994): 33, 37–38, 39.

Kier, Kathleen E. "*White-Jacket* 's Classical Oration." *SNNTS* 23.2 (1991): 237–244.

Stephenson, Will; Stephenson, Mimosa. "Melville's *White-Jacket.*" *Expl* 51.4 (1993): 221–223.

Whitsitt, Sam. "Fall Before the Fall: The Game of Identity, Language, and Voice in Melville's *White-Jacket.*" *ArQ* 48.2 (1992): 57–78.

METALIOUS, GRACE (1924–1964)

Peyton Place (1956)

Sypher, F. J. "Return to Grace Metalious." *CLC* 43.1 (1993): 3–11.
Wood, Ruth Pirsig. *Lolita in Peyton Place*, 3–13.

MICHALSKA, MADELEINE OUELETTE (1935–)

La Maison Trestler (1984)

Guillemette, Lucie. "L'Amérique déconstruite et les voix/voies féminines dans *La Maison Trestler* de Madeleine Ouellette-Michalska." *DFS* 23 (1992): 61–67.
Moss, Jane. "House Divided: Power Relations in Madeleine Ouellette-Michalska's *La Maison Trestler*." *QS* 12 (1991): 59–65.
Paterson, Janet M. *Postmodernism*, 53–67.

MILLER, SUE (1943–)

Good Mother (1986)

Perry, Ruth. "Mary Gordon's Mothers," in Daly, Brenda O., ed. *Narrating Mothers*, 209–210.
Rosenfelt, Deborah Silverton. "Feminism, 'Postfeminism,' and Contemporary Women's Fiction," in Howe, Florence, ed. *Tradition and the Talents of Women*, 279, 280, 281–282, 284, 285–286.

MILLER, WALTER M. (1923–)

Canticle for Leibowitz (1959)

House, Marilyn. "Miller's Anti-Utopian Vision: A Reading of *A Canticle for Leibowitz*." *RQ* 8.4 (1991): 253–271.
Senior, W. A. " 'From the Begetting of Monsters': Distortion as Unifier in *A Canticle for Leibowitz*." *Extrapolation* 34.4 (1993): 329–339.
Spencer, Susan. "Post-Apocalyptic Library: Oral and Literate Culture in *Fahrenheit 451* and *A Canticle for Leibowitz*." *Extrapolation* 32.4 (1991): 335–341.

MISTRY, ROHINTON (1952–)

Such a Long Journey (1991)

Malak, Amin. "Shahrazadic Tradition: Rohinton Mistry's *Such a Long Journey* and the Art of Storytelling." *JCL* 29.2 (1993): 108–118.

MITCHELL, ISAAC (1759–1812)

Alonzo and Melissa see *Asylum*

Asylum (1811)

Cowell, Pattie. "Class, Gender, and Genre: Deconstructing Social Formulas on the Gothic Frontier," in Mogen, David, ed. *Frontier Gothic*, 134–136.

MITCHELL, MARGARET (1900–1949)

Gone with the Wind (1936)

Bauer, Margaret D. " 'Put Your Heart in the Land': An Intertextual Reading of *Barren Ground* and *Gone with the Wind*," in Scura, Dorothy M., ed. *Ellen Glasgow*, 162–180.

Cantrell, James P. "Irish Culture and the War between the States: *Paddy McGann* and *Gone with the Wind*." *Eire* 27.2 (1992): 10–15.

Hanson, Elizabeth I. *Margaret Mitchell*, 51–67, 75–89.

Hapke, Laura. *Daughters of the Great Depression*, 214–217.

Harrison, Elizabeth Jane. *Female Pastoral*, 43–64.

Limon, John. *Writing After War*, 188–194.

MITCHELL, W. O. (1914–)

Vanishing Point (1973)

Davidson, Arnold E. *Coyote Country*, 157–168.

Who Has Seen the Wind (1947)

Harrison, Dick. *Intimations of Mortality: W. O. Mitchell's Who Has Seen the Wind*. Toronto: ECW Press, 1993.

MOMADAY, N. SCOTT (1934–)

Ancient Child (1989)

Owens, Louis. *Other Destinies*, 118–127.

Roemer, Kenneth M. "Ancient Children at Play—Lyric, Peteroglyphic, and Ceremonial," in Fleck, Richard F., ed. *Critical Perspectives*, 99–111.

House Made of Dawn (1969)

Evers, Lawrence J. Evers. "Words and Place: A Reading of *House Made of Dawn*," in Fleck, Richard F., ed. *Critical Perspectives*, 114–129.

Hogan, Linda. "Who Puts Together," in Fleck, Richard F., ed. *Critical Perspectives*, 134–142.

Owens, Louis. *Other Destinies*, 93–117.

Roemer, Kenneth M. "Ancient Children at Play—Lyric, Peteroglyphic, and Ceremonial," in Fleck, Richard F., ed. *Critical Perspectives*, 108–111.

Ruppert, James. *Mediation in Contemporary Native American Fiction*, 36–55.

Tusmith, Bonnie. *All My Relatives*, 105–119.

MONETTE, MADELEINE (1951–)

Double Suspect see *Le double suspect*

Le double suspect (1980)

Aas-Rouxparis, Nicole. "Inscriptions et transgressions dans *Le double suspect* de Madeleine Monette." *FR* 64.5 (1991): 754–761.

Raoul, Valerie. *Distinctly Narcissistic*, 162–166.

Petites violences (1982)

Ricouart, Janine. "Entre le miroir et le porte-clés: *Petites violences* de Madeleine Monette." *DFS* 23 (1992): 11–19.

MONETTE, PAUL (1945–1995)

Taking Care of Mrs. Carroll (1978)

Koponen, Wilfrid R. *Embracing Gay Identity*, 119–135.

MONTGOMERY, L. M. (1874–1942)

Anne of Avonlea (1909)

Epperly, Elizabeth Rollins. *Fragrance of Sweet Grass*, 39–55.

Gay, Carol. " 'Kindred Spirits' All: Green Gables Revisited." *Children's Literature Association Quarterly* 11 (1986): 9–12. Rpt. in Reimer, Mavis, ed. *Such a Simple Little Tale*, 106–108.

Anne of Green Gables (1908)

Berg, Temma F. "*Anne of Green Gables:* A Girl's Reading." *Children's Literature Association Quarterly* 13 (1988): 124–128. Rpt. in Reimer, Mavis, ed. *Such a Simple Little Tale*, 153–164,

Drain, Susan. "Community and the Individual in *Anne of Green Gables:* The Meaning of Belonging." *Children's Literature Association Quarterly* 11 (1986): 15–19. Rpt. in Reimer, Mavis, ed. *Such a Simple Little Tale*, 119–129.

Epperly, Elizabeth Rollins. *Fragrance of Sweet Grass*, 17–38.

Gay, Carol. " 'Kindred Spirits' All: Green Gables Revisited." *Children's Literature Association Quarterly* 11 (1986): 9–12. Rpt. in Reimer, Mavis, ed. *Such a Simple Little Tale*, 103–106.

Huse, Nancy. "Journeys of the Mother in the World of Green Gables." *Proceedings of the Thirteenth Annual Conference of the Children's Literature Assocation held at the University of Missouri–Kansas City, May 16–18, 1986.* Ed. Susan R. Gannon and Ruth Anne Thompson. West Lafayette, IN: Children's Literature Association, 1988. 60–63. Rpt. in Reimer, Mavis, ed. *Such a Simple Little Tale*, 131–137.

MacLulich, T.D. "L.M. Montgomery's Portraits of the Artist: Realism, Idealism, and the Domestic Imagination." *English Studies in Canada* 11 (1985): 459–473. Rpt. in Reimer, Mavis, ed. *Such a Simple Little Tale*, 92–93.

Nodelman, Perry. "Progressive Utopia: Or, How to Grow Up Without Growing Up." *Proceedings of the Sixth Annual Conference of the Children's Literature Association, University of Toronto, March 1979.* Ed. Perry Nodelman. Vol. 1. West Lafayette, IN: Children's Literature Association, 1985. 173–187. Rpt. in Reimer, Mavis, ed. *Such a Simple Little Tale*, 29–38.

Ross, Catherine. "Calling Back the Ghost of the Old-Time Heroine: Duncan, Montgomery, Atwood, Laurence and Munro." *Studies in Canadian Literature* 4.1 (1979): 43–58. Rpt. in Reimer, Mavis, ed. *Such a Simple Little Tale*, 42–44, 46–47.

Rubio, Mary. "*Anne of Green Gables:* Architect of Adolescence." *Touchstones: Reflections on the Best in Children's Literature.* Ed. Perry Nodelman. Vol. 1. West Lafayette, IN: Children's Literature Association, 1985. 173–187. Rpt. in Reimer, Mavis, ed. *Such a Simple Little Tale*, 65–81.

Solt, Marilyn. "Uses of Setting in *Anne of Green Gables.*" *Children's Literature Association Quarterly* 9 (1984–85): 179–180, 198. Rpt. in Reimer, Mavis, ed. *Such a Simple Little Tale*, 57–63.

Thomas, Gillian. "Decline of Anne: Matron vs. Child." *Canadian Children's Liter-*

ature 3 (1975): 37–41. Rpt. in Reimer, Mavis, ed. *Such a Simple Little Tale*, 23–28.

Waterson, Elizabeth. *Kindling Spirit: L.M. Montgomery's Anne of Green Gables*. Toronto: ECW Press, 1993.

Weiss-Townsend, Janet. "Sexism Down on the Farm?: *Anne of Green Gables*." *Children's Literature Association Quarterly* 11 (1986): 12–15. Rpt. in Reimer, Mavis, ed. *Such a Simple Little Tale*, 109–117.

Whitaker, Muriel A. " 'Queer Children': L.M. Montgomery's Heroines." *Canadian Children's Literature* 3 (1975): 50–59. Rpt. in Reimer, Mavis, ed. *Such a Simple Little Tale*, 11–22.

Anne of Ingleside (1939)

Epperly, Elizabeth Rollins. *Fragrance of Sweet Grass*, 138–142.

Anne of the Island (1915)

Epperly, Elizabeth Rollins. *Fragrance of Sweet Grass*, 56–74.

Anne of Windy Poplars (1936)

Epperly, Elizabeth Rollins. *Fragrance of Sweet Grass*, 133–138.

Anne's House of Dreams (1917)

Epperly, Elizabeth Rollins. *Fragrance of Sweet Grass*, 75–94.

Blue Castle (1926)

Epperly, Elizabeth Rollins. *Fragrance of Sweet Grass*, 234–239.

Thompson, Elizabeth. *Pioneer Woman*, 121, 127, 129, 134, 135, 151.

Emily Climbs (1925)

Epperly, Elizabeth Rollins. *Fragrance of Sweet Grass*, 168–181.

Emily of New Moon (1923)

Epperly, Elizabeth Rollins. *Fragrance of Sweet Grass*, 149–167.

MacLulich, T.D. "L.M. Montgomery's Portraits of the Artist: Realism, Idealism, and the Domestic Imagination." *English Studies in Canada* 11 (1985): 459–473. Rpt. in Reimer, Mavis, ed. *Such a Simple Little Tale*, 93–96.

Emily's Quest (1927)

Epperly, Elizabeth Rollins. *Fragrance of Sweet Grass*, 182–207.

Golden Road (1913)

Epperly, Elizabeth Rollins. *Fragrance of Sweet Grass*, 231–234.

Jane of Lantern Hill (1937)

Epperly, Elizabeth Rollins. *Fragrance of Sweet Grass*, 220–227.

Kilmeny of the Orchard (1910)

Epperly, Elizabeth Rollins. *Fragrance of Sweet Grass*, 228–231.

Magic for Marigold (1929)

Epperly, Elizabeth Rollins. *Fragrance of Sweet Grass*, 239–243.

Mistress Pat (1935)

Epperly, Elizabeth Rollins. *Fragrance of Sweet Grass*, 217–220.

Pat of Silver Bush (1933)

Epperly, Elizabeth Rollins. *Fragrance of Sweet Grass*, 212–217.

Rainbow Valley (1919)

Epperly, Elizabeth Rollins. *Fragrance of Sweet Grass*, 95–111.

Rilla of Ingleside (1920)

Epperly, Elizabeth Rollins. *Fragrance of Sweet Grass*, 112–130.

Story Girl (1911)

Epperly, Elizabeth Rollins. *Fragrance of Sweet Grass*, 231–234.

Tangled Web (1931)

Epperly, Elizabeth Rollins. *Fragrance of Sweet Grass*, 243–248.

MOORE, BRIAN (1921–)

Answer from Limbo (1962)

O'Donoghue, Jo. *Brian Moore*, 82–84, 86–89, 95–97, 105–116, 130–132.

Black Robe (1985)

O'Donoghue, Jo. *Brian Moore*, 187–204, 205–209.

O'Donoghue, Jo. "Historical Themes, Missionary Endeavour and Spiritual Colonialism in Brian Moore's *Black Robe*." *Studies* 82.326 (1993): 131–139.

Catholics (1972)

O'Donoghue, Jo. *Brian Moore*, 142–144.

Cold Heaven (1983)

O'Donoghue, Jo. *Brian Moore*, 164–186, 205–209.

Colour of Blood (1987)

O'Donoghue, Jo. *Brian Moore*, 219–228.

Doctor's Wife (1976)

O'Donoghue, Jo. *Brian Moore*, 84–85, 93–95, 98–99, 125–129, 130–132.

Emperor of Ice Cream (1965)

O'Donoghue, Jo. *Brian Moore*, 71–74.

Feast of Lupercal (1957)

O'Donoghue, Jo. *Brian Moore*, 46–59.

Fergus (1970)

O'Donoghue, Jo. *Brian Moore*, 74–75.

Great Victorian Collection (1975)

O'Donoghue, Jo. *Brian Moore*, 75–76.

I Am Mary Dunne (1968)

Mulryan, John. "Genderfication of Literature: Cross-Gender Writing in Joyce Carol Oates's *Expensive People* and Brian Moore's *I Am Mary Dunne*." *CEA* 56.1 (1993): 121–124.

O'Donoghue, Jo. *Brian Moore*, 89–93, 97–98, 101–102, 117–124, 130–132.

Judith Hearne (1955)

O'Donoghue, Jo. *Brian Moore*, 16–45.

Lies of Silence (1990)

O'Donoghue, Jo. *Brian Moore*, 229–242.

Luck of Ginger Coffey (1960)

O'Donoghue, Jo. *Brian Moore*, 69–71.

Mangan Inheritance (1979)

O'Donoghue, Jo. *Brian Moore*, 76–77.

Temptation of Eileen Hughes (1981)

O'Donoghue, Jo. *Brian Moore*, 149–163, 205–209.

MORALES, ALEJANDRO (1944–)

Brick People (1988)

Gutierrez-Jones, Carl. "Resisting Cultural Dependency: The Manipulation of Surveillance and Paranoia in Alejandro Morales' *The Brick People*." *AmRev* 22.1–2 (1994): 230–243.

MORLEY, CHRISTOPHER DARLINGTON (1890–1957)

Kitty Foyle (1941)

Hapke, Laura. *Daughters of the Great Depression*, 204–209.

MORRIS, WRIGHT (1910–)

Ceremony in Lone Tree (1960)

Dyck, Reginald. "Frontier Violence in the Garden of America," in Heyne, Eric, ed. *Desert, Garden*, 64–69.

Field of Vision (1956)

Hall, Joe. "Wright Morris' *The Field of Vision:* A Re-Reading of the Scanlon Story." *JACult* 14.2 (1991): 53–57.

MORRISON, TONI (1931–)

Beloved (1987)

Askeland, Lori. "Remodeling the Model Home in *Uncle Tom's Cabin* and *Beloved*." *AL* 64.4 (1992): 787–802.

Badt, Karin Luisa. "Roots of the Body in Toni Morrison: A Mater of 'Ancient Properties.' " *AAR* 29.4 (1995): 569, 571.

Broad, Robert L. "Giving Blood to the Scraps: Haints, History, and Hosea in *Beloved*." *AAR* 28.2 (1994): 189–196.

Budick, Emily Miller. "Absence, Loss, and the Space of History in Toni Morrison's *Beloved*." *ArQ* 48.2 (1992): 117–138.

Budick, Emily Miller. *Engendering Romance*, 193–197, 202–218.

Chandler, Marilyn R. *Dwelling in the Text*, 291–295, 307–318.

Crouch, Stanley. "Aunt Medea." *New Republic* (19 October 1987): 41–43. Rpt. in Bloom, Harold, ed. *Contemporary Black American Fiction Writers*, 112–113.

Crouch, Stanley. "Aunt Medea." *New Republic* (19 October 1987): 41–43. Rpt. in Bloom, Harold, ed. *Major Modern Black American Writers*, 127–128.

Daily, Gary W. "Toni Morrison's *Beloved* : Rememory, History, and the Fantastic," in Morse, Donald E., ed. *Celebration of the Fantastic*, 141–146.

Davies, Carole Boyce. "Mother Right/Write Revisited: *Beloved* and *Dessa Rose* and the Construction of Motherhood in Black Women's Fiction," in Daly, Brenda O., ed. *Narrating Mothers*, 44–56.

Doyle, Laura. *Bordering on the Body*, 209–230.

Epstein, Grace A. "Out of Blue Water: Dream Flight and Narrative Construction in the Novels of Toni Morrison," in Ruddick, Nicholas, ed. *State of the Fantastic*, 145–147.

FitzGerald, Jennifer. "Selfhood and Community: Psychoanalysis and Discourse in *Beloved*." *MFS* 39.3–4 (1993): 669–687.

Freeman, Barbara Claire. *Feminine Sublime*, 122–148.

Guth, Deborah. " 'Wonder What God Had in Mind': *Beloved*'s Dialogue with Christianity." *JNT* 24.2 (1994): 83–97.

Harding, Wendy and Jacky Martin. "Reading at the Cultural Interface: The Corn Symbolism of *Beloved*." *MELUS* 19.2 (1994): 85–97.

Harris, Trudier. "Escaping Slavery but Not Its Images," in Gates, Henry Louis, Jr., ed. *Toni Morrison*, 330–340.

Harris, Trudier. "Toni Morrison: Solo Flight through Literature into History." *WLT* 68.1 (1994): 12, 13.

Hirsch, Marianne. "Maternal Narratives: 'Cruel Enough to Stop the Blood," in Gates, Henry Louis, Jr., ed. *Toni Morrison*, 271–272.

Jones, Carolyn M. "*Sula* and *Beloved:* Images of Cain in the Novels of Toni Morrison." *AAR* 27.4 (1993): 615–620, 625–626.

Koolish, Lynda. "Fictive Strategies and Cinematic Representations in Toni Morrison's *Beloved*: Postcolonial Theory/Postcolonial Text." *AAR* 29.3 (1995): 421–437.

Krumholz, Linda. "Ghosts of Slavery: Historical Recovery in Toni Morrison's *Beloved*." *AAR* 26.3 (1992): 395–407.

Kubitschek, Missy Dehn. *Claiming the Heritage*, 165–176.

Lawrence, David. "Fleshly Ghosts and Ghostly Flesh: The Word and the Body in *Beloved*." *SAF* 19.2 (1991): 189–201.

Leake, Katherine. "Morrison's *Beloved*." *Expl* 53.2 (1995): 120–123.

Ledbetter, Mark. "An Apocalypse of Race and Gender: Body Violence and Forming Identity in Toni Morrison's *Beloved*," in Doty, William G., ed. *Picturing Cultural Values*, 158–171.

Lee, Rachel. "Missing Peace in Toni Morrison's *Sula* and *Beloved*." *AAR* 28.4 (1994): 571, 577–582.

Levy, Andrew. "Telling *Beloved*." *TSLL* 33.1 (1991): 114–123.

Lewis, Charles. "Ironic Romance of New Historicism: *The Scarlet Letter* and *Beloved* Standing in Side by Side." *ArQ* 51.1 (1995): 37–42, 48–51.

Limon, John. *Writing After War*, 194–200.

Liscio, Lorraine. "*Beloved*'s Narrative: Writing Mother's Milk." *TSWL* 11.1 (1992): 31–46.

McKible, Adam. " 'These Are the Facts of the Darky's History': Thinking History and Reading Names in Four African American Texts." *AAR* 28.2 (1994): 225, 229, 231–232.

Malmgren, Carl D. " Mixed Genres and the Logic of Slavery in Toni Morrison's *Beloved.*" *Crit* 36.2 (1995): 96–106.
Mayer, Elsie F. "Morrison's *Beloved.*" *Expl* 51.3 (1993): 192–194.
Mobley, Marilyn Sanders. "Different Remembering: Memory, History, and Meaning in *Beloved,*" in Gates, Henry Louis, Jr., ed. *Toni Morrison*, 356–363.
Mobley, Marilyn Sanders. "Mellow Moods and Difficult Truths of Toni Morrison." *SoR* 29.3 (1993): 620.
Moreland, Richard C. " 'He Wants to Put His Story Next to Hers': Putting Twain's Story Next to Hers in Morrison's *Beloved.*" *MFS* 39.3–4 (1993): 501–524.
Mullen, Harryette. "Runaway Tongue: Resistant Orality in *Uncle Tom's Cabin, Incidents in the Life of a Slave Girl*, and *Beloved,*" in Samuels, Shirley, ed. *Culture of Sentiment*, 258–264.
Osagie, Iyunolu. "Is Morrison Also among the Prophets?: 'Psychoanalytic' Strategies in *Beloved.*" *AAR* 28.3 (1994): 423–439.
Otten, Terry. "Horrific Love in Toni Morrison's Fiction." *MFS* 39.3–4 (1993): 657–660.
Peach, Linden. *Toni Morrison*, 93–111.
Perez-Torres, Rafael. "Knitting and Knotting the Narrative Thread—*Beloved* as Postmodern Novel." *MFS* 39.3–4 (1993): 689–707.
Perry, Ruth. "Mary Gordon's Mothers," in Daly, Brenda O., ed. *Narrating Mothers*, 210.
Pesch, Josef. "*Beloved:* Toni Morrison's Post-Apocalyptic Novel." *CRCL* 20.3–4 (1993): 397–408.
Phelan, James. "Toward a Rhetorical Reader-Response Criticism: The Difficult, The Stubborn, and the Ending of *Beloved.*" *MFS* 39.3–4 (1993): 709–728.
Powell, Betty Jane. " 'Will the Parts Hold?': The Journey Toward a Coherent Self in *Beloved.*" *ClQ* 31.2 (1995): 105–113.
Rainwater, Catherine. "Worthy Messengers: Narrative Voices in Toni Morrison's Novels." *TSLL* 33.1 (1991): 100–101, 102, 106–107.
Rigney, Barbara Hill. " 'A Story to Pass On': Ghosts and the Significance of History in Toni Morrison's *Beloved,*" in Carpenter, Lynette, ed. *Haunting the House of Fiction*, 229–234.
Rodrigues, Eusebio L. "Telling of *Beloved.*" *JNT* 21.2 (1991): 153–169.
Rushdy, Ashraf H. A. "Daughters Signifyin(g) History: The Example of Toni Morrison's *Beloved.*" *AL* 64.3 (1992): 567–597.
Scarpa, Giulia. "Narrative Possibilities at Play in Toni Morrison's *Beloved.*" *MELUS* 17.4 (1991–92): 91–103.
Schmudde, Carol. "Morrison's *Beloved.*" *Expl* 50.3 (1992): 187–188.
Schmudde, Carol E. "Haunting of 124." *AAR* 26.3 (1992): 409–415.
Scruggs, Charles. "Invisible City in Toni Morrison's *Beloved.*" *ArQ* 48.3 (1992): 95–132.
Scruggs, Charles. *Sweet Home*, 167–204.
Segal, Carolyn Foster. "Morrison's *Beloved.*" *Expl* 51.1 (1992): 59–61.
Smith, Valerie. " 'Circling the Subject': History and Narrative in *Beloved,*" in Gates, Henry Louis, Jr., ed. *Toni Morrison*, 342–354.
Stave, Shirley A. "Toni Morrison's *Beloved* and the Vindication of Lilith." *SoAR* 58.1 (1993): 49–66.
Travis, Molly Abel. "Speaking from the Silence of the Slave Narrative: *Beloved* and African-American Women's History." *TexasR* 13.1–2 (1992): 69–81.
Tucker, Lindsey. *Textual Excap(e)ades*, 95–106.

Tusmith, Bonnie. *All My Relatives*, 99–101.
Winter, Kari J. *Subjects of Slavery*, 115–118.
Woidat, Caroline M. "Talking Back to Schoolteacher: Morrison's Confrontation with Hawthorne in *Beloved*." *MFS* 39.3–4 (1993): 527–546.
Wyatt, Jean. "Giving Body to the Word: The Maternal Symbolic in Toni Morrison's *Beloved*." *PMLA* 108.3 (1993): 474–488.

Bluest Eye (1970)

Awkward, Michael. " 'Evil of Fulfillment': Scapegoating and Narration in *The Bluest Eye*," in Gates, Henry Louis, Jr., ed. *Toni Morrison*, 175–207.
Bennett, Paula. "Mother's Part: Incest and Maternal Deprivation in Woolf and Morrison," in Daly, Brenda O., ed. *Narrating Mothers*, 131–136.
Bishop, John. "Morrison's *The Bluest Eye*." *Expl* 51.4 (1993): 252–255.
Byerman, Keith E. "Beyond Realism," in Gates, Henry Louis, Jr., ed. *Toni Morrison*, 100–106.
Christian, Barbara. "Contemporary Fables of Toni Morrison," in Gates, Henry Louis, Jr., ed. *Toni Morrison*, 59–74, 95–98.
Doyle, Laura. *Bordering on the Body*, 207–208.
Dubey, Madhu. *Black Women Novelists*, 33–50.
Epstein, Grace A. "Out of Blue Water: Dream Flight and Narrative Construction in the Novels of Toni Morrison," in Ruddick, Nicholas, ed. *State of the Fantastic*, 142–144.
Gibson, Donald B. "Text and Countertext in *The Bluest Eye*," in Gates, Henry Louis, Jr., ed. *Toni Morrison*, 159–172.
Kester, Gunilla Theander. *Writing the Subject*, 71–79, 93–94, 95–99.
Kubitschek, Missy Dehn. "Toward a New Order: Shakespeare, Morrison, and Gloria Naylor's *Mama Day*." *MELUS* 19.3 (1994): 86.
Kuenz, Jane. "*The Bluest Eye:* Notes on History, Community, and Black Female Subjectivity." *AAR* 27.3 (1993): 421–431.
Mobley, Marilyn Sanders. "Mellow Moods and Difficult Truths of Toni Morrison." *SoR* 29.3 (1993): 616–617.
Napieralski, Edmund A. "Morrison's *The Bluest Eye*." *Expl* 53.1 (1994): 59–62.
Ogunyemi, Chikwenye Okonjo. "Womanism: The Dynamics of the Contemporary Black Female Novel in English," in Clark, VèVé A., ed. *Revising the Word*, 242.
Otten, Terry. "Horrific Love in Toni Morrison's Fiction." *MFS* 39.3–4 (1993): 653–654.
Peach, Linden. *Toni Morrison*, 24–38.
Rainwater, Catherine. "Worthy Messengers: Narrative Voices in Toni Morrison's Novels." *TSLL* 33.1 (1991): 98, 100, 101–102, 106, 107–108.
Rubenstein, Roberta. "Pariahs and Community," in Gates, Henry Louis, Jr., ed. *Toni Morrison*, 127–130, 136, 140, 141–142, 144, 146–148.
Willis, Susan. "Eruptions of Funk: Historicizing Toni Morrison," in Gates, Henry Louis, Jr., ed. *Toni Morrison*, 308–312.
Wright, Lee Alfred. *Identity, Family, and Folklore*, 75–94.

Jazz (1992)

Aguiar, Sarah Appleton. " 'Everywhere and Nowhere': Beloved's 'Wild' Legacy in Toni Morrison's *Jazz*." *NConL* 25.4 (1995): 11–12.
Badt, Karin Luisa. "Roots of the Body in Toni Morrison: A Mater of 'Ancient Properties.' " *AAR* 29.4 (1995): 568, 569–571, 572, 573, 575.
Bawer, Bruce. "All That Jazz." *NewC* 10.9 (1992): 10–17.

Chadwick-Joshua, Jocelyn. "Metonymy and Synecdoche: The Rhetoric of the City in Toni Morrison's *Jazz*," in Hakutani, Yoshinobu, ed. *City in African-American Literature*, 168–177.

Eckard, Paula Gallant. "Interplay of Music, Language, and Narrative in Toni Morrison's *Jazz*." *CLAJ* 38.1 (1994): 11–19.

Griffin, Farah Jasmine. *"Who Set You Flowin'?"*, 184–197.

Hardack, Richard. " 'A Music Seeking Its Own Words': Double-Timing and Double Consciousness in Toni Morrison's *Jazz*." *Callaloo* 18.2 (1995): 451–471.

Harris, Trudier. "Toni Morrison: Solo Flight through Literature into History." *WLT* 68.1 (1994): 12–13.

Mbalia, Dorothea Drummond. "Women Who Run with Wild: The Need for Sisterhoods in *Jazz*." *MFS* 39.3–4 (1993): 623–646.

Miller, Jane. "New Romance." *London Review of Books* (14 May 1992): 12. Rpt. in Bloom, Harold, ed. *Major Modern Black American Writers*, 133–134.

Mobley, Marilyn Sanders. "Mellow Moods and Difficult Truths of Toni Morrison." *SoR* 29.3 (1993): 621–624.

Otten, Terry. "Horrific Love in Toni Morrison's Fiction." *MFS* 39.3–4 (1993): 660–664.

Page, Philip. "Traces of Derrida in Toni Morrison's *Jazz*." *AAR* 29.1 (1995): 55–66.

Peach, Linden. *Toni Morrison*, 112–127.

Rice, Alan J. "Jazzing It Up a Storm: The Execution and Meaning of Toni Morrison's Jazzy Prose Style." *JAmS* 28.3 (1994): 423–432.

Rodrigues, Eusebio L. "Experiencing *Jazz*." *MFS* 39.3–4 (1993): 733–754.

Song of Solomon (1978)

Ashe, Bertram D. " 'Why Don't He Like My Hair?': Constructing African-American Standards of Beauty in Toni Morrison's *Song of Solomon* and Zora Neale Hurston's *Their Eyes Were Watching God*." *AAR* 29.4 (1995): 585–590.

Blake, Susan L. "Folklore and Community in *Song of Solomon*." *MELUS* 7.3 (1980): 77–79. Rpt. in Bloom, Harold, ed. *Black American Women Fiction Writers*, 150–151.

Blake, Susan L. "Folklore and Community in *Song of Solomon*." *MELUS* 7.3 (1980): 77–79. Rpt. in Bloom, Harold, ed. *Contemporary Black American Fiction Writers*, 108–109.

Blake, Susan L. "Folklore and Community in *Song of Solomon*." *MELUS* 7.3 (1980): 77–79. Rpt. in Bloom, Harold, ed. *Major Modern Black American Writers*, 123–124.

Branch, Eleanor. "Through the Maze of the Oedipal: Milkman's Search for Self in *Song of Solomon*." *L&P* 41.1–2 (1995): 52–84.

Budick, Emily Miller. *Engendering Romance*, 197–202.

Byerman, Keith E. "Beyond Realism," in Gates, Henry Louis, Jr., ed. *Toni Morrison*, 113–118.

Clayton, Jay. "Narrative Turn in Minority Fiction," in Carlisle, Janice,ed. *Narrative and Culture*, 66–67.

Coser, Stellamaris. *Bridging the Americas*, 81–106.

Duvall, John N. "Doe Hunting and Masculinity: *Song of Solomon* and *Go Down, Moses*." *ArQ* 47.1 (1991): 96–103, 104–115.

Farrell, Susan. " 'Who'd He Leave Behind?': Gender and History in Toni Morrison's *Song of Solomon*." *BuR* 39.1 (1995): 131–150.

Forrest, Leon. *Relocations of the Spirit*, 161–163.
Griffin, Farah Jasmine. *"Who Set You Flowin'?"*, 40–43, 171–178.
Guth, Deborah. "Blessing and a Burden: The Relation to the Past in *Sula*, *Song of Solomon* and *Beloved*." *MFS* 39.3–4 (1993): 579–584, 588–591.
Harris, Trudier. "Toni Morrison: Solo Flight through Literature into History." *WLT* 68.1 (1994): 11–12, 13.
Heyman, Richard. "Universalization and Its Discontents: Morrison's *Song of Solomon*—A (W)hol(e)y Black Text." *AAR* 29.3 (1995): 381–391.
Hirsch, Marianne. "Knowing Their Names: Toni Morrison's *Song of Solomon*," in Smith, Valerie, ed. *New Essays on Song of Solomon*, 69–90.
Hubbard, Dolan. "In Quest of Authority: Toni Morrison's *Song of Solomon* and the Rhetoric of the Black Preacher." *CLAJ* 35.3 (1992): 288–302.
Krumholz, Linda. "Dead Teachers: Rituals of Manhood and Rituals of Reading in *Song of Solomon*." *MFS* 39.3–4 (1993): 551–574.
Kubitschek, Missy Dehn. *Claiming the Heritage*, 126–129.
Kubitschek, Missy Dehn. "Toward a New Order: Shakespeare, Morrison, and Gloria Naylor's *Mama Day*." *MELUS* 19.3 (1994): 78–80, 86.
Lubiano, Wahneema. "Postmodernist Rag: Political Identity and the Vernacular in *Son of Solomon*," in Smith, Valerie, ed. *New Essays on Song of Solomon*, 93–113.
Middleton, Joyce Irene. "From Orality to Literacy: Oral Memory in Toni Morrison's *Song of Solomon*," in Smith, Valerie, ed. *New Essays on Song of Solomon*, 19–37.
Mobley, Marilyn Sanders. "Call and Response: Voice, Community, and Dialogic Strutures in Toni Morrison's *Song of Solomon*," in Smith, Valerie, ed. *New Essays on Song of Solomon*, 41–63.
Mobley, Marilyn Sanders. "Mellow Moods and Difficult Truths of Toni Morrison." *SoR* 29.3 (1993): 617–618.
Peach, Linden. *Toni Morrison*, 55–74.
Rainwater, Catherine. "Worthy Messengers: Narrative Voices in Toni Morrison's Novels." *TSLL* 33.1 (1991): 97–98, 100, 103–105, 108–109, 110.
Rubenstein, Roberta. "Pariahs and Community," in Gates, Henry Louis, Jr., ed. *Toni Morrison*, 135–136, 138–139, 141, 143, 145, 148, 150–152.
Smith, Valerie. "*Song of Solomon:* Continuities of Community," in Gates, Henry Louis, Jr., ed. *Toni Morrison*, 274–283.
Stryz, Jan. "Inscribing an Origin in *Song of Solomon*." *SAF* 19.1 (1991): 31–40.
Wilentz, Gay Alden. *Binding Cultures*, 81–98.
Willis, Susan. "Eruptions of Funk: Historicizing Toni Morrison," in Gates, Henry Louis, Jr., ed. *Toni Morrison*, 312–313, 315–320.

Sula (1974)

Badt, Karin Luisa. "Roots of the Body in Toni Morrison: A Mater of 'Ancient Properties.' " *AAR* 29.4 (1995): 567–568, 569, 571.
Baker, Houston A., Jr. "When Lindbergh Sleeps with Bessie Smith: The Writing of Place in *Sula*," in Gates, Henry Louis, Jr., ed. *Toni Morrison*, 236–258.
Bryant, Jerry H. "Something Ominous Here," *Nation* (6 July 1974): 23–24. Rpt. in Bloom, Harold, ed. *Major Modern Black American Writers*, 121.
Byerman, Keith E. "Beyond Realism," in Gates, Henry Louis, Jr., ed. *Toni Morrison*, 106–113.
Christian, Barbara. "Contemporary Fables of Toni Morrison," in Gates, Henry Louis, Jr., ed. *Toni Morrison*, 74–98.

Dubey, Madhu. *Black Women Novelists*, 51–71.

Epstein, Grace A. "Out of Blue Water: Dream Flight and Narrative Construction in the Novels of Toni Morrison," in Ruddick, Nicholas, ed. *State of the Fantastic*, 144–145.

Forrest, Leon. *Relocations of the Spirit*, 152–161.

Guth, Deborah. "Blessing and a Burden: The Relation to the Past in *Sula*, *Song of Solomon* and *Beloved*." *MFS* 39.3–4 (1993): 576–579, 588–591.

Hirsch, Marianne. "Maternal Narratives: 'Cruel Enough to Stop the Blood," in Gates, Henry Louis, Jr., ed. *Toni Morrison*, 261–271.

Hoffarth-Zelloe, Monika. "Resolving the Paradox?: An Interlinear Reading of Toni Morrison's *Sula*." *JNT* 22.2 (1992): 114–127.

Hunt, Patricia. "War and Peace: Transfigured Categories and the Politics of *Sula*." *AAR* 27.3 (1993): 443–459.

Jones, Carolyn M. "*Sula* and *Beloved:* Images of Cain in the Novels of Toni Morrison." *AAR* 27.4 (1993): 615–616, 620–626.

Kubitschek, Missy Dehn. "Toward a New Order: Shakespeare, Morrison, and Gloria Naylor's *Mama Day*." *MELUS* 19.3 (1994): 78.

Lee, Rachel. "Missing Peace in Toni Morrison's *Sula* and *Beloved*." *AAR* 28.4 (1994): 571, 572–577, 582.

McDowell, Deborah E. *"The Changing Same"*, 101–117.

Mobley, Marilyn Sanders. "Mellow Moods and Difficult Truths of Toni Morrison." *SoR* 29.3 (1993): 617.

Otten, Terry. "Horrific Love in Toni Morrison's Fiction." *MFS* 39.3–4 (1993): 654–656.

Peach, Linden. *Toni Morrison*, 39–54.

Pessoni, Michele. " 'She Was Laughing at Their God': Discovering the Goddess within in *Sula*." *AAR* 29.3 (1995): 439–451.

Rainwater, Catherine. "Worthy Messengers: Narrative Voices in Toni Morrison's Novels." *TSLL* 33.1 (1991): 99, 102–103, 108.

Rosenfelt, Deborah Silverton. "Feminism, "Postfeminism," and Contemporary Women's Fiction," in Howe, Florence, ed. *Tradition and the Talents of Women*, 274–275.

Rubenstein, Roberta. "Pariahs and Community," in Gates, Henry Louis, Jr., ed. *Toni Morrison*, 128, 131–135, 136–138, 143, 144–145, 148–149.

Spillers, Hortense J. "Hateful Passion, a Lost Love," in Gates, Henry Louis, Jr., ed. *Toni Morrison*, 210–214, 225–233.

Tucker, Lindsey. *Textual Excap(e)ades*, 89–95.

Willis, Susan. "Eruptions of Funk: Historicizing Toni Morrison," in Gates, Henry Louis, Jr., ed. *Toni Morrison*, 320–321.

Wright, Lee Alfred. *Identity, Family, and Folklore*, 99–128.

Tar Baby (1981)

Backus, Margot Gayle. " 'Looking for That Dead Girl': Incest, Pornography, and the Capitalist Family Romance in *Nightwood*, *The Years* and *Tar Baby*." *American Imago* 51.4 (1994): 533–541.

Badt, Karin Luisa. "Roots of the Body in Toni Morrison: A Mater of 'Ancient Properties.' " *AAR* 29.4 (1995): 567, 572, 573–574.

Byerman, Keith E. "Beyond Realism," in Gates, Henry Louis, Jr., ed. *Toni Morrison*, 118–125.

Cooper, Carolyn. " 'Something Ancestral Recaptured': Spirit Possession as Trope in Selected Feminist Fictions of the African Diaspora," in Nasta, Susheila, ed. *Motherlands*, 77–81.

Coser, Stellamaris. *Bridging the Americas*, 106–118.

Elkins, Marilyn. "Expatriate Afro-American Women as Exotics," Brown, Anne E., ed. *International Women's Writing*, 264–271.

Erickson, Peter B. "Images of Nurturance in *Tar Baby*," in Gates, Henry Louis, Jr., ed. *Toni Morrison*, 293–306.

Harris, Trudier. "Toni Morrison: Solo Flight through Literature into History." *WLT* 68.1 (1994): 13.

Kubitschek, Missy Dehn. *Claiming the Heritage*, 129–142.

Mbalia, Dorothea Drummond. *Toni Morrison's Developing Class Consciousness*. Selinsgrove, PA: Susquehanna University Press, 1991. 26–27. Rpt. in Bloom, Harold, ed. *Contemporary Black American Fiction Writers*, 117–118.

Mbalia, Dorothea Drummond. *Toni Morrison's Developing Class Consciousness*. Selinsgrove, PA: Susquehanna University Press, 1991. 26–27. Rpt. in Bloom, Harold, ed. *Major Modern Black American Writers*, 132–133.

Mobley, Marilyn Sanders. "Mellow Moods and Difficult Truths of Toni Morrison." *SoR* 29.3 (1993): 618–620.

Mobley, Marilyn Sanders. "Narrative Dilemma: Jadine as Cultural Orphan in *Tar Baby*," in Gates, Henry Louis, Jr., ed. *Toni Morrison*, 284–292.

Otten, Terry. "Horrific Love in Toni Morrison's Fiction." *MFS* 39.3–4 (1993): 656.

Peach, Linden. *Toni Morrison*, 75–92.

Rubenstein, Roberta. "Pariahs and Community," in Gates, Henry Louis, Jr., ed. *Toni Morrison*, 130–131, 139–140, 143, 145–146, 152–154.

Ryan, Judylyn S. "Contested Visions/Double-Vision in *Tar Baby*." *MFS* 39.3–4 (1993): 597–621.

Smith, Felipe. "White Witch and Black Madonna: Reclamations of the Feminine in Toni Morrison's *Tar Baby*," in Carlisle, Janice,ed. *Narrative and Culture*, 77–93.

Smith-Wright, Geraldine. "In Spite of the Klan: Ghosts in the Fiction of Black Women Writers," in Carpenter, Lynette, ed. *Haunting the House of Fiction*, 153–159.

Willis, Susan. "Eruptions of Funk: Historicizing Toni Morrison," in Gates, Henry Louis, Jr., ed. *Toni Morrison*, 313–315, 321–323.

MORROW, HONORÉ WILLSIE (1880–1940)

Exile of the Lariat (1923)

Yates, Norris. *Gender and Genre*, 92–100.

Forbidden Trail (1919)

Yates, Norris. *Gender and Genre*, 87.

Heart of the Desert (1912)

Yates, Norris. *Gender and Genre*, 82–86.

Judith of the Godless Valley (1922)

Yates, Norris. *Gender and Genre*, 89–92.

Still Jim (1914)

Yates, Norris. *Gender and Genre*, 87.

MOSLEY, WALTER (1952–)

Devil in a Blue Dress (1990)

Mason, Theodore O., Jr. "Walter Mosley's Easy Rawlins: The Detective and Afro-American Fiction." *KR* 14.4 (1992): 173–183.

MOTLEY, WILLARD (1905–1965)

Knock on Any Door (1947)

Conder, John. "Selves of the City, Selves of the South: The City in the Fiction of William Attaway and Willard Motley," in Hakutani, Yoshinobu, ed. *City in African-American Literature*, 111–112, 116–119.

Hughes, Carl Milton. *Negro Novelist: A Discussion of the Writings of American Negro Novelists 1940–1950*. New York: Citadel Press, 1953. Rpt. in Bloom, Harold, ed. *Modern Black American Fiction Writers*, 111–112.

Schraufnagel, Noel. *From Apology to Protest: The Black American Novel*. Deland, FL: Everett/Edwards, 1973. 44–46. Rpt. in Bloom, Harold, ed. *Modern Black American Fiction Writers*, 115–116.

Let No Man Write My Epitaph (1958)

Conder, John. "Selves of the City, Selves of the South: The City in the Fiction of William Attaway and Willard Motley," in Hakutani, Yoshinobu, ed. *City in African-American Literature*, 111–112, 119–122.

We Fished All Night (1951)

Giles, James R. and Karen Magee Myers. "Naturalism as Principle and Trap: The Theory and Execution in Willard Motley's *We Fished All Night*." *Studies in Black Literature* 7.1 (1976): 19, 21. Rpt. in Bloom, Harold, ed. *Modern Black American Fiction Writers*, 116–117.

MOURNING DOVE (1888(?)–1936)

Co-ge-we-a (1927)

Owens, Louis. *Other Destinies*, 40–48.

MUKHERJEE, BHARATI (1940–)

Jasmine (1989)

Carter-Sanborn, Kristin. " 'We Murder Who We Were': *Jasmine* and the Violence of Identity." *AL* 66.3 (1994): 573–593.

Kehde, Suzanne. "Colonial Discourse and Female Identity: Bharati Mukherjee's *Jasmine*," in Brown, Anne E., ed. *International Women's Writing*, 70–76.

San Juan, E., Jr. *Hegemony and Strategies*, 177–181.

Wong, Sau-ling Cynthia. *Reading Asian American Literature*, 53–55.

MURAYAMA, MILTON

All I Asking for Is My Body (1959)

Wong, Sau-ling Cynthia. *Reading Asian American Literature*, 47, 48.

MURRAY, ALBERT L. (1916–)

Spyglass Tree (1991)

Carson, Warren. "Albert Murray: Literary Reconstruction of the Vernacular Community." *AAR* 27.2 (1993): 294–295.

Train Whistle Guitar (1974)

Carson, Warren. "Albert Murray: Literary Reconstruction of the Vernacular Community." *AAR* 27.2 (1993): 290–294.

NABOKOV, VLADIMIR (1899–1977)

Ada (1969)

Giblett, Rodney. "Childhood Secret Languages as Antilanguage." *Neophil* 75.1 (1991): 1–10.
Morrison, James. "Nabokov's Third-Person Selves." *PQ* 71.4 (1992): 497–499, 505–507..
Rampton, David. *Vladimir Nabokov*, 112–119.
Wood, Michael. *Magician's Doubts*, 206–231.

Bend Sinister (1947)

Boyd, Brian. "Nabokov's *Bend Sinister*." *Shenandoah* 41.1 (1991): 12–28.
Rampton, David. *Vladimir Nabokov*, 70–78.
Wood, Michael. *Magician's Doubts*, 57–64.

Defense (1930)

Rampton, David. *Vladimir Nabokov*, 35–40.

Despair (1936)

Rampton, David. *Vladimir Nabokov*, 50–55.

Eye (1938)

Morrison, James. "Nabokov's Third-Person Selves." *PQ* 71.4 (1992): 499–501.
Rampton, David. *Vladimir Nabokov*, 40–45.

Gift (1937)

Rampton, David. *Vladimir Nabokov*, 15–32.
Waite, Sarah Tiffany. "On the Linear Structure of Nabokov's *Dar:* Three Keys, Six Chapters." *SEEJ* 39.1 (1995): 54–72.

Glory (1932)

Rampton, David. *Vladimir Nabokov*, 11–15.

Invitation to a Beheading (1938)

Blackwell, Stephen. "Reading and Rupture in Nabokov's *Invitation to a Beheading*." *SEEJ* 39.1 (1995): 38–53.
Rampton, David. *Vladimir Nabokov*, 57–63.

Laughter in the Dark (1938)

Rampton, David. *Vladimir Nabokov*, 45–50.

Lolita (1955)

Bergenholtz, Rita A. "Nabokov's *Lolita*." *Expl* 53.4 (1995): 231–235.
Blum, Virginia L. *Hide and Seek*, 201–238.
Kennedy, Colleen. "White Man's Guest, or Why Aren't More Feminists Reading *Lolita*?," in Carlisle, Janice, ed. *Narrative and Culture*, 46–56.
Olsen, Lance. *Lolita: A Janus Text*. New York: Twayne Publishers, 1995.
Rampton, David. *Vladimir Nabokov*, 79–102.
Wood, Michael. *Magician's Doubts*, 103–142.
Wood, Ruth Pirsig. *Lolita in Peyton Place*, 3–13.

Look at the Harlequins! (1974)

Rampton, David. *Vladimir Nabokov*, 119–123.

Mary (1925)

Rampton, David. *Vladimir Nabokov*, 7–10.

Pale Fire (1962)

Cowart, David. *Literary Symbiosis*, 66–84.
English, James F. "Modernist Joke-Work: *Pale Fire* and the Mock Transcendence of Mockery." *ConL* 33.1 (1992): 74–90.
Hennard, Martine. "Playing a Game of Worlds in Nabokov's *Pale Fire*." *MFS* 40.2 (1994): 299–317.
Monroe, William. "Sequestered Imagination: Nabokov versus the Materialists." *PQ* 70.3 (1991): 379–394.
Morrison, James. "Nabokov's Third-Person Selves." *PQ* 71.4 (1992): 501–503.
Pier, John. "Between Text and Paratext: Vladimir Nabokov's *Pale Fire*." *Style* 26.1 (1992): 12–32.
Rampton, David. *Vladimir Nabokov*, 104–112.
Wood, Michael. *Magician's Doubts*, 173–205.

Pnin (1957)

Burns, Christy L. "Art of Conspiracy: Punning and Paranoid Response in Nabokov's *Pnin*." *Mosaic* 28.1 (1995): 99–117.
Wood, Michael. *Magician's Doubts*, 157–172.

Real Life of Sebastian Knight (1941)

Booker, M. Keith. "Fiction and 'Real Life': Vargas Llosa's *The Real Life of Alejandro Mayta* and Nabokov's *The Real Life of Sebastian Knight*." *Crit* 35.2 (1994): 114–125.
Rampton, David. *Vladimir Nabokov*, 63–70.
Wood, Michael. *Magician's Doubts*, 29–54.

Speak, Memory (1951)

Wood, Michael. *Magician's Doubts*, 83–102.

NAYLOR, GLORIA (1950–)

Bailey's Café (1992)

Eder, Richard. "Grounds for the City." *Los Angeles Times Book Review* (30 August 1992): 2. Rpt. in Bloom, Harold, ed. *Black American Women Fiction Writers*, 176–178.

Eder, Richard. "Grounds for the City." *Los Angeles Times Book Review* (30 August 1992): 2. Rpt. in Bloom, Harold, ed. *Contemporary Black American Fiction Writers*, 134–136.

Montgomery, Maxine Lavon. "Authority, Multivocality, and the New World Order in Gloria Naylor's *Bailey's Café*." *AAR* 29.1 (1995): 27–33.

Puhr, Kathleen M. "Healers in Gloria Naylor's Fiction." *TCL* 40.4 (1994): 525–526.

Linden Hills (1985)

Christian, Barbara. "Gloria Naylor's Geography: Community, Class, and Patriarchy in *The Women of Brewster Place* and *Linden Hills*." *Reading Black, Reading Feminist: A Critical Anthology*. Ed. Henry Louis Gates, Jr. New York: Meridian, 1990. 351–352. Rpt. in Bloom, Harold, ed. *Black American Women Fiction Writers*, 172–173.

Christian, Barbara. "Gloria Naylor's Geography: Community, Class, and Patriarchy in *The Women of Brewster Place* and *Linden Hills*." *Reading Black, Reading Feminist: A Critical Anthology*. Ed. Henry Louis Gates, Jr. New York: Meridian, 1990. 351–352. Rpt. in Bloom, Harold, ed. *Contemporary Black American Fiction Writers*, 130–131.

Kubitschek, Missy Dehn. *Claiming the Heritage*, 111–126.

Levy, Helen Fiddyment. *Fiction of the Home Place*, 204–214.

Lynch, Michael F. "Wall and the Mirror in the Promised Land: The City in the Novels of Gloria Naylor," in Hakutani, Yoshinobu, ed. *City in African-American Literature*, 189–192.

Massé, Michelle A. *In the Name of Love*, 240–250.

Puhr, Kathleen M. "Healers in Gloria Naylor's Fiction." *TCL* 40.4 (1994): 520–521.

Sandiford, K. A. "Gothic and Intertextual Constructions in *Linden Hills*." *ArQ* 47.3 (1991): 117–138.

Toombs, Charles P. "Confluence of Food and Identity in Gloria Naylor's *Linden Hills*: 'What We Eat Is Who We Is'." *CLAJ* 37.1 (1993): 1–18.

Ward, Catherine C. "Gloria Naylor's *Linden Hills*: A Modern *Inferno*." *ConL* 28.1 (Spring 1987): 67, 69–70. Rpt. in Bloom, Harold, ed. *Black American Women Fiction Writers*, 167–168.

Ward, Catherine C. "Gloria Naylor's *Linden Hills*: A Modern *Inferno*." *ConL* 28.1 (Spring 1987): 67, 69–70. Rpt. in Bloom, Harold, ed. *Contemporary Black American Fiction Writers*, 125–126.

Mama Day (1988)

Andrews, Larry R. "Black Sisterhood in Gloria Naylor's Novels." *CLA Journal* 33.1 (September 1989): 18–19. Rpt. in Bloom, Harold, ed. *Black American Women Fiction Writers*, 169–170.

Andrews, Larry R. "Black Sisterhood in Gloria Naylor's Novels." *CLA Journal* 33.1 (September 1989): 18–19. Rpt. in Bloom, Harold, ed. *Contemporary Black American Fiction Writers*, 127–128.

Brown, Rita Mae. "Black Laughter in an Offshore Showoff Novel." *Los Angeles Times Book Review* 6 March 1988: 2. Rpt. in Bloom, Harold, ed. *Contemporary Black American Fiction Writers*, 126–127.

Donlon, Joycelyn Hazelwood. "Hearing Is Believing: Southern Racial Communities and Strategies of Story-Listening in Gloria Naylor and Lee Smith." *TCL* 41.1 (1995): 22–27.

Kubitschek, Missy Dehn. "Toward a New Order: Shakespeare, Morrison, and Gloria Naylor's *Mama Day*." *MELUS* 19.3 (1994): 75–89.

Levy, Helen Fiddyment. *Fiction of the Home Place*, 214–222.

Lynch, Michael F. "Wall and the Mirror in the Promised Land: The City in the Novels of Gloria Naylor," in Hakutani, Yoshinobu, ed. *City in African-American Literature*, 192–194.

Meisenhelder, Susan. " 'The Whole Picture' in Gloria Naylor's *Mama Day*." *AAR* 27.3 (1993): 405–419.

Puhr, Kathleen M. "Healers in Gloria Naylor's Fiction." *TCL* 40.4 (1994): 521–523.

Storhoff, Gary. "Only Voice Is Your Own' Gloria Naylor's Revision of *The Tempest*." *AAR* 29.1 (1995): 35–45.

Tucker, Lindsey. "Recovering the Conjure Woman: Texts and Contexts in Gloria Naylor's *Mama Day*." *AAR* 28.2 (1994): 173–187.

Women of Brewster Place (1982)

Awkward, Michael. "Authorial Dreams of Wholeness: (Dis)Unity, (Literary) Parentage, and *The Women of Brewster Place*." *Inspiring Influences: Tradition, Revision, and Afro-American Women's Novels.* New York: Columbia University Press, 1989. 98. Rpt. in Bloom, Harold, ed. *Contemporary Black American Fiction Writers*, 128–129.

Bande, Usha. "Murder as Social Revenge in *The Street* and *The Women of Brewster Place*." *NConL* 23.1 (1993): 4–5.

Christian, Barbara. "Gloria Naylor's Geography: Community, Class, and Patriarchy in *The Women of Brewster Place* and *Linden Hills*." *Reading Black, Reading Feminist: A Critical Anthology*. Ed. Henry Louis Gates, Jr. New York: Meridian, 1990. 351–352. Rpt. in Bloom, Harold, ed. *Black American Women Fiction Writers*, 172–173.

Christian, Barbara. "Gloria Naylor's Geography: Community, Class, and Patriarchy in *The Women of Brewster Place* and *Linden Hills*." *Reading Black, Reading Feminist: A Critical Anthology*. Ed. Henry Louis Gates, Jr. New York: Meridian, 1990. 351–352. Rpt. in Bloom, Harold, ed. *Contemporary Black American Fiction Writers*, 130–131.

Grenier, Donald J. *Women Enter the Wilderness*, 124–129.

Griffin, Farah Jasmine. *"Who Set You Flowin'?"*, 43–45, 91–94, 119–123.

Kelly, Lori Duin. "Dream Sequence in *The Women of Brewster Place*." *NConL* 21.4 (1991): 8–10.

Levy, Helen Fiddyment. *Fiction of the Home Place*, 199–214.

Lynch, Michael F. "Wall and the Mirror in the Promised Land: The City in the Novels of Gloria Naylor," in Hakutani, Yoshinobu, ed. *City in African-American Literature*, 186–189.

Matus, Jill L. "Dream, Deferral, and Closure in *The Women of Brewster Place*." *Black American Literature Forum* 24.1 (Spring 1990): 49–50. Rpt. in Bloom, Harold, ed. *Black American Women Fiction Writers*, 171–172.

Matus, Jill L. "Dream, Deferral, and Closure in *The Women of Brewster Place*." *Black American Literature Forum* 24.1 (Spring 1990): 49–50. Rpt. in Bloom, Harold, ed. *Contemporary Black American Fiction Writers*, 129–130.

Meisenhelder, Susan. " 'Eating Cane' in Gloria Naylor's *The Women of Brewster Place* and Zora Neale Hurston's 'Sweat'." *NConL* 23.2 (1993): 5–7.

Montgomery, Maxine L. "Fathomless Dream: Gloria Naylor's Use of the Descent Motif in *The Women of Brewster Place*." *CLAJ* 36.1 (1992): 1–11.
Puhr, Kathleen M. "Healers in Gloria Naylor's Fiction." *TCL* 40.4 (1994): 520.
Saunders, James Robert. *Wayward Preacher*, 105–124.
Smith, Barbara. "Truth That Never Hurts: Black Lesbians in Fiction in the 1980's." *Wild Women in the Whirlwind: Afra-American Culture and the Contemporary Literary Renaissance*. Ed. Joanne M. Braxton and Andrée Nicola McLaughlin. New Brunswick, NJ: Rutgers University Press, 1990. 227–230. Rpt. in Bloom, Harold, ed. *Black American Women Fiction Writers*, 174–175.
Smith, Barbara. "Truth That Never Hurts: Black Lesbians in Fiction in the 1980's." *Wild Women in the Whirlwind: Afra-American Culture and the Contemporary Literary Renaissance*. Ed. Joanne M. Braxton and Andrée Nicola McLaughlin. New Brunswick, NJ: Rutgers University Press, 1990. 227–230. Rpt. in Bloom, Harold, ed. *Contemporary Black American Fiction Writers*, 132–133.

NEPVEU, PIERRE (1946–)

L'Hiver de Mira Christophe (1986)

Aas-Rouxparis, Nicole. "La Thématique de l'hiver dans *L'Hiver de Mira Christophe* de Pierre Nepveu." *FR* 66.1 (1992): 89–97.
Aas-Rouxparis, Nicole. "Une Conque abandonnée: Mira Christophe dans *L'Hiver de Mira Christophe* de Pierre Nepveu." *DFS* 22 (1992): 53–62.
Gobin, Pierre. "Montréal et Vancouver, métro-poles d'un univers: *L'Hiver de Mira Christophe* de Pierre Nepveu." *Tangence* 48 (1995): 10–23.
Whitfield, Agnes. "Silences du corps: *L'Hiver de Mira Christophe* de Pierre Nepveu." *V&I* 18.52 (1992): 52–61.

NEWHOUSE, EDWARD (1911–)

This Is Your Day (1937)

Hapke, Laura. *Daughters of the Great Depression*, 76–77, 129–131.

NICHOLS, MARY SARGENT GOVE (1810–1884)

Mary Lyndon (1855)

Danielson, Susan Steinberg. "Healing Women's Wrongs: Water-Cure as (Fictional) Autobiography." *SAR* 16 (1992): 247–260.

NOËL, FRANCINE (1945–)

Babel (1990)

Barrett, Caroline. "La Voix(e) dialogique: Une Lecture bakhtinienne de *Babel, prise deux*." *V&I* 18.2 (1993): 304–312.
Potvin, Claudine. "De l'Eden a *Babel*: Écrire l'utopie." *V&I* 18.2 (1993): 287–303.
Raoul, Valerie. *Distinctly Narcissistic*, 254–261.

Maryse (1983)

Benedict, Francesca. "La Prise de la parole dans *Maryse* de Francine Noel." *V&I* 18.2 (1993): 264–272.

NORMAN, GURNEY (1937–)

Divine Right's Trip (1971)

Dawkins, Susan. "*Divine Right's Trip:* A Campbellian Journey in the American Counterculture." *BWVACET* 13.2 (1991): 132–143.

O'Dell, R. Keith. "Divine Right Davenport: Cultivating Phenomenology," in Lanier, Parks, Jr.,ed. *Poetics*, 81–85.

Parks, Lanier, Jr. "Divine Right and the Red Tent," in Lanier, Parks, Jr.,ed. *Poetics*, 86–93.

NORRIS, FRANK (1870–1902)

Blix (1899)

McElrath, Joseph R., Jr. *Frank Norris Revisited*, 73–82.

McTeague (1899)

Campbell, Donna M. "Frank Norris' 'Drama of a Broken Teacup': The Old Grannis-Miss Baker Plot in *McTeague*." *ALR* 26.1 (1993): 40–49.

Cassuto, Leonard. " 'Keeping Company' with the Old Folks: Unravelling the Edges of *McTeague*'s Deterministic Fabric." *ALR* 25.2 (1993): 46–55.

Fine, David. "Running Out of Space: Vanishing Landscapes in California Novels." *WAL* 26.3 (1991): 210–211.

Giles, James R. *Naturalistic Inner-City Novel in America*, 26–34.

Heddendorf, David. "*Octopus* in *McTeague:* Frank Norris and Professionalism." *MFS* 37.4 (1991): 677–683, 684–687.

Hug, William J. "*McTeague* as Metafiction? Frank Norris' Parodies of Bret Harte and the Dime Novel." *WAL* 26.3 (1991): 219–228.

McElrath, Joseph R., Jr. *Frank Norris Revisited*, 35–53.

Pizer, Donald. *Theory and Practice*, 88–91.

Man's Woman (1900)

McElrath, Joseph R., Jr. *Frank Norris Revisited*, 82–90.

Moran of the Lady Letty (1898)

McElrath, Joseph R., Jr. *Frank Norris Revisited*, 23–34.

Octopus (1901)

Duncan, Charles. " 'If Your View Be Large Enough': Narrative Growth in *The Octopus*." *ALR* 25.2 (1993): 56–66.

Eby, Clare Virginia. "*The Octupus*: Big Business as Art." *ALR* 26.3 (1994): 33–51.

Ellis, Reuben J. " 'A Little Turn through the Country': Presley's Bicycle Ride in Frank Norris's *The Octopus*." *JACult* 17.3 (1994): 17–22.

Heddendorf, David. "*Octopus* in *McTeague:* Frank Norris and Professionalism." *MFS* 37.4 (1991): 683–685, 686–687.

McElrath, Joseph R., Jr. *Frank Norris Revisited*, 91–105.

Pit (1903)

Eby, Clare Virginia. "Domesticating Naturalism: The Example of *The Pit*." *SAF* 22.2 (1994): 149–168.

McElrath, Joseph R., Jr. *Frank Norris Revisited*, 107–121.

Vandover and the Brute (1914)

McElrath, Joseph R., Jr. *Frank Norris Revisited*, 55–71.
Pizer, Donald. *Theory and Practice*, 111–114.

OATES, JOYCE CAROL (1938–)

American Appetites (1989)

Creighton, Joanne V. *Joyce Carol Oates*, 94–99.
Wagner-Martin, Linda. "Panoramic, Unpredictable, and Human: Joyce Carol Oates's Recent Novels," in Friedman, Melvin J., ed. *Traditions, Voices, and Dreams*, 202–205.

Angel of Light (1981)

Creighton, Joanne V. *Joyce Carol Oates*, 27–35.

Because It Is Bitter, and Because It Is My Heart (1990)

Creighton, Joanne V. *Joyce Carol Oates*, 99–104.

Bellefleur (1980)

Bender, Eileen T. "History as Woman's Game: *Bellefleur* as Texte de Jouissance." *Soundings* 76.2–3 (1993): 39–381.
Creighton, Joanne V. *Joyce Carol Oates*, 38–43.

Bloodsmore Romance (1982)

Creighton, Joanne V. *Joyce Carol Oates*, 43–47.

Cybele (1979)

Creighton, Joanne V. *Joyce Carol Oates*, 23–27.
Wagner-Martin, Linda. "Panoramic, Unpredictable, and Human: Joyce Carol Oates's Recent Novels," in Friedman, Melvin J., ed. *Traditions, Voices, and Dreams*, 205–207.

Expensive People (1968)

Mulryan, John. "Genderfication of Literature: Cross-Gender Writing in Joyce Carol Oates's *Expensive People* and Brian Moore's *I Am Mary Dunne*." *CEA* 56.1 (1993): 117–121.

Lives of the Twins (1987)

Creighton, Joanne V. *Joyce Carol Oates*, 82–86.

Marya, A Life (1986)

Creighton, Joanne V. *Joyce Carol Oates*, 62–69.
Wagner-Martin, Linda. "Panoramic, Unpredictable, and Human: Joyce Carol Oates's Recent Novels," in Friedman, Melvin J., ed. *Traditions, Voices, and Dreams*, 197–202.

Mysteries of Winterthurn (1984)

Creighton, Joanne V. *Joyce Carol Oates*, 47–56.
Wagner-Martin, Linda. "Panoramic, Unpredictable, and Human: Joyce Carol Oates's Recent Novels," in Friedman, Melvin J., ed. *Traditions, Voices, and Dreams*, 207–208.

Nemesis (1990)

Creighton, Joanne V. *Joyce Carol Oates*, 89–93.

Solstice (1986)

Creighton, Joanne V. *Joyce Carol Oates*, 58–62.

Son of the Morning (1978)

Creighton, Joanne V. *Joyce Carol Oates*, 12–18.

Soul/Mate (1989)

Creighton, Joanne V. *Joyce Carol Oates*, 86–89.

them (1969)

Pizer, Donald. *Theory and Practice*, 171–175.

Unholy Loves (1979)

Creighton, Joanne V. *Joyce Carol Oates*, 18–23.

You Must Remember This (1987)

Creighton, Joanne V. *Joyce Carol Oates*, 69–76.

Wagner-Martin, Linda. "Panoramic, Unpredictable, and Human: Joyce Carol Oates's Recent Novels," in Friedman, Melvin J., ed. *Traditions, Voices, and Dreams*, 198–202.

O'BRIEN, DAN (1947–)

Spirit of the Hills (1988)

Witkowsky, Paul. "If Prairies Had Trees: East, West, Environmentalist Fiction, and the Great Plains." *WAL* 28.3 (1993): 196, 200–206.

O'BRIEN, TIM (1946–)

Going After Cacciato (1975)

Bonn, Maria S. "Can Stories Save Us? Tim O'Brien and the Efficacy of the Text." *Crit* 36.1 (1994): 8–12.

Froelich, Vera P. "O'Brien's *Going After Cacciato.*" *Expl* 53.3 (1995): 181–183.

Palm, Edward F. "Falling In and Out: Military Idiom as Metaphoric Motif in *Going after Cacciato.*" *NConL* 22.5 (1992): 8.

Ringnalda, Don. *Fighting and Writing*, 92–93, 94, 98–100, 110–111.

Things They Carried (1990)

Bonn, Maria S. "Can Stories Save Us? Tim O'Brien and the Efficacy of the Text." *Crit* 36.1 (1994): 12–15.

Calloway, Catherine. " 'How to Tell a True War Story': Meta-fiction in *The Things They Carried.*" *Crit* 36.4 (1995): 249–257.

Kaplan, Steven. "Undying Uncertainty of the Narrator in Tim O'Brien's *The Things They Carried.*" *Crit* 35.1 (1993): 43–52.

Ringnalda, Don. *Fighting and Writing*, 91–92, 100–102, 104–105, 106–110, 111–114.

Smith, Lorrie N. " 'The Things Men Do': The Gendered Subtext in Tim O'Brien's Esquire Stories." *Crit* 36.1 (1994): 16–39.

O'CONNOR, FLANNERY (1925–1965)

Violent Bear It Away (1960)

Baker, J. Robert. "Flannery O'Connor's Four-Fold Method of Allegory." *FCB* 21 (1992): 84–96.
Benoit, Raymond. "Existential Intuition of Flannery O'Connor in *The Violent Bear It Away.*" *NConL* 23.4 (1993): 2–3.
Budick, Emily Miller. *Engendering Romance*, 164–180.
Donahoo, Robert. "Tarwater's March Toward the Feminine: The Role of Gender in O'Connor's *The Violent Bear It Away.*" *CEA* 56.1 (1993): 96–106.
Gillespie, Michael Patrick. "Baroque Catholicism in Southern Fiction: Flannery O'Connor, Walker Percy, and John Kennedy Toole," in Friedman, Melvin J., ed. *Traditions, Voices, and Dreams*, 36–37.
Kowalewski, Michael. *Deadly Musings*, 201–203.
Orvell, Miles. *Flannery O'Connor*, 96–125.

Wise Blood (1949)

Butler, Robert. "Visions of Southern Life and Religion in O'Connor's *Wise Blood* and Walker's *The Third Life of Grange Copeland.*" *CLAJ* 36.4 (1993): 360–368.
Carson, Ricks. "O'Connor's *Wise Blood.*" *Expl* 49.3 (1991): 186–187.
Donahoo, Robert. "Problem with Peelers: *Wise Blood* as Social Criticism." *FCB* 21 (1992): 43–57.
Kowalewski, Michael. *Deadly Musings*, 213–220.
Kowalewski, Michael. "On Flannery O'Connor." *Raritan* 10.3 (1991): 85–104.
Myers, Michael. "*Wise Blood* and the Japanese Yugen Aesthetic." *FCB* 21 (1992): 58–72.
Orvell, Miles. *Flannery O'Connor*, 66–95.
Witt, Jonathan. "*Wise Blood* and the Irony of Redemption." *FCB* 22 (1993–94): 12–24.

O'HAGAN, HOWARD (1902–1982)

Tay John (1939)

Davidson, Arnold E. *Coyote Country*, 39–57.
Granofsky, Ronald. "Country of Illusion: Vision, Change, and Misogyny in Howard O'Hagan's *Tay John,*" in Fee, Margery, ed. *Silence Made Visible*, 109–125.
Keith, W. J. "Howard O'Hagan, *Tay John*, and the Growth of Story," in Fee, Margery, ed. *Silence Made Visible*, 73–84.
Maud, Ralph. "Ethnographic Notes on Howard O'Hagan's *Tay John,*" in Fee, Margery, ed. *Silence Made Visible*, 92–95.

O'HARA, JOHN (1905–1970)

Appointment in Samarra (1934)

Castronovo, David. *American Gentleman*, 126–131.

Lockwood Concern (1965)

Castronovo, David. *American Gentleman*, 133–137.

Ten North Frederick (1955)

Castronovo, David. *American Gentleman*, 131–132.

OKADA, JOHN (1923–)

No-No Boy (1957)

Ling, Jinqi. "Race, Power, and Cultural Politics in John Okada's *No-No Boy*." *AL* 67.2 (1995): 359–381.

San Juan, E., Jr. *Hegemony and Strategies*, 184–187.

Sato, Gayle K. Fujita. "Momotaro's Exile: John Okada's *No-No Boy*," in Lim, Shirley Geok-lin , ed. *Reading the Literatures of Asian America*, 239–257.

OLLIVIER, ÉMILE (1940–)

Passages (1991)

Aas-Rouxparis, Nicole. "*Passages* d'Émile Ollivier: Dérive et diversité." *QS* 15 (1992–93): 31–39.

OLSEN, TILLIE (1913–)

Yonnondio (1974)

Cantalupo, Barbara. "Reclaiming the Inadvertent: Olsen's Visceral Voice in *Yonnondio:* From the Thirties." *SAJL* 11.2 (1992): 128–138.

Hapke, Laura. *Daughters of the Great Depression*, 79–88.

Orr, Elaine. "On the Side of the Mother: *Yonnondio* and *Call It Sleep*." *SAF* 21.2 (1993): 209–216.

Pearlman, Mickey. *Tillie Olsen*, 38–52.

OLSON, TOBY (1937–)

Dorit in Lesbos (1990)

Antin, David. "Thinking about Novels." *RCF* 11.2 (1991): 212–213, 214–216.

Life of Jesus (1976)

Perkins, Judith. "Toby Olson's *Life of Jesus*." *RCF* 11.2 (1991): 181–186.

Seaview (1982)

Barone, Dennis. "*Seaview:* Postmodernism and the Drive to Community." *RCF* 11.2 (1991): 187–193.

Woman Who Escaped from Shame (1986)

Abrams, Linsey. "Rose Is a Rose Is a Rose: The Structure of Meaning in *The Woman Who Escaped from Shame*." *RCF* 11.2 (1991): 194–198.

Antin, David. "Thinking about Novels." *RCF* 11.2 (1991): 212–214.

Farrell, Susan. "Sexual Relationships in *The Woman Who Escaped from Shame*." *RCF* 11.2 (1991): 199–209.

ONDAATJE, MICHAEL (1943–)

Collected Works of Billy the Kid (1970)

Barbour, Douglas. *Michael Ondaatje*, 36–66.
Davis, Robert Murray. *Playing Cowboys*, 86–92.

Coming Through the Slaughter (1976)

Barbour, Douglas. *Michael Ondaatje*, 99–135.
Siemerling, Winfried. *Discoveries of the Other*, 110–136.
Verhoeven, W.M. "(De)Facing the Self: Michael Ondaatje and (Auto)Biography," in D'haen, Theo, ed. *Postmodern Fiction in Canada*, 186–192.

English Patient (1992)

Barbour, Douglas. *Michael Ondaatje*, 206–212.
Totosy de Zepetnek, Steven. "*The English Patient:* 'Truth Is Stranger than Fiction'." *ECW* 53 (1994): 141–153.

In the Skin of the Lion (1987)

Acheson, Katherine. "Anne Wilkinson in Michael Ondaatje's *In the Skin of a Lion:* Writing and Reading Class." *CanL* 145 (1995): 107–119.
Barbour, Douglas. *Michael Ondaatje*, 179–205.
Bok, Christian. "Secular Opiate: Marxism as an Ersatz Religion in Three Canadian Texts." *CanL* 147 (1995): 11–22.
Gamlin, Gordon. "Michael Ondaatje's *In the Skin of a Lion* and the Oral Narrative." *CanL* 135 (1992): 68–77.
Heble, Ajay. "Putting Together Another Family: *In the Skin of the Lion*, Affiliation, and the Writing of Canadian (Hi)stories." *ECW* 56 (1995): 236–254.
Overbye, Karen. "Re-Membering the Body: Constructing the Self as Hero in *In the Skin of a Lion*." *SCL* 17.2 (1992): 1–13.
Siemerling, Winfried. *Discoveries of the Other*, 153–171.

Running in the Family (1982)

Barbour, Douglas. *Michael Ondaatje*, 136–160.
Giltrow, Janet and David Stouck. " 'Mute Dialogues': Michael Ondaatje's *Running in the Family* and the Language of Postmodern Pastoral," in D'haen, Theo, ed. *Postmodern Fiction in Canada*, 161–177.
Russell, John. "Travel Memoir as Nonfiction Novel: Michael Ondaatje's *Running in the Family*." *ArielE* 22.2 (1991): 23–40.
Siemerling, Winfried. *Discoveries of the Other*, 137–153.
Tapping, Craig. "South Asia Writes North America: Prose Fictions and Autobiographies from the Indian Diaspora," in *Lim*, Shirley Geok-lin, ed. *Reading the Literatures of Asian America*, 292–293.
Thieme, John A. " 'Historical Relations': Modes of Discourse in Michael Ondaatje's *Running in the Family*," in Howells, Coral Ann, ed. *Narrative Strategies*, 40–48.
Verhoeven, W.M. "(De)Facing the Self: Michael Ondaatje and (Auto)Biography," in D'haen, Theo, ed. *Postmodern Fiction in Canada*, 193–200.

OSTENSO, MARTHA (1900–1963)

O River, Remember (1943)

Atherton, Stanley S. "Martha Ostenso," in Lecker, Robert, ed. *Canadian Writers and Their Works* (Vol. 4), 235–239.

Wild Geese (1925)

Atherton, Stanley S. "Martha Ostenso," in Lecker, Robert, ed. *Canadian Writers and Their Works* (Vol. 4), 225–230.

Davidson, Arnold E. *Coyote Country*, 99–100.

Young May Moon (1929)

Atherton, Stanley S. "Martha Ostenso," in Lecker, Robert, ed. *Canadian Writers and Their Works* (Vol. 4), 230–235.

OTIS, JAMES see KALER, JAMES OTIS

OUVRARD, HÉLÈNE (1938–)

La noyante (1980)

Mauguiere, Benedicte. "Mythe, symbole et idéologie du pays dans *La noyante* d'Hélène Ouvrard." *FR* 65.5 (1992): 754–764.

L'herbe et le varech (1980)

Raoul, Valerie. *Distinctly Narcissistic*, 214–216.

OWENS, LOUIS (1948–)

Wolfsong (1991)

LaLonde, Chris. "Trickster, Trickster Discourse, and Identity in Louis Owens' *Wolfsong*." *SAIL* 7.1 (1995): 27–42.

OZICK, CYNTHIA (1928–)

Cannibal Galaxy (1983)

Friedman, Lawrence S. *Understanding Cynthia Ozick*, 146–157.

Sokoloff, Naomi B. *Imagining the Child*, 197–205.

Messiah of Stockholm (1987)

Friedman, Lawrence S. *Understanding Cynthia Ozick*, 157–170.

Lakritz, Andrew. "Cynthia Ozick at the End of the Modern." *ChiR* 40.1 (1994): 98–117.

Trust (1966)

Friedman, Lawrence S. *Understanding Cynthia Ozick*, 30–56.

PAGE, DOROTHY MYRA

Gathering Storm (1932)

Hapke, Laura. *Daughters of the Great Depression*, 163–166.

PAGE, THOMAS NELSON (1853–1922)

Red Rock (1898)

Michaels, Walter Benn. "Race into Culture: A Critical Genealogy of Cultural Identity." *CritI* 18.4 (1992): 655–685.

PANNETON, PHILLIPE see RINGUET

PAREDES, AMÉRICO (1915–)

George Washington Gomez (1990)

Saldívar, Ramón. "Looking for a Master Plan: Faulkner, Paredes, and the Colonial Postcolonial Subject," in Weinstein, Philip M., ed. *Cambridge Companion*, 108–120.

Sanchez, Rosaura. "Discourses of Gender, Ethnicity and Class in Chicano Literature." *AmRev* 20.2 (1992): 79–82.

PARKER, ROBERT B. (1932–)

Catskill Eagle (1985)

Grenier, Donald J. *Women Enter the Wilderness*, 103–110.

PARTON, SARA PAYSON WILLIS see FERN, FANNY

PATERSON, KATHERINE (1932–)

Come Sing, Jimmy Jo (1985)

Schmidt, Gary D. *Katherine Paterson*, 83–90.

Jacob Have I Loved (1980)

Schmidt, Gary D. *Katherine Paterson*, 72–81.

Lyddie (1991)

Schmidt, Gary D. *Katherine Paterson*, 99–109.

Master Puppeteer (1976)

Schmidt, Gary D. *Katherine Paterson*, 136–142.

Of Nightingales That Weep (1974)

Schmidt, Gary D. *Katherine Paterson*, 29–36.

Rebels of the Heavenly Kingdom (1983)

Schmidt, Gary D. *Katherine Paterson*, 42–52.

PAUL, ELLIOT (1891–1958)

Life and Death of a Spanish Town (1937)

Goldman, Arnold. "Town That Did Not Die." *JAmS* 25.1 (1991): 71–99.

PAXSON, DIANA L.

White Raven (1988)

Byfield, Bruce. "Secret Queen: Two Views of the Heroine in Diana Paxson's *The White Raven*." *Mythlore* 18.1 (1991): 30–33, 48.

Hughes, Melinda. "Dark Sisters and Light Sisters: Sister Doubling and the Search for Sisterhood in The *Mists of Avalon* and *The White Raven*." *Mythlore* 19.1 (1993): 24–27.

Wolf and the Raven (1993)

Kondratiev, Alexei. "Tales Newly Told: A Column on Current Modern Fantasy." *Mythlore* 19.3 (1993): 31–32.

PEATTIE, ELIA WILKINSON (1862–1935)

Precipice (1914)

Szuberla, Guy. "Peattie's *Precipice* and the 'Settlement House' Novel." *Midamerica* 20 (1993): 59–75.

PENNELL, JOSEPH STANLEY (1908–1963)

History of Rome Hanks and Kindred Matters (1944)

Madden, David. "On Joseph Stanley Pennell's *The History of Rome Hanks and Kindred Matters*," in Madden, David, ed. *Classics of Civil War Fiction*, 181–202.

PERCY, WALKER (1916–1990)

Lancelot (1977)

Blair, John. "To Attend to One's Own Soul: Walker Percy and the Southern Cultural Tradition." *MissQ* 46.1 (1992–93): 84–87.

Brinkmeyer, Robert H., Jr. "*Lancelot* and the Dynamics of the Intersubjective Community," in Gretlund, Jan Nordby, ed. *Walker Percy*, 155–166.

Ciuba, Gary M. *Walker Percy*, 171–201.

Desmond, John F. "Revisioning the Fall: Walker Percy and *Lancelot*." *MissQ* 47.4 (1994): 619–631.

Donaldson, Susan V. "Tradition in Amber: Walker Percy's *Lancelot* as Southern Metafiction," in Gretlund, Jan Nordby, ed. *Walker Percy*, 65–73.

Folks, Jeffrey J. *Southern Writers*, 146–148.

Gretlund, Jan Nordby. "On the Porch with Marcus Aurelius: Walker Percy's Stoicism," in Gretlund, Jan Nordby, ed. *Walker Percy*, 81–82.

Hobson, Linda Whitney. " 'Darkness That is Part of Light': *Lancelot* and 'The Grand Inquisitor,' " in Gretlund, Jan Nordby, ed. *Walker Percy*, 119–130.

Oleksy, Elzbieta H. "Walker Percy's Demonic Vision," in Gretlund, Jan Nordby, ed. *Walker Percy*, 199–209.

Scullin, Kathleen. "*Lancelot* and Walker Percy's Dispute with Sartre over Ontology," in Gretlund, Jan Nordby, ed. *Walker Percy*, 110–118.

Wilhelm, Arthur W. "Moviemaking and the Mythological Framework of Walker Percy's *Lancelot*." *SLJ* 27.2 (1995): 62–73.

Last Gentleman (1969)

Blair, John. "To Attend to One's Own Soul: Walker Percy and the Southern Cultural Tradition." *MissQ* 46.1 (1992–93): 82–83.

Ciuba, Gary M. *Walker Percy*, 96–130.

Folks, Jeffrey J. *Southern Writers*, 149–150.

Gillespie, Michael Patrick. "Baroque Catholicism in Southern Fiction: Flannery

O'Connor, Walker Percy, and John Kennedy Toole," in Friedman, Melvin J., ed. *Traditions, Voices, and Dreams*, 41–42.

Godshalk, W. L. "Engineer, Then and Now; or, Barrett's Choice," in Gretlund, Jan Nordby, ed. *Walker Percy*, 33–41.

Gretlund, Jan Nordby. "On the Porch with Marcus Aurelius: Walker Percy's Stoicism," in Gretlund, Jan Nordby, ed. *Walker Percy*, 79–80.

Hardy, John Edward. "Man, Beast, and Others in Walker Percy," in Gretlund, Jan Nordby, ed. *Walker Percy*, 145, 148.

Lawson, Lewis. " 'Parent in the Percept' in *The Last Gentleman*." *MissQ* 46.1 (1992–93): 39–59.

Lawson, Lewis A. "Will Barrett and 'the Fat Rosy Temple of Juno'." *SLJ* 26.2 (1991): 58–76.

Prenshaw, Peggy Whitman. "Elegies for Gentlemen: Walker Percy's *The Last Gentlemen* and Eudora Welty's 'The Demonstrators,' " in Gretlund, Jan Nordby, ed. *Walker Percy*, 89–92.

Stephenson, Will and Mimosa Stephenson. "Abraham of the Ur-Plain in Percy's *The Last Gentleman*." *NConL* 23.4 (1993): 5–6.

Stephenson, Will and Mimosa Stephenson. "*Der Zauberberg* and *The Last Gentleman*." *ANQ* 7.4 (1994): 228–231.

Stephenson, Will and Mimosa Stephenson. "Dr. Gamow and Dr. Duk: The Inadequacy of Science in Walker Percy's Novels." *NConL* 23.3 (1993): 7–8.

Stephenson, Will and Mimosa Stephenson. "Father Boomer as Boanerges in Walker Percy's *The Last Gentleman*." *NConL* 22.3 (1992): 2–3.

Stephenson, Will and Mimosa Stephenson. "Keats Allusion in Walker Percy's *The Last Gentleman*." *NConL* 22.3 (1992): 3–4.

Love in the Ruins (1971)

Bizup, Joseph. "Hopkins' Influence on Percy's *Love in the Ruins*." *Renascence* 46.4 (1994): 247–259.

Blair, John. "To Attend to One's Own Soul: Walker Percy and the Southern Cultural Tradition." *MissQ* 46.1 (1992–93): 83–84.

Ciuba, Gary M. *Walker Percy*, 131–170.

Gillespie, Michael Patrick. "Baroque Catholicism in Southern Fiction: Flannery O'Connor, Walker Percy, and John Kennedy Toole," in Friedman, Melvin J., ed. *Traditions, Voices, and Dreams*, 42–43.

Gretlund, Jan Nordby. "On the Porch with Marcus Aurelius: Walker Percy's Stoicism," in Gretlund, Jan Nordby, ed. *Walker Percy*, 82–83.

Hardy, John Edward. "Man, Beast, and Others in Walker Percy," in Gretlund, Jan Nordby, ed. *Walker Percy*, 145, 147, 152–153.

Moviegoer (1961)

Blair, John. "To Attend to One's Own Soul: Walker Percy and the Southern Cultural Tradition." *MissQ* 46.1 (1992–93): 79–82, 83.

Castronovo, David. *American Gentleman*, 181–185.

Ciuba, Gary M. *Walker Percy*, 56–95.

Gretlund, Jan Nordby. "On the Porch with Marcus Aurelius: Walker Percy's Stoicism," in Gretlund, Jan Nordby, ed. *Walker Percy*, 79.

Hardy, John Edward. "Man, Beast, and Others in Walker Percy," in Gretlund, Jan Nordby, ed. *Walker Percy*, 142–147, 154.

Lawson, Lewis A. "Dream Screen in *The Moviegoer*." *PLL* 30.1 (1994): 25–56.

Lawson, Lewis. "*The Moviegoer* Dates the Love Goddess." *SoQ* 33.1 (1994): 7–25.

Simmons, Philip E. "Toward the Postmodern Historical Imagination: Mass Culture in Walker Percy's *The Moviegoer* and Nicholson Baker's *The Mezzanine*." *ConL* 33.4 (1992): 603–623.

Second Coming (1980)

Ciuba, Gary M. *Walker Percy*, 203–247.

Derwin, Susan. *Ambivalence of Form*, 147–178.

Desmond, John F. "Language, Suicide, and the Writer: Walker Percy's Advancement of William Faulkner," in Gretlund, Jan Nordby, ed. *Walker Percy*, 135–140.

Gillespie, Michael Patrick. "Baroque Catholicism in Southern Fiction: Flannery O'Connor, Walker Percy, and John Kennedy Toole," in Friedman, Melvin J., ed. *Traditions, Voices, and Dreams*, 43–44.

Gretlund, Jan Nordby. "On the Porch with Marcus Aurelius: Walker Percy's Stoicism," in Gretlund, Jan Nordby, ed. *Walker Percy*, 80–81.

Hardy, John Edward. "Man, Beast, and Others in Walker Percy," in Gretlund, Jan Nordby, ed. *Walker Percy*, 145, 148–150, 151–153.

Schwartz, Joseph. "Will Barrett Redux?," in Gretlund, Jan Nordby, ed. *Walker Percy*, 42–51.

Stephenson, Will and Mimosa Stephenson. "Dr. Gamow and Dr. Duk: The Inadequacy of Science in Walker Percy's Novels." *NConL* 23.3 (1993): 7–8.

Thanatos Syndrome (1987)

Allen, William Rodney. " 'Father Smith's Confession' in *The Thanatos Syndrome*," in Gretlund, Jan Nordby, ed. *Walker Percy*, 189–198.

Blair, John. "To Attend to One's Own Soul: Walker Percy and the Southern Cultural Tradition." *MissQ* 46.1 (1992–93): 87–88.

Ciuba, Gary M. *Walker Percy*, 248–296.

Crowley, Sue Mitchell. "*The Thanatos Syndrome:* Walker Percy's Tribute to Flannery O'Connor," in Gretlund, Jan Nordby, ed. *Walker Percy*, 225–237.

Folks, Jeffrey J. *Southern Writers*, 152–155.

Gretlund, Jan Nordby. "On the Porch with Marcus Aurelius: Walker Percy's Stoicism," in Gretlund, Jan Nordby, ed. *Walker Percy*, 82.

Hardy, John Edward. "Man, Beast, and Others in Walker Percy," in Gretlund, Jan Nordby, ed. *Walker Percy*, 144, 149–151, 153.

Pitavy, François. "Walker Percy's Brave New World: *The Thanatos Syndrome*," in Gretlund, Jan Nordby, ed. *Walker Percy*, 177–188.

Poteat, Patricia Lewis. "Pilgrim's Progress; or, A Few Night Thoughts of Tenderness and the Will to Power," in Gretlund, Jan Nordby, ed. *Walker Percy*, 210–224.

Samway, Patrick, S.J. "Two Conversations in Walker Percy's *The Thanatos Syndrome:* Text and Context," in Gretlund, Jan Nordby, ed. *Walker Percy*, 24–32.

PERETTI, FRANK (1951–)

Piercing the Darkness (1989)

Howard, Jay R. "Vilifying the Enemy: The Christian Right and the Novels of Frank Peretti." *JPC* 28.3 (1994): 197–205.

This Present Darkness (1986)

Howard, Jay R. "Vilifying the Enemy: The Christian Right and the Novels of Frank Peretti." *JPC* 28.3 (1994): 197–205.

PETRY, ANN (1912–1997)

Narrows (1953)

McDowell, Margaret B. "*The Narrows:* A Fuller View View of Ann Petry." *Black American Literature Forum* 14.4 (1980): 137. Rpt. in Bloom, Harold, ed. *Modern Black American Fiction Writers*, 129–130.

Street (1946)

Andrews, Larry R. "Sensory Assault of the City in Ann Petry's *The Street*," in Hakutani, Yoshinobu, ed. *City in African-American Literature*, 196–211.
Bande, Usha. "Murder as Social Revenge in *The Street* and *The Women of Brewster Place*." *NConL* 23.1 (1993): 4–5.
Clark, Keith. "Distaff Dream Deferred? Ann Petry and the Art of Subversion." *AAR* 26.3 (1992): 495–505.
Clark, Keith. "Distaff Dream Deferred? Ann Petry and the Art of Subversion." *African American Review* 26.3 (1992): 495–497. Rpt. in Bloom, Harold, ed. *Black American Women Fiction Writers*, 191–193.
Clark, Keith. "Distaff Dream Deferred? Ann Petry and the Art of Subversion." *African American Review* 26.3 (1992): 495–497. Rpt. in Bloom, Harold, ed. *Modern Black American Fiction Writers*, 134–136.
De Jongh, James. *Vicious Modernism: Black Harlem and the Literary Imagination.* New York: Cambridge University Press, 1990. 89–92. Rpt. in Bloom, Harold, ed. *Black American Women Fiction Writers*, 187–189.
De Jongh, James. *Vicious Modernism: Black Harlem and the Literary Imagination.* New York: Cambridge University Press, 1990. 89–92. Rpt. in Bloom, Harold, ed. *Modern Black American Fiction Writers*, 130–132.
Griffin, Farah Jasmine. *"Who Set You Flowin'?"*, 114–119.
McKay, Nellie Y. "Ann Petry's *The Street and The Narrows:* A Study of the Influence of Class, Race, and Gender on Afro-American Women's Lives," in Diedrich, Maria and Dorothea Fischer-Hornung, eds. *Women and War: The Changing Status of American Women from the 1930's to the 1950's.* New York: Berg, 1990. 134–135. Rpt. in Bloom, Harold, ed. *Modern Black American Fiction Writers*, 133–134.
Wright, Lee Alfred. *Identity, Family, and Folklore*, 29–32.

PHELPS, ELIZABETH STUART (1844–1911)

Doctor Zay (1882)

Morris, Timothy. "Professional Ethics and Professional Erotics in Elizabeth Stuart Phelps' *Doctor Zay*." *SAF* 21.2 (1993): 141–152.

Gates Ajar (1868)

Jones, E. Michael. *Angel and the Machine*, 105–116.
Schnog, Nancy. " 'The Comfort of My Fancying': Loss and Recuperation in *The Gates Ajar*." *ArQ* 49.1 (1993): 21–47.

Story of Avis (1877)

Wilson, Jack H. "Competing Narratives in Elizabeth Stuart Phelps' *The Story of Avis*." *ALR* 26.1 (1993): 60–75

PHILLIPS, JAYNE ANNE (1952–)

Machine Dreams (1984)

Carter, Susanne. "Variations on Vietnam: Women's Innovative Interpretations of the Vietnam War Experience." *Extrapolation* 32.2 (1991): 172–173.

Price, Joanna. "Remembering Vietnam: Subjectivity and Mourning in American New Realist Writing." *JAmS* 27.2 (1993): 175–178, 180–182.

PIERCY, MARGE (1936–)

He, She, It (1991)

Booker, M. Keith. "Woman on the Edge of a Genre: The Feminist Dystopias of Marge Piercy." *SFS* 21.3 (1994): 342–348.

Kuznets, Lois Rostow. *When Toys Come Alive*, 197–203.

Woman on the Edge of Time (1977)

Booker, M. Keith. "Woman on the Edge of a Genre: The Feminist Dystopias of Marge Piercy." *SFS* 21.3 (1994): 339–342.

Hansen, Elaine Tuttle. "Mothers Tomorrow and Mothers Yesterday, But Never Mothers Today: *Woman on the Edge of Time* and *The Handmaid's Tale*," in Daly, Brenda O., ed. *Narrating Mothers*, 22–28, 34–40.

Maciunas, Billie. "Feminist Epistemology in Piercy's *Woman on the Edge of Time*." *WS* 20.3–4 (1992): 249–258.

Orr, Elaine. "Mothering as Good Fiction: Instances from Marge Piercy's *Woman on the Edge of Time*." *JNT* 23.2 (1993): 61–79.

Rosenfelt, Deborah Silverton. "Feminism, "Postfeminism," and Contemporary Women's Fiction," in Howe, Florence, ed. *Tradition and the Talents of Women*, 272–273, 277.

PINEDA, CECILE (1942–)

Face (1985)

Johnson, David E. "Face Value (An Essay on Cecile Pineda's *Face*)." *AmRev* 19.2 (1991): 73–93.

PINSONNEAULT, JEAN-PAUL

Les abîmes de l'aube (1962)

Raoul, Valerie. *Distinctly Narcissistic*, 140–143.

PLANTE, DAVID (1940–)

Country (1981)

Bergman, David. *Gaiety Transfigured*, 201–203.

Gordon, Mary. *Good Boys and Dead Girls*, 108–111.

PLATH, SYLVIA (1932–1963)

Bell Jar (1963)

Greene, Gayle. *Changing the Story*, 66–69.

Leonard, Garry M. " 'The Woman Is Perfected. Her Dead Body Wears the Smile of Accomplishment': Sylvia Plath and *Mademoiselle Magazine*." *CollL* 19.2 (1992): 60–82.

Martin, Robert A. "Esther's Dilemma in *The Bell Jar*." *NConL* 21.1 (1991): 6–8.

Tucker, Lindsey. *Textual Excap(e)ades*, 17–34.

POHL, FREDERIK (1919–)

Gateway (1977)

Heyne, Eric. "Gateway to an Erotics of Narrative." *Extrapolation* 35.4 (1994): 298–311.

PORTER, ELEANOR (1868–1920)

Pollyanna (1913)

Griswold, Jerry. *Audacious Kids*, 215–236.

POULIN, JACQUES (1937–)

Le vieux chagrin (1989)

Jarque, Alexandra. "Sur les traces de la lectrice dans *Le vieux chagrin* de Jacques Poulin." *QS* 18 (1994): 137–148.

Lintvelt, Jaap. "Le Double thématique et narratif dans *Le vieux chagrin* de Jacques Poulin." *DFS* 23 (1992): 87–96.

Volkswagen Blues (1984)

Navarro Pardinas, Blanca. "Phénoménologie de l'acte de lecture: L'Exemple de *Volkswagen Blues* de Jacques Poulin." *Tangence* 36 (1992): 52–62.

Paterson, Janet M. "Ni l'un, ni l'autre: L'Ambivalence du discours de l'hétérogene dans *Volkswagen Blues*." *UTQ* 63.4 (1994): 605–613.

Shek, Ben-Z. *French-Canadian*, 125–128.

POWELL, PADGETT (1952–)

Edisto (1984)

Grenier, Donald J. *Women Enter the Wilderness*, 98–103.

PRICE, REYNOLDS (1933–)

Kate Vaiden (1986)

Dewey, Joseph. "Time to Bolt: Suicide, Androgyny, and the Dislocation of the Self in Reynolds Price's *Kate Vaiden*." *MissQ* 45.1 (1991–92): 9–28.

Hartin, Edith T. "Reading as a Woman: Reynolds Price and Creative Androgyny in *Kate Vaiden*." *SoQ* 29.3 (1991): 37–52.

Long and Happy Life (1962)

Jones, Gloria G. "Reynolds Price's *A Long and Happy Life:* Style and the Dynamics of Power." *CEA* 56.1 (1993): 77–85.

Love and Work (1968)

Ciuba, Gary M. "Price's *Love and Work:* Discovering the 'Perfect Story'." *Renascence* 44.1 (1991): 45–60.

Source of Light (1981)

Schiff, James A. "Fathers and Sons in the Fiction of Reynolds Price: A Sense of Crucial Ambiguity." *SoR* 29.1 (1993): 20–29.

Surface of the Earth (1975)

Orr, Linda. "Duplicity of the Southern Story: Reflections on Reynolds Price's *The Surface of Earth* and Eudora Welty's 'The Wide Net'." *SAQ* 91.1 (1992): 111–137.

Schiff, James A. "Fathers and Sons in the Fiction of Reynolds Price: A Sense of Crucial Ambiguity." *SoR* 29.1 (1993): 20–29.

PROUTY, OLIVE HIGGINS (1882(?)–1974)

Stella Dallas (1923)

Chandler, Karen M. "Agency and *Stella Dallas:* Audience, Melodramatic Directives, and Social Determinism in 1920s America." *ArQ* 51.4 (1995): 29–35.

PUZO, MARIO (1920–)

Godfather (1969)

Torgovnick, Marianna De Marco. *Crossing Ocean Parkway*, 109–134.

PYNCHON, THOMAS (1937–)

Crying of Lot 49 (1965)

Castillo, Debra A. "Borges and Pynchon: The Tenuous Symmetries of Art," in O'Donnell, Patrick, ed. *New Essays on The Crying of Lot 49*, 21–44.

Chambers, Judith. *Thomas Pynchon*, 96–122.

Das, Prasanta. "Oedipa's Night Journey in Pynchon's *The Crying of Lot 49.*" *NConL* 23.2 (1993): 4–5.

Duyfhuizen, Bernard. " 'Hushing Sick Transmissions': Disrupting Story in *The Crying of Lot 49*," in O'Donnell, Patrick, ed. *New Essays on The Crying of Lot 49*, 79–93.

Fine, David. "Running Out of Space: Vanishing Landscapes in California Novels." *WAL* 26.3 (1991): 212.

Freese, Peter. "Surviving the End: Apocalypse, Evolution, and Entropy in Bernard Malamud, Kurt Vonnegut, and Thomas Pynchon." *Crit* 36.3 (1995): 171–174.

Gleason, William. "Postmodern Labyrinths of Lot 49." *Crit* 34.2 (1993): 83–99.

Hall, Chris. " 'Behind the Hieroglyphic Streets': Pynchon's Oedipa Maas and the Dialectics of Reading." *Crit* 33.1 (1991): 63–77.

Harper, Phillip Brian. *Framing the Margins*, 164–171.

Hayles, N. Katherine. " 'A Metaphor of God Knew How Many Parts': The Engine that Drives *The Crying of Lot 49*," in O'Donnell, Patrick, ed. *New Essays on The Crying of Lot 49*, 97–122.

Johnston, John. "Toward the Schizo-Text: Paranoia as Semiotic Regime in *The Crying of Lot 49*," in O'Donnell, Patrick, ed. *New Essays on The Crying of Lot 49*, 47–76.

Moddelmog, Debra A. *Readers and Mythic Signs*, 78–81.

O'Donnell, Patrick. "Engendering Paranoia in Contemporary Narrative." *BoundaryII* 19.1 (1992): 190–193.

Petillon, Pierre-Yves. "Re-cognition of Her Errand into the Wilderness," in O'Donnell, Patrick, ed. *New Essays on The Crying of Lot 49*, 127–162.

Putz, Manfred. "Art of the Acronym in Thomas Pynchon." *SNNTS* 23.3 (1991): 374–375, 378–379.

Safer, Elaine. "Dreams and Nightmares: 'High-Tech Paranoia' and the Jamesonian Sublime—An Approach to Thomas Pynchon's Postmodernism," in Friedman, Melvin J., ed. *Traditions, Voices, and Dreams*, 287–290.

White, Eric Charles. "Negentropy, Noise, and Emancipatory Thought," in Hayles, N. Katherine, ed. *Chaos and Order*, 269–273

Gravity's Rainbow (1973)

Best, Steven. "Creative Paranoia: A Postmodern Aesthetic of Cognitive Mapping in *Gravity's Rainbow*." *CentR* 36.1 (1992): 59–87.

Black, Joel. "Hermeneutics of Extinction: Denial and Discovery in Scientific Literature." *CCrit* 13 (1991): 147–169.

Chambers, Judith. "Dazzle of Violet and a Green-Doped Hound: Pynchon's Miracle of De-Struction in *Gravity's Rainbow*." *Crit* 32.4 (1991): 258–275.

Chambers, Judith. *Thomas Pynchon*, 123–183.

Granofsky, Ronald. *Trauma Novel*, 162–170.

Hume, Kathryn. "Repetition and the Construction of Character in *Gravity's Rainbow*." *Crit* 33.4 (1992): 243–254.

Limon, John. *Writing After War*, 139–153.

McCarron, William E. "Pynchon and Kesey." *NConL* 21.5 (1991): 8–9.

Putz, Manfred. "Art of the Acronym in Thomas Pynchon." *SNNTS* 23.3 (1991): 374, 375.

Safer, Elaine. "Dreams and Nightmares: 'High-Tech Paranoia' and the Jamesonian Sublime—An Approach to Thomas Pynchon's Postmodernism," in Friedman, Melvin J., ed. *Traditions, Voices, and Dreams*, 290.

Schwenger, Peter. "Hiroshima in the Morning," MacCannell, Juliet Flower, ed. *Textual Bodies*, 114–119.

Strehle, Susan. *Fiction in the Quantum Universe*, 27–65.

Turier, Christine. "Pynchon's *Gravity's Rainbow*." *Expl* 50.4 (1992): 244–246.

Weisenburger, Steven. "Hysteron Proteron in *Gravity's Rainbow*." *TSLL* 34.1 (1992): 87–105.

V. (1963)

Chambers, Judith. *Thomas Pynchon*, 41–95.

Cooley, Ronald W. "Hothouse or the Street: Imperialism and Narrative in Pynchon's *V.*" *MFS* 39.2 (1993): 307–325.

Kowalewski, Michael. *Deadly Musings*, 235–245.

Safer, Elaine. "Dreams and Nightmares: 'High-Tech Paranoia' and the Jamesonian

Sublime—An Approach to Thomas Pynchon's Postmodernism," in Friedman, Melvin J., ed. *Traditions, Voices, and Dreams*, 285–287.

Vineland (1990)

Booker, M. Keith. *Dystopian Impulse*, 152–162.
Chambers, Judith. *Thomas Pynchon*, 184–207.
Doxey, William. "Pinochle-Playing Worms in Pynchon's *Vineland.*" *NConL* 21.3 (1991): 11–12.
Hinds, Elizabeth Jane Wall. "Visible Tracks, Historical Method and Thomas Pynchon's *Vineland.*" *CollL* 19.1 (1992): 91–103.
Leithauser, Brad. *Penchants and Places*, 164–174.
Myers, Marsa C. "Prairie as Hero: Pynchon's *Vineland.*" *BWVACET* 13.2 (1991): 103–111.
Putz, Manfred. "Art of the Acronym in Thomas Pynchon." *SNNTS* 23.3 (1991): 376.
Robberds, Mark. "New Historicist Creepers of *Vineland.*" *Crit* 36.4 (1995): 237–248.
Rushdie, Salman. *Imaginary Homelands*, 352–357.
Safer, Elaine. "Dreams and Nightmares: 'High-Tech Paranoia' and the Jamesonian Sublime—An Approach to Thomas Pynchon's Postmodernism," in Friedman, Melvin J., ed. *Traditions, Voices, and Dreams*, 290–294.
Wilde, Alan. "Love and Death in and around Vineland, U.S.A." *BoundaryII* 18.2 (1991): 166–180.

RADDALL, THOMAS (1903–)

Governor's Lady (1960)

Morgan, Hubert. "Aspirant and Ondine: Hope and Vision in Thomas Raddall's Novels," in Young, Alan R., ed. *Time and Place*, 177, 179.
Smyth, Donna E. "Raddall's Desiring Machine: Narrative Strategies in the Historical Fiction," in Young, Alan R., ed. *Time and Place*, 76–80.

Hangman's Beach (1966)

Croft, Clary. "Use of Folklore in Selected Works of Thomas H. Raddall," in Young, Alan R., ed. *Time and Place*, 118–119.
Moody, Barry. "Novelist as Historian: The Nova Scotia Identity in the Novels of Thomas H. Raddall," in Young, Alan R., ed. *Time and Place*, 147–148.
Morgan, Hubert. "Aspirant and Ondine: Hope and Vision in Thomas Raddall's Novels," in Young, Alan R., ed. *Time and Place*, 174, 175, 176, 180–181.
Smyth, Donna E. "Raddall's Desiring Machine: Narrative Strategies in the Historical Fiction," in Young, Alan R., ed. *Time and Place*, 80–84.

His Majesty's Yankees (1942)

Croft, Clary. "Use of Folklore in Selected Works of Thomas H. Raddall," in Young, Alan R., ed. *Time and Place*, 111, 112–113, 115, 116.
Fern, Chris. "Building a Country; Losing an Empire: The Historical Fiction of Thomas H. Raddall and J.G. Farrell," in Young, Alan R., ed. *Time and Place*, 155–156, 161, 163.
Lacombe, Michèle. "Gender in the Fiction of Thomas H. Raddall," in Young, Alan R., ed. *Time and Place*, 88–91.

Moody, Barry. "Novelist as Historian: The Nova Scotia Identity in the Novels of Thomas H. Raddall," in Young, Alan R., ed. *Time and Place*, 143–146, 148–150.

Morgan, Hubert. "Aspirant and Ondine: Hope and Vision in Thomas Raddall's Novels," in Young, Alan R., ed. *Time and Place*, 174, 175, 176, 177, 179, 181.

Smyth, Donna E. "Raddall's Desiring Machine: Narrative Strategies in the Historical Fiction," in Young, Alan R., ed. *Time and Place*, 63–68.

Nymph and the Lamp (1950)

Buss, Helen M. "*The Nymph and the Lamp* and the Canadian Heroine of Conciousness," in Young, Alan R., ed. *Time and Place*, 43–59.

Lacombe, Michèle. "Gender in the Fiction of Thomas H. Raddall," in Young, Alan R., ed. *Time and Place*, 90–91, 95–97.

MacDonald, Bruce F. "Life and the Way Out in Thomas Raddall's Novels," in Young, Alan R., ed. *Time and Place*, 168–169, 170, 173.

Moody, Barry. "Novelist as Historian: The Nova Scotia Identity in the Novels of Thomas H. Raddall," in Young, Alan R., ed. *Time and Place*, 150, 152.

Morgan, Hubert. "Aspirant and Ondine: Hope and Vision in Thomas Raddall's Novels," in Young, Alan R., ed. *Time and Place*, 176, 178, 179–180, 181.

Pride's Fancy (1946)

Croft, Clary. "Use of Folklore in Selected Works of Thomas H. Raddall," in Young, Alan R., ed. *Time and Place*, 113–114, 115.

Fern, Chris. "Building a Country; Losing an Empire: The Historical Fiction of Thomas H. Raddall and J.G. Farrell," in Young, Alan R., ed. *Time and Place*, 160, 161.

Moody, Barry. "Novelist as Historian: The Nova Scotia Identity in the Novels of Thomas H. Raddall," in Young, Alan R., ed. *Time and Place*, 147.

Morgan, Hubert. "Aspirant and Ondine: Hope and Vision in Thomas Raddall's Novels," in Young, Alan R., ed. *Time and Place*, 174, 175, 176, 177, 181.

Smyth, Donna E. "Raddall's Desiring Machine: Narrative Strategies in the Historical Fiction," in Young, Alan R., ed. *Time and Place*, 75–76.

Roger Sudden (1944)

Beeler, Karin E. "Divided Loyalties in Eighteenth-Century Nova Scotia/Acadia: Nationalism and Cultural Affiliation in Thomas Raddall's *Roger Sudden* and A. E. Johann's *Ans dunkle Ufer*." *DR* 72.1 (1992): 66–72, 79.

Croft, Clary. "Use of Folklore in Selected Works of Thomas H. Raddall," in Young, Alan R., ed. *Time and Place*, 110–111, 118.

Fern, Chris. "Building a Country; Losing an Empire: The Historical Fiction of Thomas H. Raddall and J.G. Farrell," in Young, Alan R., ed. *Time and Place*, 155–156, 159–160, 161–162.

Moody, Barry. "Novelist as Historian: The Nova Scotia Identity in the Novels of Thomas H. Raddall," in Young, Alan R., ed. *Time and Place*, 141–143, 148.

Morgan, Hubert. "Aspirant and Ondine: Hope and Vision in Thomas Raddall's Novels," in Young, Alan R., ed. *Time and Place*, 175, 176, 177–176, 179, 181.

Smyth, Donna E. "Raddall's Desiring Machine: Narrative Strategies in the Historical Fiction," in Young, Alan R., ed. *Time and Place*, 68–75.

Tidefall (1953)

Croft, Clary. "Use of Folklore in Selected Works of Thomas H. Raddall," in Young, Alan R., ed. *Time and Place*, 112, 113.

Lacombe, Michèle. "Gender in the Fiction of Thomas H. Raddall," in Young, Alan R., ed. *Time and Place*, 87–88, 90, 92–94.
Moody, Barry. "Novelist as Historian: The Nova Scotia Identity in the Novels of Thomas H. Raddall," in Young, Alan R., ed. *Time and Place*, 150–151.
Morgan, Hubert. "Aspirant and Ondine: Hope and Vision in Thomas Raddall's Novels," in Young, Alan R., ed. *Time and Place*, 178–179, 181.

Wings of the Night (1956)

Croft, Clary. "Use of Folklore in Selected Works of Thomas H. Raddall," in Young, Alan R., ed. *Time and Place*, 111–112.
MacDonald, Bruce F. "Life and the Way Out in Thomas Raddall's Novels," in Young, Alan R., ed. *Time and Place*, 166–168, 171–172.
Moody, Barry. "Novelist as Historian: The Nova Scotia Identity in the Novels of Thomas H. Raddall," in Young, Alan R., ed. *Time and Place*, 150, 151–152.
Morgan, Hubert. "Aspirant and Ondine: Hope and Vision in Thomas Raddall's Novels," in Young, Alan R., ed. *Time and Place*, 175–176, 181.

RASKIN, HELEN (1928–1984)

Figgs & phantoms (1974)

Olson, Marilynn Strasser. *Ellen Raskin*, 67–80.

tattooed Potato (1975)

Olson, Marilynn Strasser. *Ellen Raskin*, 81–92.

Westing Game (1978)

Olson, Marilynn Strasser. *Ellen Raskin*, 93–104.

RECHY, JOHN (1934–)

City of Night (1963)

Christian, Karen. "Will the 'Real Chicano' Please Stand Up? The Challenge of John Rechy and Sheila Ortiz Taylor to Chicano Essentialism." *AmRev* 20.2 (1992): 92–93, 95–96, 98–99, 101–102.
Giles, James R. *Naturalistic Inner-City Novel in America*, 139–158.
Koponen, Wilfrid R. *Embracing Gay Identity*, 41–49.

REED, ISHMAEL (1938–)

Flight to Canada (1976)

Cowley, Julian. "What If I Write Circuses? The Space of Ishmael Reed's Fiction." *Callaloo* 17.4 (1994): 1238, 1241.
Walsh, Richard. " 'A Man's Story Is His Gris-Gris': Cultural Slavery, Literary Emancipation and Ishmael Reed's *Flight to Canada*." *JAmS* 27.1 (1993): 57–71.
Walsh, Richard. " 'A Man's Story Is His Gris-Gris': Cultural Slavery, Literary Emancipation and Ishmael Reed's *Flight to Canada*." *Journal of American Studies* 27.1 (1993): 61–63. Rpt. in Bloom, Harold, ed. *Contemporary Black American Fiction Writers*, 150–152.
Walsh, Richard. " 'A Man's Story Is His Gris-Gris': Cultural Slavery, Literary Emancipation and Ishmael Reed's *Flight to Canada*." *Journal of American Stud-*

ies 27.1 (1993): 61–63. Rpt. in Bloom, Harold, ed. *Major Modern Black American Writers*, 149–151.

Weixlmann, Joe. “Politics, Piracy, and Other Games: Slavery and Liberation in *Flight to Canada.*” *MELUS* 6.3 (Fall 1979): 41–42, 45–46. Rpt. in Bloom, Harold, ed. *Contemporary Black American Fiction Writers*, 142–143.

Free-Lance Pallbearers (1967)

Hume, Kathryn. “Ishmael Reed and the Problematics of Control.” *PMLA* 108.3 (1993): 514.

Kinnamon, Keneth. [Review of *Free-Lance Pallbearers*]. *Negro American Literature Forum* 1.2 (Winter 1967): 18. Rpt. in Bloom, Harold, ed. *Contemporary Black American Fiction Writers*, 138–139.

Last Days of Louisiana Red (1974)

Cowley, Julian. “What If I Write Circuses? The Space of Ishmael Reed's Fiction.” *Callaloo* 17.4 (1994): 1239.

Hume, Kathryn. “Ishmael Reed and the Problematics of Control.” *PMLA* 108.3 (1993): 513–514.

Klinkowitz, Jerome. “Ishmael Reed's Multicultural Aesthetic.” *Literary Subversions*. Carbondale, IL: Southern Illinois Press, 1985. 18–19, 21. Rpt. in Bloom, Harold, ed. *Contemporary Black American Fiction Writers*, 145–146.

Mumbo Jumbo (1972)

Cowley, Julian. “What If I Write Circuses? The Space of Ishmael Reed's Fiction.” *Callaloo* 17.4 (1994): 1240–1241.

Fox, Robert Elliot. *Conscientious Sorcerers: The Black Postmodernist Fiction of LeRoi Jones/Amiri Baraka, Ishmael Reed, and Samuel R. Delaney*. New York: Greenwood Press, 1987. 50–51. Rpt. in Bloom, Harold, ed. *Contemporary Black American Fiction Writers*, 146–147.

Fox, Robert Elliot. *Conscientious Sorcerers: The Black Postmodernist Fiction of LeRoi Jones/Amiri Baraka, Ishmael Reed, and Samuel R. Delaney*. New York: Greenwood Press, 1987. 50–51. Rpt. in Bloom, Harold, ed. *Major Modern Black American Writers*, 146–147.

Hardack, Richard. “Swing to the White, Back to the Black: Writing and 'Sourcery' in Ishamel Reed's *Mumbo Jumbo.*” *ArQ* 49.4 (1993): 117–138.

Hoffmann, Donald L. “Darker Shade of Grail: Questing at the Crossroads in Ishmael Reed's *Mumbo Jumbo.*” *Callaloo* 17.4 (1994): 1245–1256.

Hume, Kathryn. “Ishmael Reed and the Problematics of Control.” *PMLA* 108.3 (1993): 509–511.

Johnson, Carol Siri. “Limbs of Osiris: Reed's *Mumbo Jumbo* and Hollywood's *The Mummy.*” *MELUS* 17.4 (1991–92): 105–114.

Terrible Twos (1982)

Crouch, Stanley. “Kinships and Aginships.” *Nation* (May 22, 1982): 618–619. Rpt. in Bloom, Harold, ed. *Contemporary Black American Fiction Writers*, 143–145.

Yellow Back Radio Broke-Down (1969)

Cowley, Julian. “What If I Write Circuses? The Space of Ishmael Reed's Fiction.” *Callaloo* 17.4 (1994): 1237–1238, 1239–1240.

Davis, Robert Murray. *Playing Cowboys*, 132–143.

RENAUD, JACQUES (1943–)

Broke City see *Le cassé*

Le cassé (1964)

Shek, Ben-Z. *French-Canadian*, 58–59.

RESSLER, LILLIAN see "LILLIAN JANET"

RICCI, NINO (1959–)

Lives of the Saints (1990)

Imboden, Roberta. "Hyperbolical Project of Cristina: A Derridean Analysis of Ricci's *Lives of the Saints.*" *DR* 72.1 (1992): 38–51.

RICHARD, JEAN-JULES (1911–1975)

Journal d'un hobo (1965)

Raoul, Valerie. *Distinctly Narcissistic*, 149–154.

RICHARDS, DAVID ADAMS (1950–)

Blood Ties (1976)

Mathews, Lawrence. "David Adams Richards," in Lecker, Robert, ed. *Canadian Writers and Their Works: Fiction Series* (Vol. 12), 213–218.

Coming of Winter (1974)

Mathews, Lawrence. "David Adams Richards," in Lecker, Robert, ed. *Canadian Writers and Their Works: Fiction Series* (Vol. 12), 207–213.

Evening Snow Will Bring Such Peace (1990)

Mathews, Lawrence. "David Adams Richards," in Lecker, Robert, ed. *Canadian Writers and Their Works: Fiction Series* (Vol. 12), 240–243.

For Those Who Hunt the Wounded Down (1993)

Mathews, Lawrence. "David Adams Richards," in Lecker, Robert, ed. *Canadian Writers and Their Works: Fiction Series* (Vol. 12), 244–248.

Lives of Short Duration (1981)

Mathews, Lawrence. "David Adams Richards," in Lecker, Robert, ed. *Canadian Writers and Their Works: Fiction Series* (Vol. 12), 221–227.

Nights Below Station Street (1988)

Mathews, Lawrence. "David Adams Richards," in Lecker, Robert, ed. *Canadian Writers and Their Works: Fiction Series* (Vol. 12), 235–240.

Road to the Stilt House (1985)

Mathews, Lawrence. "David Adams Richards," in Lecker, Robert, ed. *Canadian Writers and Their Works: Fiction Series* (Vol. 12), 227–234.

RICHARDSON, JOHN (1796–1852)

Canadian Brothers (1840)

Hurley, Michael. *Borders of Nightmare*, 110–155.

Monk Knight of St. John (1850)

Hurley, Michael. "Double Entendre: Rebel Angels and Beautiful Losers in John Richardson's *The Monk Knight of St. John.*" *CanL* 128 (1991): 107–118.

Wacousta (1832)

Duffy, Dennis. *Tale of Sad Reality: John Richardson's Wacousta.* Toronto: ECW Press, 1993.
Hurley, Michael. *Borders of Nightmare*, 27–68, 69–109.
Hurley, Michael. "*Wacousta* as Trickster: 'The Enemy of Boundaries'." *JCSR* 26.3 (1991): 68–79.
Kuester, Martin. *Framing Truths*, 32–38.
Turner, Margaret E. *Imagining Culture*, 23–46.

Westbrook, the Outlaw (1851)

Hurley, Michael. *Borders of Nightmare*, 195–199.

RIDGE, JOHN ROLLIN (1827–1867)

Life and Adventures of Joaquin Murieta (1854)

Christensen, Peter G. "Minority Interaction in John Rollin Ridge's *The Life and Adventures of Joaquin Murieta.*" *MELUS* 17.2 (1991–92): 61–72.
Lowe, John. "Space and Freedom in the Golden Republic: Yellow Bird's *The Life and Adventures of Joaquin Murieta, the Celebrated California Bandit.*" *SAIL* 4.2–3 (1992): 106–122.
Mondragon, Maria. " 'The (Safe) White Side of the Line': History and Disguise in John Rollin Ridge's *The Life and Adventures of Joaquin Murieta: The Celebrated California Bandit.*" *ATQ* 8.3 (1994): 173–186.
Owens, Louis. *Other Destinies*, 32–40.

RIIS, SHARON (1947–)

True Story of Ida Johnson (1976)

Davidson, Arnold E. *Coyote Country*, 100–101.

RINGUET (1895–1960)

Thirty Acres See *Trente arpents*

Trente arpents (1938)

Beaudoin, Rejean. "La Langue de Ringuet ne parle pas: Elle écrit." *Tangence* 40 (1993): 39–48.
Shek, Ben-Z. *French-Canadian*, 27–30.
Smart, Patricia. *Writing in the Father's House*, 62–71, 77–79, 94–98.

RIVARD, YVON (1945–).

Les silences du corbeau (1986)

Huggan, Graham. "Orientalism Reconfirmed? Stereotypes of East-West Encounter in Janette Turner Hospital's *The Ivory Swing* and Yvon Rivard's *Les silences du corbeau.*" *CanL* 132 (1992): 44–55.

Mort et naissance de Christophe Ulric (1976)

Beaudoin, Rejean. "Quelques citations blanches dans un roman d'Yvon Rivard." *EF* 29.1 (1993): 47–58.

RIVERA, TOMÁS (1935–1984)

. . . y no se lo tragó la tierra . . . (1971)

Calderón, Héctor. "The Novel and the Community of Readers: Rereading Tomás Rivera's *y no se lo tragó la tierra*," in Calderón, Héctor, ed. *Criticism in the Borderlands*, 97–113.

Tusmith, Bonnie. *All My Relatives*, 140–156.

ROBERTS, ELIZABETH MADOX (1886–1941)

Time of Man (1926)

Joyner, Nancy Carol. "Poetics of the House in Appalachian Fiction," in Lanier, Parks, Jr.,ed. *Poetics*, 23–26.

Tate, Linda. *Southern Weave of Women*, 13–15.

ROBERTSON, MARGARET MURRAY (1821–1897)

Bairns (1870)

MacMillan, Carrie. *Silenced Sextet*, 93–97.

By a Way She Knew Not (1888)

MacMillan, Carrie. *Silenced Sextet*, 101–103.

Christie; or the Way Home see *Christie Redfern's Troubles*

Christie Redfern's Troubles (1866)

MacMillan, Carrie. *Silenced Sextet*, 87–90.

Inglises (1872)

MacMillan, Carrie. *Silenced Sextet*, 97–98.

Shenac's Work at Home (1866)

MacMillan, Carrie. *Silenced Sextet*, 90–92.

Two Miss Dawsons (1880)

MacMillan, Carrie. *Silenced Sextet*, 100–101.

ROBINSON, MARILYNNE (1944–)

Housekeeping (1982)

Bohannan, Heather. "Quest-tioning Tradition: Spiritual Transformation Images in Women's Narratives and *Housekeeping*, by Marilynne Robinson." *WF* 51.1 (1992): 65–79.

Burke, William. "Border Crossings in Marilynne Robinson's *Housekeeping*." *MFS* 37.4 (1991): 716–724.

Champagne, Rosaria. "Women's History and *Housekeeping:* Memory, Representation, and Reinscription." *WS* 20.3–4 (1992): 321–329.

Chandler, Marilyn R. *Dwelling in the Text*, 291–307.

Rosenfelt, Deborah Silverton. "Feminism, 'Postfeminism,' and Contemporary Women's Fiction," in Howe, Florence, ed. *Tradition and the Talents of Women*, 275, 277–278.

Schaub, Thomas. "Lingering Hopes, Faltering Dreams: Marilynne Robinson and the Politics of Contemporary American Fiction," in Friedman, Melvin J., ed. *Traditions, Voices, and Dreams*, 308–319.

Toles, George. " 'Sighs Too Deep for Words': Mysteries of Need in Marilynne Robinson's *Housekeeping*." *ArQ* 47.4 (1991): 137–155.

Tyan, Maureen. "Marilynne Robinson's *Housekeeping:* The Subversive Narrative and the New American Eve." *SoAR* 56.1 (1991): 79–86.

Williams, Gary. "Resurrecting Carthage: *Housekeeping* and Cultural History." *ELN* 29.2 (1991): 70–78

ROCHON, ESTHER (1948–)

Coquillage (1986)

Ketterer, David and Esther Rochon. "Outside and Inside Views of Rochon's *The Shell*." Trans. Steven Lehman. *SFS* 19.1 (1992): 17–31.

Shell see *Coquillage*

ROE, VINGIE E. (1879–1958)

Black Belle Rides the Uplands (1935)

Yates, Norris. *Gender and Genre*, 69–72.

Golden Tide (1940)

Yates, Norris. *Gender and Genre*, 72–77.

Nameless River (1923)

Yates, Norris. *Gender and Genre*, 61–66.

Wild Hearts (1932)

Yates, Norris. *Gender and Genre*, 77–78.

ROIPHE, ANNE RICHARDSON (1935–)

Lovingkindness (1987)

Fried, Lewis. "Living the Riddle: The Sacred and Profane in Anne Roiphe's *Lovingkindness*." *SAJL* 11.2 (1992): 174–181.

Glazer, Miriyam. "Male and Female, King and Queen: The Theological Imagination of Anne Roiphe's *Lovingkindness*." *SAJL* 10.1 (1991): 81–92.

Rosenfelt, Deborah Silverton. "Feminism, 'Postfeminism,' and Contemporary Women's Fiction," in Howe, Florence, ed. *Tradition and the Talents of Women*, 278–279.

Up the Sandbox (1970)

Greene, Gayle. *Changing the Story*, 71–73.

RÖLVAAG, OLE E. (1876–1931)

Giants in the Earth (1927)

Dyck, Reginald. "Frontier Violence in the Garden of America," in Heyne, Eric, ed. *Desert, Garden, Margin, Range*, 62–63.

Gross, Davis S. "No Place to Hide: Gothic Naturalism in O. E. Rölvaag's *Giants in the Earth*," in Mogen, David, ed. *Frontier Gothic*, 42–52.

Pickle, Linda S. "Foreign-Born Immigrants on the Great Plains Frontier in Fiction and Nonfiction," in Heyne, Eric, ed. *Desert, Garden, Margin, Range*, 79–82.

ROQUEBRUNE, ROBERT DE (1889–1978)

Testament de mon enfance (1958)

Dufault, Roseanna Lewis. *Metaphors of Identity*, 19–25..

ROSE, JOEL (1948–)

Kill the Poor (1988)

Young, Elizabeth. *Shopping in Space*,130–141.

ROSS, SINCLAIR (1908–)

As for Me and My House (1941)

Buss, Helen M. "Who are you, Mrs. Bentley?: Feminist Re-vision and Sinclair Ross's *As for Me and My House*," in Stouck, David, ed. *Sinclair Ross's As for Me and My House*, 190–209.

Compton, Anne. " 'As if I Really Mattered': The Narrator of Sinclair Ross's *As for Me and My House*." *SCL* 17.1 (1992): 62–77.

Cude, Wilfred. "Beyond Mrs. Bentley: A Study of *As for Me and My House*." *Journal of Canadian Studies* 8 (February 1973): 3–18. Rpt. in Stouck, David, ed. *Sinclair Ross's As for Me and My House*, 76–95.

Daniells, Roy. " 'Introduction' to *As for Me and My House*." Ross, Sinclair. *As for Me and My House*. New Canadian Library, no. 4. Toronto: Mclelland and Stewart, 1957. Rpt. in Stouck, David, ed. *Sinclair Ross's As for Me and My House*, 35–40.

Davey, Frank. "Conflicting Signs of *As for Me and My House*," in Stouck, David, ed. *Sinclair Ross's As for Me and My House*, 178–190.

Djwa, Sandra. "No Other Way: Sinclair Ross's Stories and Novels.' " *Canadian Literature* 47 (Winter 1971): 49–66. Rpt. in Stouck, David, ed. *Sinclair Ross's As for Me and My House*, 54–65.

Giltrow, Janet. "Linguistic Analysis of Sample Passages from *As for Me and My House*," in Stouck, David, ed. *Sinclair Ross's As for Me and My House*, 209–224.

Godard, Barbara. "El Greco in Canada: Sinclair Ross's *As for Me and My House*." *Mosaic* 14.2 (Spring 1981): 55–75. Rpt. in Stouck, David, ed. *Sinclair Ross's As for Me and My House*, 120–138.

Hinz, Evelyn J. and John J. Teunissen. "Who's the Father of Mrs. Bentley's Child?:

As for Me and My House and the Conventions of Dramatic Monologue." *Canadian Literature* 111 (Winter 1986): 101–113. Rpt. in Stouck, David, ed. *Sinclair Ross's As for Me and My House*, 148–161.

Jones, D.G. *Butterfly on the Rock: A Study of the Themes and Images in Canadian Literature.* Toronto: University of Toronto Press, 1970. 38–42. Rpt. in Stouck, David, ed. *Sinclair Ross's As for Me and My House*, 44–48.

Kroetsch, Robert. *Crossing Frontiers: Papers in American and Canadian Western Literature.* Ed. Dick Harrison. Edmonton, AL: University of Alberta Press, 1979. 73–83. Rpt. in Stouck, David, ed. *Sinclair Ross's As for Me and My House*, 111–120.

McMullen, Lorraine. *Sinclair Ross*. Boston: Twayne, 1979. 58–63, 81–87. Rpt. in Stouck, David, ed. *Sinclair Ross's As for Me and My House*, 103–111.

Matheson, T.J. "'But Do your Thing': Conformity, Self Reliance, and Sinclair Ross's *As for Me and My House*." *Dalhousie Review* 66 (Autumn 1986): 497–512. Rpt. in Stouck, David, ed. *Sinclair Ross's As for Me and My House*, 162–177.

Moss, John. *Modern Times.* Ed. John Moss. Toronto: NC Press. 81–92. Rpt. in Stouck, David, ed. *Sinclair Ross's As for Me and My House*, 138–147.

New, W.H. "Sinclair Ross's Ambivalent World." *Canadian Literature* 40 (Spring 1969): 26–32. Rpt. in Stouck, David, ed. *Sinclair Ross's As for Me and My House*, 48–54.

Ricou, Laurence. *Vertical Man / Horizontal World: Man and Landscape in Canadian Prairie Fiction.* Vancouver, BC: University of British Columbia Press, 1973. 81–94. Rpt. in Stouck, David, ed. *Sinclair Ross's As for Me and My House*, 66–75.

Ross, Morton L. "Sinclair Ross," in Lecker, Robert, ed. *Canadian Writers and Their Works*, (Vol.4), 273–280.

Stouck, David. "Mirror and the Lamp in Sinclair Ross's *As for Me and My House*," in Stouck, David, ed. *Sinclair Ross's As for Me and My House*, 95–103.

Tallman, Warren. "Wolf in the Snow. Part Two: The House Repossessed." *Canadian Literature* 6 (Autumn 1960): 41–48. Rpt. in Stouck, David, ed. *Sinclair Ross's As for Me and My House*, 41–44.

Williams, David. *Confessional Fictions*, 105–129, 130–146.

Sawbones Memorial (1974)

Ross, Morton L. "Sinclair Ross," in Lecker, Robert, ed. *Canadian Writers and Their Works*, (Vol.4), 286–290.

Well (1958)

Ross, Morton L. "Sinclair Ross," in Lecker, Robert, ed. *Canadian Writers and Their Works*, (Vol.4), 280–284.

Whir of Gold (1970)

Ross, Morton L. "Sinclair Ross," in Lecker, Robert, ed. *Canadian Writers and Their Works*, (Vol.4), 284–286.

ROTH, HENRY (1906–)

Call It Sleep (1934)

Goldsmith, Arnold L. *Modern American Urban Novel*, 59–83.

Orr, Elaine. "On the Side of the Mother: *Yonnondio* and *Call It Sleep*." *SAF* 21.2 (1993): 209–210, 216–221.

Sokoloff, Naomi B. *Imagining the Child*, 87–106.

ROTH, PHILIP (1933–)

Anatomy Lesson (1983)

Halio, Jay L. *Philip Roth Revisited*, 170–177.

Breast (1972)

Halio, Jay L. *Philip Roth Revisited*, 152–156.

Counterlife (1987)

Halio, Jay L. *Philip Roth Revisited*, 181–196.
Shostak, Debra. " 'This Obsessive Reinvention of the Real': Speculative Narrative in Philip Roth's *The Counterlife*." *MFS* 37.2 (1991): 197–215.

Deception (1990)

Halio, Jay L. *Philip Roth Revisited*, 196–201.

Epilogue: The Prague Orgy (1985)

Halio, Jay L. *Philip Roth Revisited*, 177–180.

Facts (1989)

Rushdie, Salman. *Imaginary Homelands*, 347–348.

Ghost Writer (1979)

Halio, Jay L. *Philip Roth Revisited*, 156–165.

Great American Novel (1973)

Halio, Jay L. *Philip Roth Revisited*, 111–125.

Letting Go (1962)

Halio, Jay L. *Philip Roth Revisited*, 37–56.

My Life as a Man (1974)

Halio, Jay L. *Philip Roth Revisited*, 126–141.

Portnoy's Complaint (1969)

Halio, Jay L. *Philip Roth Revisited*, 67–82.

Professor of Desire (1977)

Halio, Jay L. *Philip Roth Revisited*, 143–152.

Sabbath's Theater (1995)

Wolcott, James. "Last Swinger." *NewC* 14.1 (1995): 62–67.

When She Was Good (1967)

Halio, Jay L. *Philip Roth Revisited*, 57–66.

Zuckerman Unbound (1981)

Halio, Jay L. *Philip Roth Revisited*, 165–170.

ROWSON, SUSANNA (1762(?)–1824)

Charlotte Temple (1791)

Cherniavsky, Eva. "Charlotte Temple's Remains," in *Discovering Difference*, 35–46.
Clark, Suzanne. *Sentimental Modernism*, 24–25.

Forcey, Blythe. "*Charlotte Temple* and the End of Epistolarity." *AL* 63.2 (1991): 225–241.
Stern, Julia. "Working through the Frame: *Charlotte Temple* and the Poetics of Maternal Melancholia." *ArQ* 49.4 (1993): 1–30.

Reuben and Rachel (1798)

Castiglia, Christopher. "Susanna Rowson's *Reuben and Rachel:* Captivity, Colonization, and the Domestication of Columbus," in Harris, Sharon M., ed. *Redefining the Political Novel*, 23–39.

Sarah (1805)

Hansen, Klaus P. "Sentimental Novel and Its Feminist Critique." *EAL* 26.1 (1991): 48–53.

Trials of the Human Heart (1795)

Hansen, Klaus P. "Sentimental Novel and Its Feminist Critique." *EAL* 26.1 (1991): 45–48.

ROY, GABRIELLE (1909–1983)

Alexandre Chenevert (1954)

Kwaterko, Jozef. "La Problématique interculturelle dans *Alexandre Chenevert* de Gabrielle Roy." *UTQ* 63.4 (1994): 566–574.
Shek, Ben-Z. *French-Canadian*, 36–38.

Bonheur d'occasion (1945)

Bourbonnais, Nicole. "Gabrielle Roy: la représentation du corps féminin," in Saint-Martin, Lori, ed. *L'autre lecture*, (Tome 1), 98–116.
Coleman, Patrick. *Limits of Sympathy: Gabrielle Roy's The Tin Flute*. Toronto: ECW Press, 1993.
Saint-Martin, Lori. "Mère et monde chez Gabrielle Roy," in Saint-Martin, Lori, ed. *L'autre lecture*, (Tome 1), 125–126, 130–137.
Shek, Ben-Z. *French-Canadian*, 34–36.
Smart, Patricia. *Writing in the Father's House*, 159–187.

Cashier see *Alexandre Chenevert*

La Route d'Altamont (1966)

Roy, Alain. "Écriture et désir chez Gabrielle Roy: Lecture d'un récit de *La Route d'Altamont*." *V&I* 20.1 (1994): 133–161.
Saint-Martin, Lori. "Mère et monde chez Gabrielle Roy," in Saint-Martin, Lori, ed. *L'autre lecture*, (Tome 1), 119–122, 124–125, 126–127, 130–137.
Williams, David. *Confessional Fictions*, 174–190.

Road Past Altamont see *La Route d'Altamont*

Rue Deschambault (1955)

Dufault, Roseanna Lewis. *Metaphors of Identity*, 72–75.

Street of Riches see *Rue Deschambault*

Tin Flute see *Bonheur d'occasion*

RULE, JANE (1931–)

This Is Not for You (1970)

Roof, Judith. " 'This Is Not for You': The Sexuality of Mothering," in Daly, Brenda O., ed. *Narrating Mothers*, 167–172.

RUSHING, JANE GILMORE (1925–)

Winds of Blame (1983)

Thompson, Joyce. "Seeing Through the Veil: Concepts of Truth in Two West Texas Novels." *JACult* 14.2 (1991): 69–74.

RUSS, JOANNA (1937–)

Female Man (1975)

Ayres, Susan. " 'Straight Mind' in Russ's *The Female Man*." *SFS* 22.1 (1995): 22–34.

We Who Are About to . . . (1977)

Murphy, Patrick D. "Suicide, Murder, Culture, and Castastrophe: Joanna Russ's *We Who Are About To . . . ,* " in Ruddick, Nicholas, ed. *State of the Fantastic*, 121–130.

RUSSO, RICHARD (1949–)

Risk Pool (1988)

Grenier, Donald J. *Women Enter the Wilderness*, 89–98.

RYAN, MARAH ELLIS (1866(?)–1934)

Squaw Élouise (1892)

Yates, Norris. *Gender and Genre*, 118–121.

SAFIRE, WILLIAM (1929–)

Freedom (1987)

Hammer, Dean C. "Historical Novelist as Didactician: Safire's Lincoln." *JPC* 28.2 (1994): 105–112.

SAINT-ONGE, PAULE

Ce qu'il faut de regrets (1961)

Raoul, Valerie. *Distinctly Narcissistic*, 200–203.

La saison de l'inconfort (1968)

Raoul, Valerie. *Distinctly Narcissistic*, 203–205.

SALAMANCA, J. R. (1922–)

Lilith (1961)

Robb, Kenneth A. "Aberrant Place and Time in J. R. Salamanca's *Lilith.*" *NConL* 22.5 (1992): 6–7.

SALINGER, J. D. (1919–)

Catcher in the Rye (1951)

Brookeman, Christopher. "Pencey Preppy: Cultural Codes in *The Catcher in the Rye*," in Salzman, Jack, ed. *New Essays*, 57–75.

Cowan, Michael. "Holden's Museum Pieces: Narrator and Nominal Audience in *The Catcher in the Rye*," in Salzman, Jack, ed. *New Essays*, 35–54.

Kincaid, James R. *Child-Loving,* 309–320.

Mitchell, Susan K. " 'To Tell You the Truth'." *CLAJ* 36.2 (1992): 145–156.

Pinsker, Sanford. *Catcher in the Rye: Innocence Under Pressure.* New York: Twayne Publishers, 1993.

Roemer, Danielle M. "Personal Narrative and Salinger's *Catcher in the Rye.*" *WF* 51.1 (1992): 5–10.

Rowe, Joyce. "Holden Caulfield and American Protest," in Salzman, Jack, ed. *New Essays*, 77–92.

Seelye, John. "Holden in the Museum," in Salzman, Jack, ed. *New Essays*, 23–33.

Shaw, Peter. "Love and Death in *The Catcher in the Rye*," in Salzman, Jack, ed. *New Essays*, 97–112.

Franny and Zooey (1961)

Dev, Jai. "Franny and Flaubert." *JAmS* 25.1 (1991): 81–85.

SANDERS, DORI (1934–)

Clover (1990)

Tate, Linda. *Southern Weave of Women*, 61–72.

SANDOZ, MARI (1896–1966)

Beaver Men (1964)

Villiger, Laura R. *Mari Sandoz,* 147–157, 176–178, 180–182, 183–184.

Buffalo Hunters (1954)

Villiger, Laura R. *Mari Sandoz*, 147–149, 157–166, 178–180, 182–184.

Cattlemen (1958)

Villiger, Laura R. *Mari Sandoz*, 147–149, 166–175, 183–184.

Cheyenne Autumn (1953)

Villiger, Laura R. *Mari Sandoz*, 82–87, 92–93, 95, 99–101, 102–113.

Crazy Horse (1942)

Villiger, Laura R. *Mari Sandoz*, 82–87, 89–92, 94, 98–101, 102–113.

Old Jules (1935)

Villiger, Laura R. *Mari Sandoz*, 116–145.

Slogum House (1937)

Villiger, Laura R. *Mari Sandoz*, 116–145.

SANTAYANA, GEORGE (1863–1952)

Last Puritan (1935)

Castronovo, David. *American Gentleman*, 100–104.

SARGENT, PAMELA (1948–)

Shore of Women (1986)

Fitting, Peter. "Reconsiderations of the Separatist Paradigm in Recent Feminist Science Fiction." *SFS* 19.1 (1992): 33–36, 41–44.

SARTON, MAY (1912–1995)

As We Are Now (1973)

Stout, Janis P. "Wordless Balm: Silent Communication in the Novels of May Sarton." *ELWIU* 20.2 (1993): 318–321.

Faithful Are the Wounds (1955)

Stout, Janis P. "Wordless Balm: Silent Communication in the Novels of May Sarton." *ELWIU* 20.2 (1993): 312–314.

Kinds of Love (1970)

Stout, Janis P. "Wordless Balm: Silent Communication in the Novels of May Sarton." *ELWIU* 20.2 (1993): 316–318.

Mrs. Stevens Hears the Mermaids Sing (1965)

Stout, Janis P. "Wordless Balm: Silent Communication in the Novels of May Sarton." *ELWIU* 20.2 (1993): 314–316.

SAVARD, FELIX (1896–1982)

Master of the River see *Menaud, mâitre-draveur*

Menaud, mâitre-draveur (1937)

Shek, Ben-Z. *French-Canadian*, 21–23.
Smart, Patricia. *Writing in the Father's House*, 69–71, 72–75, 88–93.

SCARBOROUGH, ELIZABETH (1947–)

Healer's War (1988)

Carter, Susanne. "Variations on Vietnam: Women's Innovative Interpretations of the Vietnam War Experience." *Extrapolation* 32.2 (1991): 173–174.

SCHAEFER, JACK (1907–1991)

Shane (1949)

Quinones, Ricardo J. *Changes of Cain*, 144–146.

SCHAEFFER, SUSAN FROMBERG (1941–)

Buffalo Afternoon (1989)

Jason, Philip K. "How Dare She? Susan Fromberg Schaeffer's *Buffalo Afternoon* and the Issue of Authenticity." *Crit* 34.3 (1993): 183–192.

SCHUYLER, GEORGE SAMUEL (1895–1977)

Black No More (1931)

Faulkner, Howard J. "Vanishing Race." *CLAJ* 37.3 (1994): 274–292.

SCOTT, EVELYN (1893–1963)

Wave (1929)

Bach, Peggy. "On Evelyn Scott's *The* Wave," in Madden, David, ed. *Classics of Civil War Fiction*, 96–108.

SCOTT, GAIL (1945–)

Heroine (1987)

Waring, Wendy. " 'Mother's of Confusion': End Bracket," in Hutcheon, Linda, ed. *Double Talking*, 147–148.

SCOTT, MELISSA

Dreamships (1992)

Schleifer, Paul C. "Fear of the 'Other' in Melissa Scott's *Dreamships*." *Extrapolation* 35.4 (1994): 312–318.

SEDGWICK, CATHERINE MARIA (1789–1867)

Hope Leslie (1827)

Garvey, T. Gregory. "Risking Reprisal: Catharine Sedgwick's *Hope Leslie* and the Legitimation of Public Action by Women." *ATQ* 8.4 (1994): 287–298.

Gould, Philip. "Catharine Sedgwick's 'Recital' of the Pequot War." *AL* 66.4 (1994): 641–662.

Maddox, Lucy. *Removals*, 103–111.

Nelson, Dana. "Sympathy as Strategy in Sedgwick's *Hope Leslie*," in Samuels, Shirley, ed. *Culture of Sentiment*, 191–202.

Singley, Carol J. "Catherine Maria Sedgwick's *Hope Leslie*," in Heyne, Eric, ed. *Desert, Garden, Margin, Range*, 110–122.

Zagarell, Sandra A. "Expanding "America": Lydia Sigourney's *Sketch of Connect-*

icut, Catherine Sedgwick's *Hope Leslie*," in Harris, Sharon M., ed. *Redefining the Political Novel*, 43, 51–59.

New England Tale (1822)

Bromell, Nicholas K. *By the Sweat of the Brow*, 137–141, 144–145.

SEID, RUTH see SINCLAIR, JO

SELBY, HUBERT (1928–)

Last Exit to Brooklyn (1964)

Giles, James R. *Naturalistic Inner-City Novel in America*, 119–136.

SHINER, LEWIS (1950–)

Deserted Cities of the Heart (1988)

Donahoo, Robert and Chuck Etheridge. "Lewis Shiner and the 'Good' Anarchist," in Slusser, George, ed. *Fiction 2000*, 185–187, 188–190.

Porush, David. "Prigogine, Chaos, and Contemporary Science Fiction." *SFS* 18.3 (1991): 374–376.

Frontera (1984)

Donahoo, Robert and Chuck Etheridge. "Lewis Shiner and the 'Good' Anarchist," in Slusser, George, ed. *Fiction 2000*, 186–188.

SHULMAN, ALIX KATES (1932–)

Memoirs of an Ex-Prom Queen (1972)

Greene, Gayle. *Changing the Story*, 78–80.

SIGOURNEY, LYDIA (1791–1865)

Sketch of Connecticut (1824)

Baym, Nina. "Reinventing Lydia Sigourney," in Harris, Sharon M., ed. *Redefining the Political Novel*, 71–74.

Zagarell, Sandra A. "Expanding "America": Lydia Sigourney's *Sketch of Connecticut*, Catherine Sedgwick's *Hope Leslie*," in Harris, Sharon M., ed. *Redefining the Political Novel*, 43–51, 58–59.

SILKO, LESLIE (1948–)

Almanac of the Dead (1991)

Holland, Sharon P. " 'If You Know I Have a History, You Will Respect Me': A Perspective on Afro-Native American Literature." *Callaloo* 17.1 (1994): 342–348.

Ceremony (1977)

Allen, Paula Gunn. "Feminine Landscape of Leslie Marmon Silko's *Ceremony*," in Fleck, Richard F., ed. *Critical Perspectives*, 233–239.

Benediktsson, Thomas E. "Reawakening of the Gods: Realism and the Supernatural in Silko and Hulme." Crit 33.2 (1992): 122–125, 126–127.

Bennani, Benjamin and Catherine Warner Bennani. "No Ceremony for Men in the Sun: Sexuality, Personhood, and Nationhood in Ghassan Kanafani's *Men in the Sun*, and Leslie Marmon Silko's *Ceremony*," in Fleck, Richard F., ed. *Critical Perspectives*, 246–255.

Clayton, Jay. "Narrative Turn in Minority Fiction," in Carlisle, Janice,ed. *Narrative and Culture*, 59–60.

Harvey, Valerie. "Navajo Sandpainting in *Ceremony*," in Fleck, Richard F., ed. *Critical Perspectives*, 256–258.

Hobbs, Michael. "Living In-Between: Tayo as Radical Reader in Leslie Marmon Silko's *Ceremony*." *WAL* 28.4 (1994): 301–312.

Oandasan, William. "Familiar Love Component of Love in *Ceremony*," in Fleck, Richard F., ed. *Critical Perspectives*, 240–243.

Owens, Louis. *Other Destinies*, 167–192.

Ruppert, James. "Dialogism and Mediation in Leslie Silko's *Ceremony*." *Expl* 51.2 (1993): 129–134.

Ruppert, James. *Mediation in Contemporary Native American Fiction*, 74–91.

Sanders, Scott P. "Southwestern Gothic: On the Frontier between Landscape and Locale," in Mogen, David, ed. *Frontier Gothic*, 64–67.

Scheninger, Lee. "Writing Nature: Silko and Native Americans as Nature Writers." *MELUS* 18.2 (1992): 47–60.

Stonestreet, Linda. "Tayo's Ceremonial Quest." *BWVACET* 16 (1994): 26–31.

Swan, Edith. "Feminine Perspectives at Laguna Pueblo: Silko's *Ceremony*." *TSWL* 11.2 (1992): 309–327.

Swan, Edith. "Laguna Prototypes of Manhood in *Ceremony*." *MELUS* 17.1 (1991–92): 39–61.

Truesdale, C. W. "Tradition and *Ceremony:* Leslie Marmon Silko as an American Novelist." *NDQ* 59.4 (1991): 200–228.

Tusmith, Bonnie. *All My Relatives*, 119–129.

SILVERBERG, ROBERT (1935–)

Downward to the Earth (1970)

Dudley, Joseph M. "Transformational SF Religions: Philip Jose Farmer's *Night of Light* and Robert Silverberg's *Downward to the Earth*." *Extrapolation* 35.4 (1994): 343–349.

SIMARD, JEAN

Mon fils pourtant heureux (1956)

Raoul, Valerie. *Distinctly Narcissistic*, 101–108.

SIMMS, WILLIAM GILMORE (1806–1870)

Beauchampe (1842)

Johanyak, Debra. "William Gilmore Simms: Deviant Paradigms of Southern Womanhood?" *MissQ* 46.4 (1993): 578–580.

Border Beagles (1840)

Johanyak, Debra. "William Gilmore Simms: Deviant Paradigms of Southern Womanhood?" *MissQ* 46.4 (1993): 581–582.

Cassique of Kiawah (1859)

Johanyak, Debra. "William Gilmore Simms: Deviant Paradigms of Southern Womanhood?" *MissQ* 46.4 (1993): 585–587.

Charlemont (1836)

Johanyak, Debra. "William Gilmore Simms: Deviant Paradigms of Southern Womanhood?" *MissQ* 46.4 (1993): 576–578.

Katharine Walton (1854)

Johanyak, Debra. "William Gilmore Simms: Deviant Paradigms of Southern Womanhood?" *MissQ* 46.4 (1993): 583–584.

Paddy McGuane (1863)

Cantrell, James P. "Irish Culture and the War between the States: *Paddy McGann* and *Gone with the Wind*." *Eire* 27.2 (1992): 8–10, 15.

Scout (1854)

Johanyak, Debra. "William Gilmore Simms: Deviant Paradigms of Southern Womanhood?" *MissQ* 46.4 (1993): 584–585.

Yemassee (1835)

Johanyak, Debra. "William Gilmore Simms: Deviant Paradigms of Southern Womanhood?" *MissQ* 46.4 (1993): 580–581.

SINCLAIR, JO (1913–1995)

Changelings (1955)

Uffen, Ellen Serlen. "America, 1945: Jo Sinclair's *The Changelings*," in Noe, Marcia, ed. *Exploring the Midwestern*, 167–178.

SINCLAIR, UPTON (1878–1968)

Jungle (1906)

Derrick, Scott. "What a Beating Feels Like: Authorship, Dissolution, and Masculinity in Sinclair's *The Jungle*." *SAF* 23.1 (1995): 85–100.

SKINNER, B. F. (1904–1990)

Walden Two (1948)

Booker, M. Keith. *Dystopian Impulse*, 91–98.

SLESINGER, TESS (1905–1945)

Unpossessed (1935)

Hapke, Laura. *Daughters of the Great Depression*, 196–200.

SLOAN, KAY (1951–)

Worry Beads (1991)

Chappell, Fred. "Family Time." *SoR* 28.4 (1992): 937–940.

SLONCZEWSKI, JOAN

Door into Ocean (1986)

Fitting, Peter. "Reconsiderations of the Separatist Paradigm in Recent Feminist Science Fiction." *SFS* 19.1 (1992): 39–44.

SMEDLEY, AGNES (1892–1950)

Daughter of Earth (1929)

Hapke, Laura. *Daughters of the Great Depression*, 22–23, 95–100.

Hoffman, Nancy. "Journey into Knowing: Agnes Smedley's *Daughter of Earth*," in Howe, Florence, ed. *Tradition and the Talents of Women*, 171–182.

SMITH, LEE (1944–)

Black Mountain Breakdown (1980)

Hill, Dorothy. *Lee Smith*, 41–50, 123.

Lanier, Parks. "Psychic Space in Lee Smith's *Black Mountain Breakdown*," in Lanier, Parks, Jr.,ed. *Poetics*, 58–66.

Devil's Dream (1992)

Chappell, Fred. "Family Time." *SoR* 28.4 (1992): 940–942.

Fair and Tender Ladies (1988)

Hill, Dorothy. *Lee Smith*, 103–120.

Family Linen (1985)

Hill, Dorothy. *Lee Smith*, 83–102.

Fancy Strut (1973)

Hill, Dorothy. *Lee Smith*, 35–41.

Last Day the Dogbushes Bloomed (1968)

Hill, Dorothy. *Lee Smith*, 23–30.

Oral History (1983)

Donlon, Joycelyn Hazelwood. "Hearing Is Believing: Southern Racial Communities and Strategies of Story-Listening in Gloria Naylor and Lee Smith." *TCL* 41.1 (1995): 27–31.

Hill, Dorothy. *Lee Smith*, 51–81, 125–126.

Parrish, Nancy C. " 'Ghostland': Tourism in Lee Smith's *Oral History*." *SoQ* 32.2 (1994): 37–47.

Tate, Linda. *Southern Weave of Women*, 93–111.

Something in the Wind (1971)

Hill, Dorothy. *Lee Smith*, 30–34.

SMITH, LILLIAN (1897–1966)

Killers of the Dream (1949)

Berstein, Elizabeth. "Bread and Race: Communion in Lillian Smith's *Killers of the Dream*." *SoQ* 30.2–3 (1992): 77–80.

Romine, Scott. "Framing Southern Rhetoric Lillian Smith's Narrative Persona in *Killers of the Dream.*" *SoAR* 59.2 (1994): 95–111.

SMITH, MICHAEL

Lost Virgin of the South (1831)

Beidler, Philip D. " 'The First Production of the Kind, in the South': A Backwoods Literary Incognito and His Attempt at the Great American Novel." *SLJ* 24.2 (1992): 106–124.

SMITH, ROSAMOND see OATES, JOYCE CAROL

SMOODIN, ROBERTA (1952–)

Inventing Ivanov (1985)

Schuman, Samuel. "Inventing Nabokov." *NConL* 22.3 (1992): 7–9.

SONTAG, SUSAN (1933–)

Benefactor (1963)

Kennedy, Liam. *Susan Sontag*, 37–40.

Death Kit (1967)

Kennedy, Liam. *Susan Sontag*, 54–61.

Volcano Lover (1992)

Bawer, Bruce. "That Sontag Women." *NewC* 11.1 (1992): 31–37.
Kennedy, Liam. *Susan Sontag*, 119–126.
Olster, Stacey. "Remakes, Outtakes, and Updates in Susan Sontag's *The Volcano Lover.*" *MFS* 41.1 (1995): 117–139.

SOUTHWORTH, E.D.E.N. (1819–1899)

Hidden Hand (1859)

Hudock, Amy E. "Challenging the Definition of Heroism in E. D. E. N Southworth's *The Hidden Hand.*" *ATQ* 9.1 (1995): 5–19.

Retribution (1849)

Bakker, Jan. "Twists of Sentiment in Antebellum Southern Romance." *SLJ* 26.1 (1993): 8–12.

SPEARE, ELIZABETH GEORGE (1908–)

Bronze Bow (1961)

Apseloff, Marilyn Fain. *Elizabeth George Speare*, 64–73.

Calico Captive (1957)

Apseloff, Marilyn Fain. *Elizabeth George Speare*, 23–46.

Prospering (1967)

Apseloff, Marilyn Fain. *Elizabeth George Speare*, 112–125.

Witch of Blackbird Pond (1958)

Apseloff, Marilyn Fain. *Elizabeth George Speare*, 48–62.

SPENCER, ELIZABETH (1921–)

Crooked Way (1952)

Roberts, Terry. "This Crooked Narrative Way." *MissQ* 46.1 (1992–93): 61–75.

Night Travellers (1991)

Greene, Sally. "Re-Placing the Hero: *The Night Travellers* as Novel of Female of Self-Discovery." *SoQ* 33.1 (1994): 33–39.

STEFFLER, JOHN (1947–)

Afterlife of George Cartwright (1992)

Jaeger, Peter. " 'The Land Created a Body of Lore': The Green Story in John Steffler's *The Afterlife of George Cartwright*." *ESC* 21.1 (1995): 41–54.

STEIN, GERTRUDE (1874–1946)

Making of Americans (1925)

Johnston, Georgia. "Reading Anna Backwards: Gertrude Stein Writing Modernism Out of the Nineteenth Century." *SLitI* 25.2 (1992): 31–37.

STEINBECK, JOHN (1902–1968)

Cannery Row (1945)

French, Warren. *John Steinbeck's Fiction Revisited*, 95–104.

Gladstein, Mimi R. "*Cannery Row:* A Male World and the Female Reader." *StQ* 25.3–4 (1992): 87–97.

Hattenhauer, Darryl. "Frog as a Metaphor in *Cannery Row*." *NConL* 21.4 (1991): 7–8.

Hearle, Kevin. " 'The Boat Shaped Mind': Steinbeck's Sense of Language as Discourse in *Cannery Row* and *Sea of Cortez*," in Donald V. Coers, ed., *After The Grapes of Wrath*, 101–102, 103, 108–111.

Meyer, Michael J. "Steinbeck's *Cannery Row*," in Tetsumaro Hayashi, ed. *New Study Guide*, 53–62.

Cup of Gold (1929)

Astro, Richard. "Phlebas Sails the Caribbean: Steinbeck, Hemingway, and the American Waste Land," in French, Warren, ed. *Twenties: Fiction, Poetry, Drama*. DeLand, FL: Everett/Edwards, Inc., 1975. 215–233. Rpt. in Hayashi, Tesumaro, ed. *Steinbeck's Literary Dimension*, 30–43.

French, Warren. *John Steinbeck's Fiction Revisited*, 38–41.

East of Eden (1952)

Gladstein, Mimi R. "Strong Female Principle of Good— or Evil: The Women of *East of Eden*." *StQ* 24.1–2 (1991): 30–40.

Heavilin, Barbara A. "Steinbeck's Exploration of Good and Evil: Structural and Thematic Unity in *East of Eden.*" *StQ* 26.3–4 (1993): 90–100.

Mulder, Steven. "Reader's Story: *East of Eden* as Postmodernist Metafiction." *StQ* 25.3–4 (1992): 109–118.

Owens, Louis. "Steinbeck's *East of Eden,*" in Tetsumaro Hayashi, ed. *New Study Guide*, 73–86.

Quinones, Ricardo J. *Changes of Cain*, 135–144.

Simmonds, Roy S. "Cathy Ames and Rhoda Penmark: Two Child Monsters." *Mississippi Quarterly* 39 (Spring 1986): 91–101. Rpt. in Hayashi, Tesumaro, ed. *Steinbeck's Literary Dimension*, 103–112.

Grapes of Wrath (1939)

Carr, Duane R. "Steinbeck's Blakean Vision in *The Grapes of Wrath.*" *Steinbeck Quarterly* 8 (Summer-Fall 1975): 67–73. Rpt. in Hayashi, Tesumaro, ed. *Steinbeck's Literary Dimension*, 1–8.

Cassuto, David. "Turning Wine into Water: Water as Privileged Signifier in *The Grapes of Wrath.*" *PLL* 29.1 (1993): 67–95.

Dircks, Phyllis T. "Steinbeck's Statement on the Inner Chapters of *The Grapes of Wrath.*" *StQ* 24.3–4 (1991): 86–94.

French, Warren. *John Steinbeck's Fiction Revisited*, 75–84.

Gladstein, Mimi Reisel. "*The Grapes of Wrath:* Steinbeck and the Eternal Immigrant," in Hayashi, Tetsumaro, ed. *John Steinbeck*, 132–144.

Hapke, Laura. *Daughters of the Great Depression*, 18–19, 35–39.

Kanoza, Theresa. "Steinbeck's *The Grapes of Wrath.*" *Expl* 51.3 (1993): 187–189.

Owens, Louis. "Steinbeck's *The Grapes of Wrath,*" in Tetsumaro Hayashi, ed. *New Study Guide*, 97–111.

Visser, Nicholas. "Audience and Closure in *The Grapes of Wrath.*" *SAF* 22.1 (1994): 19–36.

In Dubious Battle (1936)

French, Warren. *John Steinbeck's Fiction Revisited*, 69–72.

Lojeck, Helen. "Steinbeck's *In Dubious Battle,*" in Tetsumaro Hayashi, ed. *New Study Guide*, 121–134.

Owens, Louis. "Writing 'in Costume': The Missing Voices of *In Dubious Battle,*" in Hayashi, Tetsumaro, ed. *John Steinbeck*, 78–94.

Pressman, Richard S. "Individualists or Collectivists? Steinbeck's In Dubious Battle and Hemingway's *To Have and Have Not.*" *StQ* 25.3–4 (1992): 123–126, 128–130.

Werlock, Abby H. P. "Looking at Lisa: The Function of the Feminine in Steinbeck's *In Dubious Battle,*" in Hayashi, Tetsumaro, ed. *John Steinbeck*, 46–63.

Sea of Cortez (1941)

Adams, Bett Yates. "Form of the Narrative Section of *Sea of Cortez:* A Specimen Collected From Reality." *Steinbeck Quarterly* 9 (Spring 1976): 36–44. Rpt. in Hayashi, Tesumaro, ed. *Steinbeck's Literary Dimension*, 135–142.

Hearle, Kevin. "'The Boat Shaped Mind': Steinbeck's Sense of Language as Discourse in *Cannery Row* and *Sea of Cortez,*" in Donald V. Coers, ed., *After The Grapes of Wrath*, 102–103, 104–108.

Sweet Thursday (1954)

DeMott, Robert. "*Sweet Thursday* Revisited: An Excursion in Suggestiveness," in Donald V. Coers, ed., *After The Grapes of Wrath*, 172–193.

To an Unknown God (1933)

French, Warren. *John Steinbeck's Fiction Revisited*, 41–43.

Shillinglaw, Susan. "Steinbeck and Ethnicity," in Donald V. Coers, ed., *After The Grapes of Wrath*, 45–47.

Wayward Bus (1947)

Busch, Christopher S. "Steinbeck's *The Wayward Bus:* An Affirmation of the Frontier Myth." *StQ* 25.3–4 (1992): 98–108.

Ditsky, John. "Work, Blood, and *The Wayward Bus*," in Donald V. Coers, ed., *After The Grapes of Wrath*, 136–147.

French, Warren. *John Steinbeck's Fiction Revisited*, 108–110.

Railsback, Brian. "*Wayward Bus:* Misogyny or Sexual Selection," in Donald V. Coers, ed., *After The Grapes of Wrath*, 125–134.

Winter of Our Discontent (1961)

French, Warren. *John Steinbeck's Fiction Revisited*, 126–131

Hughes, Robert S., Jr. "What Went Wrong? How a 'Vintage' Steinbeck Short Story Became the Flawed *Winter of Our Discontent.*" *StQ* 26.1–2 (1993): 7–12.

Meyer, Michael. "Citizen Cain: Ethan Hawley's Double Identity in *The Winter of Our Discontent*," in Donald V. Coers, ed., *After The Grapes of Wrath*, 197–213.

Meyer, Michael J. "Steinbeck's *The Winter of Our Discontent*," in Tetsumaro Hayashi, ed. *New Study Guide*, 252–269.

Meyer, Michael J. "Transforming Evil to Good: The Image of Iscariot in *The Winter of Our Discontent.*" *StQ* 26.3–4 (1993): 101–110.

Stone, Donal. "Steinbeck, Jung, and *The Winter of Our Discontent.*" *Steinbeck Quarterly* 11 (Summer-Fall 1978): 87–96. Rpt. in Hayashi, Tesumaro, ed. *Steinbeck's Literary Dimension*, 91–100.

Valenti, Peter. "Steinbeck's Geographical Seasons: *The Winter of Our Discontent.*" *StQ* 26.3–4 (1993): 111–117.

STERLING, BRUCE (1954–)

Difference Engine (1990)

Booker, M. Keith. *Dystopian Impulse*, 151–152.

Porush, David. "Prigogine, Chaos, and Contemporary Science Fiction." *SFS* 18.3 (1991): 379–384.

Sussman, Herbert. "Cyberpunk Meets Charles Babbage: *The Difference Engine* as Alternative Victorian History." *VS* 38.1 (1994): 1–23.

Schismatrix (1985)

Thompson, Craig. "Searching for Totality: Antinomy and the 'Absolute' in Bruce Sterling's *Schismatrix.*" *SFS* 18.2 (1991): 198–208.

STILL, JAMES (1906–)

River of Earth (1940)

Turner, Martha Billips. "Vision of Change: Appalachia in James Still's *River of Earth.*" *SLJ* 24.2 (1992): 11–25.

STODDARD, ELIZABETH (1843–1902)

Morgesons (1862)

Alaimo, Stacy. "Elizabeth Stoddard's *The Morgesons:* A Feminist Dialogue of Bildung and Descent." *Legacy* 8.1 (1991): 29–37.

Henwood, Dawn. "First-Person Storytelling in Elizabeth Stoddard's *Morgesons:* Realism, Romance, and the Psychology of the Narrating Self." *ESQ* 41.1 (1995): 41–63.

STONE, ROBERT (1937–)

Children of Light (1986)

Solotaroff, Robert. *Robert Stone*, 115–137.

Dog Soldiers (1974)

Solotaroff, Robert. *Robert Stone*, 52–81.

Flag for Sunrise (1981)

Pizer, Donald. *Theory and Practice*, 181–185.
Solotaroff, Robert. *Robert Stone*, 82–114.

Hall of Mirrors (1967)

Solotaroff, Robert. *Robert Stone*, 25–51.

Outerbridge Reach (1992)

Solotaroff, Robert. *Robert Stone*,138–172.

STOWE, HARRIET BEECHER (1811–1896)

Dred (1856)

Boyd, Richard. "Violence and Sacrificial Displacement in Harriet Beecher Stowe's *Dred*." *ArQ* 50.2 (1994): 51–71.

Sánchez-Eppler, Karen. "Bodily Bonds: The Intersecting Rhetorics of Feminism and Abolition," in Samuels, Shirley, ed. *Culture of Sentiment*, 100–102.

Minister's Wooing (1859)

Harris, Susan K. "Female Imaginary in Harriet Beecher Stowe's *The Minister's Wooing*." *NEQ* 66.2 (1993): 179–198.

MacFarlane, Lisa Watt. "New England Kitchen Goes Uptown: Domestic Displacements in Harriet Beecher Stowe's New York." *NEQ* 64.2 (1991): 272–291.

Schultz, Nancy Lusignan. "Artist's Craftiness: Miss Prissy in *The Minister's Wooing*." *SAF* 20.1 (1992): 33–44.

My Wife and I (1871)

Hovet, Grace Ann and Theodore R. Hovet. "TABLEAUX VIVANTS: Masculine Vision and Feminine Reflections in Novels by Warner, Alcott, Stowe, and Wharton." *ATQ* 7.4 (1993): 335–338, 344–348, 352–355.

MacFarlane, Lisa Watt. "New England Kitchen Goes Uptown: Domestic Displacements in Harriet Beecher Stowe's New York." *NEQ* 64.2 (1991): 272–291.

Romines, Ann. *Home Plot*, 21–23.

Oldtown Folks (1869)

MacFarlane, Lisa Watt. "New England Kitchen Goes Uptown: Domestic Displacements in Harriet Beecher Stowe's New York." *NEQ* 64.2 (1991): 272–291.

Pearl of Orr's Island (1862)

Baker, Dorothy Z. "Puritan Providences in Stowe's *The Pearl of Orr's Island:* The Legacy of Cotton Mather." *SAF* 22.1 (1994): 61–79.

MacFarlane, Lisa Watt. "New England Kitchen Goes Uptown: Domestic Displacements in Harriet Beecher Stowe's New York." *NEQ* 64.2 (1991): 272–291.

Romines, Ann. *Home Plot*, 20–21.

Poganuc People (1878)

Romines, Ann. *Home Plot*, 29–30.

Uncle Tom's Cabin (1852)

Anderson, Beatrice A. "Uncle Tom: A Hero at Last." *ATQ* 5.2 (1991): 95–108.

Askeland, Lori. "Remodeling the Model Home in *Uncle Tom's Cabin* and *Beloved.*" *AL* 64.4 (1992): 787–788.

Bellin, Joshua D. "Up to Heaven's Gate, Down in Earth's Dust: The Politics of Judgment in *Uncle Tom's Cabin.*" *AL* 65.2 (1993): 275–295.

Bense, James. "Myths and Rhetoric of the Slavery Debate and Stowe's Comic Vision of Slavery," in Lowance, Mason I., Jr., ed. *Stowe Debate*, 187–203.

Bentley, Nancy. "White Slaves: The Mulatto Hero in Antebellum Fiction." *AL* 65.3 (1993): 501–502, 505–506, 508.

Boyd, Richard. "Models of Power in Harriet Beecher Stowe's *Dred.*" *SAF* 19.1 (1991): 15–30.

Brodhead, Richard H. *Cultures of Letters*, 35–42.

Bromell, Nicholas K. *By the Sweat of the Brow*, 152–172.

Budick, Emily Miller. *Engendering Romance*, 109–113.

De Prospo, R. C. "Afterword/Afterward: Auntie Harriet and Uncle Ike—Prophesying a Final Stowe Debate," in Lowance, Mason I., Jr., ed. *Stowe Debate*, 271–291.

Donovan, Josephine. *Uncle Tom's Cabin: Evil, Affliction, and Redemptive Love.* Boston: Twayne Publishers, 1991.

Dorsey, Peter A. "De-Authorizing Slavery: Realism in Stowe's *Uncle Tom's Cabin* and Brown's *Clotel.*" *ESQ* 41.4 (1995): 274–282.

Ducksworth, Sarah Smith. "Stowe's Construction of an African Persona and the Creation of White Identity for a New World Order," in Lowance, Mason I., Jr., ed. *Stowe Debate*, 205–254.

Fluck, Winfried. "Power and Failure of Representation in Harriet Beecher Stowe's *Uncle Tom's Cabin.*" *NLH* 23.2 (1992): 319–338.

Foreman, P. Gabrielle. " 'This Promiscuous Housekeeping': Death, Transgression, and Homoeroticism in *Uncle Tom's Cabin.*" *Representations* 43 (1993): 51–72.

Jenkins, Jennifer L. "Failed Mothers and Fallen Houses: The Crisis of Domesticity in *Uncle Tom's Cabin.*" *ESQ* 38.2 (1992): 161–187.

Kisthardt, Melanie J. "Flirting with Patriarchy: Feminist Dialogics," in Lowance, Mason I., Jr., ed. *Stowe Debate*, 37–56.

Lang, Amy Schrager. "Class and the Strategies of Sympathy," in Samuels, Shirley, ed. *Culture of Sentiment*, 131–132, 135–136, 137–139, 140–142.

Levin, David. *Forms of Uncertainty*, 249–258.

Lowance, Mason I., Jr. "Biblical Typology and the Allegorical Mode: The Prophetic Strain," in Lowance, Mason I., Jr., ed. *Stowe Debate*, 159–184.

Meyer, Michael J. "Toward a Rhetoric of Equality: Reflective and Refractive Images in Stowe's Language," in Lowance, Mason I., Jr., ed. *Stowe Debate*, 236–254.

Nuernberg, Susan Marie. "Rhetoric of Race," in Lowance, Mason I., Jr., ed. *Stowe Debate*, 255–270.

O'Connell, Catharine E. " 'Magic of the Real Presence of Distress': Sentimentality and Competing Rhetorics of Authority," in Lowance, Mason I., Jr., ed. *Stowe Debate*, 13–35.

Pilditch, Jan. "Rhetoric and Satire," in Lowance, Mason I., Jr., ed. *Stowe Debate*, 57–70.

Railton, Stephen. *Authorship and Audience*, 74–89.

Riss, Arthur. "Racial Essentialism and Family Values in *Uncle Tom's Cabin*." *AQ* 46.4 (1994): 513–544.

Roberson, Susan L. "Matriarchy and the Rhetoric of Domesticity," in Lowance, Mason I., Jr., ed. *Stowe Debate*, 116–136.

Romines, Ann. *Home Plot*, 19.

Shaw, S. Bradley. "Pliable Rhetoric of Domesticity," in Lowance, Mason I., Jr., ed. *Stowe Debate*, 73–97.

Vrettos, Athena. *Somatic Fictions*, 99–102.

Wardley, Lynn. "Relic, Fetish, Femmage: The Aesthetics of Sentiment in the Work of Stowe," in Samuels, Shirley, ed. *Culture of Sentiment*, 203–218.

Wardley, Lynn. "Relic, Fetish, Femmage: The Aesthetics of Sentiment in the Work of Stowe." *YJC* 5.3 (1992): 165–191.

Westra, Helen Petter. "Confronting Antichrist: The Influence of Jonathan Edwards's Millennial Vision," in Lowance, Mason I., Jr., ed. *Stowe Debate*, 141–158.

White, Isabelle. "Sentimentality and the Uses of Death," in Lowance, Mason I., Jr., ed. *Stowe Debate*, 99–115.

Whitney, Lisa. "In the Shadow of *Uncle Tom's Cabin:* Stowe's Vision of Slavery from the Great Dismal Swamp." *NEQ* 66.4 (1993): 552–569.

Wolff, Cynthia Griffin. " 'Masculinity' in *Uncle Tom's Cabin*." *AQ* 47.4 (1995): 595–618.

We and Our Neighbors (1873)

MacFarlane, Lisa Watt. "New England Kitchen Goes Uptown: Domestic Displacements in Harriet Beecher Stowe's New York." *NEQ* 64.2 (1991): 272–291.

Romines, Ann. *Home Plot*, 23–27.

STRATTON-PORTER, GENE (1863–1924)

Girl of the Limberlost (1909)

Ford, Elizabeth. "How to Cocoon a Butterfly: Mother and Daughter in *A Girl of the Limberlost*." *CLAQ* 18.4 (1993–94): 148–153.

STRAUB, PETER (1943–)

Ghost Story (1979)

Andriano, Joseph. *Our Lady of Darkness*, 136–139.

Koko (1988)

Ringnalda, Don. *Fighting and Writing*, 115–135.

STRIBLING, T. S. (1881–1965)

Birthright (1922)

McLendon, Jacquelyn . *Politics of Color*, 22–26.

STUART, JESSE (1907–1984)

Daughter of the Legend (1965)

Lanier, Parks, Jr. "Love, Loss, and the Poetics of Space in Jesse Stuart's *Daughter of the Legend*," in Lanier, Parks, Jr.,ed. *Poetics*, 183–191.

STYRON, WILLIAM (1925–)

Confessions of Nat Turner (1968)

Allen, Joe. "Blues in *The Confessions of Nat Turner*." *NConL* 24.5 (1994): 2–3.
Coale, Samuel. *William Styron Revisited*, 73–102.
Cologne-Brookes, Gavin. *Novels of William Styron*, 98–155.
Davis, Mary Kemp. "William Styron's Nat Turner as an Archetypal." *SLJ* 28.1 (1995): 67–84.
Folks, Jeffrey J. *Southern Writers*, 116–119.
Stewart, Anthony. "William Turnergraystyron, Novelist(s): Reactivating State Power in *The Confessions of Nat Turner*." *SNNTS* 27.2 (1995): 169–185.
West, James L. W., III "Voices Interior and Exterior: William Styron's Narrative Personae," in Friedman, Melvin J., ed. *Traditions, Voices, and Dreams*, 55–58.

Lie Down in Darkness (1951)

Coale, Samuel. *William Styron Revisited*, 40–49.
Cologne-Brookes, Gavin. *Novels of William Styron*, 10–44.
Nostrandt, Jeanne R. "William Styron's *Lie Down in Darkness:* A Parable." *SLJ* 28.1 (1995): 58–66.
West, James L. W., III "Voices Interior and Exterior: William Styron's Narrative Personae," in Friedman, Melvin J., ed. *Traditions, Voices, and Dreams*, 48–52.

Long March (1952)

Coale, Samuel. *William Styron Revisited*, 50–58.
Cologne-Brookes, Gavin. *Novels of William Styron*, 45–67.
Folks, Jeffrey J. *Southern Writers*, 108–111.
West, James L. W., III "Voices Interior and Exterior: William Styron's Narrative Personae," in Friedman, Melvin J., ed. *Traditions, Voices, and Dreams*, 52–53.

Set This House on Fire (1960)

Coale, Samuel. *William Styron Revisited*, 59–72.
Cologne-Brookes, Gavin. *Novels of William Styron*, 68–97.
West, James L. W., III "Voices Interior and Exterior: William Styron's Narrative Personae," in Friedman, Melvin J., ed. *Traditions, Voices, and Dreams*, 53–55.

Sophie's Choice (1980)

Coale, Samuel. *William Styron Revisited*, 103–134.
Cologne-Brookes, Gavin. *Novels of William Styron*, 156–201.
Fiedler, Leslie. *Fiedler on the Roof*, 103–110.
Folks, Jeffrey J. *Southern Writers*, 111–116, 119–121.
Langer, Lawrence L. *Admitting the Holocaust*, 79–84.
Lupack, Barbara Tepa. *Insanity as Redemption*, 156–202.
Stanford, Janet M. "Whisper of Violins in Styron's *Sophie's Choice*." *SLJ* 25.1 (1992): 106–117.
West, James L. W., III "Voices Interior and Exterior: William Styron's Narrative Personae," in Friedman, Melvin J., ed. *Traditions, Voices, and Dreams*, 58–60.

SUCH, PETER (1939–)

Riverrun (1973)

Davidson, Arnold E. *Coyote Country*, 140–156.

SWAN, SUSAN (1944–)

Biggest Modern Woman of the World (1983)

Heffernan, Teresa. "Tracing the Travesty: Constructing the Female Subject in Susan Swan's *The Biggest Modern Woman of the World*." *CanL* 133 (1992): 24–37.
Kambourelli, Smaro. "*Biggest Modern Woman of the World:* Canada as the Absent Spouse." *SCL* 16.2 (1991): 1–16.

TAN, AMY (1952–)

Joy Luck Club (1989)

Boldt, Chris. "Why Is the Moon Lady in Amy Tan's *The Joy Luck Club* Revealed to Be a Man?" *NConL* 24.4 (1994): 9–10.
Heung, Marina. "Daughter-Text/Mother-Text: Matrilineage in Amy Tan's *Joy Luck Club*." *FSt* 19.3 (1993): 597–616.
Shear, Walter. "Generation Differences and the Diaspora in *The Joy Luck Club*." *Crit* 34.3 (1993): 193–199.
Shen, Gloria. "Born of a Stranger: Mother-Daughter Relationships and Storytelling in Amy Tan's *The Joy Luck Club*," in Brown, Anne E., ed. *International Women's Writing*, 233–3243.
Souris, Stephen. " 'Only Two Kinds of Daughters': Inter-Monologue Dialogicity in *The Joy Luck Club*." *MELUS* 19.2 (1994): 99–123.
Tusmith, Bonnie. *All My Relatives*, 67–68.
Wong, Sau-ling Cynthia. *Reading Asian American Literature*, 40, 44–45, 69–70.

Kitchen God's Wife (1991)

Caesar, Judith. "Patriarchy, Imperialism, and Knowledge in *The Kitchen God's Wife*." *NDQ* 62.4 (1994–95): 164–174.
Davis, Rocio G. "Amy Tan's *The Kitchen God's Wife:* An American Dream Come True—in China." *NConL* 24.5 (1994): 3–5.

TARKINGTON, BOOTH (1869–1946)

Magnificient Ambersons (1918)

Castronovo, David. *American Gentleman*, 120–123.

Penrod (1914)

Jacobson, Marcia. *Being a Boy Again*, 134–149.

TATE, ALLEN (1899–1979)

Fathers (1938)

Hanson, Elizabeth I. *Margaret Mitchell*, 82–84.

Strawn, John R. "Lacy Buchan as the Voice of Allen Tate's Modernist Aesthetic in *The Fathers*." *SLJ* 26.1 (1993): 64–77.

Wicker, Tom. "On Allen Tate's *The Fathers*," in Madden, David, ed. *Classics of Civil War Fiction*, 174–180.

TAYLOR, PETER (1917–1994)

Summons to Memphis (1986)

Brinkmeyer, Robert H., Jr. "Memory, Rewriting, and the Authoritarian Self in *A Summons to Memphis*," in Stephens, Ralph, ed. *Craft of Peter Taylor*, 111–121.

Castronovo, David. *American Gentleman*, 177–180.

Lindsay, Creighton. "Phillip Carver's Ethical Appeal in Peter Taylor's *A Summons to Memphis*." *MissQ* 44.2 (1991): 167–181.

Metress, Christopher. "Expenses of Silence in *A Summons to Memphis*," in McAlexander, Hubert H., ed. *Critical Essays on Peter Taylor*, 201–214.

Richmond, Linda. "Peter Taylor and the Paternal Metaphor," in Stephens, Ralph, ed. *Craft of Peter Taylor*, 57–60, 63.

Woman of Means (1950)

Brown, Ashley. "Early Fiction of Peter Taylor," in McAlexander, Hubert H., ed. *Critical Essays on Peter Taylor*, 85–86.

Lindsay, Creighton. "Trouble Gardens: Peter Taylor's Pastoral Equations," in Stephens, Ralph, ed. *Craft of Peter Taylor*, 39.

Smith, James Penny. "Narration and Theme in Taylor's *A Woman of Means*," in McAlexander, Hubert H., ed. *Critical Essays on Peter Taylor*, 98–106.

TEPPER, SHERI (1929–)

Beauty (1991)

Kondratiev, Alexei. "Tales Newly Told: A Column on Current Modern Fantasy." *Mythlore* 18.1 (1991): 28–29.

Gate to Women's Country (1988)

Fitting, Peter. "Reconsiderations of the Separatist Paradigm in Recent Feminist Science Fiction." *SFS* 19.1 (1992): 36–39, 41–44.

TÉTREAU, JEAN (1923–)

Les nomades (1967)

Colas-Charpentier, Helene. "Four Quebecois Dystopias, 1963–1972." Trans. ABE and Carine Deschanel. *SFS* 20.3 (1993): 388–390.

THÉORET, FRANCE (1942–)

L'homme qui peignait Staline (1989)

Gould, Karen. "Autobiographical History and the Lure of the Recent Past: France Theoret's *L'homme qui peignait Staline*." *ECr* 33.2 (1993): 83–93.

Nous parlerons comme on écrit (1982)

Den Tandt, Catherine. "Mapping Identity in Quebec: France Theoret." *Diacritics* 23.3 (1993): 91–108.

Green, Mary Jean. "Private Life and Collective Experience in Quebec: The Autobiographical Project of France Theoret." *StTCL* 17.1 (1993): 119–129.

Shek, Ben-Z. *French-Canadian*, 93–96.

Smart, Patricia. "Un réalisme moderne: l'approche du réel dans l'oeuvre de France Théoret," in Saint-Martin, Lori, ed. *L'autre lecture* (Tome II), 87–99.

THÉRIAULT, YVES (1915–1983)

Aaron (1954)

Hesse, M.G. *Yves Thériault*, 92–98.

Shek, Ben-Z. *French-Canadian*, 42–43.

Agaguk (1958)

Berube, Renald. "L'Intrigue policière et la loi dans *Agaguk* d'Yves Thériault." *Tangence* 38 (1992): 33–41.

Hesse, M.G. *Yves Thériault*, 111–128.

Agoak (1975)

Hesse, M.G. *Yves Thériault*, 111–128.

Ashini (1960)

Hesse, M.G. *Yves Thériault*, 140–150.

Cul-de-sac (1961)

Hesse, M.G. *Yves Thériault*, 102–107.

La fille laide (1950)

Hesse, M.G. *Yves Thériault*, 57–66.

Roy, Fernand. "Figures de l'écrit dans le roman," in Duchet, Claude, ed. *Recherche littéraire*, 222–223.

La mort d'eau (1968)

Hesse, M.G. *Yves Thériault*, 98–102.

La quête de l'ourse (1980)

Hesse, M.G. *Yves Thériault*, 129–136.

Le dernier Havre (1970)

Hesse, M.G. *Yves Thériault*, 107–109.

Le ru d'Ikoué (1963)

Hesse, M.G. *Yves Thériault*, 136–140.

Les commettants de Caridad (1961)

Hesse, M.G. *Yves Thériault*, 66–71.

N'Tsuk (1968)

Hesse, M.G. *Yves Thériault*, 140–150.

Tayaout (1969)

Hesse, M.G. *Yves Thériault*, 111–128.

THEROUX, ALEXANDER (1939–)

Adultery (1987)

Pinker, Michael. "Rhetoric of Disintegration: Alexander Theroux's *An Adultery*." *RCF* 11.1 (1991): 117–126.

Darconville's Cat (1981)

Chenetier, Marc. " 'A Prose of Love, a Prose of Hate': Figuring with a Vengeance: A Morlock's View of Alexander Theroux's *Darconville's Cat*." *RCF* 11.1 (1991): 86–106.

O'Rourke, William. "Causes of Immortal Conceptions." *RCF* 11.1 (1991): 107–116.

O'Rourke, William. *Signs of the Literary Times*, 21–27.

THEROUX, PAUL (1941–)

Happy Isle of Oceania (1992)

Lyons, Paul. "From Man-Eaters to Spam-Eaters: Literary Tourism and the Discourse of Cannibalism from Herman Melville to Paul Theroux." *ArQ* 51.2 (1995): 37, 46–47, 48, 49–54.

Picture Palace (1978)

MacLaine, Brent. "Photofiction as Family Album: David Galloway, Paul Theroux and Anita Booker." *Mosaic* 24.2 (1991): 132, 142–145.

THOMAS, THOMAS T.

Mask of Loki (1990)

Lindskold, Jane M. *Roger Zelazny*, 55, 60.

THOMPSON, HUNTER S. (1939–)

Curse of Lono (1983)

Stull, James N. *Literary Selves*, 91–93, 96–97, 98–99.

Fear and Loathing in Las Vegas (1971)

Cooper, Ken. " 'Zero Pays the House': The Las Vegas Novel and Atomic Roulette." *ConL* 33.3 (1992): 540–542.

Stull, James N. *Literary Selves*, 89–90, 91–92, 93, 96–97.

Fear and Loathing: On the Campaign Trail '72 (1973)

Stull, James N. *Literary Selves*, 95–96.

THOMPSON, JIM (1906–1977)

After Dark My Sweet (1955)

Haut, Woody. *Pulp Culture*, 59–61.

Cropper's Cabin (1952)

Haut, Woody. *Pulp Culture*, 51–52.

Grifters (1963)

Haut, Woody. *Pulp Culture*, 62–63.

Heed the Thunder (1946)

Haut, Woody. *Pulp Culture*, 49–51.

Hell of a Women (1954)

Haut, Woody. *Pulp Culture*, 55–56.

Kill-Off (1957)

Haut, Woody. *Pulp Culture*, 61–62.

Killer Inside Me (1952)

Haut, Woody. *Pulp Culture*, 49, 52–54.

Nothing Man (1954)

Haut, Woody. *Pulp Culture*, 58–59.

Nothing More Than Murder (1949)

Haut, Woody. *Pulp Culture*, 51.

Savage Night (1953)

Haut, Woody. *Pulp Culture*, 56–58.

Swell Looking Babe (1954)

Haut, Woody. *Pulp Culture*, 58.

Hendershot, Cyndy. "Imaginary Fantasy and Oedipal Tyranny: Jim Thompson's *A Swell-Looking Babe*." *NConL* 23.2 (1993): 2–4.

Wild Town (1957)

Haut, Woody. *Pulp Culture*, 54–55.

THURMAN, WALLACE (1902–1934)

Blacker the Berry (1929)

Gaither, Renoir W. "Moment of Revision: A Reappraisal of Wallace Thurman's Aesthetics in *The Blacker the Berry* and *Infants of the Spring*." *CLAJ* 37.1 (1993): 81–93.

Hapke, Laura. *Daughters of the Great Depression*, 59–61.

Infants of Spring (1932)

Gaither, Renoir W. "Moment of Revision: A Reappraisal of Wallace Thurman's Aesthetics in *The Blacker the Berry* and *Infants of the Spring*." *CLAJ* 37.1 (1993): 81–93.

TILLMAN, LYNNE

Haunted Houses (1987)

Young, Elizabeth. *Shopping in Space*, 198–201.

Motion Sickness (1991)

Young, Elizabeth. *Shopping in Space*, 207–210.

TOOLE, JOHN KENNEDY (1937–1969)

Confederacy of Dunces (1980)

Fennell, Barbara A. and John Bennett. "Sociolinguistic Concepts and Literary Analysis." *AQ* 66.4 (1991): 371–379.

Gillespie, Michael Patrick. "Baroque Catholicism in Southern Fiction: Flannery O'Connor, Walker Percy, and John Kennedy Toole," in Friedman, Melvin J., ed. *Traditions, Voices, and Dreams*, 37–40.

Neon Bible (1989)

Rudnicki, Robert Walter. "Toole's Proboscis: Some Effluvial Concerns in *The Neon Bible*." *MissQ* 47.2 (1994): 221–236.

TORRES, OMAR (1945–)

Fallen Angels Sing (1991)

Alvarez-Borland, Isabel. "Displacements and Autobiography in Cuban-American Fiction." *WLT* 68.1 (1994): 45–46.

TOUGAS, GÉRALD

La mauvaise foi (1990)

Mesavage, Ruth Matilde. "Le Délire de l'écriture et *La mauvaise foi* de Gerald Tougas." *QS* 17 (1993–94): 169–176.

TOURGÉE, ALBION (1838–1905)

Figs and Thistles (1879)

Limon, John. *Writing After War*, 71–75.

Fool's Errand (1879)

Limon, John. *Writing After War*, 70–71.

Royal Gentleman see *'Toinette*

'Toinette (1874)

Limon, John. *Writing After War*, 67–70.

TRACY, ANN (1941–)

Winter Hunger (1990)

Atwood, Margaret. *Strange Things*, 109–114.

TRAILL, CATHARINE PARR (1802–1899)

Canadian Crusoes (1852)

Fleming, Robert. "Supplementing Self: A Postcolonial Quest(ion) for (of) National Essence in Indigenous Form in Catharine Parr Traill's *Canadian Crusoes*." *ECW* 56 (1995): 198–223.

Thompson, Elizabeth. *Pioneer Woman*, 21–27.

Lady Mary and Her Nurse (1856)

Thompson, Elizabeth. *Pioneer Woman*, 18–21.

Young Emigrants (1826)

Thompson, Elizabeth. *Pioneer Woman*, 12–17.

TRAN VAN DIHN (1923–)

Blue Dragon, White Tiger (1983)

Christopher, Renny. "*Blue Dragon, White Tiger:* The Bicultural Stance of Vietnamese American Literature," in *Lim*, Shirley Geok-lin, ed. *Reading the Literatures of Asian America*, 259–269.

TRAVEN, B. ((?)–1969)

Rebellion of the Hanged (1950)

Payne, Kenneth. "*Rebellion of the Hanged:* B. Traven's Anti-Fascist Novel of the Mexican Revolution." *IFR* 18.2 (1991): 96–107.

TREMBLAY, MICHEL (1942–)

Des nouvelles d'Edouard (1984)

Forget, Danielle. "Des paroles qui n'en sont pas: Conséquences argumentatives et narratives." *ELit* 25.1–2 (1992): 137–146.

Gauvin, Lise. "Théâtre de la langue," in David, Gilbert, ed. *Monde*, 352–353, 356.

Gobin, Pierre. "Portrait de l'artiste en Protée androgyne," in David, Gilbert, ed. *Monde*, 388–397.

Raoul, Valerie. *Distinctly Narcissistic*, 155–162.

First Quarter of the Moon see *Le premier quartier de la lune*

La duchesse et le roturier (1982)

Brochu, André. "D'une Lune l'autre ou les Avatars du Rêve," in David, Gilbert, ed. *Monde*, 270–273.

Gauvin, Lise. "Théâtre de la langue," in David, Gilbert, ed. *Monde*, 355.
Gobin, Pierre. "Portrait de l'artiste en Protée androgyne," in David, Gilbert, ed. *Monde*, 395.

La grosse femme d'à côté est enceinte (1978)

Brochu, André. "D'une Lune l'autre ou les Avatars du Rêve," in David, Gilbert, ed. *Monde*, 261–267.
Gauvin, Lise. "Théâtre de la langue," in David, Gilbert, ed. *Monde*, 351–352, 355.
Gobin, Pierre. "Portrait de l'artiste en Protée androgyne," in David, Gilbert, ed. *Monde*, 385, 387.
Popovic, Pierre. "La rue fable," in David, Gilbert, ed. *Monde*, 276–282.
Vachon, Georges-André. "L'enfant de la Grosse Femme," in David, Gilbert, ed. *Monde*, 289–303.

Le premier quartier de la lune(1989)

Gauvin, Lise. "Théâtre de la langue," in David, Gilbert, ed. *Monde*, 356.
Gobin, Pierre. "Portrait de l'artiste en Protée androgyne," in David, Gilbert, ed. *Monde*, 379–380, 384
Popovic, Pierre. "La rue fable," in David, Gilbert, ed. *Monde*, 282–288.
Vachon, Georges-André. "L'enfant de la Grosse Femme," in David, Gilbert, ed. *Monde*, 289–303.

Thérèse et Pierrette à l'école des Saints-Anges (1980)

Brochu, André. "D'une Lune l'autre ou les Avatars du Rêve," in David, Gilbert, ed. *Monde*, 267–270.
Gauvin, Lise. "Théâtre de la langue," in David, Gilbert, ed. *Monde*, 355.
Vachon, Georges-André. "L'enfant de la Grosse Femme," in David, Gilbert, ed. *Monde*, 302.

TRILLING, LIONEL (1905–1975)

Middle of the Journey (1947)

Seed, David. "Style of Politics in Lionel Trilling's *The Middle of the Journey*." *DUJ* 86.1 (1994): 119–28.

TWAIN, MARK (1835–1910)

Adventures of Huckleberry Finn (1885)

Allingham, Philip V. "Patterns of Deception in *Huckleberry Finn* and *Great Expectations*." *NCF* 46.4 (1992): 447–472.
Anspaugh, Kelly. " 'I Been There Before': Biblical Typology and *Adventures of Huckleberry Finn*." *ANQ* 7.4 (1994): 219–222.
Barksdale, Richard K. "History, Slavery, and Thematic Irony in *Huckleberry Finn*," in Leonard, James S., ed. *Satire or Evasion?*, 49–55.
Bell, Bernard W. "Twain's 'Nigger' Jim: The Tragic Face behind the Minstrel Mask," in Leonard, James S., ed. *Satire or Evasion?*, 124–138.
Blair, Walter. *Essays on American Humor*, 179–196, 215–220.
Brodwin, Stanley. "Mark Twain's Theology: The Gods of a Brevet Presbyterian," in Robinson, Forrest G., ed. *Cambridge Companion*, 238–239.
Camfield, Gregg. " 'I Wouldn't Be as Ignorant as You for Wages': Huck Talks Back to His Conscience." *SAF* 20.2 (1992): 169–175.

Camfield, Gregg. "Sentimental Liberalism and the Problems of Race in *Huckleberry Finn.*" *NCF* 46.1 (1991): 96–113.

Carton, Evan. "Speech Acts and Social Action: Mark Twain and the Politics of Literary Performance," in Robinson, Forrest G., ed. *Cambridge Companion*, 165–168.

Cummings, Sherwood. "Mark Twain's Moveable Farm and the Evasion." *AL* 63.3 (1991): 440–458.

Davis, Mary Kemp. "Veil Rent in Twain: Degradation and Revelation in *Adventures of Huckleberry Finn,*" in Leonard, James S., ed. *Satire or Evasion?*, 77–89.

Derwin, Susan. "Impossible Commands: Reading *Adventures of Huckleberry Finn.*" *NCF* 47.4 (1993): 437–454.

Fishkin, Shelley Fisher. "Mark Twain and Women," in Robinson, Forrest G., ed. *Cambridge Companion*, 60.

Gardner, Richard M. "*Huck Finn*'s Ending: The Intimacy and Disappointment of Tourism." *JNT* 24.1 (1994): 55–68.

Griswold, Jerry. *Audacious Kids*, 42–72.

Henrickson, Gary P. "Biographers' Twain, Critics' Twain, Which of the Twains Wrote the 'Evasion'?" *SLJ* 26.1 (1993): 14–29.

Henry, Peaches. "Struggle for Tolerance: Race and Censorship in *Huckleberry Finn,*" in Leonard, James S., ed. *Satire or Evasion?*, 25–44.

Hill, Richard. "Overreaching: Critical Agenda and the Ending of *Adventures of Huckleberry Finn.*" *TSLL* 33.4 (1991): 492–513.

Hirsh, James. "Samuel Clemens and the Ghost of Shakespeare." *SNNTS* 24.3 (1992): 260–267.

Hunt, Alan and Carol Hunt. "Practical Joke in *Huckleberry Finn.*" *WF* 51.2 (1992): 197–202.

Jacobson, Marcia. *Being a Boy Again*, 60–70.

Jehlen, Myra. "Banned in Concord: *Adventures of Huckleberry Finn* and Classic American Literature," in Robinson, Forrest G., ed. *Cambridge Companion*, 93–114.

Jones, Betty H. "Huck and Jim: A Reconsideration," in Leonard, James S., ed. *Satire or Evasion?*, 154–172.

Jones, Rhett S. "Nigger and Knowledge: White Double-Consiousness in *Adventures of Huckleberry Finn,*" in Leonard, James S., ed. *Satire or Evasion?*, 173–193.

Knoper, Randall. *Acting Naturally*, 71–73, 108–111.

Lester, Julius. "Morality and *Adventures of Huckleberry Finn,*" in Leonard, James S., ed. *Satire or Evasion?*, 199–207.

Lott, Eric. "Mr. Clemens and Jim Crow: Twain, Race, and Blackface," in Robinson, Forrest G., ed. *Cambridge Companion*, 133–142.

Magistrale, Tony. "Science, Politics, and the Epic Imagination: *The Talisman,*" in Magistrale, Tony, ed. *Dark Descent*, 115–119.

Mandia, Patricia M. *Comedic Pathos*, 29–49.

Moreland, Richard C. " 'He Wants to Put His Story Next to Hers': Putting Twain's Story Next to Hers in Morrison's *Beloved.*" *MFS* 39.3–4 (1993): 501–524.

Morrison, Toni. "Black Matter(s)." *GrandS* 10.4 (1991): 219–225.

Nichols, Charles H. " 'A True Book— With Some Stretchers': *Huck Finn* Today," in Leonard, James S., ed. *Satire or Evasion?*, 208–214.

Nilon, Charles H. "Ending of *Huckleberry Finn:* 'Freeing the Free Negro'," in Leonard, James S., ed. *Satire or Evasion?*, 62–75.

Pitcher, E. W. "Huck Finn as Sarah Williams: A Precedent for the Discovery Trick." *N&Q* 38.3 (1991): 324.

Powell, Jon. "Trouble and Joy from 'A True Story' to *Adventures of Huckleberry Finn:* Mark Twain and the 'Book of Jeremiah.' " *SAF* 20.2 (1992): 145–154.

Prioleau, Elizabeth. " 'That Abused Child of Mine': Huck Finn as Child of an Alcoholic." *EAS* 22 (1993): 85–98.

Quirk, Tom. *Coming to Grips with Huckleberry Finn: Essays on a Book, a Boy, and a Man.* Columbia, MO: University of Missouri Press, 1993.

Rampersad, Arnold. "*Adventures of Huckleberry Finn* and Afro-American Literature," in Leonard, James S., ed. *Satire or Evasion?*, 216–227.

Rogers, Franklin R. *Occidental Ideographs*, 100–129.

Rosenthal, M. L. "Alice, Huck, Pinocchio, and the Blue Fairy: Bodies Real ." *SoR* 29.3 (1993): 487.

Schmitz, Neil. "Mark Twain's Civil War: Humor's Reconstructive Writing," in Robinson, Forrest G., ed. *Cambridge Companion*, 81–91.

Segal, Harry G. "Life without Father: The Role of the Paternal in the Opening Chapters of *Huckleberry Finn.*" *JAmS* 27.1 (1993): 19–33.

Shaw, Peter. *Recovering American Literature*, 100–126.

Smith, David L. "Huck, Jim, and American Racial Discourse," in Leonard, James S., ed. *Satire or Evasion?*, 103–117.

Subryan, Carmen. "Mark Twain and the Black Challenge," in Leonard, James S., ed. *Satire or Evasion?*, 91–102.

Williams, Kenny J. "*Adventures of Huckleberry Finn;* or, Mark Twain's Racial Ambiguity," in Leonard, James S., ed. *Satire or Evasion?*, 228–237.

Wonham, Henry B. "Disembodied Yarnspinner and the Reader of *Adventures of Huckleberry Finn.*" *ALR* 24.1 (1991): 2–22.

Woodward, Fredrick and Donnarae MacCann. "Minstrel Shackles and Nineteenth-Century 'Liberality' in *Huckleberry Finn,*" in Leonard, James S., ed. *Satire or Evasion?*, 141–151.

Adventures of Tom Sawyer (1876)

Aspiz, Harold. "*Tom Sawyer*'s Games of Death." *SNNTS* 27.2 (1995): 141–153.

Blair, Walter. *Essays on American Humor*, 154–164.

Briden, Earl F. "Tom Sawyer's Funeral—Shades of Charley Warner?" *ANQ* 4.2 (1991): 75–77.

Brodwin, Stanley. "Mark Twain's Theology: The Gods of a Brevet Presbyterian," in Robinson, Forrest G., ed. *Cambridge Companion*, 225–226.

Burde, Edgar J. "Slavery and the Boys: *Tom Sawyer* and the Germ of Huck Finn." *ALR* 24.1 (1991): 86–88.

Griswold, Jerry. *Audacious Kids*, 143–155.

Hendler, Glenn. "Tom Sawyer's Masculinity." *ArQ* 49.4 (1993): 33–56.

Jacobson, Marcia. *Being a Boy Again*, 46–60.

Knoper, Randall. *Acting Naturally*, 79–80, 111–112.

MacLeod, Anne Scott. *American Childhood*, 69–76.

Connecticut Yankee in King Arthur's Court (1889)

Berkove, Lawrence I. "Gospel according to Hank Morgan's Newspaper." *EAS* 20 (1991): 32–42.

Carton, Evan. "Speech Acts and Social Action: Mark Twain and the Politics of Literary Performance," in Robinson, Forrest G., ed. *Cambridge Companion*, 168–170.

Fulton, Joe Boyd. "Twain's *A Connecticut Yankee in King Arthur's Court.*" *Expl* 53.1 (1994): 34–36.
George, Roger. " 'The Road Lieth Not Straight': Maps and Mental Models in *A Connecticut Yankee in King Arthur's Court.*" *ATQ* 5.1 (1991): 57–67.
Knoper, Randall. *Acting Naturally*, 81–86, 112, 135–138, 142–143, 155–169.
Limon, John. *Writing After War*, 50–55.
Mandia, Patricia M. *Comedic Pathos*, 84–100.
Maragou, Helena. "Game Playing and Fantasy in Twain's *A Connecticut Yankee.*" *ALR* 26.1 (1993): 26–39.
Michelson, Bruce. "Realism, Romance, and Dynamite: The Quarrel of *A Connecticut Yankee in King Arthur's Court.*" *NEQ* 64.4 (1991): 609–632.
Pfitzer, Gregory M. " 'Iron Dudes and White Savages in Camelot': The Influence of Dime-Novel Sensationalism on Twain's *A Connecticut Yankee in King Arthur's Court.*" *ALR* 27.1 (1994): 47–58.
Rogers, Franklin R. *Occidental Ideographs*, 235–238.
Rowe, John Carlos. "How the Boss Played the Game: Twain's Critique of Imperialism in *A Connecticut Yankee in King Arthur's Court,*" in Robinson, Forrest G., ed. *Cambridge Companion*, 175–189.
Yim, Jin-hee. "Modern American Adam's Utopian Experiment in *A Connecticut Yankee in King Arthur's Court.*" *JELL* 40.4 (1994): 675–687.
Zlatic, Thomas D. "Language Technologies in *A Connecticut Yankee.*" *NCF* 45.4 (1991): 453–477.

Gilded Age (1873)

Goldner, Ellen J. "Tangled Webs: Lies, Capitalist Expansion, and the Dissolution of the Subject in *The Gilded Age.*" *ArQ* 49.3 (1993): 59–91.
Zheng, Da. "Twain's and Warner's *The Gilded Age:* The Economy of Insanity." *CLAJ* 39.1 (1995): 71–93.

Personal Recollections of Joan of Arc (1896)

Fishkin, Shelley Fisher. "Mark Twain and Women," in Robinson, Forrest G., ed. *Cambridge Companion*, 61.
Knoper, Randall. *Acting Naturally*, 171–180.
Zlatic, Thomas D. " 'Seeing Eye' and the 'Creating Mouth': Literacy and Orality in Mark Twain's *Joan of Arc.*" *ClioI* 21.3 (1992): 285–304.

Prince and the Pauper (1881)

Griswold, Jerry. *Audacious Kids*, 121–139.
Knoper, Randall. *Acting Naturally*, 104–105, 150–155.

Tragedy of Pudd'nhead Wilson (1894)

Carton, Evan. "Speech Acts and Social Action: Mark Twain and the Politics of Literary Performance," in Robinson, Forrest G., ed. *Cambridge Companion*, 170–172.
Brodwin, Stanley. "Mark Twain's Theology: The Gods of a Brevet Presbyterian," in Robinson, Forrest G., ed. *Cambridge Companion*, 238.
Fishkin, Shelley Fisher. "Mark Twain and Women," in Robinson, Forrest G., ed. *Cambridge Companion*, 61–62.
Gillman, Susan. "The Mulatto, Tragic or Triumphant? The Nineteenth-Century American Race Melodrama," in Samuels, Shirley, ed. *Culture of Sentiment*, 227–231.

Howe, Lawrence. "Race, Genealogy, and Genre in Mark Twain's *Pudd'nhead Wilson*." *NCF* 46.4 (1992): 495–516.

Knoper, Randall. *Acting Naturally*, 86–95, 113–114.

Lott, Eric. "Mr. Clemens and Jim Crow: Twain, Race, and Blackface," in Robinson, Forrest G., ed. *Cambridge Companion*, 144–149.

Mandia, Patricia M. *Comedic Pathos*, 51–67.

Sundquist, Eric J. *To Wake the Nations*, 225–270.

Wonham, Henry B. "Getting to the Bottom *of Pudd'nhead Wilson;* Or, a Critical Vision Focused (Too Well?) for Irony." *ArQ* 50.3 (1994): 111–126.

TYLER, ANNE (1941–)

Accidental Tourist (1985)

Almond, Barbara R. "Accidental Therapist: Intrapsychic Change in a Novel." *L&P* 38.1–2 (1992): 84–104.

Cuningham, Henry. "Accidental Tourist's Best Friend: Edward as Four-Legged Literary Device." *NConL* 23.4 (1993): 10–12.

Evans, Elizabeth. *Anne Tyler*, 82–83, 84–88, 102–103, 110–111.

Breathing Lessons (1988)

Evans, Elizabeth. *Anne Tyler*, 77, 83–84, 92, 124, 125, 131–132.

Koppel, Gene. "Maggie Moran, Anne Tyler's Madcap Heroine: A Game-Approach to *Breathing Lessons*." *ELWIU* 18.2 (1991): 276–287.

Celestial Navigation (1974)

Evans, Elizabeth. *Anne Tyler*, 79–80, 90–91, 93, 101–102, 108–110, 111, 112–113, 118, 121–122, 126.

Papadimas, Julie Persing. "America Tyler Style: Surrogate Families and Transiency." *JACult* 15.3 (1992): 46–47, 50.

Clock Winder (1972)

Evans, Elizabeth. *Anne Tyler*, 74–77, 80–81, 82, 94, 103–105, 124–125, 128, 137.

Dinner at the Homesick Restaurant (1982)

Evans, Elizabeth. *Anne Tyler*, 95–97, 102, 103, 107, 113–116, 130, 132–133, 135–136.

Papadimas, Julie Persing. "America Tyler Style: Surrogate Families and Transiency." *JACult* 15.3 (1992): 47–48.

Town, Caren J. "Rewriting the Family during *Dinner at the Homesick Restaurant*." *SoQ* 31.1 (1992): 13–23.

Earthly Possessions (1977)

Evans, Elizabeth. *Anne Tyler*, 116–118, 122–123, 124, 126, 128–129.

Papadimas, Julie Persing. "America Tyler Style: Surrogate Families and Transiency." *JACult* 15.3 (1992): 48–50.

If Morning Ever Comes (1964)

Evans, Elizabeth. *Anne Tyler*, 45–56.

Ladder of Years (1995)

Allen, Brooke. "Anne Tyler in Mid-Course." *NewC* 13.9 (1995): 31–34.

Morgan's Passing (1980)

Evans, Elizabeth. *Anne Tyler*, 119–120, 121, 125.
Papadimas, Julie Persing. "America Tyler Style: Surrogate Families and Transiency." *JACult* 15.3 (1992): 50.

Saint Maybe (1991)

Caesar, Judith. "Foreigners in Anne Tyler's *Saint Maybe*." *Crit* 37.1 (1995): 71–79.
Evans, Elizabeth. *Anne Tyler*, 77–78, 92.
Hauerwas, Stanley. *Dispatches from the Front*, 80–86.

Searching for Caleb (1976)

Evans, Elizabeth. *Anne Tyler*, 69–72, 83, 118–119, 129–130.

Slipping-Down Life (1970)

Evans, Elizabeth. *Anne Tyler*, 72–74, 81–82, 93–94, 102, 111, 120–121, 125, 136–137.

Tin Can Tree (1964)

Evans, Elizabeth. *Anne Tyler*, 56–65.
Papadimas, Julie Persing. "America Tyler Style: Surrogate Families and Transiency." *JACult* 15.3 (1992): 45–46.

UPDIKE, JOHN (1932–)

Centaur (1963)

Sethuraman, Ramchandran. "Updike's *The Centaur:* On Aphanisis, Gaze, Eyes, and the Death Drive." *L&P* 39.3 (1993): 38–65.

Coup (1979)

Schueller, Malini. "Containing the Third World: John Updike's *The Coup*." *MFS* 37.1 (1991): 113–128.

Couples (1968)

Singh, Sukhbir. "Updike's *Couples*." *Expl* 52.2 (1994): 125–128.

Marry Me (1976)

Leckie, Barbara. " 'The Adulterous Society': John Updike's *Marry Me*." *MFS* 37.1 (1991): 61–79.

Rabbit at Rest (1990)

Clausen, Jan. "Native Fathers." *KR* 14.2 (1992): 44–46, 47, 48–52.
El Moncef, Salah. "Sounding the Black Box: Linear Reproduction and Chance Bifurcations in *Rabbit at Rest*." *ArQ* 51.4 (1995): 69–107.
Olster, Stacey. "Rabbit Rerun: Updike's Replay of Popular Culture in *Rabbit at Rest*." *MFS* 37.1 (1991): 45–59.
Wilson, Matthew. "Rabbit Tetralogy: From Solitude to Society to Solitude Again." *MFS* 37.1 (1991): 5–24.

Rabbit Is Rich (1981)

Wilson, Matthew. "Rabbit Tetralogy: From Solitude to Society to Solitude Again." *MFS* 37.1 (1991): 5–24.

Rabbit Redux (1971)

Clausen, Jan. "Native Fathers." *KR* 14.2 (1992): 49, 51.

DeBellis, Jack. " 'The Awful Power': John Updike's Use of Kubrick's 2001: A Space Odyssey in *Rabbit Redux*." *LFQ* 21.3 (1993): 209–217.

Limon, John. *Writing After War*, 169–170.

Wilson, Matthew. "Rabbit Tetralogy: From Solitude to Society to Solitude Again." *MFS* 37.1 (1991): 5–24.

Rabbit, Run (1960)

Clausen, Jan. "Native Fathers." *KR* 14.2 (1992): 51.

Klinkowitz, Jerome. "Toward a New American Mainstream: John Updike and Kurt Vonnegut," in Friedman, Melvin J., ed. *Traditions, Voices, and Dreams*, 161–163.

Limon, John. *Writing After War*, 168–169.

Rogers, Franklin R. *Occidental Ideographs*, 242–243.

Wilson, Matthew. "Rabbit Tetralogy: From Solitude to Society to Solitude Again." *MFS* 37.1 (1991): 5–24.

Wright, Derek. "Mapless Motion: Form and Space in Updike's *Rabbit, Run*." *MFS* 37.1 (1991): 35–44.

Roger's Version (1986)

Duvall, John N. "Pleasure of Textual/Sexual Wrestling: Pornography and Heresy in *Roger's Version*." *MFS* 37.1 (1991): 81–95.

URQUHART, JANE (1949–)

Whirlpool (1986)

Gottschalk, Katherine K. "Isabel Huggan and Jane Urquhart: Feminine in This?," in Pearlman, Mickey, ed. *Canadian Women*, 104–109.

Hancu, Laura. "Escaping the Frame: Circumscribing the Narrative in *The Whirlpool*." *SCL* 20.1 (1995): 45–64.

Turner, Margaret E. *Imagining Culture*, 94–107.

Changing Heaven (1990)

Gottschalk, Katherine K. "Isabel Huggan and Jane Urquhart: Feminine in This?," in Pearlman, Mickey, ed. *Canadian Women*, 109–112.

VAN HERK, ARITHA (1954–)

Judith (1978)

Davidson, Arnold E. *Coyote Country*, 101–110.

Thompson, Elizabeth. *Pioneer Woman*, 122, 134, 135, 150.

No Fixed Address (1986)

Becker, Susanne. "Ironic Transformations: The Feminine Gothic in Aritha Van Herk's *No Fixed Address*," in Hutcheon, Linda, ed. *Double Talking*, 115–133.

Goldman, Marlene. "Earth-Quaking the Kingdom of the Male Virgin: A Deleuzian Analysis of Aritha van Herk's *No Fixed Address* and *Places Far from Ellesmere*." *CanL* 137 (1993): 26–30, 36.

Lutz, H.; Hindersmann, J. "Uses of Mythology in Aritha Van Herk's *No Fixed Address*." *IFR* 18.1 (1991):15–20.

Places Far from Ellesmere (1990)

Beeler, Karin E. "Re-Creating Cassandra and Anna Karenina: Unheard Voices in Christa Wolf's *Cassandra* and Aritha van Herk's *Places Far from Ellesmere.*" *Crit* 36.4 (1995): 231–234.

Goldman, Marlene. "Earth-Quaking the Kingdom of the Male Virgin: A Deleuzian Analysis of Aritha van Herk's *No Fixed Address* and *Places Far from Ellesmere.*" *CanL* 137 (1993): 30–36.

Manera, Matthew. "Act of Being Read: Fictional Process in *Places Far from Ellesmere.*" *CanL* 146 (1995): 87–94.

Tent Peg (1981)

Davidson, Arnold E. *Coyote Country*, 110–118.

VARLEY, JOHN (1947–)

Millennium (1983)

Kramer, Reinhold. "Machine in the Ghost: Time and Presence in Varley's *Millennium.*" *Extrapolation* 32.2 (1991): 156–169.

VAUGHN, ELIZABETH DEWBERRY (1962–)

Break the Heart of Me (1994)

Cronin, Gloria L. "Fundamentalist Views and Feminist Dilemmas: Elizabeth Dewberry Vaughn's *Many Things Have Happened Since He Died* and *Break the Heart of Me*," in Friedman, Melvin J., ed. *Traditions, Voices, and Dreams*, 258–260, 273–276.

Many Things Have Happened Since He Died (1992)

Cronin, Gloria L. "Fundamentalist Views and Feminist Dilemmas: Elizabeth Dewberry Vaughn's *Many Things Have Happened Since He Died* and *Break the Heart of Me*," in Friedman, Melvin J., ed. *Traditions, Voices, and Dreams*, 260–267, 268–273.

VIDAL, GORE (1925–)

Messiah (1954)

Booker, M. Keith. *Dystopian Impulse*, 105–106.

VILLARREAL, JOSÉ ANTONIO (1924–)

Clemente Chacon (1984)

Hernandez-G., Manuel de Jesus. "Villarreal's *Clemente Chacon* (1984): A Precursor's Accommodationist Dialogue." *BR/RB* 16.1 (1991): 35–43.

Pocho (1959)

Myers, Inma Minoves. "Language and Style in *Pocho.*" *BR/RB* 16.2–3 (1991): 180–187.

VILLEMAIRE, YOLANDE (1949–)

La Vie en prose (1980)

Paterson, Janet M. *Postmodernism*, 85–96.
Shek, Ben-Z. *French-Canadian*, 97–99.

Meurtres à blanc (1974)

Green, Mary Jean. "Postmodern Agents: Cultural Representation in Hubert Aquin's *Prochain épisode* and Yolande Villemaire's *Meurtres à blanc*." *UTQ* 63.4 (1994): 584–596.

VIZENOR, GERALD (1934–)

Bearheart: The Heirship Chronicles see *Darkness in Saint Louis Bearheart*

Darkness in Saint Louis Bearheart (1978)

Hauss, Jon. "Real Stories: Memory, Violence, and Enjoyment in Gerald Vizenor's *Bearheart*." *L&P* 41.4 (1995): 1–16.
Hochbruck, Wolfgang. "Breaking Away: The Novels of Gerald Vizenor." *WLT* 66.2 (1992): 274, 277.
Owens, Louis. " 'Ecstatic Strategies' Gerald Vizenor's *Darkness in Saint Louis Bearheart*," in Fleck, Richard F., ed. *Critical Perspectives*, 145–154.
Owens, Louis. " 'Grinning Aboriginal Demons': Gerald Vizenor's *Bearheart* and the Indian's Escape from Gothic," in Mogen, David, ed. *Frontier Gothic*, 71–81.
Owens, Louis. *Other Destinies*, 228–240.
Ruppert, James. *Mediation in Contemporary Native American Fiction*, 92–108.
Velie, Alan R. "Gerald Vizenor's Indian Gothic." *MELUS* 17.1 (1991–92): 75–85.

Griever (1987)

Hochbruck, Wolfgang. "Breaking Away: The Novels of Gerald Vizenor." *WLT* 66.2 (1992): 275–276, 277.
Owens, Louis. *Other Destinies*, 240–250.
Sims, Cecilia. "Rebirth of Indian and Chinese Mythology in Gerald Vizenor's *Griever: An American Monkey King in China*," in Fleck, Richard F., ed. *Critical Perspectives*, 171–177.

Heirs of Columbus (1991)

Hochbruck, Wolfgang. "Breaking Away: The Novels of Gerald Vizenor." *WLT* 66.2 (1992): 277–278.

Trickster of Liberty (1988)

Boyarin, Jonathan. "Europe's Indian, America's Jew: Modiano and Vizenor." *BoundaryII* 19.3 (1992): 197–222.
Hochbruck, Wolfgang. "Breaking Away: The Novels of Gerald Vizenor." *WLT* 66.2 (1992): 276.
Owens, Louis. *Other Destinies*, 250–254.
Schmidt, Kerstin. "Subverting the Dominant Paradigm: Gerald Vizenor's Trickster Discourse." *SAIL* 7.1 (1995): 65–76.

VOIGT, CYNTHIA (1942–)

Callendar Papers (1983)

Reed, Suzanne Elizabeth. *Presenting Cynthia Voigt*, 17–23.

Come a Stranger (1986)
Reed, Suzanne Elizabeth. *Presenting Cynthia Voigt*, 43–44.

David and Jonathan (1991)
Reed, Suzanne Elizabeth. *Presenting Cynthia Voigt*, 81–84.

Dicey's Song (1983)
Reed, Suzanne Elizabeth. *Presenting Cynthia Voigt*, 37–39.

Glass Mountain (1992)
Reed, Suzanne Elizabeth. *Presenting Cynthia Voigt*, 84–90.

Homecoming (1981)
Reed, Suzanne Elizabeth. *Presenting Cynthia Voigt*, 32–37.

Izzy, Willy-Nilly (1986)
Reed, Suzanne Elizabeth. *Presenting Cynthia Voigt*, 52–54.

Jackaroo (1985)
Reed, Suzanne Elizabeth. *Presenting Cynthia Voigt*, 63–68.

On Fortune's Wheel (1990)
Reed, Suzanne Elizabeth. *Presenting Cynthia Voigt*, 68–73.

Runner (1985)
Reed, Suzanne Elizabeth. *Presenting Cynthia Voigt*, 41–43.

Seventeen Against the Dealer (1989)
Reed, Suzanne Elizabeth. *Presenting Cynthia Voigt*, 46–48

Solitary Blue (1983)
Reed, Suzanne Elizabeth. *Presenting Cynthia Voigt*, 39–41.

Sons from Afar (1987)
Reed, Suzanne Elizabeth. *Presenting Cynthia Voigt*, 44–46.

Tell Me If the Lovers Are Losers (1982)
Reed, Suzanne Elizabeth. *Presenting Cynthia Voigt*, 23–30.

Tree by Leaf (1988)
Reed, Suzanne Elizabeth. *Presenting Cynthia Voigt*, 56–59.

Vandemark Mummy (1991)
Reed, Suzanne Elizabeth. *Presenting Cynthia Voigt*, 59–61.

When She Hollers (1994)
Reed, Suzanne Elizabeth. *Presenting Cynthia Voigt*, 99–102.

Wings of the Falcon (1993)
Reed, Suzanne Elizabeth. *Presenting Cynthia Voigt*, 73–78.

VOLLMANN, WILLIAM T. (1959–)

Rifles (1993)
Smith, Carlton. "Arctic Revelations: Vollmann's *Rifles* and the Frozen Landscape of the Self." *RCF* 13.2 (1993): 53.

You Bright and Risen Angels (1987)

Laidlaw, Marc. "Suicide Notes on William T. Vollmann's *You Bright and Risen Angels*." *RCF* 13.2 (1993): 46–52.

VONNEGUT, KURT (1922–)

Bluebeard (1987)

Klinkowitz, Jerome. "Toward a New American Mainstream: John Updike and Kurt Vonnegut," in Friedman, Melvin J., ed. *Traditions, Voices, and Dreams*, 164–166.

Kopper, Edward A., Jr. "Abstract Expressionism in Vonnegut's *Bluebeard*." *JML* 17.4 (1991): 583–584.

Rampton, David. "Into the Secret Chamber: Art and the Artist in Kurt Vonnegut's *Bluebeard*." *Crit* 35.1 (1993): 16–26.

Cat's Cradle (1963)

Bland, Michael. "Game of Black Humor in Vonnegut's *Cat's Cradle*." *NConL* 24.4 (1994): 8–9.

Byun, Jong-min. "Some Aspects of Confucianism in Vonnegut's *Cat's Cradle*." *JELL* 37.4 (1991): 973–981.

Galápagos (1985)

Freese, Peter. "Surviving the End: Apocalypse, Evolution, and Entropy in Bernard Malamud, Kurt Vonnegut, and Thomas Pynchon." *Crit* 36.3 (1995): 167–171.

Hocus Pocus (1990)

Rushdie, Salman. *Imaginary Homelands*, 358–361.

Player Piano (1952)

Booker, M. Keith. *Dystopian Impulse*, 99–105.

Slaughterhouse-Five (1969)

Granofsky, Ronald. *Trauma Novel*, 53–54.

Lee, Cremilda Toledo. "Fantasy and Reality in Kurt Vonnegut's *Slaughterhouse-Five*." *JELL* 37.4 (1991): 983–991.

Limon, John. *Writing After War*, 139–153.

Lupack, Barbara Tepa. *Insanity as Redemption*, 100–134.

Stralen, Hans van. "*Slaughterhouse Five*, Existentialist Themes Elaborated in a Postmodernist Way." *Neophil* 79.1 (1995): 3–12.

VORSE, MARY HEATON (1874–1966)

Strike! (1930)

Hapke, Laura. *Daughters of the Great Depression*, 153–161.

WALKER, ALICE (1944–)

Color Purple (1982)

Abbandonato, Linda. " 'A View from 'Elsewhere': Subversive Sexuality and the Rewriting of the Heroine's Story in *The Color Purple*." *PMLA* 106.5 (1991): 1106–1115.

Babb, Valerie. "Women and Words: Articulating the Self in *Their Eyes Were Watching God* and *The Color Purple*," in Howard, Lillie P., ed. *Alice Walker and Zora Neale Hurston*, 83–85, 89–93.

Berlant, Lauren. "Race, Gender, and Nation in *The Color Purple*." *Critical Inquiry* 14.4 (1988): 857–858. Rpt. in Bloom, Harold, ed. *Black American Women Fiction Writers*, 202–203.

Berlant, Lauren. "Race, Gender, and Nation in *The Color Purple*." *Critical Inquiry* 14.4 (1988): 857–858. Rpt. in Bloom, Harold, ed. *Contemporary Black American Fiction Writers*, 162–163.

Berlant, Lauren. "Race, Gender, and Nation in *The Color Purple*." *Critical Inquiry* 14.4 (1988): 857–858. Rpt. in Bloom, Harold, ed. *Major Modern Black American Writers*, 175–176.

Brown, Robert McAfee. *Persuade Us To Rejoice*, 127–134.

Christophe, Marc A. "*The Color Purple:* An Existential Novel." *CLAJ* 36.3 (1993): 280–290.

Clark, Suzanne. *Sentimental Modernism*, 182–190.

Dawson, Emma J. Waters. "Redemption Through Redemption of Self in *Their Eyes Were Watching God* and *The Color Purple*," in Howard, Lillie P., ed. *Alice Walker and Zora Neale Hurston*, 69–70, 77–81.

Fannin, Alice. "Sense of Wonder: The Pattern for Psychic Survival in *Their Eyes Were Watching God* and *The Color Purple*." *Zora Neale Hurston Forum* 1.1 (1986): 1–11. Rpt. in Howard, Lillie P., ed. *Alice Walker and Zora Neale Hurston*, 45–46, 52–56.

Harrison, Elizabeth Jane. *Female Pastoral*, 101–116.

Henke, Suzette A. "Women's Life-Writing and the Minority Voice: Maya Angelou, Maxine Hong Kingston, and Alice Walker," in Friedman, Melvin J., ed. *Traditions, Voices, and Dreams*, 224–230.

Jamison-Hall, Angelene. "She's Just Too Womanish For Them: Alice Walker and *The Color Purple*," in Karolides, Nicholas J., ed., *Censored Books*, 191–200.

Karanja, Ayana. "Zora Neale Hurston and Alice Walker: A Transcendent Relationship—*Jonah's Gourd Vine* and *The Color Purple*," in Howard, Lillie P., ed. *Alice Walker and Zora Neale Hurston*, 121–124, 128–133.

King-Kok Cheung. " 'Don't Tell': Imposed Silences in *The Color Purple* and *The Woman Warrior*," in Lim, Shirley Geok-lin, ed. *Reading the Literatures of Asian America*, 163–185.

McDowell, Deborah E. *"The Changing Same"*, 34–37, 41–57.

Manzulli, Mia. "Edith Wharton's Gardens as a Legacy to Alice Walker." *EWhR* 11.2 (1994): 9–12.

Marvin, Thomas F. " 'Preachin' the Blues': Bessie Smith's Secular Religion and Alice Walker's *The Color Purple*." *AAR* 28.3 (1994): 411–420.

Massé, Michelle A. *In the Name of Love*, 62–63.

Ogunyemi, Chikwenye Okonjo. "Womanism: The Dynamics of the Contemporary Black Female Novel in English," in Clark, VéVé A., ed. *Revising the Word*, 246.

Phillips, Rebecca. "Thousand and First Face of the Hero." *BWVACET* 13.2 (1991): 91–102.

Powers, Peter Kerry. " 'Pa Is Not Our Pa': Sacred History and Political Imagination in *The Color Purple*." *SoAR* 60.2 (1995): 69–72.

Reddy, Maureen T. "Maternal Reading: Lazarre and Walker," in Daly, Brenda O., ed. *Narrating Mothers*, 226, 227, 228–229, 230–231, 233.

Rosenfelt, Deborah Silverton. "Feminism, 'Postfeminism,' and Contemporary

Women's Fiction," in Howe, Florence, ed. *Tradition and the Talents of Women*, 273–274, 276, 277, 279–280.

Scholl, Diane Gabrielsen. "With Ears to Hear and Eyes to See: Alice Walker's Parable *The Color Purple*." *C&L* 40.3 (1991): 255–266.

Selzer, Linda. "Race and Domesticity in *The Color Purple*." *AAR* 29.1 (1995): 67–82.

Stanford, Ann Folwell. "Dynamics of Change: Men and Co-Feeling in the Fiction of Zora Neale Hurston and Alice Walker," in Howard, Lillie P., ed. *Alice Walker and Zora Neale Hurston*, 115, 117–118.

Tate, Linda. *Southern Weave of Women*, 115–132.

Turner, Daniel E. "Cherokee and Afro-American Interbreeding in *The Color Purple*." *NConL* 21.5 (1991): 10–11.

Tusmith, Bonnie. *All My Relatives*, 71–83.

Wilentz, Gay Alden. *Binding Cultures*, 61–80.

Wilson, Mary Ann. " 'That Which the Soul Lives By': Spirituality in the Works of Zora Neale Hurston and Alice Walker," in Howard, Lillie P., ed. *Alice Walker and Zora Neale Hurston*, 60–61, 63–65.

Winchell, Donna Haisty. *Alice Walker*, 85–99.

Wright, Lee Alfred. *Identity, Family, and Folklore*, 51–69.

Meridian (1976)

Daly, Brenda O. "Teaching Alice Walker's *Meridian:* Civil Rights According to Mothers," in Daly, Brenda O., ed. *Narrating Mothers*, 239–256.

Downey, Anne M. " 'A Broken and Bloody Hoop': The Intertexuality of *Black Elk Speaks* and Alice Walker's *Meridian*." *MELUS* 19.3 (1994): 37–45.

Dubey, Madhu. *Black Women Novelists*, 126–144.

Kubitschek, Missy Dehn. *Claiming the Heritage*, 155–165.

Porter, Nancy. "Women's Interracial Friendships and Visions of Community in *Meridian, The Salt Eaters,* and *Dessa Rose*," in Howe, Florence, ed. *Tradition and the Talents of Women*, 252–255, 265–266.

Reddy, Maureen T. "Maternal Reading: Lazarre and Walker," in Daly, Brenda O., ed. *Narrating Mothers*, 225, 227, 228, 229, 231–234.

Tucker, Lindsey. *Textual Excap(e)ades*, 71–86.

Wilson, Mary Ann. " 'That Which the Soul Lives By': Spirituality in the Works of Zora Neale Hurston and Alice Walker," in Howard, Lillie P., ed. *Alice Walker and Zora Neale Hurston*, 65–66.

Winchell, Donna Haisty. *Alice Walker*, 59–68.

Possessing the Secret of Joy (1992)

Applegate, Nancy. "Feminine Sexuality in Alice Walker's *Possessing the Secret of Joy*." *NConL* 24.4 (1994): 11.

Bass, Margaret Kent. "Alice's Secret." *CLAJ* 38.1 (1994): 1–10.

Buckman, Alyson R. "Body as a Site of Colonization: Alice Walker's *Possessing the Secret of Joy*." *JACult* 18.2 (1995): 89–94.

Howard, Lillie P. "Benediction: A Few Words About *The Temple of My Familiar*, Variously Experienced, and *Possessing the Secret of Joy*," in Howard, Lillie P., ed. *Alice Walker and Zora Neale Hurston*, 143–146.

Temple of My Familiar (1989)

Coetzee, J. M. "The Beginnings of (Wo)man in Africa." *New York Times Book Review* 30 April 1989, 7. Rpt. in Bloom, Harold, ed. *Contemporary Black American Fiction Writers*, 164–165.

Dieke, Ikenna. "Toward a Monastic Idealism: The Thematics of Alice Walker's *The Temple of My Familiar.*" *AAR* 26.3 (1992): 507–513.

Howard, Lillie P. "Benediction: A Few Words About *The Temple of My Familiar*, Variously Experienced, and *Possessing the Secret of Joy*," in Howard, Lillie P., ed. *Alice Walker and Zora Neale Hurston*, 140–143.

Reddy, Maureen T. "Maternal Reading: Lazarre and Walker," in Daly, Brenda O., ed. *Narrating Mothers*, 227, 233.

Winchell, Donna Haisty. *Alice Walker*, 115–130.

Third Life of Grange Copeland (1970)

Butler, Robert James. "Alice Walker's Vision of the South in *The Third Life of Grange Copeland.*" *AAR* 27.2 (1993): 195–203.

Butler, Robert. "Visions of Southern Life and Religion in O'Connor's *Wise Blood* and Walker's *The Third Life of Grange Copeland.*" *CLAJ* 36.4 (1993): 353–360.

Cornwell, JoAnne. "Searching For Zora in Alice's Garden: Rites of Passage in Hurston's *Their Eyes Were Watching God* and Walker's *The Third Life of Grange Copeland*," in Howard, Lillie P., ed. *Alice Walker and Zora Neale Hurston*, 97–98, 103–106.

Dubey, Madhu. *Black Women Novelists*, 106–125.

Harris, Trudier. "Folklore in the Fiction of Alice Walker: A Perpetuation of Historical and Literary Traditions." *Black American Literature Forum* 11.1 (1977): 7–8. Rpt. in Bloom, Harold, ed. *Black American Women Fiction Writers*, 198–200.

Harris, Trudier. "Folklore in the Fiction of Alice Walker: A Perpetuation of Historical and Literary Traditions." *Black American Literature Forum* 11.1 (1977): 7–8. Rpt. in Bloom, Harold, ed. *Contemporary Black American Fiction Writers*, 158–160.

Harris, Trudier. "Folklore in the Fiction of Alice Walker: A Perpetuation of Historical and Literary Traditions." *Black American Literature Forum* 11.1 (1977): 7–8. Rpt. in Bloom, Harold, ed. *Major Modern Black American Writers*, 171–173.

Stanford, Ann Folwell. "Dynamics of Change: Men and Co-Feeling in the Fiction of Zora Neale Hurston and Alice Walker," in Howard, Lillie P., ed. *Alice Walker and Zora Neale Hurston*, 115–117.

Winchell, Donna Haisty. *Alice Walker*, 43–56.

WALKER, MARGARET (1915–)

Jubilee (1966)

Goodman, Charlotte. "From *Uncle Tom's Cabin* to Vyry's Kitchen: The Black Female Folk Tradition in Margaret Walker's *Jubilee*," in Howe, Florence, ed. *Tradition and the Talents of Women*, 328–337.

Ogunyemi, Chikwenye Okonjo. "Womanism: The Dynamics of the Contemporary Black Female Novel in English," in Clark, VéVé A., ed. *Revising the Word*, 238–239.

Spillers, Hortense J. "Hateful Passion, a Lost Love," in Gates, Henry Louis, Jr., ed. *Toni Morrison*, 214–220.

WALLACE, DAVID FOSTER (1962–)

Broom of the System (1987)

Olsen, Lance. "Termite Art, or Wallace's Wittgenstein." *RCF* 13.2 (1993): 199–215.

WALLACE, LEW (1827–1905)

Ben-Hur (1880)

Gutjahr, Paul. " 'To the Heart of Solid Puritans': Historicizing the Popularity of *Ben-Hur*." *Mosaic* 26.3 (1993): 53–68.

WALLANT, EDWARD LEWIS (1926–1962)

Pawnbroker (1961)

Goldsmith, Arnold L. *Modern American Urban Novel*, 119–132.

WARFIELD, CATHERINE ANN (1816–1877)

Household of Bouverie (1860)

Wyatt-Brown, Bertram. "Percy Forerunners, Family History, and the Gothic Tradition," in Gretlund, Jan Nordby, ed. *Walker Percy*, 57–63.

WARNER, CHARLES DUDLEY (1829–1900)

Gilded Age (1873)

Goldner, Ellen J. "Tangled Webs: Lies, Capitalist Expansion, and the Dissolution of the Subject in *The Gilded Age*." *ArQ* 49.3 (1993): 59–91.

Zheng, Da. "Twain's and Warner's *The Gilded Age:* The Economy of Insanity." *CLAJ* 39.1 (1995): 71–93.

WARNER, SUSAN BOGERT (1819–1885)

Wide, Wide World (1850)

Brodhead, Richard H. *Cultures of Letters*, 30–35.

Bromell, Nicholas K. *By the Sweat of the Brow*, 137–141, 145–151.

Goshgarian, G. M. *To Kiss the Chastening Rod*, 76–120.

Foster, Shirley. *What Katy Read*, 36–59.

Hovet, Grace Ann and Theodore R. Hovet. "Identity Development in Susan Warner's *The Wide, Wide World:* Relationship, Performance and Construction." *Legacy* 8.1 (1991): 3–16.

Hovet, Grace Ann and Theodore R. Hovet. "TABLEAUX VIVANTS: Masculine Vision and Feminine Reflections in Novels by Warner, Alcott, Stowe, and Wharton." *ATQ* 7.4 (1993): 335–342, 352–355.

Stewart, Veronica. "Wild Side of *The Wide, Wide World*." *Legacy* 11.1 (1994): 1–16.

WARREN, ROBERT PENN (1905–1989)

All the King's Men (1946)

Blair, John. " 'The Lie We Must Learn to Live By': Honor and Tradition in *All the King's Men*." *SNNTS* 457–472.

Clark, William Bedford. *American Vision of Robert Penn Warren*, 89–98.

Cunningham, Henry. "Jack Burden Investigates." *SoQ* 31.1 (1992): 35–49.

Drake, Robert. "Robert Penn Warren's Enormous Spider Web." *MissQ* 48.1 (1994–95): 11–15.

Ferriss, Lucy. "Sleeping with the Boss: Female Subjectivity in Robert Penn Warren's Fiction." *MissQ* 48.1 (1994–95): 151–155.

Koppelman, Robert. "*All the King's Men*, Spiritual Aesthetics, and the Reader." *MissQ* 48.1 (1994–95): 105–114.

Robinson, Forrest G. "Combat with the Past: Robert Penn Warren on Race and Slavery." *AL* 67.3 (1995): 511–530.

At Heaven's Gate (1943)

Clark, William Bedford. *American Vision of Robert Penn Warren*, 81–89.

Ferriss, Lucy. "Sleeping with the Boss: Female Subjectivity in Robert Penn Warren's Fiction." *MissQ* 48.1 (1994–95): 157–158.

Band of Angels (1955)

Clark, William Bedford. *American Vision of Robert Penn Warren*, 111–112.

Ferriss, Lucy. "Sleeping with the Boss: Female Subjectivity in Robert Penn Warren's Fiction." *MissQ* 48.1 (1994–95): 164–167.

Cave (1959)

Clark, William Bedford. *American Vision of Robert Penn Warren*, 121–123.

Ferriss, Lucy. "Sleeping with the Boss: Female Subjectivity in Robert Penn Warren's Fiction." *MissQ* 48.1 (1994–95): 151–155.

Flood (1964)

Clark, William Bedford. *American Vision of Robert Penn Warren*, 123–124.

Ferriss, Lucy. "Sleeping with the Boss: Female Subjectivity in Robert Penn Warren's Fiction." *MissQ* 48.1 (1994–95): 159–161.

Meet Me in the Green Glen (1971)

Ferriss, Lucy. "Sleeping with the Boss: Female Subjectivity in Robert Penn Warren's Fiction." *MissQ* 48.1 (1994–95): 164–167.

Night Rider (1939)

Clark, William Bedford. *American Vision of Robert Penn Warren*, 71–81.

Ferriss, Lucy. "Sleeping with the Boss: Female Subjectivity in Robert Penn Warren's Fiction." *MissQ* 48.1 (1994–95):155–157.

Winn, Thomas H. "*Night Rider* Revisited: A Historical Perspective." *SoQ* 31.4 (1993): 68–74.

Place to Come Home To (1977)

Justus, James H. "Warren's Terra." *MissQ* 48.1 (1994–95): 133–146.

Wilderness (1961)

Hendricks, Randy J. "Warren's *Wilderness* and the Defining 'If'." *MissQ* 48.1 (1994–95): 115–131.

World Enough and Time (1950)

Barry, Michael G. "Interpretation and Justice: The Heart of *World Enough and Time*." *SLJ* 25.2 (1993): 57–68.

Clark, William Bedford. *American Vision of Robert Penn Warren*, 104–108.

Ferriss, Lucy. "Sleeping with the Boss: Female Subjectivity in Robert Penn Warren's Fiction." *MissQ* 48.1 (1994–95): 161–164.

WATSON, SHEILA (1909–)

Double Hook (1959)

Davidson, Arnold E. *Coyote Country*, 58–73.
Deer, Glenn. *Postmodern Canadian Fiction*, 28–46.
Turner, Margaret E. *Imagining Culture*, 64–78.

WATTERSTON, GEORGE (1783–1854)

Lawyer (1808)

Watts, Edward. "Peculiar Birthright of Every American: George Watterston's *The Lawyer*." *SAF* 23.1 (1995): 55–71.

WEBSTER, ALICE JANE CHANDLER see WEBSTER, JEAN

WEBSTER, JEAN (1876–1916)

Daddy Long-Legs (1912)

Alkalay-Gut, Karen. " 'If Mark Twain Had a Sister': Gender-Specific Values and Structure in *Daddy Long-Legs*." *JACult* 16.4 (1993): 91–99.

WELCH, JAMES (1940–)

Death of Jim Loney (1979)

Lincoln, Kenneth. "Blackfeet Winter Blues: James Welch," in Fleck, Richard F., ed. *Critical Perspectives*, 221–226.
Owens, Louis. *Other Destinies*, 147–156.
Purdy, John. "Bha'a and *The Death of Jim Loney*." *SAIL* 5.2 (1993): 67–71.
Riley In-The-Woods, Patricia. "*Death of Jim Loney:* A Ritual of Re-Creation." *Fiction International* 20 (1991): 157–166.

Fools Crow (1986)

Ballard, Charles G. "Question of Survival in *Fools Crow*." *NDQ* 59.4 (1991): 251–259.
Barry, Nora. " 'A Myth to Be Alive': James Welch's *Fools Crow*." *MELUS* 17.1 (1991–92): 3–20.
Murphree, Bruce. "Welch's *Fools Crow*." *Expl* 52.3 (1994): 186–187.
Owens, Louis. *Other Destinies*, 156–166.

Winter in the Blood (1974)

Ballard, Charles G. "Theme of the Helping in *Winter in the Blood*." *MELUS* 17.1 (1991–92): 63–74.
Eisenstein, Paul. "Finding Lost Generations: Recovering Omitted History in *Winter in the Blood*." *MELUS* 19.3 (1994): 3–18.
Lincoln, Kenneth. "Blackfeet Winter Blues: James Welch," in Fleck, Richard F., ed. *Critical Perspectives*, 212–221.
Nelson, Emmanuel. "Fourth World Fictions: A Comparative Commentary on James Welch's *Winter in the Blood* and Mudrooroo Narogin's *Wild Cat Falling*," in Fleck, Richard F., ed. *Critical Perspectives*, 59–62.

Owens, Louis. *Other Destinies*, 128–147.

Ruoff, A. Lavonne. "Alienation and the Female Principle in Broken Narrative in *Winter in the Blood*," in Fleck, Richard F., ed. *Critical Perspectives*, 195–207.

Ruppert, James. *Mediation in Contemporary Native American Fiction*, 56–73.

Sands, Kathleen M. "Alienation and Broken Narrative in *Winter in the Blood*," in Fleck, Richard F., ed. *Critical Perspectives*, 181–188.

Tardieu, Betty. "Communion in James Welch's *Winter in the Blood*." *SAIL* 5.4 (1993): 69–80.

Velie, Alan R. "*Winter in the Blood* as Comic Novel," in Fleck, Richard F., ed. *Critical Perspectives*, 189–194.

WELTY, EUDORA (1909–)

Delta Wedding (1946)

Fuller, Danielle. " 'Making a Scene': Some Thoughts on Female Sexuality and Marriage in Eudora Welty's *Delta Wedding* and *The Optimist's Daughter*." *MissQ* 48.2 (1995):295–309, 317–318.

Hanson, Elizabeth I. *Margaret Mitchell*, 86–89.

Levy, Helen Fiddyment. *Fiction of the Home Place*, 167–175.

Marrs, Suzanne. " 'The Treasure Most Dearly Regarded': Memory and Imagination in *Delta Wedding*." *SLJ* 25.2 (1993): 79–91.

Romines, Ann. *Home Plot*, 211–230.

Tate, Linda. *Southern Weave of Women*, 18–20.

Westling, Louise. "Food, Landscape and the Feminine in *Delta Wedding*." *SoQ* 30.2–3 (1992): 29–40.

Yakimenko, Natalia. "Idyllic Chronotope in *Delta Wedding*." *SoQ* 32.1 (1993): 21–26.

Losing Battles (1970)

Bass, Eben E. "Languages of *Losing Battles*." *SAF* 21.1 (1993): 67–82.

Gretlund, Jan Nordby. "Welty's *Losing Battles*." *Expl* 51.1 (1992): 49–50.

Levy, Helen Fiddyment. *Fiction of the Home Place*, 183–188.

Romines, Ann. *Home Plot*, 269–289.

Zverev, Aleksei. "*Losing Battles* against the Background of the Sixties." *SoQ* 32.1 (1993): 27–30.

Optimist's Daughter (1972)

Brinkmeyer, Robert H., Jr. "New Orleans, Mardi Gras, and Eudora Welty's *The Optimist's Daughter*." *MissQ* 44.4 (1991): 429–441.

Fuller, Danielle. " 'Making a Scene': Some Thoughts on Female Sexuality and Marriage in Eudora Welty's *Delta Wedding* and *The Optimist's Daughter*." *MissQ* 48.2 (1995): 310–318.

Levy, Helen Fiddyment. *Fiction of the Home Place*, 188–195.

Romincs, Ann. *Homc Plot*, 257–269.

Wolff, Sally. " 'Among Those Missing': Phil Hand's Disappearance from *The Optimist's Daughter*." *SLJ* 25.1 (1992): 74–88.

Ponder Heart (1954)

Seaman, Gerda and Ellen L. Walker. " 'It's All in a Way of Speaking': A Discussion of *The Ponder Heart*." *SLJ* 23.2 (1991): 65–76.

Varis, Sharon Deykin. "Welty's Philosophy of Friendship: Meanings Treasured in *The Ponder Heart.*" *SLJ* 27.2 (1995): 43–61.

Robber Bridegroom (1942)

Hattenhauer, Darryl. "Absurdism and Dark Humor in Welty's *The Robber Bridegroom.*" *UMSE* 10 (1992): 167–169.

Hattenhauer, Darryl. "Welty's *The Robber Bridegroom.*" *SDR* 30.4 (1992): 98–111.

Wilson, Deborah. "Altering/Alterity of History in Eudora Welty's *The Robber Bridegroom.*" *SoQ* 32.1 (1993): 62–71.

WEST, DOROTHY (1907–)

Living Is Easy (1948)

Griffin, Farah Jasmine. *"Who Set You Flowin'?"*, 83–87.

WEST, PAUL (1930–)

Alley Jaggers (1966)

Irwin, Ivor S. "Paul West's *Alley Jaggers:* Escaping the Trap of British Proletarian Fiction." *RCF* 11.1 (1991): 219–226.

Place in the Flowers Where the Pollen Rests (1988)

Bosworth, David. "Being and Becoming: The Canvas of Paul West's Work." *RCF* 11.1 (1991): 280–288.

Lingis, Alphonso. "From under Dismembered Bodies." *RCF* 11.1 (1991): 289–297.

Rat Man of Paris (1986)

Schreiner, Christopher S. "Of Involutes, a Rat, and Hugh's Guitar." *RCF* 11.1 (1991): 231–239.

Very Rich Hours of Count von Stauffenberg (1980)

Young, Philip. " 'Stauff'." *RCF* 11.1 (1991): 249–251.

Women of Whitechapel (1991)

Saltzman, Arthur M. "Beholding Paul West and *The Women of Whitechapel.*" *TCL* 40.2 (1994): 256–271.

West, Paul. "Deep Sixed into the Atlantic." *RCF* 11.3 (1991): 260–262.

WHARTON, EDITH (1862–1937)

Age of Innocence (1920)

Bentley, Nancy. " 'Hunting for the Real': Wharton and the Science of Manners," in Bell, Millicent, ed. *Cambridge Companion*, 51–56, 59–60.

Castronovo, David. *American Gentleman*, 53–57.

Chandler, Marilyn R. *Dwelling in the Text*, 149–179.

Eby, Clare Virginia. "Silencing Women in Edith Wharton's *The Age of Innocence.*" *ClQ* 28.2 (1992): 93–104.

Fedorko, Kathy A. *Gender and the Gothic*, 85–100.

Fracasso, Evelyn E. "Transparent Eyes of May Welland in Wharton's *The Age of Innocence*." *MLS* 21.4 (1991): 43–48.

Hadley, Kathy Miller. "Ironic Structure and Untold Stories in *The Age of Innocence*." *SNNTS* 23.2 (1991): 262–272.

Joslin, Katherine. *Edith Wharton*, 89–107.

Knights, Pamela. "Forms of Disembodiment: The Social Subject in *The Age of Innocence*," in Bell, Millicent, ed. *Cambridge Companion*, 20–46.

Miller, D. Quentin. " 'A Barrier of Words': The Tension between Narrative Voice and Vision in the Writings of Edith Wharton." *ALR* 27.1 (1994): 19–21.

Murphy, John J. "Filters, Portraits, and History's Mixed Bag': *A Lost Lady* and *The Age of Innocence*." *TCL* 38.4 (1992): 481, 483–484.

Pimple, Kenneth D. "Edith Wharton's 'Inscrutable Totem Terrors': Ethnography and *The Age of Innocence*." *SFolk* 51.2 (1994): 137–152.

Pizer, Donald. "American Naturalism in Its 'Perfected' State: *The Age of Innocence* and *An American Tragedy*," in Bendixen, Alfred, ed. *Edith Wharton*, 127–140.

Pizer, Donald. *Theory and Practice*, 157–166.

Rogers, Franklin R. *Occidental Ideographs*, 246–249.

Singley, Carol J. *Edith Wharton*, 164–183.

Buccaneers (1938)

Tintner, Adeline R. "Consuelo Vanderbilt and *The Buccaneers*." *EWhR* 10.2 (1993): 15–19.

Children (1928)

Sensibar, Judith L. "Edith Wharton Reads the Bachelor Type: Her Critique of Modernism's Representative Man," in Bendixen, Alfred, ed. *Edith Wharton*, 159–176.

Custom of the Country (1913)

Bentley, Nancy. " 'Hunting for the Real': Wharton and the Science of Manners," in Bell, Millicent, ed. *Cambridge Companion*, 63–64.

Castronovo, David. *American Gentleman*, 65–69.

Joslin, Katherine. *Edith Wharton*, 70–88.

Showalter, Elaine. "Spragg: The Art of the Deal," in Bell, Millicent, ed. *Cambridge Companion*, 87–97.

Waid, Candace. *Edith Wharton's Letters from the Underworld*, 129–172.

Fruit of the Tree (1907)

Carlin, Deborah. "To Form a More Imperfect Union: Gender, Tradition, and the Text in Wharton's *The Fruit of the Tree*," in Bendixen, Alfred, ed. *Edith Wharton*, 57–76.

Tuttleton, James W. "Justine: or, the Perils of Abstract Idealism," in Bell, Millicent, ed. *Cambridge Companion*, 157–168.

Gods Arrive (1932)

Bauer, Dale M. *Edith Wharton's Brave New Politics*, 137–144.

Singley, Carol J. *Edith Wharton*, 196–208.

Werlock, Abby H. P. "Edith Wharton's Subtle Revenge?: Morton Fullerton and the Female Artist in *Hudson River Bracketed* and *The Gods Arrive*," in Bendixen, Alfred, ed. *Edith Wharton*, 181–197.

House of Mirth (1905)

Abbott, Reginald. " 'A Moment's Ornament': Wharton's Lily Bart and Art Nouveau." *Mosaic* 24.2 (1991): 73–91.

Ammons, Elizabeth. "Edith Wharton and the Issue of Race," in Bell, Millicent, ed. *Cambridge Companion*, 77–82.

Bentley, Nancy. " 'Hunting for the Real': Wharton and the Science of Manners," in Bell, Millicent, ed. *Cambridge Companion*, 62–63.

Budick, Emily Miller. *Engendering Romance*, 133–135.

Colquitt, Clare. "Succumbing to the 'Literary Style': Arrested Desire in *The House of Mirth*." *WS* 20.2 (1991): 153–162.

Fedorko, Kathy A. "Edith Wharton's Haunted Fiction: 'The Lady's Maid's Bell' and *The House of Mirth*," in Carpenter, Lynette, ed. *Haunting the House of Fiction*, 80–105.

Fedorko, Kathy A. *Gender and the Gothic*, 31–47.

Freeman, Barbara Claire. *Feminine Sublime*, 55–67.

Fryer, Judith. "Reading *Mrs. Lloyd*," in Bendixen, Alfred, ed. *Edith Wharton*, 27–52.

Gabler-Hover, Janet and Kathleen Plate. "*House of Mirth* and Edith Wharton's 'Beyond!' " *PQ* 72.3 (1993): 357–378.

Goldner, Ellen J. "Lying Woman and the Cause of Social Anxiety: Interdependence and the Woman's Body in *The House of Mirth*." *WS* 21.3 (1992): 285–305.

Hapke, Laura. *Tales of the Working Girl*, 63–65.

Hochman, Barbara. "Rewards of Representation: Edith Wharton, Lily Bart and the Writer/Reader Interchange." *Novel* 24.2 (1991): 147–161.

Hovet, Grace Ann and Theodore R. Hovet. "TABLEAUX VIVANTS: Masculine Vision and Feminine Reflections in Novels by Warner, Alcott, Stowe, and Wharton." *ATQ* 7.4 (1993): 335–338, 348–351, 352–355.

Howard, Maureen. "Bachelor and the Baby: *The House of Mirth*," in Bell, Millicent, ed. *Cambridge Companion*, 137–156.

Joslin, Katherine. *Edith Wharton*, 49–69.

Macnaughton, William R. "Wharton's *The Reef*." *Expl* 51.4 (1993): 227–230.

Miller, D. Quentin. " 'A Barrier of Words': The Tension between Narrative Voice and Vision in the Writings of Edith Wharton." *ALR* 27.1 (1994): 15.

Orr, Elaine N. "Contractual Law, Relational Whisper: A Reading of Edith Wharton's *The House of Mirth*." *MLQ* 52.1 (1991): 53–70.

Riegel, Christian. "Rosedale and Anti-Semitism in *The House of Mirth*." *SAF* 20.2 (1992): 219–224.

Rogers, Franklin R. *Occidental Ideographs*, 238–241.

Sapora, Carol Baker. "Female Doubling: The Other Lily Bart in Edith Wharton's *The House of Mirth*." *PLL* 29.4 (1993): 371–394.

Showalter, Elaine. "Death of the Lady (Novelist): Wharton's *House of Mirth*," in Bendixen, Alfred, ed. *Edith Wharton*, 3–23.

Showalter, Elaine. *Sister's Choice*, 85–102.

Singley, Carol J. *Edith Wharton*, 67–88.

Tyson, Lois. "Beyond Morality: Lily Bart, Lawrence Selden and the Aesthetic Commodity in *The House of Mirth*." *ESQ* 9.2 (1992): 3–10.

Waid, Candace. *Edith Wharton's Letters from the Underworld*, 15–49.

Yeazell, Ruth Bernard. "Conspicuous Wasting of Lily Bart." *ELH* 59.3 (1992): 713–734.

Hudson River Bracketed (1929)

Bauer, Dale M. *Edith Wharton's Brave New Politics*, 118–120, 122–126, 128–133.

Singley, Carol J. *Edith Wharton*, 196–208.

Werlock, Abby H. P. "Edith Wharton's Subtle Revenge?: Morton Fullerton and the Female Artist in *Hudson River Bracketed* and *The Gods Arrive*," in Bendixen, Alfred, ed. *Edith Wharton*, 181–197.

Mother's Recompense (1925)

Bauer, Dale M. *Edith Wharton's Brave New Politics*, 52–82.

Joslin, Katherine. *Edith Wharton*, 108–127.

Tonkovich, Nicole. "An Excess of Recompense: The Feminine Economy of The *Mother's Recompense*." *ALR* 26.3 (1994): 12–32.

Reef (1912)

DeShong, Scott. "Protagonism in *The Reef:* Wharton's Novelistic Discourse." *EWhR* 8.2 (1991): 19–23.

Faery, Rebecca Blevins. "Wharton's *Reef:* The Inscription of Female Sexuality," in Bendixen, Alfred, ed. *Edith Wharton*, 79–94.

Inness, Sherrie A. "Nature, Culture, and Sexual Economics in Edith Wharton's *The Reef*." *ALR* 26.1 (1993): 76–90.

Jones, Wendell, Jr. "Holding up the Revealing Lamp: The Myth of Psyche in Edith Wharton's *The Reef*." *CollL* 19.1 (1992): 75–90.

Keyser, Elizabeth Lennox. " 'The Ways in Which the Heart Speaks': Letters in *The Reef*." *SAF* 19.1 (1991): 95–106.

Macnaughton, William R. "Edith Wharton, *The Reef* and Henry James." *ALR* 26.2 (1994): 48–50, 51, 53–56.

Macnaughton, William R. "Edith Wharton's 'Bad Heroine': Sophy Viner in *The Reef*." *SNNTS* 25.2 (1993): 213–225.

Singley, Carol J. *Edith Wharton*, 128–147.

Son at the Front (1923)

Higonnet, Margaret R. "Women in the Forbidden Zone: War, Women, and Death," in Goodwin, Sarah Webster, ed. *Death and Representation*, 201–203.

Limon, John. *Writing After War*, 205–210.

Summer (1918)

Bentley, Nancy. " 'Hunting for the Real': Wharton and the Science of Manners," in Bell, Millicent, ed. *Cambridge Companion*, 60–62.

Blackall, Jean Frantz. "Charity at the Window: Narrative Technique in Edith Wharton's *Summer*," in Bendixen, Alfred, ed. *Edith Wharton*, 115–125.

Fedorko, Kathy A. *Gender and the Gothic*, 70–82.

Miller, D. Quentin. " 'A Barrier of Words': The Tension between Narrative Voice and Vision in the Writings of Edith Wharton." *ALR* 27.1 (1994): 18–19.

Pfeiffer, Kathleen. "*Summer* and Its Critics' Discomfort." *WS* 20.2 (1991): 141–152.

Singley, Carol J. *Edith Wharton*, 147–161.

Skillern, Rhonda. "Becoming a 'Good Girl': Law, Language, and Ritual in Edith Wharton's *Summer*," in Bell, Millicent, ed. *Cambridge Companion*, 117–136.

Voorhees-Whitehead, Kathryn. " 'The Long Flame' of Edith Wharton's Summer: The Novella as Medium for the 'Dangerous'." *BWVACET* 13.1 (1991): 21–28.

Waid, Candace. *Edith Wharton's Letters from the Underworld*, 87–125.

Touchstone (1900)

Ammons, Elizabeth. *Conflicting Stories*, 143–145.

Olin-Ammentorp, Julie. "Edith Wharton, Margaret Aubyn, and the Woman Novelist." *WS* 20.2 (1991): 133–139.

Witzig, Denise. "Letter(s) from an Unknown Woman: Edith Wharton's Correspondence with Authority." *WS* 20.2 (1991): 169–176.

Twilight Sleep (1927)

Bauer, Dale M. *Edith Wharton's Brave New Politics*, 96–105.

Valley of Decision (1902)

Balestra, Gianfranca. "Italian Foregrounds and Backgrounds: *The Valley of Decision*." *EWhR* 9.1 (1992): 12–14, 27.

Vance, William L. "Edith Wharton's Italian Mask: *The Valley of Decision*," in Bell, Millicent, ed. *Cambridge Companion*, 169–198.

WHITE, EDMUND (1940–)

Beautiful Room Is Empty (1988)

Koponen, Wilfrid R. *Embracing Gay Identity*, 73–96.

Boy's Own Story (1983)

Bergman, David. *Gaiety Transfigured*, 192–195.

Nocturnes for the King of Naples (1978)

Bergman, David. *Gaiety Transfigured*, 195–196.

WHITE, LIONEL (1905–)

Big Caper (1955)

Haut, Woody. *Pulp Culture*, 159–162.

Clean Break see *Killing*

Killing (1955)

Haut, Woody. *Pulp Culture*, 156–159.

WHITE, WALTER (1893–1955)

Fire in the Flint (1924)

Rhodes, Chip. "Writing Up the New Negro: The Construction of Consumer Desire in the Twenties." *JACult* 28.2 (1994): 191–192.

WIDEMAN, JOHN EDGAR (1941–)

Hiding Place (1981)

Berben, Jacqueline. "Beyond Discourse: The Unspoken Versus Words in the Fiction of John Edgar Wideman." *Callaloo* 8.3 (Fall 1985): 525, 528. Rpt. in Bloom, Harold, ed. *Contemporary Black American Fiction Writers*, 174–176.

Tusmith, Bonnie. *All My Relatives*, 84–85.

Philadelphia Fire (1990)

Clausen, Jan. "Native Fathers." *KR* 14.2 (1992): 44–46, 48, 52–55.

Sent for You Yesterday (1983)
Tusmith, Bonnie. *All My Relatives*, 88–94.

WIESEL, ELIE (1928–)

Accident see *Le Jour*

Beggar of Jerusalem see *Le Mendiant de Jérusalem*

Dawn see *L'Aube*

Fifth Son see *Le Cinquième Fils*

Gates of the Forest see *Les Portes de la forêt*

La Ville de la chance (1962)
Davis, Colin. *Elie Wiesel's Secretive Texts*, 67–85.

L'Aube (1960)
Davis, Colin. *Elie Wiesel's Secretive Texts*, 62–67, 144–146.

Le Cinquième Fils (1983)
Davis, Colin. *Elie Wiesel's Secretive Texts*, 123–124, 148–149, 157–158.

Le Crépuscule, au loin (1987)
Davis, Colin. *Elie Wiesel's Secretive Texts*, 103–112.

Le Jour (1961)
Davis, Colin. *Elie Wiesel's Secretive Texts*, 62–67.

Le Mendiant de Jérusalem (1968)
Davis, Colin. *Elie Wiesel's Secretive Texts*, 35–44, 104–111.

Le Serment de Kolvillàg (1973)
Davis, Colin. *Elie Wiesel's Secretive Texts*, 97–103.

Le Testament d'un poete juif assassine (1980)
Davis, Colin. *Elie Wiesel's Secretive Texts*, 147–148, 150–151, 153–156.
Sibelman, Simon P. "Phylacteries as Metaphor in Elie Wiesel's *La Testament d'un poete juif assassine*." *StTCL* 18.2 (1994): 267–275.

Les Portes de la forêt (1964)
Davis, Colin. *Elie Wiesel's Secretive Texts*, 86–97.
Lazarus, Joyce B. "Expanding Time: The Art of Eli Wiesel in *The Gates of the Forest*." *MLS* 24.4 (1994): 39–46.

L'Oublié (1989)
Davis, Colin. *Elie Wiesel's Secretive Texts*, 129–138, 176–182.

Oath see *Le Serment de Kolvillàg*

Testament see *Le Testament d'un poète juif assassiné*

Town Beyond the Wall see *La Ville de la chance*

Twilight see *Le Crépuscule, au loin*

WIGGIN, KATE DOUGLAS (1856–1923)

Rebecca of Sunnybrook Farm (1903)
Griswold, Jerry. *Audacious Kids*, 73–90.

WIGGINS, MARIANNE (1947–)

John Dollar (1989)

Dohrmann, Gail V. "*John Dollar:* Marianne Wiggins' Anti-Utopian Novel." *EJ* 80.4 (1991): 69–72.

Grenier, Donald J. *Women Enter the Wilderness*, 120–123.

WILDER, LAURA INGALLS (1867–1957)

Farmer Boy (1933)

Erisman, Fred. "*Farmer Boy:* The Forgotten 'Little House' Book." *WAL* 28.2 (1993): 123–130.

Little House in the Big Woods (1932)

Mowder, Louise. "Domestication of Desire: Gender, Language, and Landscape in the Little House Books." *CLAQ* 17.1 (1992): 15–18.

Little House on the Prairie (1935)

Mowder, Louise. "Domestication of Desire: Gender, Language, and Landscape in the Little House Books." *CLAQ* 17.1 (1992): 15–18.

On the Banks of Plum Creek (1937)

Mowder, Louise. "Domestication of Desire: Gender, Language, and Landscape in the Little House Books." *CLAQ* 17.1 (1992): 15–18.

WILDER, THORNTON (1897–1975)

Ides of March (1948)

Christensen, Peter G. "Politics of Thornton Wilder's *The Ides of March.*" *CML* 12.1 (1991): 69–79.

WILLEFORD, CHARLES (1919–)

Pick-Up (1955)

Haut, Woody. *Pulp Culture*, 177–182.

Woman Chaser (1960)

Haut, Woody. *Pulp Culture*, 182–188.

WILLIAMS, CHARLES (1909–)

Big Bite (1957)

Haut, Woody. *Pulp Culture*, 171–176.

WILLIAMS, JOHN A. (1925–)

Angry Ones (1960)

Munroe, C. Lynn. "Culture and Quest in the Fiction of John A. Williams." *College Language Association Journal* 22.2 (1978): 74. Rpt. in Bloom, Harold, ed. *Modern Black American Fiction Writers*, 146.

Junior Bachelor Society (1976)

Ramsey, Priscilla R. "John A. Williams: The Black American Narrative and the City, " in Hakutani, Yoshinobu, ed. *City in African-American Literature*, 221–225.

Man Who Cried I Am (1967)

Bryant, Jerry H. "John A. Williams: The Political Use of the Novel." *Critique* 16.3 (1975): 99–100. Rpt. in Bloom, Harold, ed. *Modern Black American Fiction Writers*, 145–146.

Burke, William M. "Resistance of John A. Williams: *The Man Who Cried I Am.*" *Critique* 15.3 (1973): 11. Rpt. in Bloom, Harold, ed. *Modern Black American Fiction Writers*, 141–142.

Ramsey, Priscilla R. "John A. Williams: The Black American Narrative and the City," in Hakutani, Yoshinobu, ed. *City in African-American Literature*, 215–217.

Reilly, John M. "Thinking History in *The Man Who Cried I Am.*" *Black American Literature Forum* 21.1–2 (1987): 39–40. Rpt. in Bloom, Harold, ed. *Modern Black American Fiction Writers*, 150–151.

Walcott, Ronald. "*The Man Who Cried I Am:* Crying in the Dark." *Studies in Black Literature* 3.1 (1972): 25–26. Rpt. in Bloom, Harold, ed. *Modern Black American Fiction Writers*, 139–140.

Mothersill and the Foxes (1975)

Ramsey, Priscilla R. "John A. Williams: The Black American Narrative and the City," in Hakutani, Yoshinobu, ed. *City in African-American Literature*, 219–221.

Night Song (1961)

Ramsey, Priscilla R. "John A. Williams: The Black American Narrative and the City," in Hakutani, Yoshinobu, ed. *City in African-American Literature*, 213–215.

Sissie (1963)

Schraufnagel, Noel. *From Apology to Protest: The Black American Novel.* Deland, FL: Everett, Edwards, 1973. Rpt. in Bloom, Harold, ed. *Modern Black American Fiction Writers*, 142–143.

Sons of Darkness, Sons of Light (1969)

Ramsey, Priscilla R. "John A. Williams: The Black American Narrative and the City," in Hakutani, Yoshinobu, ed. *City in African-American Literature*, 217–219.

WILLIAMS, SHERLEY ANNE (1944–)

Dessa Rose (1986)

Davies, Carole Boyce. "Mother Right/Write Revisited: *Beloved* and *Dessa Rose* and the Construction of Motherhood in Black Women's Fiction," in Daly, Brenda O., ed. *Narrating Mothers*, 44–56.

Harrison, Elizabeth Jane. *Female Pastoral*, 117–131.

Kester, Gunilla Theander. *Writing the Subject*, 107–110, 125–134.

King, Nicole R. "Meditations and Mediations: Issues of History and Fiction in *Dessa Rose.*" *Soundings* 76.2–3 (1993): 351–368.

McDowell, Deborah E. *"The Changing Same"*, 141–155.

McKible, Adam. " 'These Are the Facts of the Darky's History': Thinking History and Reading Names in Four African American Texts." *AAR* 28.2 (1994): 223, 224, 227, 228, 232–234.

Porter, Nancy. "Women's Interracial Friendships and Visions of Community in *Meridian, The Salt Eaters,* and *Dessa Rose*," in Howe, Florence, ed. *Tradition and the Talents of Women*, 252, 260–266.

Rushdy, Ashraf H. "Reading Mammy: The Subject of Relation in Sherley Anne Williams' *Dessa Rose*." *AAR* 27.3 (1993): 365–389.

Sanchez, Marta E. "Estrangement Effect in Sherley Anne Williams' *Dessa Rose*." *Genders* 15 (1992): 21–36.

Trapasso, Ann E. "Returning to the Site of Violence: The Restructuring of Slavery's Legacy in Sherley Anne Williams's *Dessa Rose*," in Lashgari, Deidre, ed. *Violence, Silence, and Anger*, 219–230.

WILLIAMSON, ELLEN DOUGLAS see DOUGLAS, ELLEN

WILLIS, MEREDITH (1946–)

Higher Ground (1981)

Joyner, Nancy Carol. "Poetics of the House in Appalachian Fiction," in Lanier, Parks, Jr.,ed. *Poetics*, 17–20.

WILSON, ETHEL (1888–1980)

Swamp Angel (1954)

Atwood, Margaret. *Strange Things*, 102–103.

Thompson, Elizabeth. *Pioneer Woman*, 120–121, 133, 134, 150.

WILSON, HARRIET E. (c.1828–c.1863)

Our Nig (1859)

Bell, Bernard W. *Afro-American Novel and Its Tradition.* Amherst, MA: University of Massachusetts Press, 1987. 48–50. Rpt. in Bloom, Harold, ed. *Black American Women Fiction Writers*, 215–216

Gates, Henry Louis, Jr. "Introduction." *Our Nig; or, Sketches from the Life of a Free Black.* New York: Random House, 1983. lii–liv. Rpt. in Bloom, Harold, ed. *Black American Women Fiction Writers*, 212–213.

Jackson, Blyden. *History of Afro-American Literature*. Baton Rouge: Louisiana State University Press, 1989. Vol. 1. 362–363. Rpt. in Bloom, Harold, ed. *Black American Women Fiction Writers*, 216–217.

Mitchell, Angelyn. "Her Side of His Story: A Feminist Analysis of Two Nineteenth-Century Antebellum Novels—William Wells Browns' *Clotel* and Harriet E. Wilson's *Our Nig*." *ALR* 24.3 (1992): 13–19.

Mullen, Harryette. "Runaway Tongue: Resistant Orality in *Uncle Tom's Cabin, Incidents in the Life of a Slave Girl*, and *Beloved*," in Samuels, Shirley, ed. *Culture of Sentiment*, 254–257.

Richardson, Marilyn. "Shadow of Slavery." *Women's Review of Books* 1.1 (October 1983): 15. Rpt. in Bloom, Harold, ed. *Black American Women Fiction Writers*, 214–215.

Tate, Claudia. "Allegories of Black Female Desire; or, Rereading Nineteenth-Century Sentimental Narratives of Black Female Authority." Wall, Cheryl A., ed.

Changing Our Words: Essays on Criticism, Theory, and Writing by Black Women. New Brunswick, NJ: Rutgers University Press, 1989. 113–114. Rpt. in Bloom, Harold, ed. *Black American Women Fiction Writers*, 217–218.

Winter, Kari J. *Subjects of Slavery*, 34–35.

WILSON, SLOAN (1920–)

Man in the Gray Flannel Suit (1956)

Wood, Ruth Pirsig. *Lolita in Peyton Place*, 17–27.

WISEMAN, ADELE (1928–)

Crackpot (1974)

Panofsky, Ruth. "From Complicity to Subversion: The Female Subject in Adele Wiseman's Novels." *CanL* 137 (1993): 44–47.

Zichy, Francis. "Lurianic Background: Myths of Fragmentation and Wholeness in Adele Wiseman's *Crackpot*." *ECW* 50 (1993): 264–279.

Sacrifice (1956)

Panofsky, Ruth. "From Complicity to Subversion: The Female Subject in Adele Wiseman's Novels." *CanL* 137 (1993): 41–44.

WISTER, OWEN (1860–1938)

Virginian (1902)

Davis, Robert Murray. *Playing Cowboys*, 3–29.

WOIWODE, LARRY (1941–)

Born Brothers (1988)

Grenier, Donald J. *Women Enter the Wilderness*, 75–82.

WOLFE, BERNARD (1915–1985)

Limbo (1952)

Hayles, N. Katherine. "Life Cycle of Cyborgs: Writing the Posthuman," in Benjamin, Marina, ed. *Question of Identity*, 156–162.

WOLFE, GENE (1931–)

Nightside the Long Sun (1993)

Kondratiev, Alexei. "Tales Newly Told: A Column on Current Modern Fantasy." *Mythlore* 19.4 (1993): 30–31.

WOLFE, THOMAS (1900–1938)

Good Child's River (1991)

Fraser, Stephen Douglas. "Filters of Fiction: Wolfe, Bernstein, and the Writing of *The Good Child's River*." *TWN* 16.2 (1992): 15–22.

Stutman, Suzanne. "Image of the Child in *The Good Child's River.*" *TWN* 18.1 (1994): 19–24.

Look Homeward, Angel (1929)

Bailey, J. Todd. "Metamorphosis of the Uneeda Lunch Cafes." *TWN* 18.1 (1994): 48–52.

Bumgarner, John R. "*Look Homeward, Angel:* An Epidemiologic Study." *TWN* 19.1 (1995): 10–13.

Castronovo, David. *American Gentleman*, 189–191.

Cunningham, Cheryl. "*Look Homeward, Angel* and Ovid's *Metamorphoses.*" *TWN* 18.2 (1994): 6–12.

Jacobs, Paul. "*Look Homeward, Angel* in World War II." *TWN* 16.2 (1992): 44–46.

Mitchell, Ted. "Thomas Wolfe's Angels." *TWN* 18.1 (1994): 1–18.

Ribblett, David L. "Homeward Bound: Thomas Wolfe and the Old Kentucky Home." *TWN* 16.2 (1992): 52–65.

Snyder, Phillip A. "*Look Homeward, Angel* as Autobiography and Artist Novel." *TWN* 19.1 (1995): 44–53.

Of Time and the River (1935)

O'Neill, Heather. " 'Of Wandering Forever and the Earth Again': Mythology in Thomas Wolfe's *Of Time and the River.*" *TWN* 18.2 (1994): 40–49.

WOLFE, TOM (1931–)

Bonfire of the Vanities (1987)

Castronovo, David. *American Gentleman*, 86–88.

McKeen, William. *Tom Wolfe*, 117–124.

Porsdam, Helle. "In the Age of Lawspeak: Tom Wolfe's *The Bonfire of the Vanities* and American Litigiousness." *JAmS* 25.1 (1991): 39–57.

Smith, James F. "Tom Wolfe's *Bonfire of the Vanities:* A Dreiser Novel for the 1980s." *JACult* 14.3 (1991): 43–49.

Varsava, Jerry A. "Tom Wolfe's Defense of the New (Old) Social Novel: Or, the Perils of the Great White-Suited Hunter." *JACult* 14.3 (1991): 35–40.

WONG, SHAWN (1949–)

Homebase (1979)

Wong, Sau-ling Cynthia. *Reading Asian American Literature*, 141–146.

WOOD, JANE ROBERTS (1929–)

Train to Estelline (1987)

Thompson, Joyce. "Seeing Through the Veil: Concepts of Truth in Two West Texas Novels." *JACult* 14.2 (1991): 71–73.

WOOD, JOANNA E. (1867–1927)

Daughter of Witches (1900)

MacMillan, Carrie. *Silenced Sextet*, 190–192.

Farden Ha' (1902)

MacMillan, Carrie. *Silenced Sextet*, 193–196.

Judith Moore (1898)

MacMillan, Carrie. *Silenced Sextet*, 184–189.

Untempered Wind (1894)

MacMillan, Carrie. *Silenced Sextet*, 172–180.

WOOLSEY, SARAH CHAUNCEY see COOLIDGE, SUSAN

WOUK, HERMAN (1915–)

Caine Mutiny (1951)

Mazzeno, Laurence W. *Herman Wouk*, 25–40.
Quinones, Ricardo J. *Changes of Cain*, 146–152.

Inside Outside (1985)

Mazzeno, Laurence W. *Herman Wouk*, 101–104.

Marjorie Morningstar (1955)

Mazzeno, Laurence W. *Herman Wouk*, 52–62.

War and Remembrance (1978)

Mazzeno, Laurence W. *Herman Wouk*, 77–91.

Winds of War (1971)

Mazzeno, Laurence W. *Herman Wouk*, 77–91.

Youngblood Hawke (1962)

Mazzeno, Laurence W. *Herman Wouk*, 66–71.

WRIGHT, RICHARD (1908–1960)

Lawd Today (1963)

Burrison, William. "*Lawd Today:* Wright's Tricky Apprenticeship," in Gates, Henry Louis, Jr., ed. *Richard Wright*, 98–109.
Kostelanetz, Richard. *Politics and the African-American Novel*, 75–78.

Long Dream (1958)

Alsen, Eberhard. " 'Toward the Living Sun': Richard Wright's Change of Heart from *The Outsider* to *The Long Dream.*" *CLAJ* 38.2 (1994): 212–215, 218–221, 221–226.
Bryant, Earle V. "Sexual Initiation and Survival in *The Long Dream*," in Gates, Henry Louis, Jr., ed. *Richard Wright*, 424–431.
Kostelanetz, Richard. *Politics and the African-American Novel*, 101–104.
Margolies, Edward. *Art of Richard Wright*. Carbondale, IL: Southern Illinois University Press, 1969. 129–130. Rpt. in Bloom, Harold, ed. *Major Black American Writers Through the Harlem Renaissance*, 179.
Smith, Valerie. "Alienation and Creativity in the Fiction of Richard Wright," in Gates, Henry Louis, Jr., ed. *Richard Wright*, 435.

Native Son (1940)

Baker, Houston A., Jr. "On Knowing Our Place," in Gates, Henry Louis, Jr., ed. *Richard Wright*, 200–202, 217–223.

Baldwin, James. "Many Thousands Gone." *Notes of a Native Son*. Boston: Beacon Press, 1955. 23–24, 33–35. Rpt. in Bloom, Harold, ed. *Major Black American Writers Through the Harlem Renaissance*, 175–177.

Butler, Robert. "Farrell's Ethnic Neighborhood and Wright's Urban Ghetto: Two Visions of Chicago's South Side." *MELUS* 18.1 (1993): 102–110.

Deena, Seodial. "Irrationality of Bigger Thomas's World: A Frightening View for the Twenty-First Century Urban Population." *CLAJ* 38.1 (1994): 20–30.

Felgar, Robert. "Cultural Work of Time in *Native Son*." *NMW* 24.2 (1992): 99–103.

Foley, Barbara. "Politics of Poetics: Ideology and Narrative Form in *An American Tragedy* and *Native Son*," in Gates, Henry Louis, Jr., ed. *Richard Wright*, 188–199.

Gardner, Laurel J. "Progression of Meaning in the Images of Violence in Richard Wright's *Uncle Tom's Children* and *Native Son*." *CLAJ* 38.4 (1995): 432–440.

Giles, James R. *Naturalistic Inner-City Novel in America*, 71–93.

Griffin, Farah Jasmine. *"Who Set You Flowin'?"*, 123–130.

Hakutani, Yoshinobu. "If the Street Could Talk: James Baldwin's Search for Love and Understanding," Hakutani, Yoshinobu, ed. *City in African-American Literature*, 151–152.

Hapke, Laura. *Daughters of the Great Depression*, 62–64.

Holladay, Hilary. "*Native Son*'s Guilty Man." *CEA* 54.2 (1992): 30–36.

Joyce, Joyce Anne. "Figurative Web of *Native Son*," in Gates, Henry Louis, Jr., ed. *Richard Wright*, 171–187.

Kostelanetz, Richard. *Politics and the African-American Novel*, 78–85.

Kowalewski, Michael. *Deadly Musings*, 40–52.

McCall, Dan. *Example of Richard Wright*. New York: Harcourt, Brace and World, 1969. 64, 66–67. Rpt. in Bloom, Harold, ed. *Major Black American Writers Through the Harlem Renaissance*, 177–179.

Pudaloff, Ross. "Celebrity as Identity: *Native Son* and Mass Culture," in Gates, Henry Louis, Jr., ed. *Richard Wright*, 156–166.

Reilly, John M. "Giving Bigger a Voice: The Politics of Narrative in *Native Son*." *New Essays on Native Son*. Ed. Keneth Kinnamon. New York: Cambridge University Press, 1990. 45–46. Rpt. in Bloom, Harold, ed. *Major Black American Writers Through the Harlem Renaissance*, 184–185.

Scruggs, Charles. *Sweet Home*, 68–99.

Smith, Valerie. "Alienation and Creativity in the Fiction of Richard Wright," in Gates, Henry Louis, Jr., ed. *Richard Wright*, 439–446.

Tanner, Laura E. "Uncovering the Magical Disguise of Language: The Narrative Presence in Richard Wright's *Native Son*," in Gates, Henry Louis, Jr., ed. *Richard Wright*, 132–146.

Outsider (1953)

Alsen, Eberhard. " 'Toward the Living Sun': Richard Wright's Change of Heart from *The Outsider to The Long Dream*." *CLAJ* 38.2 (1994): 212–215, 215–218, 221.

Brignano, Russell Carl. *Richard Wright: An Introduction to the Man and His Works*. Pittsburgh: University of Pittsburgh Press, 1970. 82–83. Rpt. in Bloom,

Harold, ed. *Major Black American Writers Through the Harlem Renaissance*, 180.
Harrison, Elizabeth Jane. *Female Pastoral*, 56, 58–61.
Henderson, Mae. "Drama and Denial in *The Outsider*," in Gates, Henry Louis, Jr., ed. *Richard Wright*, 388–407.
Kostelanetz, Richard. *Politics and the African-American Novel*, 98–101.
Smith, Valerie. "Alienation and Creativity in the Fiction of Richard Wright," in Gates, Henry Louis, Jr., ed. *Richard Wright*, 434–435.
Tate, Claudia. "Christian Existentialism in *The Outsider*," in Gates, Henry Louis, Jr., ed. *Richard Wright*, 369–386.

WRIGHT, STEPHEN (1946–)

Meditations in Green (1984)

Ringnalda, Don. *Fighting and Writing*, 51–70.
Stewart, Matthew. "Stephen Wright's Style in *Meditations in Green*." *Crit* 34.2 (1993): 126–136.

WYLIE, PHILIP (1902–1971)

Disappearance (1951)

Seed, David. "Postwar Jeremiads of Philip Wylie." *SFS* 22.2 (1995): 237–238.

End of the Dream (1972)

Seed, David. "Postwar Jeremiads of Philip Wylie." *SFS* 22.2 (1995): 244–248.

Generation of Vipers (1942)

Seed, David. "Postwar Jeremiads of Philip Wylie." *SFS* 22.2 (1995): 235–236.

Tomorrow (1954)

Seed, David. "Postwar Jeremiads of Philip Wylie." *SFS* 22.2 (1995): 239–241.

Triumph (1963)

Seed, David. "Postwar Jeremiads of Philip Wylie." *SFS* 22.2 (1995): 241–244.

YATES, RICHARD (1926–)

Revolutionary Road (1961)

Castronovo, David. *American Gentleman*, 79–80.

YEP, LAURENCE (1948–)

Dragonwings (1975)

Walter, Virginia A. "Crossing the Pacific to America: The Uses of Narrative." *CLAQ* 16.2 (1991): 63–65.

YEZIERSKA, ANZIA (1885–1970)

Bread Givers (1925)

Ammons, Elizabeth. *Conflicting Stories*, 166–168.
Wilentz, Gay. "Cultural Mediation and Immigrant's Daughter: Anzia Yezierska's *Bread Givers*." *MELUS* 17.3 (1991–92): 33–41.

YOUNG, MARGUERITE (1909–)

Miss Macintosh, My Darling (1965)

Fuchs, Miriam. "Marguerite Young's *Miss Macintosh, My Darling:* Liquescence as Form," in Fuchs, Miriam, ed. *Marguerite Young, Our Darling*, 112–120.

Oboler, Suzanne. "Cultural Reality of the American Dream: Marguerite Young's *Miss Macintosh, My Darling*," in Fuchs, Miriam, ed. *Marguerite Young, Our Darling*, 90–97.

Robinson, Lillian S. "Eugene Debs, My Darling: Narrative and Redemption in the Work of Marguerite Young," in Fuchs, Miriam, ed. *Marguerite Young, Our Darling*, 66–72.

Sattler, Martha J. "Epic of the Nature and Experience of Woman: Marguerite Young's *Miss Macintosh, My Darling*," in Fuchs, Miriam, ed. *Marguerite Young, Our Darling*, 98–102.

Shaik, Fatima. "*Miss Macintosh, My Darling:* Poetry of the Subconscious," in Fuchs, Miriam, ed. *Marguerite Young, Our Darling*, 103–105.

Shaviro, Steven. "Exorbitance and Death: Marguerite Young's Vision," in Fuchs, Miriam, ed. *Marguerite Young, Our Darling*, 122–128.

Strehle, Susan. "Telling Women's Time: *Miss Macintosh, My Darling*," in Fuchs, Miriam, ed. *Marguerite Young, Our Darling*, 106–111.

ZELAZNY, ROGER (1937–1995)

Bridge of Ashes (1976)

Lindskold, Jane M. *Roger Zelazny*, 21–24.

Changeling (1980)

Lindskold, Jane M. *Roger Zelazny*, 53, 108.

Changing Land (1981)

Lindskold, Jane M. *Roger Zelazny*, 121–122, 124.

Courts of Chaos (1978)

Lindskold, Jane M. *Roger Zelazny*, 115.

Creatures of Light and Darkness (1969)

Lindskold, Jane M. *Roger Zelazny*, 53, 81–83, 141–142.

Damnation Alley (1969)

Lindskold, Jane M. *Roger Zelazny*, 94, 111–113.

Dark Traveling (1987)

Lindskold, Jane M. *Roger Zelazny*, 77–78, 118–119.

Deus Irae (1976)

Moddelmog, Debra A. *Readers and Mythic Signs*, 57, 58.

Doorways in the Sand (1976)

Lindskold, Jane M. *Roger Zelazny*, 113–114.

Eye of the Cat (1982)

Lindskold, Jane M. *Roger Zelazny*, 63–64, 83–85, 90–91, 93, 95, 100.

Isle of the Dead (1967)
Lindskold, Jane M. *Roger Zelazny*, 92, 95–100.

Jack of Shadows (1971)
Lindskold, Jane M. *Roger Zelazny*, 109–111.

Lord of Light (1967)
Lindskold, Jane M. *Roger Zelazny*, 27, 94, 107–108, 134–135.

Madwand (1981)
Lindskold, Jane M. *Roger Zelazny*, 108.

Mask of Loki (1990)
Lindskold, Jane M. *Roger Zelazny*, 55, 60.

Nine Princes in Amber (1970)
Lindskold, Jane M. *Roger Zelazny*, 28–29, 80.

Prince of Chaos (1991)
Lindskold, Jane M. *Roger Zelazny*, 117–118.

To Die in Italbar (1973)
Lindskold, Jane M. *Roger Zelazny*, 131, 138.

Trumps of Doom (1985)
Lindskold, Jane M. *Roger Zelazny*, 115–116.

ZUGSMITH, LEANE (1903–1969)

Time to Remember (1936)
Hapke, Laura. *Daughters of the Great Depression*, 131–133.

List of Books Indexed

Abramson, Edward A. *Bernard Malamud Revisited.* New York: Twayne Publishers, 1993.

Ammons, Elizabeth. *Conflicting Stories: American Women Writers at the Turn into the Twentieth Century.* New York: Oxford University Press, 1991.

Andriano, Joseph. *Our Lady of Darkness: Feminine Daemonology in Male Gothic Fiction.* University Park, PA: Pennsylvania State University Press, 1993.

Apseloff, Marilyn Fain. *Elizabeth George Speare.* New York: Twayne Publishers, 1991.

Atwood, Margaret. *Strange Things: The Malevolent North in Canadian Literature.* New York: Oxford University Press, 1995.

Babb, Valerie Melissa. *Ernest Gaines.* Boston: Twayne, 1991.

Barbour, Douglas. *Michael Ondaatje.* New York: Twayne Publishers, 1993.

Bauer, Dale M. *Edith Wharton's Brave New Politics.* Madison, WI: University of Wisconsin Press, 1994.

Bell, Ian F. A. *Henry James and the Past: Readings into Time.* New York: St. Martin's Press, 1991.

Bell, Millicent, ed. *Cambridge Companion to Edith Wharton.* New York: Cambridge University Press, 1995.

Bell, Millicent. *Meaning in Henry James.* Cambridge: Harvard University Press, 1991.

Bendixen, Alfred and Annette Zilversmit, eds. *Edith Wharton: New Critical Essays.* New York: Garland Publishing, Inc., 1992.

Benjamin, Marina, ed. *Question of Identity: Women, Science and Literature.* New Brunswick, NJ: Rutgers University Press, 1993.

Beran, Carol. *Living Over the Abyss: Margaret Atwood's Life Before Man.* Toronto: ECW Press, 1993.

Bercovitch, Sacvan. *Office of the Scarlet Letter.* Baltimore, MD: Johns Hopkins University Press, 1991.

Bergman, David. *Gaiety Transfigured: Gay Self-Representation in American Literature.* Madison, WI: University of Minnesota Press, 1991.

Berman, Ronald. *Great Gatsby and Modern Times.* Chicago: University of Illinois Press, 1994.

Blair, Walter. *Essays on American Humor: Blair Through the Ages.* Selected and edited by Hamlin Hill. Madison, WI: University of Wisconsin Press, 1993.

Blanchard, Paula. *Sarah Orne Jewett: Her World and Her Work.* Reading, MA: Addison -Wesley Publishing Company, 1994.

Bloom, Harold, ed. *Black American Women Fiction Writers.* New York: Chelsea House Publishers, 1995.
Bloom, Harold, ed. *Brett Ashley.* New York: Chelsea House Publishers, 1991.
Bloom, Harold, ed. *Contemporary Black American Fiction Writers.* New York: Chelsea House Publishers, 1995.
Bloom, Harold, ed. *Gatsby.* New York: Chelsea House Publishers, 1991.
Bloom, Harold, ed. *Major Black American Writers Through the Harlem Renaissance.* New York: Chelsea House Publishers, 1995.
Bloom, Harold, ed. *Major Modern Black American Writers.* New York: Chelsea House Publishers, 1995.
Bloom, Harold, ed. *Modern Black American Fiction Writers.* New York: Chelsea House Publishers, 1995.
Blum, Virginia L. *Hide and Seek: The Child Between Psychoanalysis and Fiction.* Chicago: University of Chicago Press, 1995.
Booker, M. Keith. *Dystopian Impulse in Modern Literature: Fiction as Social Criticism.* Westport, CT: Greenwood Press, 1994.
Bouson, J. Brooks. *Brutal Choreographies: Oppositional Strategies and Narrative Design in the Novels of Margaret Atwood.* Amherst, MA: University of Massachusetts, 1993.
Brodhead, Richard H. *Cultures of Letters: Scenes of Reading and Writing in Nineteenth-Century America.* Chicago: University of Chicago Press, 1993.
Bromell, Nicholas K. *By the Sweat of the Brow: Literature and Labor in Antebellum America.* Chicago: University of Chicago Press, 1993.
Brown, Anne E. and Marjanne E. Goozé, eds. *International Women's Writing: New Landscapes of Identity.* Westport, CT: Greenwood Press, 1995.
Brown, Robert McAfee. *Persuade Us To Rejoice: The Liberating Power of Fiction.* Louisville, KY: Westminster/John Know Press, 1992.
Budick, Emily Miller. *Engendering Romance: Women Writers and the Hawthorne Tradition, 1850–1990.* New Haven, CT: Yale University Press, 1994.
Buitenhuis, Peter. *House of the Seven Gables: Severing Family and Colonial Ties.* Boston: Twayne Publishers, 1991.
Burke, Ruth E. *Games of Poetics: Ludic Criticism and Postmodern Fiction.* New York: Peter Lang, 1994.
Busby, Mark. *Ralph Ellison.* Boston: Twayne Publishers, 1991.
Byatt, A. S. *Passions of the Mind: Selected Essays.* New York: Turtle Bay Books, 1992.
Calderón, Héctor and José David Saldívar, eds. *Criticism in the Borderlands: Studies in Chicano Literature, Culture, and Ideology.* Durham, IL: Duke University Press, 1991.
Cameron, Elspeth, ed. *Robertson Davies: An Appreciation.* Peterborough, ON: Broadview Press, 1991.
Carlisle, Janice and Daniel r. Schwarz, eds. *Narrative and Culture.* Athens, GA: University of Georgia Press, 1994.
Carpenter, Lynette and Wendy K. Kolmar, eds. *Haunting the House of Fiction: Feminist Perspectives on Ghost Stories by American Women.* Knoxville, TN: University of Tennessee Press, 1991.
Castronovo, David. *American Gentleman: Social Prestige and the Modern Literary Mind.* New York: Continuum Publishing Company, 1991.
Chambers, Judith. *Thomas Pynchon.* New York: Twayne Publishers, 1992.

Chandler, Marilyn R. *Dwelling in the Text: Houses in American Fiction.* Berkeley, CA: University of California Press, 1991.
Christophersen, Bill. *Apparition in the Glass: Charles Brockden Brown's American Gothic.* Athens, GA: University of Georgia Press, 1993.
Ciuba, Gary M. *Walker Percy: Books of Revelation.* Athens, GA: University of Georgia Press, 1991.
Clark, Suzanne. *Sentimental Modernism: Women Writers and the Revolution of the Word.* Bloomington, IN: Indiana University Press, 1991.
Clark, VéVé A., Ruth-Ellen B. Joeres and Madelon Sprengnether, eds. *Revising the Word and the World: Essays in Feminist Literary Criticism.* Chicago: University of Chicago Press, 1993.
Clark, William Bedford. *American Vision of Robert Penn Warren.* Lexington, KY: University Press of Kentucky, 1991.
Coale, Samuel. *William Styron Revisited.* Boston: Twayne Publishers, 1991.
Coers, Donald V., Paul D. Ruffin, Robert J. DeMott, eds. *After The Grapes of Wrath: Essays on John Steinbeck In Honor of Tetsumaro Hayashi.* Athens, OH: Ohio University Press, 1995.
Coleman, Patrick. *Limits of Sympathy: Gabrielle Roy's The Tin Flute.* Toronto: ECW Press, 1993.
Cologne-Brookes, Gavin. *Novels of William Styron: From Harmony to History.* Baton Rouge: Louisiana State University Press, 1995.
Comley, Nancy R. and Robert Scholes. *Hemingway's Genders: Rereading the Hemingway Text.* New Haven, CT: Yale University Press, 1994.
Coser, Stellamaris. *Bridging the Americas: The Literature of Paule Marshall, Toni Morrison, and Gayl Jones.* Philadelphia: Temple University Press, 1994.
Costa, Richard Hauer. *Alison Lurie.* New York: Twayne Publishers, 1992.
Cowan, Bainard and Joseph G. Kronick, eds. *Theorizing American Literature: Hegel, the Sign, and History.* Baton Rouge: Louisiana State University Press, 1991.
Cowart, David. *Literary Symbiosis: The Reconfigured Text in Twentieth-Century Writing.* Athens, GA: University of Georgia Press, 1993.
Creighton, Joanne V. *Joyce Carol Oates: Novels of the Middle Years.* New York: Twayne Publishers, 1992.
Cudjoe, Selwyn R. and William E. Cain, eds. *C.L.R. James: His Intellectual Legacies.* Amherst, MA: University of Massachusetts Press, 1995.
Cummings, Katherine. *Telling Tales: The Hysteric's Seduction in Fiction and Theory.* Stanford, CA: Stanford University Press, 1991.
Dahlie, Hallvard. *Isolation and Commitment: Frederick Philip Grove's Settlers of the Marsh.* Toronto: ECW Press, 1993.
Daly, Brenda O. and Maureen T. Reddy, eds. *Narrating Mothers: Theorizing Maternal Subjectivities.* Knoxville, TN: University of Tennessee Press, 1991.
David, Gilbert and Pierre Lavoie, eds. *Monde de Michel Tremblay: Des Belles-Soeurs à Marcel poursuivi par les chiens.* Montréal: Cahiers de Théâtre Jeu/Éditions Lansman, 1993.
Davidson, Arnold. *Writing Against the Silence: Joy Kogawa's Obasan.* Toronto: ECW Press, 1993.
Davidson, Arnold E. *Coyote Country: Fictions of the Canadian West.* Durham, NC: Duke University Press, 1994.
Davis, Colin. *Elie Wiesel's Secretive Texts.* Gainesville, FL: University of Florida Press, 1994.

Davis, Lloyd, ed. *Virginal Sexuality and Textuality in Victorian Literature*. Albany, NY: State University of New York Press, 1993.

Davis, Robert Murray. *Playing Cowboys: Low Culture and High Art in the Western*. Norman, OK: University of Oklahoma Press, 1991.

Dean, Misao. *Different Point of View: Sara Jeanette Duncan*. Montreal: McGill-Queen's University Press, 1991.

Deer, Glenn. *Postmodern Canadian Fiction and the Rhetoric of Authority*. Montreal: McGill-Queen's University Press, 1994.

DeKoven, Marianne. *Rich and Strange: Gender, History, Modernism*. Princeton, NJ: Princeton University Press, 1991.

Demers, Patricia. *Seasonal Romance: Louis Hemon's Maria Chapdelaine*. Toronto: ECW Press, 1993.

Denniston, Dorothy Hamer. *Fiction of Paule Marshall*. Knoxville, TN: University of Tennessee Press, 1995.

Derwin, Susan. *Ambivalence of Form: Lukács, Freud, and the Novel*. Baltimore: Johns Hopkins University Press, 1992.

D'haen, Theo and Hans Bertens, eds. *Postmodern Fiction in Canada*. Amsterdam: Rodopi, 1992.

Donovan, Josephine. *Uncle Tom's Cabin: Evil, Affliction, and Redemptive Love*. Boston: Twayne Publishers, 1991.

Doty, William G., ed. *Picturing Cultural Values in Postmodern America*. Tuscaloosa, AL: University of Alabama Press, 1995.

Dougherty, David. C. *Stanley Elkin*. Boston: Twayne Publishers, 1991.

Dowie, William. *Peter Matthiessen*. Boston: Twayne Publishers, 1991.

Doyle, Laura. *Bordering on the Body: The Racial Matrix of Modern Fiction and Culture*. New York: Oxford University Press, 1994.

Dubey, Madhu. *Black Women Novelists and the Nationalist Aesthetic*. Indianapolis: Indiana University Press, 1994.

Duchet, Claude and Stéphane Vachon, eds. *Recherche littéraire: Objets et méthodes*. Montréal: XYZ, 1993.

Dufault, Roseanna Lewis. *Metaphors of Identity: The Treatment of Childhood in Selected Québécois Novels*. Rutherford, WI: Fairleigh Dickinson University Press, 1991.

Duffy, Dennis. *Tale of Sad Reality: John Richardson's Wacousta*. Toronto: ECW Press, 1993.

Dyer, Joyce. *The Awakening: A Novel of Beginnings*. New York: Twayne Publishers, 1993.

Epperly, Elizabeth Rollins. *Fragrance of Sweet Grass: L.M. Montgomery's Heroines and the Pursuit of Romance*. Toronto: University of Toronto Press, 1992.

Estes, David C., ed. *Critical Reflections on the Fictions of Ernest J. Gaines*. Athens, GA: University of Georgia Press, 1994.

Evans, Elizabeth. *Anne Tyler*. New York: Twayne Publishers, 1993.

Fedorko, Kathy A. *Gender and the Gothic in the Fiction of Edith Wharton*. Tuscaloosa, AL: University of Alabama Press, 1995.

Fee, Margery. *Fat Lady Dances: Margaret Atwood's Lady Oracle*. Toronto: ECW Press, 1993.

Fee, Margery, ed. *Silence Made Visible: Howard O'Hagan and Tay John*. Toronto: ECW Press, 1992.

Fiedler, Leslie. *Fiedler on the Roof: Essays on Literature and Jewish Identity*. Boston: David R. Godine, Publisher, Inc., 1991.

Fleck, Richard F., ed. *Critical Perspectives on Native American Fiction*. Washington, D.C.: Three Continents Press, 1993.

Folks, Jeffrey J. *Southern Writers and the Machine: Faulkner to Percy*. New York: Peter Lang, 1993.

Forrest, Leon. *Relocations of the Spirit*. Wakefield, RI: Asphodel Press, 1994.

Foster, Frances Smith. *Written By Herself: Literary Production by African-American Women, 1746–1892*. Indianapolis: Indiana University Press, 1993.

Foster, Shirley and Judy Simons. *What Katy Read: Feminist Re-Readings of 'Classic' Stories for Girls*. Iowa City: University of Iowa Press, 1995.

Fowler, Doreen and Ann J. Abadie, eds. *Faulkner and Religion: Faulkner and Yoknapatawpha, 1989*. Jackson, MS: University Press of Mississippi, 1991.

Freeman, Barbara Claire. *Feminine Sublime: Gender and Excess in Women's Fiction*. Berkeley: University of California Press, 1995.

French, Warren. *John Steinbeck's Fiction Revisited*. New York: Twayne Publishers, 1994.

Friedman, Lawrence S. *Understanding Cynthia Ozick*. Columbia, SC: University of South Carolina Press, 1991.

Friedman, Melvin J. and Ben Siegel, eds. *Traditions, Voices, and Dreams: The American Novel since the 1960's*. Newark, DE: University of Delaware Press, 1995.

Fuchs, Miriam, ed. *Marguerite Young, Our Darling: Tribute and Essays*. Normal, IL: Dalkey Archive Press, 1994.

Gates, Henry Louis, Jr. and K. A. Appiah, eds. *Richard Wright: Critical Perspectives Past and Present*. New York: Amistad Press, 1993.

Gates, Henry Louis, Jr. and K. A. Appiah, eds. *Toni Morrison: Critical Perspectives Past and Present*. New York, Amistad Press, 1993.

Gates, Henry Louis, Jr. and K. A. Appiah, eds. *Zora Neale Hurston: Critical Perspectives Past and Present*. New York: Amistad Press, 1993.

Gerber, Philip. *Theodore Dreiser Revisited*. New York: Twayne Publishers, 1992.

Gerber, Philip. *Willa Cather*. Revised Edition. New York: Twayne Publishers, 1995.

Giles, James R. *Naturalistic Inner-City Novel in America: Encounters With the Fat Man*. Columbia, SC: University of South Carolina, 1995.

Glassman, Steve and Kathryn Lee Seidel, eds. *Zora in Florida*. Orlando, FL: University of Central Florida Press, 1991.

Glenday, Michael K. *Norman Mailer*. New York: St. Martin's Press, 1995.

Gogol, Miriam, ed. *Theodore Dreiser: Beyond Naturalism*. New York: New York University Press, 1995.

Goldsmith, Arnold L. *Modern American Urban Novel: Nature as "Interior Structure"*. Detroit, MI: Wayne State University Press, 1991.

Goodenough, Elizabeth, Mark A. Heberle and Naomi Sokoloff, eds. *Infant Tongues: The Voice of the Child in Literature*. Detroit: Wayne State University Press, 1994.

Goodwin, Sarah Webster and Elisabeth Bronfen, eds. *Death and Representation*. Baltimore, MD: Johns Hopkins University Press, 1993.

Gordon, Mary. *Good Boys and Dead Girls and Other Essays*. New York: Viking, 1991.

Goshgarian, G. M. *To Kiss the Chastening Rod: Domestic Fiction and Sexual Ideology in the American Renaissance*. Ithaca, NY: Cornell University Press, 1992.

Granofsky, Ronald. *Trauma Novel: Contemporary Symbolic Depictions of Collective Disaster*. New York: Peter Lang, 1995.

Green, Mary Jean. *Marie-Claire Blais*. New York: Twayne Publishers, 1995.

Greene, Gayle. *Changing the Story: Feminist Fiction and the Tradition*. Indianapolis: Indiana University Press, 1991.

Grenier, Donald J. *Women Enter the Wilderness: Male Bonding and the American Novel of the 1980s*. Columbia, SC: University of South Carolina Press, 1991.

Gretlund, Jan Nordby and Karl-Heinz Westarp, eds. *Walker Percy: Novelist and Philosopher*. Jackson, MS: University Press of Mississippi, 1991.

Griffin, Farah Jasmine. *"Who Set You Flowin'?": The African-American Migration Narrative*. New York: Oxford University Press, 1995.

Griswold, Jerry. *Audacious Kids: Coming of Age in America's Classic Children's Books*. New York: Oxford University Press, 1992.

Hakutani, Yoshinobu and Robert Butler, eds. *City in African-American Literature*. Madison, WI: Fairleigh Dickinson University Press, 1995.

Halio, Jay L. *Philip Roth Revisited*. New York: Twayne Publishers, 1992.

Hanks, Dorrel Thomas, Jr. *E. L. Konigsburg*. New York: Twayne Publishers, 1992.

Hanson, Elizabeth I. *Margaret Mitchell*. Boston: Twayne Publishers, 1991.

Hapke, Laura. *Daughters of the Great Depression: Women, Work, and Fiction in the American 1930's*. Athens, GA: University of Georgia Press, 1995.

Hapke, Laura. *Tales of the Working Girl: Wage-Earning Women in American Literature, 1890–1925*. New York: Twayne Publishers, 1992.

Harper, Phillip Brian. *Framing the Margins: The Social Logic of Postmodern Culture*. New York: Oxford University Press, 1994.

Harris, Sharon M., ed. *Redefining the Political Novel: American Women Writers, 1797–1901*. Knoxville, TN: University of Tennessee Press, 1995.

Harrison, Dick. *Intimations of Mortality: W. O. Mitchell's Who Has Seen the Wind*. Toronto: ECW Press, 1993.

Harrison, Elizabeth Jane. *Female Pastoral: Women Writers Re-visioning the American South*. Knoxville, TN: University of Tennessee Press, 1991.

Hauerwas, Stanley. *Dispatches from the Front: Theological Engagements with the Secular*. Durham, NC: Duke University Press, 1994.

Haut, Woody. *Pulp Culture: Hardboiled Fiction and the Cold War*. New York: Serpent's Tail, 1995.

Hayashi, Tetsumaro, ed. *John Steinbeck: The Years of Greatness, 1936–1939*. Tuscaloosa, AL: University of Alabama Press, 1993.

Hayashi, Tetsumaro, ed. *New Study Guide to Steinbeck's Major Works, With Critical Explications*. Metuchen, NJ: Scarecrow Press, 1993.

Hayashi, Tesumaro, ed. *Steinbeck's Literary Dimension: A Guide to Comparative Studies, Series II*. Metchuen, NJ: Scarecrow Press, 1991.

Hayles, N. Katherine, ed. *Chaos and Order: Complex Dynamics in Literature and Science*. Chicago: University of Chicago Press, 1991.

Heilman, Robert Bechtold. *Workings of Fiction*. Columbia, MO: University of Missouri Press, 1991.

Hernández, Guillermo E. *Chicano Satire: A Study in Literary Culture*. Austin, TX: University of Texas Press, 1991.

Herreshoff, David Sprague. *Labor Into Art: The Theme of Work in Nineteenth-Century American Literature*. Detroit, MI: Wayne State University Press, 1991.

Hesse, M.G. *Yves Thériault, Master Storyteller*. New York: Peter Lang, 1993.

Heyne, Eric, ed. *Desert, Garden, Margin, Range: Literature on the American Frontier*. New York: Twayne Publishers, 1992.

Higonnet, Margaret R. and Joan Templeton, eds. *Reconfigured Spheres: Feminist Explorations of Literary Space*. Amherst, MA: University of Massachusetts Press, 1994.

Hill, Dorothy. *Lee Smith*. New York: Twayne Publishers, 1992.

Hill, Jane. *Gail Godwin.* New York: Twayne Publishers, 1992.
Hlavsa, Virginia V. James. *Faulkner and the Thoroughly Modern Novel.* Charlottesville, VA: University Press of Virginia, 1991.
Hollahan, Eugene. *Crisis-Consciousness and the Novel.* Newark, DE: University of Delaware Press, 1992.
Hook, Andrew. *F. Scott Fitzgerald.* New York: Edward Arnold, 1992.
Howard, Lillie P., ed. *Alice Walker and Zora Neale Hurston: The Common Bond.* Westport, CT: Greenwood Press, 1993.
Howe, Florence, ed. *Tradition and the Talents of Women.* Urbana, IL: University of Illinois Press, 1991.
Howells, Coral Ann. *Margaret Atwood.* New York: St. Martins Press, 1995.
Howells, Coral Ann and Lynette Hunter, eds. *Narrative Strategies in Canadian Literature: Feminism and Postcolonialism.* Philadelphia: Open University Press, 1991.
Hurley, Michael. *Borders of Nightmare: The Fiction of John Richardson.* Toronto: University of Toronto Press, 1992.
Hussey, Mark, ed. *Virginia Woolf and War: Fiction, Reality, and Myth.* Syracuse, NY: Syracuse University Press, 1991.
Hutcheon, Linda, ed. *Double Talking: Essays on Verbal and Visual Ironies in Canadian Contemporary Art and Literature.* Toronto: ECW Press, 1992.
Irvine, Lorna. *Collecting Clues: Margaret Atwood's Bodily Harm.* Toronto: ECW Press, 1993.
Jacobson, Marcia. *Being a Boy Again: Autobiography and the American Boy Book.* Tuscaloosa, AL: University of Alabama Press, 1994.
James, Henry. *Portrait of a Lady: an Authoritative Text, Reviews and Criticism.* Ed. Robert D. Bamberg. 2nd ed. New York: W.W. Norton, 1995.
Jennings, La Vinia Delois. *Alice Childress.* New York: Twayne Publishers, 1995.
Johnson, Claudia Durst. *To Kill a Mockingbird: Threatening Boundaries.* New York: Twayne Publishers, 1994.
Johnson, Claudia Durst. *Understanding the Scarlet Letter: A Student Casebook to Issues, Sources, and Historical Documents.* Westport, CT: Greenwood Press, 1995.
Johnson, Claudia Durst. *Understanding To Kill a Mockingbird: A Student Casebook to Issues, Sources, and Historic Documents.* Westport, CT: Greenwood Press, 1994.
Jones, E. Michael. *Angel and the Machine: The Rational Psychology of Nathaniel Hawthorne.* Peru, IL: Sherwood Sugden and Company Publishers, 1991.
Joslin, Katherine. *Edith Wharton.* New York: St. Martin's Press, 1991.
Kadar, Marlene, ed. *Essays on Life Writing: From Genre to Critical Practice.* Toronto: University of Toronto Press, 1992.
Karolides, Nicholas J., Less Burress and John M. Kean, eds. *Censored Books: Criticial Viewpoints.* Metuchen, NJ: Scarecrow Press, Inc., 1993.
Karpinski, Joanne B., ed. *Critical Essays on Charlotte Perkins Gilman.* New York: G. K. Hall & Co., 1992.
Kartiganer, Donald M. and Ann J. Abadie, eds. *Faulkner and Ideology: Faulkner and Yoknapatawpha, 1992.* Jackson, MS: University of Mississippi Press, 1995.
Kartiganer, Donald M. and Ann J. Abadie, eds. *Faulkner and Psychology: Faulkner and Yoknapatawpha.* Jackson, MS: University of Mississippi Press, 1994.
Kaufmann, Michael. *Textual Bodies: Modernism, Postmodernism, and Print.* Lewisburg, PA : Bucknell University Press, 1994
Keesey, Douglas. *Don DeLillo.* New York: Twayne Publishers, 1993.
Keith, W. J. *Life Struggle: Hugh Maclennan's The Watch That Ends the Night.* Toronto: ECW Press, 1993.

Kennedy, Liam. *Susan Sontag: Mind as Passion*. New York: Manchester University Press, 1995.

Kester, Gunilla Theander. *Writing the Subject: Bildung and the African-American Text*. New York: Peter Lang, 1995.

Keyser, Elizabeth Lennox. *Whispers in the Dark: The Fiction of Louisa May Alcott*. Knoxville, TN: University of Tennessee Press, 1993.

Kincaid, James R. *Child-Loving: The Erotic Child and Victorian Culture*. New York: Routledge, 1992.

Knoper, Randall. *Acting Naturally: Mark Twain and the Culture of Performance*. Berkeley, CA: University of California Press, 1995.

Koponen, Wilfrid R. *Embracing Gay Identity: Gay Novels as Guides*. Wesport, CT: Bergin and Garvey, 1993.

Kostelanetz, Richard. *Politics and the African-American Novel: James Weldon Johnson, W.E.B. Du Bois, Richard Wright, and Ralph Ellison*. New York: Greenwood Press, 1991.

Kowalewski, Michael. *Deadly Musings: Violence and Verbal Form in American Fiction*. Princeton, NJ: Princeton University Press, 1993.

Kubitschek, Missy Dehn. *Claiming the Heritage: African-American Women Novelists and History*. Jackson, MS: University Press of Mississippi, 1991.

Kuester, Martin. *Framing Truths: Parodic Structures in Contemporary English-Canadian Historical Novels*. Toronto: University of Toronto Press, 1992.

Kuznets, Lois Rostow. *When Toys Come Alive: Narratives of Animation, Metamorphosis, and Development*. New Haven, CT: Yale University Press, 1994.

Langer, Lawrence L. *Admitting the Holocaust: Collected Essays*. New York: Oxford University Press, 1995.

Lanier, Parks, Jr, ed. *Poetics of Appalachian Space*. Knoxville, TN: University of Tennessee Press, 1991.

Lashgari, Deidre, ed. *Violence, Silence, and Anger: Women's Writing as Transgression*. Charlottesville, VA: University Press of Virginia, 1995.

Lecker, Robert, Jack David and Ellen Quigley, eds. *Canadian Writers and Their Works: Fiction Series*. Vol. 4. Toronto: ECW Press, 1991.

Lecker, Robert, Jack David and Ellen Quigley, eds. *Canadian Writers and Their Works: Fiction Series*. Vol. 12. Toronto: ECW Press, 1995.

Leithauser, Brad. *Penchants and Places: Essays and Criticism*. New York: Alfred A. Knopf, 1995.

Lentricchia, Frank, ed. *Introducing Don DeLillo*. Durham, NC: Duke University Press, 1991.

Lentricchia, Frank, ed. *New Essays on White Noise*. New York: Cambridge University Press, 1991.

Leonard, James S., Thomas A. Tenney and Thadious M. Davis, eds. *Satire or Evasion?: Black Perspectives on Huckleberry Finn*. Durham, NC: Duke University Press, 1992.

Levenson, Michael. *Modernism and the Fate of Individuality: Character and Novelistic Form from Conrad to Woolf*. New York: Cambridge University Press, 1991.

Levin, David. *Forms of Uncertainty: Essays in Historical Criticism*. Charlottesville, VA: University Press of Virginia, 1992.

Levy, Helen Fiddyment. *Fiction of the Home Place: Jewett, Cather, Glasgow, Porter, Welty, and Naylor*. Jackson, MS: University Press of Mississippi, 1992.

Lim, Shirley Geok-lin and Amy Ling, eds. *Reading the Literatures of Asian America*. Philadelphia: Temple University Press, 1992.

Limon, John. *Writing After War: American War Fiction from Realism to Postmodernism.* New York: Oxford University Press, 1994.
Lindskold, Jane M. *Roger Zelazny.* New York: Twayne Publishers, 1993.
Lofaro, Michael A., ed. *James Agee: Reconsiderations.* Knoxville, TN: University of Tennessee Press, 1992.
Lohmann, Christoph K., ed.. *Discovering Difference: Contemporary Essays in American Culture.* Indianapolis: Indiana University Press, 1993.
Lowance, Mason I., Jr., Ellen E. Westbrook and R. C. De Prospo, eds. *Stowe Debate: Rhetorical Strategies in Uncle Tom's Cabin.* Amherst, MA: University of Massachusetts Press, 1994.
Lowe, James. *Creative Process of James Agee.* Baton Rouge: Louisiana State University Press, 1994.
Lowe, John. *Jump at the Sun: Zora Neale Hurston's Cosmic Comedy.* Chicago: University of Illinois Press, 1994.
Lustig, T. J. *Henry James and the Ghostly.* New York: Cambridge University Press, 1994.
McAlexander, Hubert H., ed. *Critical Essays on Peter Taylor.* New York: G.K. Hall, 1993.
MacCannell, Juliet Flower and Laura Zakarin, eds. *Textual Bodies.* Stanford, CA: Stanford University Press, 1994.
McDowell, Deborah E. *"The Changing Same": Black Women's Literature, Criticism, and Theory.* Bloomington, IN: Indiana University Press, 1995.
McElrath, Joseph R., Jr. *Frank Norris Revisited.* New York: Twayne Publishers, 1992.
McKeen, William. *Tom Wolfe.* New York: Twayne Publishers, 1995.
McLendon, Jacquelyn. *Politics of Color in the Fiction of Jessie Fauset and Nella Larsen.* Charlottesville, VA: University Press of Virginia, 1995.
MacLeod, Anne Scott. *American Childhood: Essays on Children's Literature of the Nineteenth and Twentieth Centuries.* Athens, GA: University of Georgia Press, 1994.
MacMillan, Carrie, Lorraine McMullen and Elizabeth Waterston. *Silenced Sextet: Six Nineteenth-Century Canadian Women Novelists.* Montreal: McGill-Queen's University Press, 1992.
McPherson, Karen S. *Incriminations: Guilty Women / Telling Stories.* Princeton, NJ: Princeton University Press, 1994.
Madden, David and Peggy Bach, eds. *Classics of Civil War Fiction.* Jackson, MS: University Press of Mississippi, 1991.
Maddox, Lucy. *Removals: Nineteenth-Century American Literature and the Politics of Indian Affairs.* New York: Oxford University Press, 1991.
Magistrale, Tony, ed. *Dark Descent: Essays Defining Stephen King's Horrorscope.* Westport, CT: Greenwood Press, 1992.
Magistrale, Tony. *Stephen King: The Second Decade, Danse Macabre to The Dark Half.* New York: Twayne Publishers, 1992.
Mandia, Patricia M. *Comedic Pathos: Black Humor in Twain's Fiction.* Jefferson, NC: McFarland and Company, Inc., 1991.
Marcato-Falzoni, Franca, ed. *Mythes et mythologies des origines dans la littérature québécoise.* Bologna: Cooperativa Libraria Universitaria Editrice Bologna, 1994.
Marchalonis, Shirley, ed. *Critical Essays on Mary Wilkins Freeman.* Boston: G.K. Hall, 1991.
Massé, Michelle A. *In the Name of Love: Women, Masochism, and the Gothic.* Ithaca, NY: Cornell University Press, 1992.

Mazzeno, Laurence W. *Herman Wouk*. New York: Twayne Publishers, 1994.
Meanor, Patrick. *John Cheever Revisited.* New York: Twayne Publishers, 1995.
Messent, Peter. *Ernest Hemingway*. New York: St. Martins Press, 1992.
Mishra, Vijay. *Gothic Sublime*. Albany, NY: State University of New York Press, 1994.
Moddelmog, Debra A. *Readers and Mythic Signs: The Oedipus Myth in Twentieth Century Fiction*. Carbondale, IL: Southern Illinois University Press, 1993.
Mogen, David, Scott P. Sanders and Joanne B. Karpinski, eds. *Frontier Gothic: Terror and Wonder at the Frontier in American Literature*. Madison, WI: Fairleigh Dickinson University Press, 1993.
Monk, Patricia. *Gilded Beaver: An Introduction to the Life and Work of James De Mille.* Toronto: ECW Press, 1991.
Monk, Patricia. *Mud and Magic Shows: Robertson Davies's Fifth Business.* Toronto: ECW Press, 1992.
Morgan, Thaïs E., ed. *Men Writing the Feminine: Literature, Theory, and the Question of Genders*. Albany, NY: State University of New York Press, 1994.
Morley, Patricia. *Margaret Laurence: The Long Journey Home.* Revised Edition. Montreal: McGill-Queen's University Press, 1991.
Morse, Donald E., Marshall B. Tymn and Csilla Bertha, eds. *Celebration of the Fantastic: Selected Papers from the. Tenth Anniversary International Conference on the Fantastic in the Arts.* Westport, CT: Greenwood Press, 1992.
Murfin, Ross C., ed. *Scarlet Letter: Complete, Authoritative Text with Biographical Background and Critical History plus Essays from Five Contemporary Critical Perspectives with Introductions and Bibliographies.* Boston: Bedford Books, 1991.
Nasta, Susheila, ed. *Motherlands: Black Women's Writing from Africa, the Caribbean and South Asia*. New Brunswick, NJ: Rutgers University Press, 1992.
Nicholson, Colin, ed. *Margaret Atwood: Writing and Subjectivity*. New York: St. Martin's Press, 1994.
Noe, Marcia, ed. *Exploring the Midwestern Literary Imagination: Essays in Honor of David D. Anderson.* Troy, NY: Whitston Publishing Company, 1993.
O'Donnell, Patrick, ed. *New Essays on The Crying of Lot 49*. New York: Cambridge University Press, 1991.
O'Donoghue, Jo. *Brian Moore: A Critical Study.* Montreal: McGill-Queen's University Press, 1991.
Olsen, Lance. *Lolita: A Janus Text*. New York: Twayne Publishers, 1995.
Olson, Lance. *William Gibson*. San Bernardino, CA: Borgo Press, 1992.
Olson, Marilynn Strasser. *Ellen Raskin*. Boston: Twayne Publishers, 1991.
Orange, John. *Orpheus in Winter: Morley Callaghan's The Loved and the Lost*. Toronto: ECW Press, 1993.
O'Rourke, William. *Signs of the Literary Times: Essays, Reviews, Profiles 1970–1992.* Albany, NY: State University of New York, 1993.
Orvell, Miles. *Flannery O'Connor: An Introduction*. Jackson, MS: University Press of Mississippi, 1991.
Owens, Louis. *Other Destinies: Understanding the American Indian Novel*. Norman, OK: University of Oklahoma Press, 1992.
Parks, John G. *E. L. Doctorow*. New York: Continuum Publishing Company, 1991.
Paterson, Janet M. *Postmodernism and the Quebec Novel*. Trans. David Homel and Charles Phillips. Toronto: University of Toronto Press, 1994.
Peach, Linden. *Toni Morrison*. New York: St. Martins Press, 1995.

Pearlman, Mickey, ed. *Canadian Women Writing Fiction.* Jackson, MS: University Press of Mississippi, 1993.

Pearlman, Mickey and Abby H. P. Werlock. *Tillie Olsen.* Boston: Twayne Publishers, 1991.

Pease, Donald, ed. *New Essays on The Rise of Silas Lapham.* New York: Cambridge University Press, 1991.

Peck, Daniel, ed. *New Essays on The Last of the Mohicans.* New York: Cambridge University Press, 1992.

Pendleton, Thomas A. *I'm Sorry About the Clock: Chronology, Composition and Narrative Technique in The Great Gatsby.* Selinsgrove, PA: Susquehanna University Press, 1993.

Penee, Donna. *Praying for Rain: Timothy Findley's Not Wanted on the Voyage.* Toronto: ECW Press, 1993.

Pettis, Joyce. *Toward Wholeness in Paule Marshall's Fiction.* Charlottesville, VA: University Press of Virginia, 1995.

Pfister, Joel. *Production of the Personal Life: Class, Gender, and the Psychological in Hawthorne's Fiction.* Stanford, CA: Stanford University Press, 1991.

Phillips, Robert L., Jr. *Shelby Foote: Novelist and Historian.* Jackson, MS: University Press of Mississippi, 1992.

Pickens, Ernestine Williams. *Charles W. Chesnutt and the Progressive Movement.* New York: Pace University Press, 1994.

Pinsker, Sanford. *Catcher in the Rye: Innocence Under Pressure.* New York: Twayne Publishers, 1993.

Pizer, Donald, ed. *New Essays on Sister Carrie.* New York: Cambridge University Press, 1991.

Pizer, Donald. *Theory and Practice of American Literary Naturalism: Selected Essays and Reviews.* Carbondale, IL: Southern Illinois University Press, 1993.

Plant, Deborah G. *Every Tub Must Sit on Its Own Bottom: The Philosophy and Politics of Zora Neale Hurston.* Chicago: University of Illinois Press, 1995.

Quinones, Ricardo J. *Changes of Cain: Violence and the Lost Brother in Cain and Abel Literature.* Princeton, NJ: Princeton University Press, 1991.

Quirk, Tom. *Coming to Grips with Huckleberry Finn: Essays on a Book, a Boy, and a Man.* Columbia, MO: University of Missouri Press, 1993.

Railton, Stephen. *Authorship and Audience: Literary Performance in the American Renaissance.* Princeton, NJ: Princeton University Press, 1991.

Rampton, David. *Vladimir Nabokov.* New York: St. Martins Press, 1993.

Rao, Eleonora. *Strategies for Identity: The Fiction of Margaret Atwood.* New York: Peter Lang, 1993.

Raoul, Valerie. *Distinctly Narcissistic: Diary Fiction in Quebec.* Toronto: University of Toronto Press, 1993.

Rebolledo, Tey Diana. *Women Singing in the Snow: A Cultural Analysis of Chicana Literature.* Tucson: University of Arizona Press, 1995.

Reed, Suzanne Elizabeth. *Presenting Cynthia Voigt.* New York: Twayne Publishers, 1995.

Reed, T. V. *Fifteen Jugglers, Five Believers: Literary Politics and the Poetics of American Social Movements.* Berkeley: University of California Press, 1992.

Reilly, Edward C. *William Kennedy.* Boston: Twayne Publishers, 1991.

Reimer, Mavis, ed. *Such a Simple Little Tale: Critical Responses to L.M. Montgomery's Anne of Green Gables.* Metuchen, NJ: Scarecrow Press, 1992.

Ringnalda, Don. *Fighting and Writing the Vietnam War.* Jackson, MS: University Press of Mississippi, 1994.

Robinson, Forrest G., ed. *Cambridge Companion to Mark Twain.* New York: Cambridge University Press, 1995.

Rogers, Franklin R. *Occidental Ideographs: Image, Sequence, and Literary History.* Cranbury, NJ: Associated University Presses, 1991.

Roman, Margaret. *Sarah Orne Jewett: Reconstructing Gender.* Tuscaloosa, AL: University of Alabama Press, 1992.

Romines, Ann. *Home Plot: Women, Writing and Domestic Ritual.* Amherst, MA: University of Massachusetts Press, 1992.

Rose, Jane Atteridge. *Rebecca Harding Davis.* New York: Twayne Publishers, 1993.

Rosen, Kenneth, ed. *Hemingway Repossessed.* Westport, CT: Praeger, 1994.

Rosenthal, Bernard, ed. *Critical Essays on Hawthorne's The House of Seven Gables.* New York: G. K. Hall & Co., 1995.

Roulston, Robert and Helen H. Roulston. *Winding Road to West Egg: The Artistic Development of F. Scott Fitzgerald.* Lewisburg, PA: Bucknell University Press, 1995.

Rovit, Earl and Gerry Brenner. *Ernest Hemingway.* Revised Edition. New York: Twayne Publishers, 1995.

Ruddick, Nicholas, ed. *State of the Fantastic: Studies in the Theory and Practice of Fantastic Literature and Film, Selected Essays from the Eleventh International Conference on the Fantastic in the Arts, 1990.* Westport, CT: Greenwood Press, 1992.

Ruppert, James. *Mediation in Contemporary Native American Fiction.* Norman, OK: University of Oklahoma Press, 1994.

Rushdie, Salman. *Imaginary Homelands: Essays an Criticism 1981–1995.* London: Granta Books, 1991.

Saint-Martin, Lori, ed. *L'autre lecture: La critique au féminin et les textes québécois.* 2 tomes. Montréal: XYZ éditeur, 1994.

Salzman, Jack, ed. *New Essays on The Catcher in the Rye.* New York: Cambridge University Press, 1991.

Samuels, Shirley, ed. *Culture of Sentiment: Race, Gender, and Sentimentality in Nineteenth- Century America.* New York: Oxford University Press, 1992.

San Juan, E., Jr. *Hegemony and Strategies of Transgression: Essays in Cultural Studies and Comparative Literature.* Albany, NY: State University Press of New York, 1995.

Sanders, David. *John Hersey Revisited.* Boston: Twayne, 1991.

Saunders, James Robert. *Wayward Preacher in the Literature of African-American Women.* Jefferson, NC: McFarland and Company, Inc., Publishers, 1995.

Scafella, Frank, ed. *Hemingway: Essays of Reassessment.* New York: Oxford University Press, 1991.

Scharnhorst, Gary, ed. *Critical Response to Nathaniel Hawthorne's The Scarlet Letter.* New York: Greenwood Press, 1992.

Schaub, Thomas Hill. *American Fiction in the Cold War.* Madison, WI: University of Wisconsin Press, 1991.

Schmidt, Gary D. *Katherine Paterson.* New York: Twayne Publishers, 1994.

Scholl, Peter A. *Garrison Keillor.* New York: Twayne Publishers, 1993.

Scruggs, Charles. *Sweet Home: Invisible Cities in the Afro-American Novel.* Baltimore, MD: Johns Hopkins University Press, 1993.

Scura, Dorothy M., ed. *Ellen Glasgow: New Perspectives*. Tennessee Studies in Lit. 36. Knoxville, TN: University of Tennessee Press, 1995.

Sedgwick, Eve Kosofsky. *Tendencies*. Durham, NC: Duke University Press, 1993.

Seed, David, ed. *Anticipations: Essays on Early Science Fiction and its Precursors.* Syracuse, NY: Syracuse University Press, 1995.

Shaw, Peter. *Recovering American Literature.* Chicago: Ivan R. Dee, 1994.

Shek, Ben-Z. *French-Canadian & Québécois Novels.* Toronto: Oxford University Press, 1991.

Showalter, Elaine. *Sister's Choice: Tradition and Change in American Women's Writing*. New York: Oxford University Press, 1991.

Siemerling, Winfried. *Discoveries of the Other: Alterity in the Work of Leonard Cohen, Hubert Aquin, Michael Ondaatje, and Nicole Brossard.* Toronto: University of Toronto Press, 1994.

Simmons, Diane. *Jamaica Kincaid.* New York: Twayne Publishers, 1994.

Singley, Carol J. *Edith Wharton: Matters of Mind and Spirit.* New York: Cambridge University Press, 1995.

Slusser, George and Tom Shippey, eds. *Fiction 2000: Cyberpunk and the Future of Narrative.* Athens, GA: University of Georgia Press, 1992.

Smart, Patricia. *Writing in the Father's House: The Emergence of the Feminine in the Quebec Literary Tradition.* Toronto: University of Toronto Press, 1991.

Smith, Valerie, ed. *New Essays on Song of Solomon*. New York: Cambridge University Press, 1995.

Smythe, Karen E. *Figuring Grief: Gallant, Munro, and the Poetics of Elegy*. Buffalo, NY: McGill-Queen's University Press, 1992.

Snodgras, Kathleen. *Fiction of Hortense Calisher.* Newark, DE: University of Delaware Press, 1993.

Söderlind, Sylvia. *MARGIN / ALIAS: Language and Colonization in Canadian and Québécois Fiction.* Toronto: University of Toronto Press, 1991.

Sokoloff, Naomi B. *Imagining the Child In Modern Jewish Fiction.* Baltimore, MD: Johns Hopkins University Press, 1992.

Solotaroff, Robert. *Robert Stone*. New York: Twayne Publishers, 1994.

Sommer, Doris. *Foundational Fictions: The National Romances of Latin America.* Berkeley, CA: University of California Press, 1991.

Stephens, C. Ralph and Lynda B. Salamon, eds. *Craft of Peter Taylor.* Tuscaloosa, AL: University of Alabama Press, 1995.

Stern, Milton R. *Tender is the Night: The Broken Universe.* New York: Twayne Publishers, 1994.

Stouck, David, ed. *Sinclair Ross's As for Me and My House: Five Decades of Criticism.* Toronto: University of Toronto Press, 1991.

Stovel, Nora. *Rachel's Children: Margaret Laurence's A Jest of God.* Toronto: ECW Press, 1992.

Stovel, Nora. *Stacey's Choice: Margaret Laurence's The Fire-Dwellers*. Toronto: ECW Press, 1993.

Strehle, Susan. *Fiction in the Quantum Universe.* Chapel Hill, NC: University of North Carolina Press, 1992.

Stull, James N. *Literary Selves: Autobiography and Contemporary American Nonfiction*. Westport, CT: Greenwood Press, 1993.

Sundquist, Eric J. *Hammer of Creation: Folk Culture in Modern African-American Fiction.* Athens, GA: University of Georgia Press, 1992.

Sundquist, Eric J. *To Wake the Nations: Race in the Making of American Literature.* Cambridge, MA: Belknap Press, 1993.

Tate, Linda. *Southern Weave of Women: Fiction of the Contemporary South.* Athens, GA: University of Georgia Press, 1994.

Thompson, Elizabeth. *Pioneer Woman: A Canadian Character Type.* Montreal: McGill-Queen's University Press, 1991.

Tiefensee, Dianne. *"The Old Dualities": Deconstructing Robert Kroetsch and His Critics.* Montreal: McGill-Queen's University Press, 1994.

Toker, Leona. *Eloquent Reticence: Withholding Information in Fictional Narrative.* Lexington, KY: University Press of Kentucky, 1993.

Torgovnick, Marianna De Marco. *Crossing Ocean Parkway: Readings by an Italian American Daughter.* Chicago: University of Chicago Press, 1994.

Touponce, William F. *Isaac Asimov.* Boston: Twayne Publishers, 1991.

Tucker, Lindsey. *Textual Excap(e)ades: Mobility, Maternity, and Textuality in Contemporary Fiction by Women.* Westport, CT: Greenwood Press, 1994.

Turner, Margaret E. *Imagining Culture: New World Narrative and the Writing of Canada.* Montreal: McGill-Queen's University Press, 1995.

Tusmith, Bonnie. *All My Relatives: Community in Contemporary Ethnic American Literature.* Ann Arbor, MI: University of Michigan Press, 1993.

Urgo, Joseph R. *Willa Cather and the Myth of American Migration.* Chicago: University of Illinois Press, 1995.

Verduyn, Christl. *Lifelines: Marian Engel's Writings.* Montreal: McGill-Queen's University Press, 1995.

Villiger, Laura R. *Mari Sandoz: A Study in Post-Colonial Discourse.* New York: Peter Lang, 1994.

Vrettos, Athena. *Somatic Fictions: Imagining Illness in Victorian Culture.* Stanford, CA: Stanford University Press, 1995.

Wagenknecht, Edward. *Willa Cather.* New York: Continuum, 1994.

Waid, Candace. *Edith Wharton's Letters from the Underworld: Fictions of Women and Writing.* Chapel Hill, NC: University of North Carolina Press, 1991.

Walker, Nancy A. *Awakening: Complete, Authoritative Text with Biographical and Historical Contexts, Critical History, and Essays from Five Contemporary Critical Perspecives.* New York: Bedford Books, 1993.

Walker, Nancy A. *Fanny Fern.* New York: Twayne Publishers, 1993.

Wall, Cheryl A. *Women of the Harlem Renaissance.* Indianapolis: Indiana University Press, 1995.

Ward, Carol M. *Rita Mae Brown.* New York: Twayne Publishers, 1993.

Warwick, Susan J. *River of Now and Then: Margaret Laurence's The Diviners.* Toronto: ECW Press, 1993.

Washington, Bryan R. *Politics of Exile: Ideology in Henry James, F. Scott Fitzgerald, and James Baldwin.* Boston: Northeastern University Press, 1995.

Waterson, Elizabeth. *Kindling Spirit: L.M. Montgomery's Anne of Green Gables.* Toronto: ECW Press, 1993.

Weinstein, Philip M., ed. *Cambridge Companion to William Faulkner.* New York: Cambridge University Press, 1995.

Weston, Elizabeth A. *International Theme in F. Scott Fitzgerald's Literature.* New York: Peter Lang, 1995.

Westrum, Dexter. *Thomas McGuane.* Boston: Twayne Publishers, 1991.

Wilentz, Gay Alden. *Binding Cultures: Black Women Writers in Africa and the Diaspora.* Bloomington, IN: Indiana University Press, 1992.

Williams, David. *Confessional Fictions: A Portrait of the Artist in the Canadian Novel.* Toronto: University of Toronto Press, 1991.

Wilson, Sharon Rose. *Margaret Atwood's Fairy-Tale Sexual Politics.* Jackson, MS: University Press of Mississippi, 1993.

Winchell, Donna Haisty. *Alice Walker.* New York: Twayne Publishers, 1992.

Winter, Kari J. *Subjects of Slavery, Agents of Change: Women and Power in Gothic Novels and Slave Narratives, 1790–1865.* Athens, GA: University of Georgia Press, 1992.

Wood, Michael. *Magician's Doubts: Nabokov and the Risks of Fiction.* Princeton, NJ: Princeton University Press, 1994.

Wood, Ruth Pirsig. *Lolita in Peyton Place: Highbrow, Middlebrow, and Lowbrow Novels of the 1950's.* New York: Garland Publishing, Inc., 1995.

Woodcock, George. *Moral Predicament: Morley Callaghan's More Joy in Heaven.* Toronto: ECW Press, 1993.

Wong, Sau-ling Cynthia. *Reading Asian American Literature.* Princeton, NJ: Princeton University Press, 1993.

Wright, Lee Alfred. *Identity, Family, and Folklore in African American Literature.* New York: Garland Publishing, 1995.

Yates, Norris. *Gender and Genre: An Introduction to Women Writers of Formula Westerns, 1900–1950.* Alburquerque: University of New Mexico Press, 1995.

Young, Alan R., ed. *Time and Place: The Life and Works of Thomas H. Raddall.* Fredericton, NB: Acadiensis Press, 1991.

Young, Elizabeth and Graham Caveney. *Shopping in Space: Essays on America's Blank Generation Fiction.* New York: Atlantic Monthly Press, 1992.

Zwinger, Lynda. *Daughters, Fathers, and the Novel: Sentimental Romance of Heterosexuality.* Madison: University of Wisconsin Press, 1991.

Index